Great Power Games

Great Power Games

From Western Decline to Eastern Ascent

Vikram Sood

JUGGERNAUT BOOKS
C-I-128, First Floor, Sangam Vihar, Near Holi Chowk,
New Delhi 110080, India

First published by Juggernaut Books 2025

Copyright © Vikram Sood 2025

10 9 8 7 6 5 4 3 2 1

P-ISBN: 9789353459291
E-ISBN: 9789353453695

The views and opinions expressed in this book are the author's own.
The facts contained herein were reported to be true as on the date of publication
by the author to the publishers of the book, and the publishers are not
in any way liable for their accuracy or veracity.

All rights reserved. No part of this publication may be reproduced,
transmitted, or stored in a retrieval system in any form or by any means without the
written permission of the publisher.

Typeset in Adobe Caslon Pro by R. Ajith Kumar, Noida

Printed at Thomson Press India Ltd

To our wonderful children
Arvind and Rupa,
Nandita and Lionel,
and
To our amazing grandchildren
Kabir,
Raghav,
Sonam,
and
Neel
who have given us immense happiness

Contents

Introduction		1
1.	Power, Money and Global Control	10
2.	Superspies: You Win Some, You Lose Some	43
3.	Philanthropy for Profit	61
4.	Decline of an Empire	90
5.	Provocation of an Old Rival	131
6.	Retaliation, Pushback	152
7.	Challenge from a Would-Be Global Power	178
8.	Clash of Civilizations	227
9.	Obstacles to India's Destiny	267
10.	Awakening, and India Has Risen	307
Acknowledgements		327
Notes		328

Introduction

Look again at that dot. That's here. That's home. That's us. On it everyone you love, everyone you know, everyone you ever heard of, every human being who ever was, lived out their lives. The aggregate of our joy and suffering ... ideologies, and economic doctrines, every hunter and forager, every hero and coward ... every king and peasant, every young couple in love ... every mother and father, hopeful child, inventor and explorer, every teacher of morals, every corrupt politician, every "superstar", every "supreme leader," every saint and sinner in the history of our species, lived there—on a mote of dust suspended in a sunbeam.[1]

— CARL SAGAN

It is on this pale blue dot that generals and emperors, prime ministers and presidents, have spilt the blood of others for their short moments of glory and triumph. The arrogance of the rich and powerful and the timidity of the rest enabled endless cruelties in history. The saga continues today in the name of science, humanity, religion, beliefs, patriotism and nationalism. I will explain more in the pages that follow.

It is on this pale blue dot that mankind is engaged in an unending struggle to dominate and kill the 'other' with the smartest weapons, to consume all of nature's bounty and leave nothing for posterity. It is on this pale blue dot that geopolitical battles are playing out, which are as much about human egos as they are about total control of the world. And yet, as Albert Einstein remarked, 'Only two things are infinite, the universe and human stupidity, and I'm not sure about the former.'

More than eight billion of us on this earth are engaged in a life-and-death struggle over religion, political beliefs and acquisition of wealth, alongside some truly wonderful achievements in the arts, science, medicine and technology. It is this pale blue dot that gives us our food and shelter, our way of life, and which, because of our collective greed, we have enshrouded in a carbon cloud that threatens our continuing existence.

What we see are the possibilities – world wars, hot wars, cold wars, trade wars, info wars, spy wars, cyber wars, pharma wars, tech wars, resource wars and more. Peace does not seem to have a chance to take root, nor is it profitable for those who reap the benefits of war. Today, as the globe seems to be on the edge of a precipice, creative chaos and deadly fears are favourite policy options of many world powers. It is in this world that India must rise and find its rightful place.

Chaos appears to be the defining characteristic of this age. The ongoing US-led tariff war is the latest in a global series of hot wars – in Yemen, Ukraine, Gaza, Iran. Each serial takes global attention away from the previous one. United States President Donald Trump's trade tariff war is not about trade and economy – that is simply the narrative that has been constructed. Its real goal is global supremacy and winning the competition against China. The narrative also involves superpower egos. As industrialist Ray Dalio argues, in the past 500 years, whenever one empire declined and another rose, there were not only military clashes but different currencies which also competed and dominated.[2] Closer to our times, the Smoot Hawley Act of 1930 raised tariffs to protect American farmers, and deepened the Great Depression as a result. Shortly after the Depression, Adolf Hitler took control of the National Socialist Party (the Nazi Party) and declared himself the Führer in 1933. Eventually World War II began in September 1939. The jury is still out on whether Trump's moves to enhance tariffs is a game changer that will 'Make America Great Again (MAGA)' or a recipe for disaster. Economists differ – as they often do.

Trump's trade tariffs are not about trade competition with China, Russia, India or anybody else. This is a desperate attempt, through threats and bullying, at reasserting control and supremacy. This is the narrative about MAGA. In this case there is ego too. Yet the basis of past global history is that as an empire declines and another rises there is inevitably a multi-pronged struggle for supremacy. This would explain the present state of creative chaos, which will have global repercussions in our lifetime as a new world order takes shape. Meanwhile, our globe teeters on the edge and it is on this globe we seek our destiny.

Maybe wars are not required to be won. They just have to be conducted – wherever, whenever, even forever. There are multiple benefits for the attacker. Hardware lying in stock gets used up, so there is more on the production chain and upgraded, with new versions being developed based on what the opposition uses. Then, a hapless, destroyed country needs to be rebuilt. The destruction and reconstruction of a country are profitable enough, sometimes both being conducted by the same country. Everybody is happy as more money rolls into home coffers or into tax-free havens. The fear of massive destruction ensures obedience. Inevitably, the overuse of this policy leads to diminishing returns.

As the US and China get ready to battle it out for the global title, for India the choice is to either be friendly with a has-been hegemon that is far away, or with a hegemon sitting right on our fence, while not forgetting the third hegemon, Russia, who frightens Europe because Europe wants to be frightened. The only answer, in India's national interest and shorn of polite verbiage, is to be a hegemon ourselves. For the present, the massive egos of Donald Trump and Xi Jinping are also involved and they will be quite ready to take down billions of us. The world needs a new order that limits this capacity to destroy, if not eliminate. The question again is: how does the world get there, or are we doomed?

Almost every crisis or change is taking place simultaneously, and not just in geopolitics. Other factors are becoming increasingly important – the economic order, military engagements, terror and retaliation, education, health and pandemics, access to food and energy sources and climate change. When a superpower that is also a self-appointed guardian of the world and its freedoms walks away from the treaties it signed and refuses to sign other treaties meant for global security, as it abandons allies on the battlefield, global uncertainty becomes the only certainty.

Howard Zinn, the famous American historian and political scientist, once said that, historically, the most terrible things – war, genocide and slavery – have resulted not from disobedience, but from obedience. And I would add – also from greed and appeasement. We are in an era of declining empires, ambitious powers, resurgent powers and rising Islamic fundamentalism, all occurring in a crucible of organized chaos.

It is into this era that my country must awake.

If we look at recent history, we can discern a pattern where Washington favours autocratic regimes to quarrelsome democratic regimes, and uses

Islamist terror organizations for its own strategic benefit, as it has done most recently in Syria. Monarchs, autocrats and dictators are easier to handle than democracies. Hence, intelligence services have been working at destabilizing democracies.

American forays since 2001 have been: the so-called Global War on Terror that began with a response to 9/11 but led to an invasion of Iraq in 2003, along with what became a 20-year war in Afghanistan, interspersed with a global financial crisis in 2008, the Arab Spring from 2010–2012, the Syrian War in 2011, the rise of ISIS in 2014 and the revival of Al Qaeda. The outbreak of the Covid-19 pandemic presented a diversion from the Afghan debacle. The ongoing Ukraine misadventure will leave Ukraine and Europe in a shambles, but the US may not have the capacity to repeat a Marshall Plan or be able to claim the right to continue as the Benevolent Global Hegemon.

These have all been opportunities, for some, to profit. If the war machinery provides gains to the military–industrial complex, which in turn favours wars, pharma and tech stand to gain during pandemics and with revolutionary changes in diagnosis and treatment. In today's world, social media, information and technology earn profits all the time. Since acquisition of wealth and dominance are the primary goals of all nations, aspects of acquisition – control of resources and markets – are also at risk and need to be secured. One could see a military–industrial–pharma–technology–media–philanthropy–intelligence complex working together. There resides, somewhere, a Deep State in most countries under the convenient narrative of democracy. Therefore, total secret intelligence from every conceivable means is a part of these arrangements.

The dollar, for long the symbol of American power, is losing ground as countries switch to dealing bilaterally with other countries in their own currencies. Quite clearly the US has entered, as all empires eventually do, a period of imperial overstretch. Decline sets in when its abilities to have its way do not match its self-described goal and total domination becomes near impossible. That is why there is talk of a 'Great Reset' being worked out by some senior and powerful gentlemen sitting in a village in Switzerland, which means establishing a new kind of autocratic democracy. At the same time, China is praised for its totalitarian method of governance that includes compulsory digital IDs and biometric surveillance of individuals and their social credits systems. The coming

Age of Technology, looking beyond Artificial Intelligence (AI), could make this Chinese form of surveillance compulsory everywhere, but it would first be implemented in the developed world.

With the world in turbulence from the cumulative impacts of the after-effects of the pandemic, the fall of America in Afghanistan, the Ukraine face-off between a resurgent Russia and a distracted America, and a new superpower rivalry between China and the US, the Pentagon will react the only way it can. It will want to push for increased military budgets with a renewed focus on emerging and frontier technologies where it has global advantage, and prepare for information and economic warfare fought in the world of cyber tech, AI, as the new threats and weapons in this age of Big Tech and Big Pharma. President Trump has already announced an increase in the Pentagon budget to $1 trillion for 2026, up from $893 billion in 2025,[3] much to the delight, one can imagine, of the military–industrial complex.

The West–Russia animosity resurfaced early in 2022 in Ukraine, but strangely, for the US, not every country was prepared to oppose Russia for invading Ukraine. The twenty-first-century world was beginning to understand the difference between 'interests' and 'narratives'. The memory of the US failure in Afghanistan and its duplicity in Iraq were all too fresh. American moves to safeguard its own interests had left local populations suffering and their countries in tatters; the world was not going to take a chance again, so soon. Yet at the time of writing this, the Ukraine–NATO war against Russia has escalated sharply when the Russians reacted with all their conventional might against Ukraine's destruction of Russian war planes deep inside Russian territory. The Russians have used their deadly Oreshnik intermediate range ballistic missiles with multiple powerful warheads against several targets all over Ukraine.

In the immediate future, apart from purely military threats, there are other issues that will be the cause for turmoil, conflict or even war. Terror in its many manifestations, but chiefly Islamic, will grow, especially to the west of India. The quest for energy remains vital, as do mineral resources, especially rare earths and markets. Pandemics, water shortage, demographic pressures and climate change will cause human dislocations and anguish. The wealthy nations would want to control populations, even reduce them, because they fear that the cake is not large enough to allow the underprivileged to have a larger slice of it.

China, in pursuit of its dream of empire, will not only target markets and resource bases in Latin America and Africa, but also in the United States and Europe. It will continue its hostility towards India, directly or through Pakistan. Today, thanks to American and European buccaneers, China mines for coal in the Tennessee mountains, and controls the lithium reserves in Chile, which is about 40 per cent of the global total, and produces 90 per cent of the globe's supply of rare earths. China is now the number one trading nation in the world and has more foreign currency reserves than any other country. China's control over critical commodities and strategic terrain, its penetration in the US and more than 70 other countries, and its success in compromising dozens of key US industries, all threaten American security interests.

Ukraine apart, which has been a typical US failure, future wars would be more non-military, technology- and AI-based with reduced military hardware. These will also be increasingly about the control of resources – water, energy, food and seeds and rare earths. Adversaries and allies would be tackled through subversion espionage, propaganda and cyber-attacks, geared to turn a thriving state into an arena of fierce armed conflict; it could become the victim of foreign intervention and sink into chaos, and eventually civil war.

India may be too large to be conquered in this manner, but it can be suborned or led by leaders that pay court to the big powers. Put the two factors together and think strategically, and consider which country would really want India to be big and powerful with an independent voice, no matter what the smooth talk might be. Not China, not Pakistan, not the US or Russia – for strategic reasons, for existential reasons, for reasons of domination and control, for markets and resources. We are on our own. Above all ego – for reasons of self-adduced exceptionalism or being the centre of the earth, has increasingly become a factor in today's geopolitics.

As India becomes stronger economically and militarily, it will automatically become more than a swing state – it will become another pole in a multipolar world. India may not be the reason for this global churn, but we are very much in the midst of it. It is overtly very violent, but one wonders if there was any decade since World War II that was peaceful, or when peace was not threatened. None. Violence, organized or unconventional, which is a euphemism for terror, has been the overt sign of trouble.

Trying to mould or change behaviour, mindset and dependencies and stifling alternative voices within a country through subtle methods or authoritarian practices, have been psychological exercises. Subtle methods are used externally through extensive means of communication (media and think tanks) and using locals of a country (both part of an intelligence operation), and strategic thinkers who could be placed anywhere in these two categories. It is a subtle coercion of the mind. A country's strategists must therefore be knowledgeable enough to advise the leadership to widen the scope and the meaning of the word 'enemy'. It is not always the man with the gun who is an enemy; it could be the man who wears a smile and carries gifts. This should include all countries who claim to be friends but who act otherwise. Any country must be judged not just by its actions, but how those actions affect Indian interests.

Self-proclaimed friends could be working against India's interests. Indians cheer themselves as they progress economically and internationally. India's self-reliant nationalism is not good news in the corridors of power in the West. Two self-reliant, independent, and economic, military and nuclear giants in Asia is a horror story, especially for the Western corporate world, which really runs the show. The mistakes of the past, where the US helped China to grow to a stage where it now threatens the US, must not become a model in the case of India. The US will continue its doublespeak on India–Pakistan relations using its strong economic military relations with Pakistan to make sure India continues to look over its shoulder, while exerting pressure on India to open its trade gates and abandon military purchases from Russia in favour of American products. Any past subtlety about these pursuits has been given up by the new Trump administration.

One can see a storm gathering on the horizon. In India, keen watchers feared that this storm would reach India in full fury ahead of the general elections in 2024. The intention was that come 2024, New Delhi must either have a weak, divided government which may or may not be led by Narendra Modi, or better still, a mixed up, directionless government sitting in New Delhi with the control levers elsewhere. Conspiracy theory? No. Not if one studies the commentaries, editorials, seminars and statements emanating from the West over a period of time or when there is an episode like the recent Indian response to Pakistan-backed terror in India, or stories that appear in the media that make it look like a concerted campaign against India and against what is described as 'Hindu India' with references to the BJP as a 'Hindu nationalist ruling party'.

The sooner these are identified, without getting paranoid, the faster and better will be the preparation to handle them. It is never a bad idea to try and turn an enemy into a friend, but whatever action a strategist must take, a country should not become a naive victim. It must be armed with prudence, the ability to detect the enemy within and never ever lower one's guard, not even for friends.

The Indian liberal assumes a paternalistic attitude towards the rest of the country, arising from a sense of entitlement. He assumes he knows best for everyone and dismisses all alternative opinion as nonsensical. He finds it difficult to adjust to the new reality of India. The truth is that India is changing, and it will have to find its place in the new world that is emerging. As Sanjeev Sanyal, member of the Prime Minister's Economic Advisory Committee, mentioned recently in my discussion with him, 'The change in the global order is inevitable. The old system was breaking down anyway and a period of turbulent transition was going to occur at some point. India's strategy must be to survive the turbulence and to negotiate a better place in the new world order, whatever it is. Of course, it will require that India must build alliances that work for its interests.'

This book is not about history. It is a descriptive book about events, reasons and consequences. Each chapter could easily be the subject of more than one book. Many have already been written. This book is in a way a continuation of my first two books and the three could be considered a trilogy. My first book, *The Unending Game*, which was essentially about international espionage, had a chapter on how intelligence agencies were involved in the control of narratives. My second book, *The Ultimate Goal*, was about how narratives are created by states that wish to have or sustain global dominance. This book, *Great Power Games*, is about all this breaking down as new powers emerge to challenge the existing world order.

For many years, one saw and read about how the world was being run by the rich and the powerful, and how their narrative and interests were all that mattered. There is now a palpable decline in their ability to have their writ run all the time. Other nations and civilizations, like the Chinese, Indian and Russian, want their place at the table.

It was a major effort to compress all this into 10 chapters, and there would be many subjects that are either not adequately explored or not covered in the book at all. I have relied mostly on Western sources for chapters 1 to 8 and on Indian sources for chapters 9 and 10.

The idea is to present the book to the young, defined as those who are between 20 and 60 years old, and hopefully correct some perspectives!

Yet on this pale blue dot, all 'our posturings, our imagined self-importance, the delusion that we have some privileged position in the Universe, are challenged by this point of pale light. Our planet is a lonely speck in the great enveloping cosmic dark. In our obscurity, in all this vastness, there is no hint that help will come from elsewhere to save us from ourselves.'[4]

1

Power, Money and Global Control

Power is the ability to direct or prevent the current or future actions of other groups and individuals.

— MOSES NAIM[1]

It is difficult to define or measure power, but it is true that wealth is a source of power and the ability to project violent force adds to that power. That word 'power' is defined as the ability to make other nations, people and individuals do something one wants them to do. Or, conversely, the power to prevent them from doing something you do not want them to do. For a long time, during the Cold War, the US used this power among its allies, those it called friends and sometimes those who were neither, like India. America has had plenty of money and a large army for a long time. It has also appropriated God with the slogan, 'God Save America'. Its power and control over other nations and territories took a few decades to grow and were linked to education, skills and industrial innovation.

If one were to examine the centuries prior to America's rise to eminence, in Europe, the twelfth century onwards became an Age of Higher Learning when universities in Oxford, Bologna, Cambridge and Salamanca were established; it coincided with the Age of the Crusades as European Catholics fought to reclaim their Holy Lands. It was also the century when Muslim marauders from Central Asia destroyed Indian universities of Nalanda, Takshashila and others, in 1193.

The Age of Empire, when European powers acquired colonies, was followed by the Age of Industrialization, and then both ran simultaneously.

Each fed on the other and was Europe-led. Feudal to the core, European monarchs used their control of their populations to enable imperial conquests of non-European lands and subjugation of populations. They also used subjugated populations to fight their colonial and imperial battles. Later on, selected locals used the same tactics as their imperial masters to enslave the local population and profiteer by trading in slaves for profit.

The forced sale of opium to China led to the British-led Opium Wars – military subjugation to safeguard and push commercial interests that would, in the twentieth century, manifest in similar American acts in Latin America and elsewhere in the world. Increased wealth fuelled the search for new ways to further enhance it; for instance, through better technological innovation and exploitation of resources. This meant that imperial powers would enforce laws that forced people off their land and converted them into coolies or indentured labour to work in distant lands to profit the rich. Self-serving laws and coercion through elite control ensured that wealth from economic activity redistributed wealth from the poor to the rich.

In essence, nothing has changed in the last century, from the goals and ambitions of the rich and the powerful, the conflict of country against country and within each country, the conflict of the elite versus the poor. Europeans barely knew until the fourteenth century that humanity existed on the other side of the globe – apart from Marco Polo and one or two visitors who had travelled beyond the known world. The Age of Knowledge was followed by a very Adam Smithian age, about which the thinker wrote in 1775, 'All for ourselves, and nothing for other people, seems, in every age of the world, to have been the vile maxim of the masters of mankind.'[2] Very little has changed about the motives of the 'masters of mankind'. If anything, they have sharpened.

The Gilded Age

In 1861, just before the onset of the American Civil War, Henry Brooks Adams, a descendant of two American presidents, accompanied his father, Charles Francis Adams, to London. Charles Adams was designated US ambassador to Great Britain by Abraham Lincoln. The son, as secretary to his father, learnt wartime diplomacy monitoring Confederate diplomatic intrigues. When he returned home in 1868, barely three years after the Civil War ended, he found his country transformed. The economy was booming with a GDP of $72 billion, which jumped to $170 billion by 1890, and $400 billion two decades later. This was the kind of growth that was seen almost a century later with China and the Asian tigers.[3] The war had been an industrial bonanza for the country and by 1892, there were more than 4,000 millionaires in the United States. The Americans had learnt that a good war can be good for the economy.

The Gilded Age had arrived. The two most prominent of its early icons were Andrew Carnegie and John D. Rockefeller. Both wanted to be remembered as generous donors to society; both were shrewd businessmen, ruthless about the goals they set for themselves and frugal with their workers. Two other tycoons were Jay Gould and John Pierpont Morgan. They had all been in their late twenties or early thirties, on the first rungs of their careers, in the waning days of the Civil War in 1865. By 1899, Carnegie Steel was the largest steel company in the world. Rockefeller was already on his way to becoming the biggest oil magnate of America. These were the four men who made things happen, and by the end of the nineteenth century, the US was the richest country in the world. It had the highest industrial output, well-endowed farmlands and factories churning out products. Carnegie cornered and reinvented the steel industry, Rockefeller became the oil king, Gould specialized in railroads and the telegraph, the critical infrastructure of those times, and Morgan became the American banker and financier of the Gilded Age.[4]

The Carnegie technique was straightforward: focus on an objective, cut brutally through any conventions, competitors or ordinary people who stood in his way and dominate at all costs. He could be pointlessly cruel, even to his most loyal associates, manipulate his employees, highlight their faults and claim all the credit for their work.[5] A Scotsman, he had begun his work life in a telegraph office and climbed his way to eventually become the 'father of the steel industry'. A man of contrasts, he was not a nice man to know, but a rich, ruthless and powerful entity.

Rockefeller had a modest and largely unremarkable early life. It was his investment of $1,000 borrowed from his father to buy a partnership in another company that set him on the path to his future. Soon, he was into the oil boom of Pennsylvania. Excelsior Works, a kerosene refinery started by Rockefeller along with Samuel Andrews and Maurice B. Clark, was by 1865 one of the largest companies in the country. The characteristic Rockefeller method during those early days was to move with startling speed and minimum fanfare, display confidence and not be afraid to use the money approach when needed. He had an eye for detail while keeping his sights on the big picture. Rockefeller companies unquestionably paid bribes to local officials, but, as the English observer, Lord James Bryce, wrote about the business environment in nineteenth-century America, 'It is only by the use of money that [corporations] can ward off the attacks constantly made on them by demagogues or blackmailers.'

Rockefeller did not need to cheat to win world oil dominance; he was simply better at the business than anyone else.[6] Standard Oil was Rockefeller's empire that began in 1870, and by 1911, it controlled 90 per cent of US production, refining, transportation and marketing.[7] That is when the antitrust axe fell on Standard Oil, which had to divest, and it did so into several companies, some of whom are today's major energy corporations after several mergers, like ExxonMobil, BP, Chevron and others.

Among the 'robber barons'[8] of the day, which included Carnegie, Rockefeller, Carl Vanderbilt and, later, Henry Ford, Jay Gould had the darkest reputation. To Henry Adams, Gould was 'a spider . . . [who] spun huge webs, in corners and in the dark'. Gould's career coincided with the great epoch of American railroads, the first large, investor-financed, publicly traded corporations.[9] J.P. Morgan, who had earlier been outmanoeuvred by Gould, was always torn between keeping him at a wary distance and chasing after his business. Gould had one of the supplest business minds of his, or of any, age. The railroads were his playing field. A few clever strategic deals executed unscrupulously, and wealth and property were snatched from unsuspecting owners. Railroads became the centre of Gould's interests early in his career, and more than anyone else, he created the national railroad map that prevails to this day in the US.[10]

The US developed in the nineteenth century with the initiative, drive and ruthlessness of people like Carnegie (who gave away most of his wealth to charity), Rockefeller and his contributions to some of America's great universities through the Rockefeller Foundation and the Rockefeller Family Foundation while he influenced finance through his bank, the Chase Manhattan and Gould and Morgan – astute business dealers and entrepreneurs at one end and robber barons at the other.

Power in the nineteenth century came from the military power of the state. Where needed, the US Cavalry ensured lands were appropriated from Native Americans, who were largely exterminated in the process. British sea merchants ensured delivery of millions of slave labour from Africa for plantations in the US and the Caribbean for increasing wealth on the American East coast. Millionaires flourished in this era of unfettered growth.

The industrial revolution in Europe had led to a massive flow of money into the US during the nineteenth century and helped in the creation of millionaires Rockefeller, Carnegie, Morgan, Vanderbilt and others; the Rothschilds represented British interests directly through front companies or indirectly through agencies that they controlled. The wealthy had some very specific ideas about perpetuating control.

The Age of Money

One night in November 1910, six men, America's biggest bankers of the day, slipped away from New York for a secret 10-day conclave at an exclusive, inaccessible club, the Jekyll House Clubhouse, in Georgia. They described themselves as members of the First Name Club. Their cover was a duck hunt, but their true purpose was to work out a system that protected their interests as their wealth grew.

The six men were Senator Nelson W. Aldrich (Nelson Rockefeller's grandfather), Arthur Shelton (Rockefeller's assistant), Paul M. Warburg (a partner in Koen, Loeb and Company, representing the Rothschilds and Warburgs in Europe), A. Piatt Andrew (assistant secretary of the Treasury), Henry P. Davison (senior partner, J.P. Morgan Company) and Frank A. Vanderlip (president of the National City Bank of New York, representing William Rockefeller). At the end of the secret discussions, they created a blueprint for the Federal Reserve System, which ensured the country's biggest private banks had oversight of the nation's currency supply and over smaller banks. The entire exercise was conducted in total secrecy.[11] The six First Name Club members were concerned with financial instability. Warburg had described the American banking system as archaic and of the kind that existed in Europe at the time of the Médicis or in Asia during the time of Hammurabi (eighteenth-century Babylon).[12]

Eventually, the six were able to persuade the political leadership to accept the idea of a privately owned central bank. The Federal Reserve System was established in 1913. Its creation led to a fusion of power of the Eight Families who represented one-quarter of the total global wealth at that time and the military and diplomatic might of the United States.[13] This was a monopolistic collusion among the wealthy to stop competition from newer banks, create money as required, control reserves of all the banks and get the taxpayer to pick up the losses that they might run into.

The House of Morgan went on to finance half the US war effort in World War I while collecting commissions for arranging contractors like GE, Du Pont and US Steel. Morgan also financed the Boer War in South Africa and the Anglo–Prussian War, and was astute enough to preside over the 1919 Paris Peace Conference for reconstruction efforts among the Allied nations and Germany. Thus, Morgan gained from enforcement of both war and peace. Doubtless, Morgan had close relations with Benito Mussolini, while Nazi functionary, Dr Hjalmar Schacht, was a Morgan Bank liaison during World War II. A practice that continues in the American system till today – gaining from destruction and gaining from reconstruction.

The Four Horsemen of Banking and Oil

The Rothschilds were a unique family of adventurers who were quite focused, even ruthless, about achieving their goals. Mayer Amschel was a Jew without a family name who lived with no street address in a ghetto in Frankfurt in the mid-eighteenth century. He adopted the name of the house that he lived in, Red Shield (Rothschild). Amschel first made his money by selling rare coins, medals and antiques to aristocratic buyers and spent it wisely. His wealth increased and he located five of his sons in London, Paris, Naples, Vienna and Frankfurt, where they remained upwardly mobile, dealing with the noblest of clients and learning the art of double bookkeeping.

Close relationships with leading political figures, and salaried secret agents providing essential commercial and political news with secret messaging, helped build the Rothschild dynasty. The international bond market was their favoured means of acquiring wealth. By 1850, they were worth over $10 billion.¹⁴ The European elite preferred to work in the background and manipulate people of stature. The Rothschilds knew this art to perfection. It is believed both the royal estates of Sandringham and Balmoral were facilitated by the Rothschilds through a long-standing tradition of gifting loans. Mayer Amschel Rothschild once said, 'I care not who controls the nation's political affairs, so long as I control her currency.'¹⁵ He summed up his investment strategy with the words, 'When the streets of Paris are running in blood, I buy.'¹⁶

In times of war, the Rothschild strategy was to help both combatants. Nathan Rothschild loaned Napoleon £5 million while also loaning money to the Duke of Wellington, as they both prepared for the Battle of Waterloo. One story goes that Nathan, based in London, dispatched one of his trusted aides to locate himself north of the battlefield, close to the English Channel. As soon as the battle was over, the agent, who might well have been a family member, rushed to the Channel and crossed it to inform Nathan that Wellington had won. Wellington's own couriers arrived 24 hours later. By then Nathan had offloaded all his government bonds in the market, creating the impression that Wellington had lost. The rest of the market followed. At the same time, Nathan secretly bought the stock through others for only a fraction and gained enormously when the market resurged a few hours later when news of Wellington's victory spread.¹⁷ Secrecy was a favourite weapon and exclusivity too.

The Rothschild financial empire includes majority stakes in most world central banks. The family owns the bank BSI SA in Lugano, Switzerland, the Rothschild bank in Zurich and the Rothschild Italia in Milan. Wealth and money were the main criteria for the Rothschilds and ties to drug money or any other shady deals were acceptable. The firm N.M. Rothschild and Sons was involved in the notorious Bank of Credit and Commerce International (BCCI) scandal in the UK in the 1970s. The Rothschilds escaped dubious limelight when a warehouse full of documents conveniently burned to the ground even as the Rothschild connections with the Bank of England helped and BCCI was shut down.

After the merger of the House of Morgan with the Rockefeller Chase Manhattan group in 2000, four giants dominated the American money scene: JPMorganChase and Citigroup on the East Coast who together controlled more than 50 per cent of the New York Federal Reserve

Bank, and Bank of America and Wells Fargo who controlled the West Coast. During the 2008 banking crisis these firms got even bigger. JPMorganChase acquired Washington Mutual, Bank of America got Merrill Lynch and Countrywide, Wells Fargo got America's fifth biggest bank, Wachovia. As Dean Henderson writes in his 2010 book, *Big Oil and Their Bankers in the Persian Gulf:* 'The same banks which for decades had galloped their Four Horsemen roughshod through the Persian Gulf oil patch were now more powerful than at any time in their histories. They were the Four Horsemen of Banking.'[18]

Anthony Sampson, in his 1975 book *The Seven Sisters: The Great Oil Companies and the World They Made*, describes the oil giants, ExxonMobil, Texaco, Chevron, BP, Royal Dutch Shell and Gulf Oil, and the clout they had. These giants became even more powerful when Chevron absorbed Gulf Oil in 1984 and Exxon and Mobil merged in 1999, with Chevron partnering Texaco in 2000. This left ExxonMobil, ChevronTexaco, BP Amoco and Royal Dutch Shell as the four big players by the turn of the century. Henderson refers to them as the 'Four Horsemen of Oil' who controlled the energy sector and managed the Middle East with considerable assistance from the US government, the Central Intelligence Agency (CIA) and the Four Horsemen of Banking.

The Four Horsemen of Banking control the Four Horsemen of Oil along with the Deutsche Bank, Banque Paribas, Barclays and other European old-money giants. Their control extends beyond the Middle East oil and the same banking houses figure among the top ten stockholders in virtually every Fortune 500 corporation. Just eight families own 80 per cent of the New York Federal Reserve Bank, the most powerful federal branch, and only four of these reside in the US: Goldman Sachs, Rockefellers, Lehmans and Kuhn Loebs of New York. The Rothschilds of Paris and London, the Warburgs of Hamburg, the Lazards of Paris and the Israel Moses Seifs of Rome are the other four.[19]

These banking families operate in secrecy quite intentionally, and their influence and control over the global economy cannot be overstated. Usually, their corporate media arm is quick to discredit any information that seeks to expose the extent of their financial clout as half-baked conspiracy theories. To quote Dean Henderson, 'Anyone who dare utter the word (conspiracy) is quickly excluded from public debate and written off as insane. Yet the facts remain.'[20]

Banking, Financial Meltdown and Investment

The 'once-in-a-century' financial meltdown of 2008 revealed a great deal, not only about the deep flaws in the global financial system but also the way the financial super class exercises power. Important, well-established financial institutions like Lehman Brothers, Merrill Lynch, Bear Stearns, AIG, and mortgage lenders Fannie Mae and Freddie Mac, were either wiped out, rendered unrecognizable or taken over by the US government. JPMorgan stepped in to lead the acquisition of the remaining assets of Bear Stearns and soften the blow.

This was a repeat of the time when J.P. Morgan himself moved $65 million in gold in 1895 for the US government to help stop a run on the financial markets. Morgan later bought out Andrew Carnegie and launched U.S. Steel Corporation. Since then, this super elite class has only grown in number, and in some ways become more important than the military class, as the cost of military warfare keeps becoming increasingly unaffordable.

Some estimates put the losses of 2008 at $2 trillion yet wealthy individuals like Warren Buffet, John Paulson, a hedge fund manager, and Jamie Dimon, CEO of JPMorgan, capitalized on the fear factor. Dimon helped his bank acquire Bear Sterns and Washington Mutual. For every loss there is profit to be made by the courageous.

After the 2008 financial crisis, leaders in the very same businesses that had been greed-driven used their influence to ensure that the new financial instruments and those in the evolving global markets were self-regulating. They wanted to be trusted and their past misdemeanours ignored. It was a significant indicator of power when the super elite of the financial world, who earlier wanted the government to stay out of their business, suggested that the government intervene and save them, and the government obliged. Thus, many of those who had created and led the crisis ended up being some of its biggest beneficiaries. This feature of the super elite creating a crisis and then benefiting from it or leading to a new class of elite has often happened in the US.[21]

In fact, the way US business and finance functions has not changed in its essentials perhaps for decades. C. Wright Mills, a former Columbia professor of sociology, describes the country's power structure in his book, *The Power Elite*, written in 1956. Mills's central theme was that the top tier of the business, government and military communities showed that there was a remarkably small overlapping community of deciders. This power elite is 'composed of men whose positions enable them to transcend ordinary environments of ordinary men and women; they are in positions to make decisions having major consequences ... they are in command of the major hierarchies and organisations of modern society. They rule the big corporations. They run the machinery of the state and claim its prerogatives to direct the military establishment. They occupy strategic command posts of the social structure, in which are now centred the effective means of the power and the wealth and the celebrity which they enjoy.'[22]

This is another version of what President Dwight Eisenhower had spoken of on 17 January 1961, in his famous and often repeated farewell address when he referred to the military–industrial complex and warned against its unwarranted influence. 'The potential for the disastrous rise of misplaced power exists and will persist,' he had said.[23] Since then, this complex has undergone many changes and expansions; it has grown more powerful internationally and can exercise its power regarding the governments of the members' respective home countries or the one in which it operates.

The Big Three

America is a big country where everything is to scale, so big corporations need big money which means big investment in and beyond American territory, and big military. There are three investment companies in the US who hold the largest share of the market – BlackRock, Vanguard and State Street. Some of their employees have held positions in multiple US presidential administrations, and own part of CNN and Fox. This enables them to influence the bipartisan information flow.[24] BlackRock, Inc. is one of the biggest investment companies in the world today. It was established in 1988 by Larry Fink and seven others. Fink is now its chairman and CEO. The company specializes in asset and risk management. It grew over time – naturally, and through mergers and acquisitions. At the end of 2024, it had $11.6 trillion assets under its management.[25] BlackRock is sometimes referred to as the 'fourth branch of government' because of its immense power and influence.[26]

Not far behind BlackRock is the Vanguard Group with AUM (assets under management) valued at $10.4 trillion at the end of January 2024. Another characteristic is how these holdings are managed.[27] Vanguard holds the largest number of shares in BlackRock as of June 2024, ahead of BlackRock Fund, and BlackRock is the largest owner of stock in the Vanguard Group. The third AUM company is State Street with its assets holding at $4.7 trillion in 2024.[28] All three together hold assets under management valued at a little above $20 trillion.

In the aftermath of the 2008 financial crisis, the US Treasury Department asked BlackRock Solutions for assistance in solving problems relating to the collapsed shares of financial companies like Bear Stearns, Freddie Mac, Morgan Stanley and American International Group.[29] The next year, BlackRock became the world's largest asset manager.

The Big Three, according to S&P 500 Firms Index, were the single largest shareholders in almost 90 per cent of S&P 500 firms, including, Microsoft, ExxonMobil, General Electric, the Coca-Cola Company and PepsiCo.[30] Pepsi and Coke may be rivals but BlackRock had no problem in investing in both. BlackRock has investments in CNN, Fox News, Times Warner, MSNBC, in Exxon and Chevron, Pfizer, Merck, AstraZeneca, Northrop Grumman, Raytheon and Boeing, Facebook and Netflix, to name a few.

BlackRock's biggest shareholder is Vanguard, a private company whose shareholders are not publicly known, accentuating the monopolization of control. Such monopolization has meant concentration of wealth to an unimaginable level – as it is 1 per cent of the world owns 99 per cent of its money; or 82 per cent of the earned money some years ago went to this 1 per cent. This means that ultimately two investment companies, Vanguard and BlackRock, hold monopoly in all industries in the world, which in turn are owned by the richest families including royalty that amassed their wealth even before the Industrial Revolution, which only added to it. The intriguing aspect for some might be how little-known this fact is, just like another fact – that 90 per cent of international media is owned by nine media conglomerates.

Journalist Bill Sardi has quoted a TV documentary by a Dutch creator, called 'Big Finance Corporations', which reveals how the stocks of the world's largest corporations are owned by the same institutional investors – that is, they own each other. This means that competing brands are not really competing, since ultimately their stock is owned by the same investment companies, investment funds, insurance companies, banks and, in some cases, governments. 'The smaller investors are owned by larger investors. Those are owned by even bigger investors. The visible top of this pyramid shows only two companies whose names we have often seen ... they are Vanguard and BlackRock.'[31]

Both BlackRock and Vanguard have entered the Chinese financial market with investments in China Poly Group's subsidiaries – Poly Property and Poly Technology. Ironically, the Poly Group sent substantial supplies of gunpowder to Russia as assistance during the ongoing Ukraine War.[32] The Chinese Military Commission has an interest in Poly Technology.

The power of BlackRock and Vanguard is beyond imagination. In January 2020, Larry Fink, the CEO of BlackRock, circulated a letter addressed to his Wall Street colleagues and corporate CEOs.[33] He called it 'A Fundamental Reshaping of Finance' and said that money would 'go green', meaning that 'in the near future – and sooner than most anticipate – there will be a significant re-allocation of capital ... Climate risk is investment risk ...' and 'Every government and shareholder must confront climate change.'[34] It was a Big Finance versus Big Energy letter. He declared that BlackRock would be screening new investments in oil, gas and coal to determine if the UN Agenda 2030 was being adhered to. Fink also said BlackRock would begin to disinvest in oil, gas and coal. Fink's letter caused an immediate disinvestment in the trillion-dollar oil and gas sector. In the two years since Fink's letter, an estimated $1 trillion worth investment in oil and gas exploration was pulled out.

The same year (2020) Fink was made a member of Klaus Schwab's 'dystopian' World Economic Forum.[35] Early in his presidential bid, in late 2019, Joe Biden had a secret meeting with Fink, who is believed to have told the candidate, 'I'm here to help,' and Biden announced, 'We are going to get rid of fossil fuels ...' In December 2020, even before his inauguration in January 2021, Biden named BlackRock's global head of Sustainable Investing, Brian Deese, assistant to the president and director of the National Economic Council. Deese then quietly shaped the Biden war on fossil fuel energy.[36]

Biden's aggressive environmental rules and BlackRock ESG investing mandates had a direct impact on US refinery capacity. Without refineries the number of barrels of oil removed from the Strategic Petroleum Reserve have no significance or use. In the first two years of Biden's Presidency, the US shut down some 1 million barrels a day of gasoline and diesel refining capacity, which was the fastest decline in US history.

In June 2022, citing the heavy Wall Street disinvestment in oil and the Biden anti-oil policies, the CEO of Chevron declared that he did not believe the US would ever build another new refinery. Some might wonder if America is ruled from New York, the headquarters of BlackRock, or Washington, DC, the headquarters of the US president.

In January 2025, under pressure from Republicans, BlackRock announced that it would leave the Net Zero Asset Managers initiative and become the biggest investor firm on Wall Street to depart an environmentally focused investor group. Larry Fink, appointed as an interim chairman of the World Economic Forum in August 2025, was a colleague of Ursula von der Leyen who left the WEF Board in 2019 to become EU Commission head. Her first major act in Brussels was to push through the EU Zero Carbon Fit for 55 agenda. It imposed major carbon taxes and other constraints on oil, gas and coal in the EU well before the February 2022 Russian actions in Ukraine. The combined impact of the Fink ESG agenda in the Biden administration and the EU's Zero Carbon was a massive energy and inflation crisis.[37] President Trump is anti-climate change and the Biden-era policies are likely to be reversed, but the above example gives a glimpse into the kind of power wielded by companies like BlackRock.

War for Wealth Creation

In the 1930s, figures like Rothschild continued to wield influence on institutions to restructure the world order and make it more profitable for themselves. In his 2023 article, 'Historical Analysis of the Global Elites', researcher Robert J. Burrowes refers to Major General Smedley Butler, who was perhaps the first to spell out the role war played in wealth creation for the elite. A US Marine Corps officer, Butler wrote in his 1935 book, *War Is a Racket*, 'I spent most of my time being a high-class muscle man for big business, for Wall Street and for the bankers who ensured I was a racketeer for capitalism . . . War is a racket. It has always been. It is possibly the oldest, easily the most profitable, surely the most vicious ... the only one in which the profits are reckoned in dollars and the losses in lives.'³⁸

Soon after Butler's book was published, the world was at war again. Professor Anthony C. Sutton, a British–American economist, was able to penetrate the deception behind the origins of the Second World War with access to original documentation and eyewitness accounts to reveal one of the most unreported and remarkable facts of World War II. In his 1976 book, *Wall Street and the Rise of Hitler*, Sutton carefully documented how prominent Wall Street banks and US business houses supported Nazi Germany and Hitler's rise to power when they financed and traded with that country. Sutton concluded that the Second World War was a catastrophe that was extremely profitable for a select group of financial insiders like JP Morgan, the Rockefeller interests, General Electric, Standard Oil, Chase and Manhattan Bank, General Motors and Ford Motor Company, among scores of others.³⁹

General Motors purchased Adam Opel AG, the well-known German auto manufacturer with its modernized manufacturing plant, in 1929. By the late 1930s it was manufacturing armaments for Nazi Germany's military and going out of its way to win contracts. GM's Opel ended up making bombers for Hitler's Germany. IBM was another multinational that helped the German government in operations of the Nazi extermination and slave labour programmes by providing technology and maintenance until 1941.

I.G. Farben, the German pharmaceutical giant of the interwar years, compromised its stellar contribution to health innovation by agreeing to work with the Nazis to make chemicals for the extermination of prisoners in concentration camps.⁴⁰ Max Warburg (brother of Paul, who was on the US Federal Reserve) was on Farben's board of directors, a position from which he resigned in 1932. Farben produced all of Nazi Germany's lubricating oil, 95 per cent of its poison gas, enough to kill 200 million people, used in the gas chambers, 84 per cent of Nazi Germany's explosives, 70 per cent of its gunpowder and several other crucial requirements for the conduct of war.

War is profitable not just for the war merchants and armament manufacturers but for anyone who sees an opportunity for monetary profit. Like the reconstruction boom after the Iraq War of 2003 that was opportunity for Bechtel and Dick Cheney's Halliburton to move in, and for which the Iraqis had to pay in cash or in kind (oil).

JPMorgan and BlackRock have been helping the Ukrainian government set up a reconstruction bank to steer public seed capital into rebuilding projects that could attract hundreds of billions of dollars.[41] There have been discussions between the Ukrainian President Volodymyr Zelenskyy and BlackRock. Firms like BlackRock invest some of their assets in military–industrial complex firms.[42] During the Afghan war, shares of such firms outperformed the stock market, ultimately benefiting investors.[43]

Empires of the Cold War

To control a global empire post-World War II, the US needed to be omnipresent across the globe. Often, its interventions were on economic grounds rather than political, although the narrative was usually woven around politics and security. The intervention in Iran in the early 1950s was a regime change to depose a new democratically elected government of the leftist Mohammad Mosaddegh, whose policies threatened the interests of the Anglo-Persian Oil Company. The operation cost a few hundred thousand dollars, which made calls for similar action elsewhere more acceptable. It was indeed excellent value for money and enough encouragement for similar acts elsewhere.

US interventions for regime change, successful or otherwise, in Latin America have been numerous. These have included, in alphabetic order, Argentina, Bolivia, Brazil, Chile, Costa Rica, Cuba, Dominican Republic, Guatemala, Panama, Paraguay and Venezuela. US hyperactivity in the Middle East has been covered in several books and essays authored by American experts. Locally elected leaders have been replaced with either military dictators or individuals and parties backed by Washington, DC, and US corporate interests.

In 1951, for instance, the US was paranoid about communism in its neighbourhood and Guatemala's new president – the reformist nationalist Jacobo Árbenz – sent shivers down US corporates' spines. One of his first tasks was to bring in economic reforms to reduce the massive income disparities, where 3 per cent of the population held 70 per cent of the land. This reform would have hurt the largest landowner in the country – the American United Fruit Company. Alarmed at the prospect of loss of business, United Fruit launched a massive PR campaign with the American public and the US Congress, saying that Guatemala was being turned into a Soviet colony and that land reform was a Soviet ploy to destroy capitalism in Latin America.[44]

Lobbying by vested interests, a combination of psychological warfare, disinformation and military threats, led to the ouster of Árbenz. His replacement, Carlos Armas, reversed the reforms, leading to violent unrest that lasted 40 years. The ouster had cost the US government $3 million.[45] The United Fruit company used its close connections with the future secretary of state John Foster Dulles, who was one of their lawyers, and his brother Alan, who was at that time the deputy director of the CIA.

The storyline prevalent in Washington's ruling circles was that communism directed from Kremlin was reaching different parts of the world and that Guatemala would be a prototype for testing means and methods to combat this threat. President Eisenhower gave the signal for regime change and CIA-sponsored coups took place, first in Iran in 1953, and then in Guatemala the following year. The CIA was in business and a new kind of empire was being built. In 1957, the CIA and Israel's Mossad helped create the SAVAK, the brutal strong arm of the Shah in Iran and, therefore, of the US as well. The CIA and SAVAK had a cozy relationship in the region, and human rights were a non-issue in the days of the Cold War; control on oil and gas and high finance were the only issues that mattered.

In the early 1960s, President Sukarno of oil-rich Indonesia went on a self-reliance spree, nationalizing foreign-owned farms, real estate and mines. Sukarno had the support of communists, and this was bad news in Washington, with fears of a communist onslaught in Southeast Asia. The CIA was called to action. Alongside or before, a representative from Chas. T. Main, Inc., an international consultancy group based in Washington, was assigned to go to Indonesia.

The consultancy's operating principle for delivering tasks in a foreign country was to create a situation that would let American corporations into that country. Chas. T. Main would prepare a hugely optimistic picture of the economy if it were developed properly, which would then encourage international loans that would come back to Chas. T. Main and other companies like Bechtel, Halliburton, Brown & Root, through massive engineering and infrastructure projects. Ideally, it was desirable to bankrupt the countries which had taken loans so that they remained beholden and dependent on their creditors and amenable to pressures, such as for allowing military bases, or in the form of UN votes and access to oil and other natural resources.[46]

In Indonesia, British and American instructions to their faithful were to liquidate Sukarno if the situation demanded it and the opportunity existed. They worked on carefully compiled lists of leftists, who were rounded up, never to be found again. Some Indonesian economists at Berkeley were developing contingency plans on behalf of Sukarno's opponent, Suharto, in case of a sudden change in the Sukarno government. The free market economists, although not as radical as Milton Friedman's Chicago School, would soon find themselves in the Suharto cabinet![47]

A bloody coup led to a genocide of about a million Indonesians but at the end of it, in 1966, General Suharto was President. Recently released documents confirm that the US role in the 1965 massacre was part of its bigger Cold War strategy.[48] American assistance, along with American weapons and military aircraft sales, soon followed. Suharto's cabinet of Berkeley-led and Ford-funded economists passed laws allowing foreign companies to own 100 per cent of natural resources and oil industries. Within two years, Indonesia's copper, nickel, hardwood, rubber and oil were in foreign hands. No wonder Richard Nixon described Indonesia as 'the greatest prize in the Southeast Asia region'.[49]

Suharto's pre-emptive use of ruthless force effectively silenced nationalists. A senior CIA operations officer, Ralph McGhee, described Suharto's terror as 'a model operation', which would be used for overthrowing Salvador Allende in Chile. Indonesia also became the model for Operation Phoenix in Vietnam, where American-led death squads assassinated 50,000 Vietnamese. McGhee commented, 'You can trace back all the major, bloody events run from Washington to the way Suharto came to power. The success of that meant that it would be repeated, again and again.'[50] The coup in Chile in 1973 secured the commercial interests of AT&T. For Chile, a US Senate Committee later found that 'CIA collaborators participated in preparing an initial overall economic plan which has served as the basis for the Junta's most important economic decisions'.[51]

The shock therapy of Chile and Indonesia included the large-scale disappearances of opponents or dissenters or those who exhibited nationalist tendencies. What happened in Tiananmen Square in Beijing in June 1989 was similar shock therapy by Deng Xiaoping,[52] after which reforms in China picked up pace. In 1998, Venezuelan President Hugo Chavez's battle with the US began soon after he got elected president. Incorruptible and defiant of US oil corporations and therefore the US government, but popular among the people and his Latin American neighbourhood, his attitude of not favouring the oil empires was bound to evoke a reaction from Washington. Chavez was becoming the regional icon and that was unnerving for the US. Initial attempts to dislodge Chavez through 'economic hit men' and intelligence agencies failed.

John Perkins, author of the bestseller *Confessions of an Economic Hitman*, writes, 'Economic Hit Men (EHMs) are highly paid professionals who cheat countries around the globe out of trillions of dollars. They funnel money from the World Bank, the US Agency for International Development and other foreign aid organizations into the coffers of huge corporations and the pockets of a few wealthy families who control the planet's natural resources. Their tools include fraudulent financial reports, rigged elections, extortion, sex, and murder. They play a game as old as empire but one that has taken on new and terrifying dimensions during this time of globalization.' Perkins insists he knows what he is talking about because he was an EHM himself.[53]

During the Cold War, American foreign policy was an outgrowth of their capitalist model that demanded control over both willing and unwilling members of the global neoliberal system. In contrast, the closed Soviet model focused more on influence over governments and their contracts. The Chinese model is a hybrid of the American and Soviet models. The American narrative worked out in the past was that many underdeveloped countries needed infrastructure support, which could be arranged through finance from the World Bank, hopefully saving them from communism in the bargain. The World Bank and United States Agency for International Development (USAID) agreed with this line of thought. Sophisticated econometric models were drawn up by specialized teams to establish that investments in electricity projects, highways, ports and industrial parks would bring economic growth to the country in question. In absolute figures, the GDP showed improvement.

However, the story behind these statistics for the Global South was invariably biased in favour of 'families that owned the industries, banks, supermarkets, hotels, and other businesses'.[54] Only this category prospered. The rest of the country would remain mired in poverty – Indonesia in the Suharto regime is an example. Funds budgeted for healthcare, education and other social services would be diverted to pay interest on loans. Unable to repay the principal, countries were caught in a debt trap. The International Monetary Fund (IMF) would step in and demand that the government offer its oil or any other resources to American corporations at throwaway prices, and public utilities like electricity, water and sewerage be privatized. Big business was the winner.

A fundamental aspect of this approach was that American engineering and construction companies were involved. Consequently, most of the money never left the United States. It would simply be transferred from banks in Washington to engineering and construction companies elsewhere in the US, just as most of the trillions spent in Iraq and Afghanistan were not spent on these countries but remained in the US. This also ensured that that the country being 'helped' would buy related or other equipment, like airplanes, medicines, tractors, computer technologies and so on, from different American companies. This was corporatization of assistance, and colonization with a difference.

The countries that repaid the loans had to pay interest. Any default would lead to demands for allowing a military base on their soil, favourable voting in the UN or uninterrupted access to resources. Even if the country in question agreed to these terms, it would not automatically translate into a waiver on either the loan or the interest.[55]

A crisis for American interests arose in the 1970s in the form of the Arab–Israeli Yom Kippur war in October 1973. This was followed by the Organization of the Petroleum Exporting Countries (OPEC) embargo on oil, which sent oil prices skyrocketing, and by January 1974 it was above $8 per barrel, up from almost a dollar and a half in January 1970. This was unaffordable and unimaginable for US business; the Big Corporations, the Big Banks and the US government hunkered down to find a breakthrough. The embargo was lifted in March 1974 and the Americans probably swore 'Never Again'. Soon after this, American negotiations with the Saudis began. On offer were US military hardware, training and technical support, and everything needed for the modernization of the country to bring it to the twentieth century. What the Americans wanted in exchange were petrodollars and the assurance that there would never be another embargo. This led to the creation of the US–Saudi Joint Commission on Economic Cooperation (JECOR), where the US would assist and the Saudis would pay. The US Congress was consequently never involved.

This was probably the beginning of deep US entrenchment in the kingdom, which would progress to mutual interdependence. For the American corporates it was an unrivalled opportunity as they helped the Saudis develop using their unlimited financial resources; it tied the Saudis ever closer to the Americans. Chas. T. Main, Bechtel, Brown & Root, Halliburton, Stone and Webster, along with many others, were in clover for decades. This extensive US involvement in Saudi Arabia did not distress Saudi Islamists; it was only when American troops landed in the kingdom to stay during and after the Iraq War (2003–2011), did the Islamists become resentful.

Away from the sumptuous conference rooms and boardrooms of defence and armament manufacturers, wars look completely different on the ground. All kinds of deals were done with the dark underground where shady but powerful and ruthless arms traffickers flourished, as in all the wars that the US fought after the Cold War. Afghanistan and Iraq were extremely lucrative markets for arms dealers and brokers. Viktor Bout, a well-known Russian in the underworld business of supplying contraband to insurgents, terrorists, criminals and even governments, saw every war as an opportunity. So was the Iraq War. A hastily put together war, it quickly ran into problems of oversight and defence spending. Having made considerable sums of money in various wars in Africa, Bout had acquired an airline, Irbis Air, which was sought by the US Armed Forces for delivery in the absence other means, since US Air Force planes were under attack in Iraq. Despite his being on the CIA and FBI's wanted list, the Americans had little choice but to turn to Bout. Between 2003 and 2005, Irbis Air ran a few hundred sorties carrying material for the war. Bout was paid $60,000 per flight and he made about $60 million in total.

Interestingly, Beretta weapons meant for the Iraqi security forces, clandestinely purchased by an English company, found their way to Exeter in England and then turned up with terrorists fighting for Musab al Zarqawi, the Al Qaeda leader in Iraq.[56] Obviously, US systems to prevent such pilferage were inadequate. Eventually a mountain of weapons went missing and someone was sitting on a neat pile of dollars. But the murky underworld is a place where competition is not tolerated and is often terminated permanently. There are no comebacks. Forever wars are more than welcome here, overground and legitimate or underground and illegitimate. Permanent peace is not desirable for those who manufacture small arms and those who clandestinely smuggle these weapons. Recurrent conflict provides opportunities to manufacture, sell and profit.

Empires of Oil

The oil boom of the 1990s saw in action the same old giants and the new dictators from the 'Stans'; the region's pipelines and supply lines became security issues too. Pipeline security was a new discipline that the CIA would train its Caspian agents in, along with the US Army that trained local soldiers. The Caspian pipeline intrigues caught the fancy of Hollywood and provided the backdrop to the James Bond film, *The World Is Not Enough* (1999), while intrigues between the CIA, Kazakhstan and the oil industry inspired the 2005 film, *Syriana*.[57] The Caspian region was another theatre for a twentieth-century Great Game.

George Bush Sr.'s presidency had brought James Baker III into the corridors of power, who later benefited enormously in the world of corporate lawyers–lobbyists. Bush Jr., to recoup from his failed career in the oil business, tapped into the enormous network of his father and James Baker III. Was the famous Florida recount of 2000, which declared Bush Junior a winner against Al Gore, a climate change enthusiast, an exhibition of the reach and power of the Texan oil lobby? It is fairly plausible to say that both the Gulf Wars were fought because the Texan oil lobby wanted greater control over the oil business. The two Texans, George W. Bush Jr and Dick Cheney, had a neat little power group; they were the Big Rich Texans, and George H.W. Bush Sr and James Baker (quite the man for all seasons) were a part of this group. Others included Kenneth Lay, former CEO of Enron, and Ray Hunt, an independent oilman and chairman of the Federal Reserve Bank of Dallas, who were the giants of their time 'mingling energy, business and government for private profit'.[58]

The American economy was built on cheap oil available in abundance, which is still needed if the American standard of living is to be maintained. For the present, Dallas and Houston in Texas remain the centres of Big Oil in America. All major domestic and integrated companies are headquartered there. Many of these companies figure in the Fortune 500 list.

The American invasion of Iraq in 2003 was not aimed at targets in Baghdad or the Al Qaeda or Weapon of Mass Destructions (WMDs), nor was it about the usually declared noble goals of restoring democracy and preserving human rights. Instead, British and American forces were seizing oil fields in Kirkuk, Northern Iraq and in Basra and Rumaila. The US Navy Seals' destination was Mina al-Bakr, Iraq's main oil export terminal, which was capable of loading 2 million barrels of oil per day onto supertankers in the Persian Gulf meant for dozens of refineries all over the world.

The Mina al-Bakr terminal, although Iraqi-owned, had strong Texas connections. It was built by the well-known Texan company, Brown & Root, which was a part of Halliburton where former defence secretary Dick Cheney was CEO till the summer of 2000. He received tens of millions of dollars as a reward before he went on to become George W. Bush's vice president. Halliburton also gave Cheney about $367,000 even when he was vice president, as deferred compensation. Cheney owned $242,000 in Halliburton stock options in 2004, which jumped in value to over $8 million in 2005 when Halliburton obtained contracts worth $11 billion to rebuild Iraq's oilfields and civil infrastructure.[59] Soon after Baghdad was captured, Halliburton's first task was to reopen Mina al-Bakr for business.

The Americans did not want to totally defeat Iraq after the invasion of 2003, as that would leave the neighbouring Iranians in control of the region, politically and economically. Yet, Saddam Hussein's control of Kuwait would have meant that he would have control of 25 per cent of the oil in the world, threatening Saudi supremacy. If Iran made up with Iraq, it would add another 9 per cent to the Iraq and Iran share. As Bush Sr declared in 1990 after Saddam's invasion of Kuwait, 'Our jobs, our way of life, our own freedoms and the freedom of friendly countries around the world would all suffer if control of the world's great oil reserves fell in the hands of Saddam Hussein.'[60] The Americans would re-enter Iraq a decade or so later and ensure that their missteps would leave Iran stronger than ever before. This was geo-strategy and geo-economics gone wrong.

The 10 biggest corporations in the world in 2006 were Walmart, ExxonMobil, Royal Dutch Shell, BP, General Motors, Chevron, DaimlerChrysler, Toyota, Ford and ConocoPhillips – five of them were energy companies, and four were auto manufacturers, which meant they were a primary consumer of the product of the five energy companies. Except for Toyota, all had their head offices in the Western hemisphere. About 6 of the 10 dollars these international mega-corporations earned came from operations outside their country of origin, about 60 per cent of their employees were from outside that country, the boards were also internationalized. Global ranking by Fortune 500 had six oil companies in the top 10. 'Oil is almost like money,' exclaimed one oil tycoon.[61] All this money came in dollars and was housed in American banks, mostly. Big Oil and Big Money made this possible, with help from Big Army. By 2020, the global pecking order was: Walmart, Sinopec Group, State Grid, China National Petroleum, Royal Dutch Shell, Saudi Aramco, Volkswagen, BP, Amazon and Toyota. Five were still energy-related, except that three were Chinese owned by the Communist Party of China (CCP), and one Saudi.[62] By 2024, the top 10 companies were: Walmart, Amazon, China's State Grid, Saudi Aramco, Sinopec Group, China National Petroleum, Apple, United Health Group, Berkshire Hathaway and CVS Health – three were Chinese, one Saudi, and along with energy and tech, the list indicated the growing relevance of health and insurance.[63]

Most of the oil in the world is in autocratic and dictatorial regimes – Russia, Saudi Arabia, Iraq, Iran, Venezuela, Nigeria, Kazakhstan, Turkmenistan, Azerbaijan and other parts of Africa and Central Asia. Oil has long been an intoxicant for some and has led to unholy alliances between sworn enemies and exhibitions of unabashed sycophancy towards a dictator sitting on barrels of oil.[64] The security of oil resources for America and its allies, preventing other powers from gaining a foothold in the Middle East, and security of US private investments and supply lines had been a steady policy of the US establishment. Oil was king then; it still is, although there are other aspirants now to this title. The link between oil, economy, profits, security and control has always been obvious.

The extent of power these corporations could exercise was apparent when the 1997 Kyoto Protocol was up for signatures. The agreement required 173 signatures to come into force to reduce emission of greenhouse gases. Sweden was leading the campaign. The world's leading emitter of greenhouse gases, US, signed the protocol but the Senate did not ratify it. A group of corporations led by ExxonMobil, other oil and gas industry peers, car companies and industries that were emissions-intensive, had got together to lobby in a well-orchestrated and well-financed campaign to prevent the US from signing the agreement. Sweden lost; ExxonMobil won. The oil lobby, led by ExxonMobil and the American Petroleum Institute, had supported Bush's candidature for presidency and he owed them one.[65] Paula Dobriansky, under secretary at that time, sent a pre-briefing note to the oil lobby saying, 'POTUS rejected Kyoto in part based on input from you.'[66] Eventually, the Paris Agreement of 2015, which 196 countries signed, would take the battle against climate change forward.

It is interesting that ExxonMobile's annual sales in 2009 were $442 billion while Sweden's GDP was $406 billion. Sweden had a limited number of embassies in the world while ExxonMobil operated almost worldwide with its product marketing, exploration and production sites in 30 countries across the globe. Sweden has a small army of less than 300,000 personnel that it never deploys. ExxonMobil often hires private forces and even some local military forces for security in Africa and Asia, such as in the province of Aceh in Indonesia. It spends about half a million dollars a month for security and many of the personnel it has hired have committed human rights abuses, including murder and torture.[67]

A few years ago, the revenue of WalMart Stores Inc. exceeded the GDP of all but 25 countries. It employed more than the populations of several countries. We have already discussed the world's largest asset management company, BlackRock, which controls assets greater than the national reserves of any country on the planet. The Gates Foundation is a private philanthropic organization that spends as much on healthcare as does the World Health Organization.[68]

It is interesting to note that many of these massive organizations do not manufacture any product. The annual revenues of other giant corporations, such as Apple and Microsoft, are colossal. The scale of their profits takes on a whole new meaning when compared with the GDPs of many countries. In January 2025, Apple and Microsoft had a larger market capitalization than the individual GDPs of France, Brazil, Italy and Canada, listed among the ten biggest global economies.[69]

The rise of China and US policy errors in Iraq, Syria and Afghanistan have given an opening to both China and Russia in the region. It is not enough to have a military–industrial complex; technology, communications and intelligence, maybe even pharma, are now included in the nexus of influence. Defence contracts are profitable if there are enough buyers for the expensive equipment, which then must be used for replacements or repairs. Regime change by stealth, through military coups or 'peoples' revolutions' have been the traditional methods to preserve or enhance interests. The advent of technology and state-of-the-art all-inclusive surveillance technology as in China, has made regime change increasingly difficult.

There was a time when political, economic and military power determined the total power of a nation. There was a prosperous and a powerful military–industrial complex from the dying days of World War II and early days of the Cold War, which arranged production and sales of newer weapons and, more importantly, their periodic consumption and replenishment through endless wars. Globalization and technology altered this equation rapidly by bringing in new factors.

Elites, Cronies and the New Superclass

'No one from among the superclass – the most powerful of the world's most powerful people – would have flown higher than the financial elites,' says American foreign policy analyst, David Rothkopf in his 2008 book, *Superclass: How the Rich Ruined our World*.[70] This is a most important observation about a class that is not so visible, in sharp contrast to today's industrial or technology barons. It was this group that globalized most rapidly and played an outsized role in promoting globalization. They disregarded the bounds of national regulatory systems and flourished in the uncharted uncharitable territory beyond borders, creating fortunes for themselves and the businesses they served. They were the new icons of wealth and power, and made a difference to national policies, which earlier could be done only by electorates or armies. In the West they are called the elites, in Russia they are the oligarchs.

The global elites that have emerged over the past several decades have vastly more power than any other group on the planet. They form a 'superclass' that has had – and still does – the ability to regularly influence the lives of millions of people in multiple countries worldwide. Each exercised this elitist power, individual, group or state, on its own or sometimes along with others, thereby amplifying its reach and effect. The age of inherited lifelong power, however, is under challenge, and the new entrant now must prove his worth.

As Rothkopf says, 'That such a group exists is indisputable. Heads of state, CEOs of the world's largest companies, media barons, billionaires who are actively involved in their investments, technology entrepreneurs, hedge fund managers, private equity investors, top military commanders, a select few religious leaders, a handful of renowned writers, scientists, and artists, even terrorist leaders and master criminals meet the above criteria for membership.'[71]

The famous international private equity firm, the Carlyle Group, manages assets and funds internationally with an impressive roster of prominent employees. This included the omnipresent former secretary of state, James Baker III, former secretary of defence, Frank Carlucci, the former White House budget director, Dick Darman, among others. Also included for some time were John Major, former British prime minister, Fidel Ramos, the former Philippines president, and former US presidents George Bush Sr. and Jr. – at different times. Carlyle operated silently to build its stake in the defence industry and acquired a strong position internationally. After Carlucci joined Carlyle, the company began to buy up defence-related assets, starting with the $130 million purchase of BDM Consulting. It was not unusual to have former defence secretaries Carlucci, William Cohen, Caspar Weinberger, William Perry, Dick Cheney and Donald Rumsfeld lunching with Carlyle.

The fact that investment decisions taken by Carlyle affect several hundred thousand employees all over the world, along with countless investors and competitors, indicates the extent of group's power. David Rubenstein, one of its founders and one of the richest men in Washington, along with his editors and partners, make for a very powerful global network. They can invest people's money, support political candidates and be available for agenda-setting situations. Often, they organize their own big meetings that attract the powerful from other countries, which is also a measure of their own power. Blackstone is another similar private equity company. Among investors with Carlyle are the Hungarian–American billionaire George Soros, Prince Alwaleed bin Talal and members of the bin Laden family. Shafiq bin Laden, one of Osama's many brothers, was in fact attending a Carlyle conference in Washington on 11 September 2001.[72]

What the world sees is the effect of Big Oil, along with Big Money. To give an example of the intricate connections among the powerful, consider this. Soon after World War II, the British oil company BP sought to preserve its huge interests in Iranian oil and gas by ensuring that the Americans, led by the Dulles brothers (John as Secretary of State and Allen as head of CIA), organized a coup in Iran to replace the elected prime minister, Mossadegh, by the pliable Reza Pahlavi as the Shah. The British lost imperial control of Iran to the Americans; BP stayed on. Also, the Dulles brothers worked with the Washington law firm, Sullivan and Cromwell, before joining the US government. This firm represented BP's interests in the US. The firm had also been legal counsel to the J. Henry Schroder bank, which was controlled by the Warburg family bank, and the Hamburg bank that had financed Adolf Hitler's rise to power in Nazi Germany.

Allen Dulles had also been a lawyer for the Nazi combine, IG Farben, and headed the CIA's predecessor, Office of Strategic Services, during World War II, and the brothers were cousins of the Rockefellers.[73] The nature of Germany's Nazi regime was hardly an impediment to the Dulles brothers or indeed the US government. Some cozy nests thrived, regardless of ideology.

After the War, Allen Dulles as the US intelligence station chief in Bern, became active with the Muslim Brotherhood and former Nazis, when he helped the Swiss Nazi, François Genoud, transfer Hitler's and Joseph Goebbels's trusts into Swiss bank accounts. In 1952, Dulles helped found the Banque Commerciale Arabe in Lausanne, Switzerland. The bank represented a deal between the CIA and the Muslim Brotherhood which included members of the Saudi royal family. The same year, in 1953, when Dulles formed an alliance with the House of Saud, the CIA launched its mind control programme – MKUltra, using LSD produced by the Warburg banking dynasty's Swiss Sandoz Laboratories.[74]

Total control was all that mattered to the US as it prepared for the Cold War; morality and conscience were at a low premium in international matters and national interest was the only guiding principle. This has remained so ever since.

America's superclass has its exclusive clubs and associations. The Council on Foreign Relations (CFR), the Trilateral Commission (TC) and the Bilderberg Group form a Trinity of influence and power. These are exclusive nesting spots for the wealthy, powerful and ambitious. CFR is perhaps the most powerful of all think tanks, represents interests of monopoly capital, has links with the CIA and is sometimes referred to as 'Wall Street's think tank'.[75] They are on a high pedestal and their opinion is sometimes authority. Reaching this status of superclass clubs and associations is a long circuitous process. It requires diligence, initiative, opportunism, imagination and the ability to operate through a maze of private and exclusive pressure clubs. These were and are via revolving doors, lobbies, think tanks, media houses and business contractors of various kinds that lead to political power and control. For instance, think tanks were particularly useful in creating an intellectual perception for supporting an invasion of Iraq while acknowledging that the claim that Iraq was pursuing the nuclear weapon route was 'unpersuasive'.[76] All this was accompanied by a strong military capability that would, in times of need, keep rivals at bay, if not defeated.

Then there is the other wealth club – the Davos World Economic Forum, which has members like George Soros. There were reports in 2016 that Soros had begun to try a quiet overhaul of the US justice system when he channelled more than $3 million for campaigns for seven district attorneys. Instead of investing in high-profile presidential campaigns, Soros went under the radar to campaign for one of the progressive movement's core goals – reshaping the American justice system. Soros has also supported African-American and Hispanic candidates for powerful local roles, all of whom ran on platforms sharing major goals of his, like reducing racial disparities in sentencing and directing some drug offenders to diversion programmes instead of trial.[77] Soros has also canvassed for election of democratic candidate to the Wisconsin Supreme Court and raised a million dollars for the Democratic Party candidate.[78] Albanian President Ilir Meta asserted that Albania had managed to avoid a domestic and international conspiracy to 'capture the state' by George Soros, although he offered no evidence for his claim.[79] In June 2018 the Hungarian government passed a law to criminalize help given to illegal immigrants, which it called the 'Stop Soros' law to oppose the non-governmental organizations (NGOs) that extend such help, some of which, it said, were backed by George Soros.[80]

Soros is something of an anomaly in this superclass, which tends to be non-ideological and purely driven by profit. Soros seems to be trying to recast the system according to an ideology. Also, he is not part of the traditional 'elite' and has used his money in disruptive ways (rather than in status quoist ways). The cause of his disruptive beliefs and actions is unclear – it could be personal power and money or a supremacist leftist ideology where the state rules completely over every aspect of human existence, something even the communists did not dream of.

Imagine if two powerful American corporate houses, say the Rothschild and Rockefeller houses, were placed on the same page and the connections between them shown. The US president would not be the centrepiece, at least not Donald Trump. Featured along with the Rockefellers and Rothschilds would be the CFR, TC and the Bilderbergers, all connected to each other and to the two families. There would be George Soros and his deputy Stewart Mnuchin (now the baton has been passed to George's son, Alex Soros); Henry Kissinger (when he was alive) more or less in the middle; Dick Cheney, Goldman Sachs, ExxonMobil and Rex Tillerson; Condoleezza Rice connected to the Bilderbergers, the American Israeli Public Affairs Committee(AIPAC), BlackRock and Vanguard, the world's largest private equity companies. All the various coloured lines would converge in the CFR box. Another chart can show all American media, TV, print and their editors and journalists, from the *Los Angeles Times*, *New York Times* and *Wall Street Journal*, to BBC and CNN, to *The Times* and *Financial Times* – and they would all be connected with this Trinity (CFR, TC and the Bilderbergers).

That is true international corporate power. It is not just managing wealth; it is also about managing the storyline.

Empires of Globalization

Globalization is driven by markets, but markets are amoral and Darwinian – only the fittest, the smartest and the most ruthless survive. In March 1999, the American commentator Thomas Friedman wrote in the *New York Times*, 'From supercharged financial markets to Osama bin Laden, the emerging global order demands an enforcer. That's America's new burden.'[81]

The old model of a military–industrial complex that Eisenhower warned about, had begun to expand almost immediately after the end of the Second World War, when the era of colonialism was declared to be over and there were newly independent countries. Powerful corporates who had gained from the war effort took over from governments as they hunted for new opportunities in new areas.

The Cold War had its own stability. After it ended, the global system grew increasingly unstable and dangerous. The Soviet Union collapsed more under its own weight rather than because of the military defeat in Afghanistan. Its cumbersome unimaginative central planning in closed societies at a time when elsewhere in the world there was free flow of information and trade caused the Soviet Union to lose the race. Communism had failed, liberalism had won; there could be no complete individual freedom without capitalism, and the world celebrated the onset of modernism and globalization. Soon globalization became the religion of the corporate world. The World Bank and other American institutions, NGOs and think tanks included, aggressively began to push the agenda of deregulation and free markets.

An aspect of globalization during the 1990s was that many companies that had traditionally manufactured their own products and maintained large, stable workforces, began to change their style of operation. One was the Nike model: the management did not own any factories but manufactured the product through an intricate web of contractors and subcontractors. It diverted its resources into designing. The other was the Microsoft model, which maintained a tight control on the shareholders and employees, who were the company's core competence, but outsourced everything else to temporary workers, from running the delivery systems to code writing.[82]

Excess of consumption and production became the mantras; to get richer even quicker was the goal. There was a certain recklessness among corporations and financial centres; there was a death wish in this extravagance. The total euphoria of being the only superpower, finally, and the 'end-of-history' illusion prevented Americans from seeing that their economic activities were leading to worsening inequalities at home and abroad. America moved away from an industry-manufacturing-

and-services-led economy to a service industry with cheap imports from China. Corporate America was in clover, profits had skyrocketed and inflation was low, interest rates had fallen and the cost of borrowing was low as well. America had become an overweight financial system; so, when the 2008 financial crisis happened, many of its financial companies were just too big to fail. In less than two decades after the 'end of history', capitalism had to be saved and the political system came under tremendous strain as a result. Inflation had to be kept low and cheap imports from China doubled to $600 billion between 2008 and 2019.

As a global power, America had missed the signals of the early twenty-first century. There was political and economic upheaval around the globe. Edward Luttwak, an American military strategist, had warned of the fallout of unbridled capitalism in a prescient 1994 paper.[83] He argued that while unobstructed capitalism was an engine of growth, the structural changes imposed by cycles of relentless competition, destruction and replacement 'can inflict more disruption on working lives, firms, entire industries and their localities than individuals can absorb, or the connective tissue of friendships, families, clans, elective groupings, neighbourhoods, villages, towns, cities or even nations can withstand'.

The political ramifications of this had come to a head and bipartisan consensus on Capitol Hill had become elusive and difficult, which was worrying for long-term strategic planners. Critical legislation gets hamstrung in political bickering, rendering it inflexible in a competitive world where centralized leadership in China and Russia faced no such problems. The present stand-off over Ukraine is one evidence of this policy paralysis in Washington, DC. In 2025, as Israel continues its no-holds-barred campaign against Hamas and Hezbollah and against Iran and its nuclear capabilities, the US policy paralysis is quite evident.

Earlier this century, no one paid attention as America remained bogged down in the political, military, sectarian and economic problems of the Middle East. These were proving to be unaffordable politically, militarily and financially. Yet no one read the writing on the wall. The events of 11 September 2001 and the disproportionate American response to an act by non-state actors, destabilized the system further. Many saw the new wars as salvation for their economy.

The global financial crises in 2008 and 2009 were thus far more important in a macro sense than the destructive attack on the World

Trade Centre in New York. It made European allies and rising powers like China and India question whether the American model had failed. New powers like China had begun to grow at a phenomenal pace and others like India and Brazil were on a growth trajectory too. The German finance minister of the time, Peter Steinbruck, predicted: '[T]he U.S. will lose its status as the superpower of the world financial system . . . The world will become multipolar . . . [it] will never be the same again . . . when we look back 10 years from now, we will see 2008 as a fundamental rupture.'[84] Later the French president speaking at a G20 summit said that 'the all-powerful market that is always right is finished' and that the page had been turned on Anglo–American capitalism.[85]

Nothing changed adversely for the elite and the wealthy, though. In the middle of the decade of 2010–2020, after all the crises, 62 billionaires, globally, possessed as much wealth as the bottom half of the global population (about 3.6 billion). A few years ago, this number was 300; but later, when better figures were available, the 62 had dropped to eight. These eight had made their money in technology – Bill Gates, Mark Zuckerberg, Jeff Bezos of Amazon, Larry Ellison of Oracle, Carlos Slim of Telemax and Michael Bloomberg. The other two were Warren Buffet (who had shares in IBM and Apple) and Amancio Ortega (who had built the retailer Zara).[86]

The narrative of control has changed in the age of technology. A country that spends billions of dollars on surveillance, including of its own citizens in the name of guaranteeing freedoms, would be expected to cover social media not just for information but to prevent certain trends and guide them in a particular direction. In the process, social media made its billions, the corporates got their business and the authorities got their intelligence – a win-win arrangement for everyone except the consumer/reader/user who, along with his or her data, becomes the product on 'free' social media platforms.[87]

Despite the age of technology, or perhaps aided by it, we inhabit a turbulent world. With the hot wars raging in Eurasia and the Middle East where multiple powers and their proxies are involved, the global situation could easily roll out of control. Will the Big Powers be able to control this, or will they aggravate the mess by joining the battles themselves?

The world is taking a turn for the worse, with more Western experts talking of World War III. The financial crash on the New York market, with all the joint USAF-led air force exercises in Qatar, obviously aimed at intimidating Iran or diverting attention from the mess in US, the Le Pen sentence which is bound to bring a reaction, Europeans talking of rearming against Russia, Trump's move on what he calls 'global tariffs against US' and the Islamists talking of a separate 400-acre city in Texas, adds financial and ideological chaos to political and military chaos on the globe. Democracy, as the West taught us, may be dying.

As it is, the atomic clock is ticking towards zero hour.

2

Superspies: You Win Some, You Lose Some

One of the things that distinguishes the CIA from the State Department is that the CIA is both asked to, and authorized to, steal secrets. So, if the question is whether the CIA steals secrets, the answer is yes.[1]

— MICHAEL HAYDEN, former director, CIA

Where I see it going is toward a totalitarian state. You've got the NSA doing all this collecting of material on all of its citizens – that's what the SS, the Gestapo, the Stasi, the KGB, and the NKVD did.[2]

— WILLIAM BINNEY, former intelligence officer, National Security Agency

It was September 1945, and the Second World War was over. Hitler had died by suicide in his bunker along with his mistress; Stalin's victorious Soviet Army was sitting in Berlin, Japan had surrendered after suffering a nuclear disaster, Europe was devastated and Nazi Germany was divided into two, East and West. The allies of convenience were quickly reverting to their pre-war status of enemies vying for global control.

The Americans had fought the war along with the Office of Strategic Services headed by Col. William 'Wild Bill' Donovan, which was not strictly an intelligence agency but meant for special operations against the enemy. During the war, the Americans had relied on European intelligence, mainly British, and used signals intelligence (SIGINT) in the Pacific against Japan. This was inadequate for a country that already felt it had the right to rule the world. The hot war was over, and the Cold War had begun as Stalin pulled the Iron Curtain down across East Europe. The Americans 'imported' many of the Nazi Germany's Gestapo and Abwehr officers to help them strengthen US intelligence's Soviet network, because the Nazis had a strong network against the Soviet Union. Among those called in for this task was General Reinhard Gehlen, who worked with the US military intelligence and was sent back to Germany to establish the new Federal Intelligence Service, the BND (German external intelligence). While in captivity after the war, Gehlen had volunteered valuable information to the Americans.

The Beginning of CIA's Overt and Covert Operations

The Central Intelligence Agency was created on 18 September 1947, under the National Security Act, with a charter focused on gathering and analysing intelligence. This changed quickly. Elections were due in Italy in April 1948 and the fear was that the communist candidate would win unless the rival was supported. A budget of $250 million ($2.5 billion at today's rate) was approved. CIA proprietary media organizations like the Voice of America, Radio Free Europe and Radio Liberty were to establish a surround system on Italy, even as money was routed through the church, trade unions and the mafia. Bags of money began to reach politicians for their political and campaign expenses, posters and pamphlets. Hollywood's charm, too, was recruited for this noble cause.

Operation Gladio, an agency created for 'stay behind' operations in Italy and elsewhere, was authorized to use psychological warfare, false-flag operations and even assassinations to delegitimize left-wing politicians and parties, and to reactivate operations in case of another war.[3] Later, Miles Copeland, one of the original members of the CIA, would point out, 'Had it not been for the Mafia, the Communists would by now have been in control of Italy.'[4] Quite obviously there would have been payback between the CIA and the Mafia.

Soon the CIA was active in Latin America, arranging governments to Washington's and the American corporate world's satisfaction, and in Europe where it was tasked with keeping the Soviet Union away, even as it fought proxy wars elsewhere. The CIA thus had a dual role – collection and analysis of intelligence *and* covert operations – both global, in keeping with America's new image as the world's peacekeeper and guardian of democracy, an image that was embellished by its glossies like *Life* and *Time* magazines. The other big operation carried out successfully was the overthrow of the democratically elected Iranian prime minister Mohammed Mossadegh, who had the audacity to nationalize the British-owned Anglo-Persian Oil Company in 1951. By 1953 America ensured he was dethroned by a 'spontaneous revolution' and the Shah of Persia restored.

The Italian job was over on 18 April 1948, with the CIA-backed Christian Democracy coalition winning. This was followed by a document on 30 April 1948, called 'The Inauguration of Organized Political Warfare',[5] written by George Kennan, the father of US strategy, a forerunner of Henry Kissinger and Zbigniew Brzeziński and author of the famous seventy-page, 8000-word 'Long Telegram'. The Long Telegram, written in 1946, is considered the basis of US policy to deal with the Cold War and the Soviet Union. Some consider it a foundational document of the US along with the Declaration of Independence, the Federalist Papers and George Washington's Farewell Address.

Kennan's 'The Inauguration of Organized Political Warfare' was 'top secret' till 2005, when it was declassified. In it, he described organized political warfare as 'the employment of all the means at a nation's command, short of war, to achieve its national objective. Such operations are both overt and covert. They range from such overt actions as political alliances, economic measures and "white" propaganda, to such covert operations as clandestine support of "friendly" foreign elements, "black" psychological warfare and even encouragement of underground resistance in hostile states'.[6]

Kennan referred to aggressive Soviet tactics that led America first to the Truman Doctrine (a policy established by President Harry S. Truman in 1947 to support democratic nations against the Soviet Union) and then to covert activities like its interference in the Italian elections. This was political warfare and should be recognized as such, Kennan said, and it was of two types – overt and covert. Both should be directed and coordinated by the Department of State, he asserted. As America assumed greater international responsibilities for intelligence collection while tackling the full might of the Kremlin's political warfare, it could not also immobilize its resources for covert political warfare. America could not afford to have to scramble during a political crisis with impromptu covert operations as was done during the Italian elections. Kennan proposed a permanent structure for these activities located in the State Department with the Soviet world in mind.

To do this, Kennan recommended three long-term projects. The first was to form centres of national hope and revive a sense of purpose among political refugees from the Soviet world to provide inspiration for continuing popular resistance within these countries as well as to become a potential nucleus for all-out liberation movements in the event of war. The programme would be overt with covert American assistance in the form of funds and guidance. Publicly appointed committees in America and elsewhere would organize public support of resistance to tyranny in foreign countries.

The second project would be to organize underground activities behind the Iron Curtain. These operations would be on the traditional British and Soviet political warfare pattern where there would be 'remote and deeply concealed official control of clandestine operations so that governmental responsibility cannot be shown'. Modern terminology for this is 'plausible deniability'. The US government would provide the general direction and financial support, which would be passed through private American organizations or even business enterprises comprising private citizens of suitable calibre and reliability. These organizations would have access to field offices in Europe and Asia for establishing various national underground representatives in free countries and through their intermediaries pass on assistance and guidance to resistance movements behind the Iron Curtain.

The third project was support for indigenous anti-communist elements in countries of the free world. The purpose was to strengthen indigenous forces combating communism in countries where Soviet political warfare could become a threat to American security. This would be a covert operation utilizing private intermediaries and organizations to conduct operations that would be separate from the organizations handling projects in the previous two categories. These committees or organizations would replicate American actions during the Italian elections of April 1948 and be guided by the government and funded by it as well.

Kennan recommended the creation of a covert political warfare operations directorate within the government, guided by one person selected by the government who would be responsible for the covert phases of political warfare and be answerable to the Secretary of State. This document became the blueprint for the US intelligence services, and its recommendations have been followed by and large in both classic intelligence operations and covert psywar and influence operations.

This time was open season for US activity in its backyard, Latin America. Coups d'etat to replace left-wing governments with those that were right-wing, faithful to American interests and corporates, quickly became the norm. The replacements could be military juntas, dictators or authoritarian regimes. Originally meant to be only an exercise in containment, the US government directive NSC68 of 1950 allowed more aggressive actions against potential Soviet allies, and prepared the ground for militarization during the Cold War. There was scarcely any Latin American country that did not face US intervention in the twentieth century.

Quite early into the Cold War, intelligence agencies were experimenting with new skills and processes to improve their intelligence output. Imaginations were running riot. Operation Artichoke in 1951 tried new methods of interrogation and Operation MKUltra in 1953 experimented with drugs like LSD and barbiturates along with hypnosis and torture for mind control. It was wound down in 1973 just ahead of the Church Committee disclosures chaired by Senator Frank Church.[7]

The Church Committee was appointed after the Watergate scandal during President Richard Nixon's presidency, when there was a break-in into the Democratic Party headquarters in Watergate and it came to light that some of the burglars had an intelligence background. The ensuing scandal ultimately led to Nixon's resignation and the appointment of the Church Committee to look into the functioning of intelligence agencies. Some of the programmes that were investigated included COINTELPRO, which conducted the surveillance and infiltration of American political and civil rights organizations; Family Jewels, a CIA programme to covertly assassinate foreign leaders; and Operation Mockingbird, a propaganda campaign that used domestic and foreign journalists as CIA assets with dozens of US news organizations providing cover for CIA activity. This confirmed earlier suspicions that the CIA cultivated relationships with private institutions, including the press. The Church Committee found 50 journalists who had official, but secret, relationships with the CIA. Project Shamrock was about major telecommunications companies sharing their traffic with the NSA and thereby publicly confirmed the existence of the NSA as a signals monitoring agency.

The post-Watergate enquiries into the CIA exposed details of its covert political activities in other countries undertaken to promote US foreign policy objectives. After taking over as president in January 1977, Jimmy Carter banned such activities and imposed strict limits on the CIA's covert operations in foreign countries. After his election in November 1980, and before taking over as president in January 1981, Ronald Reagan sought recommendations from William Casey, who later became CIA director. Casey recommended the revival of covert political activities. Since there might have been opposition from the Congress and public opinion after the Church Committee findings, it was suggested that this task be given to an NGO with no ostensible links to the CIA.

National Endowment for Democracy

The National Endowment for Democracy (NED) was born under a Congressional enactment of 1983 as a 'non-profit, non-governmental, bipartisan, grant-making organization to help strengthen democratic institutions around the world'. Amongst its activities were the secret funding of individuals, political parties and NGOs favourable to US interests and the funnelling of money to counter the activities of those considered anti-US.

Since the 1980s, the NED became the main conduit for funds, ideas and decisions wherever American interests were involved.[8] Its grants programme was augmented by the International Forum for Democratic Studies, the *Journal of Democracy*, the Reagan–Fascell Fellows Program, the World Movement for Democracy and the Center for International Media Assistance. Its core institutes include the Center for International Private Enterprise, the International Republican Institute, the National Democratic Institute and the Solidarity Center.

The NED is active in more than 100 countries and apart from its four core institutes, works through several American grants recipients. It has been active in aiding democratic movements in the Soviet Union and now in Russia, East Europe, China, Cuba, Iran, Vietnam, Nicaragua, the Arab world and the Indian subcontinent. Apart from funds, the NED supplies technical know-how, training, educational material, computers, fax machines and other office equipment to selected political groups, civic organizations, labour unions, dissident movements, students' groups, publishers and news media. It has manipulated elections in Latin America, Mongolia, Bulgaria, Albania, funded the opposition to Venezuelan President Hugo Chávez, and of course, to anti-Castro groups in Cuba.

Allen Weinstein, who helped draft the legislation establishing the NED, declared in 1991, 'A lot of what we do today was done covertly 25 years ago by the CIA.'[9] In an article elaborating the role of the NED, the writer pointed out that the organization's efficacy lay in the fact that funds were being routed through a non-government organization, as receiving money from the US government directly would damage the credibility of local leadership.

In September 2024, Victoria Nuland, a former diplomat who had played a big role in the 2014 Ukraine elections, was reappointed to the NED Board of Directors. Announcing Nuland's appointment, NED president Damon Wilson said, 'As NED partners face increasing threats from autocrats around the world, ambassador Nuland's experiences will help the Endowment sharpen its approach to supporting democracy advocates.'[10] It would be wise to read between the lines about the role Nuland has played in the past in Europe. Her role in the ouster of the democratically elected government in Ukraine in 2014 was her crowning achievement.[11]

Anne Applebaum, Pulitzer-prize winning historian, a Senior Fellow at the Johns Hopkins School of Advanced International Studies and the Agora Institute where she co-directs Arena, a programme on disinformation and twenty-first century propaganda, is also on NED's Board of Directors. The international chess grandmaster Garry Kasparov, who is chairman of the US-backed Human Rights Foundation, is another famous name associated with NED.

Over the years, the NED and its partner organizations have in effect weaponized civil society and media against governments that have stood in the way of American policies of free market and corporate interests.

It has constantly interfered in elections, mobilized coups with a little assistance from supposedly unknown sources, and led public relations campaigns against nations opposed to America's global agenda.

The NED's campaigns against Russia, China and North Korea are well known. While former speaker Nancy Pelosi was evasive when asked if the US government should stop funding the NED for seeking regime change, the late CIA whistleblower Philip Agee (author of the bestseller, *Inside the Company: CIA Diary*, 1975) was more forthright. 'Nowadays, instead of having the CIA going around behind the scenes and trying to manipulate the process by inserting money here and giving instructions secretly and so forth, they now have a sidekick, which is the National Endowment for Democracy, NED.'[12]

An over-enthusiastic ally of the NED gave the plot away with its loud claim of the role of the NED in Nicaragua. It boasted that for decades, the United States' National Endowment for Democracy had played a key role in shaping Nicaragua's political arena.[13]

The Arab Spring, sparked by a fiery suicide in Tunisia in December 2010 quickly enflamed Egypt, Libya, Syria, Bahrain and Yemen. Each country followed a different route but Egypt, with the largest population in the region, reflected its importance to America when by January 2011, Tahrir Square in Cairo became a national symbol of peoples' anger against President Hosni Mubarak. They wanted him out. For the West led by America, the Egyptian control of the Suez Canal and its borders with Israel, Sudan and Libya made it a central figure in their strategic calculations in the region.

Hosni Mubarak stepped down in February 2011 as the unrest grew, and was imprisoned. Power passed into the hands of Supreme Council of the Armed Forces. Since 2014, Abdel Fattah el-Sisi has been president over successive elections. Many locally run and organized NGOs with their pro-democracy, human rights or pro-liberty slogans were offshoots of NED. In December 2011, Washington went into a spin when the Egyptian Army raided 17 NGOs, many of them US intelligence cutouts.[14] One of the NGOs raided was the National Democratic Institute, which had been inaugurated by former secretary of state Madeleine Albright and another, International Republican Institute, inaugurated by the regime-change fan, John McCain, both organizations associates of NED. It's 'completely unacceptable', fumed Secretary of State Hillary Clinton in Washington. The raids were awkward for the State Department. American friend Egypt was the recipient of about $1.5 billion military aid, (the second largest in the world at that time) but was violating the US Congress dictum about democracy and freedoms. Hillary Clinton had to issue a 'national security waiver' to avoid having to explain to Congress about freedom of expression, association and religion.

USAID

Much before the NED was created, President John F. Kennedy formed the favourite American instrument for creating narratives and establishing control in their Cold War with the Soviet Union – USAID – in 1961. The ostensible idea was to provide humanitarian assistance abroad, to fund education and fight hunger along with nutritional assistance to infants and children. It was meant to be a semi-autonomous body supervised by the State Department. Yet, it has special departments that deal with promoting democracy, which in less polite language, can also mean regime change.

USAID became an instrument of US foreign policy and after the end of Cold War I (1991), funded democracy-building programmes in the former Soviet Union 'sometimes on its own, sometimes in concert with the CIA'.[15] Within the first year of its formation, in 1961, USAID became associated with CIA's short-lived Operation Pin Cushion to train Laotian guerrillas.[16] Over time, USAID's links with the CIA grew stronger as the two worked together and trained police forces in different parts of the world. USAID also provided a cover for some covert operations of the CIA, especially during the Vietnam War. Former US State Department official Mike Benz, speaking at the *Shawn Ryan Show*, said, 'When it's too dirty for the CIA, you give it to USAID because the CIA needs to get presidential approval for every covert action they do. USAID does not.'[17]

Scott Horton, director of the Libertarian Institute, in his 2024 book, *Provoked: How Washington Started the New Cold War with Russia and the Catastrophe in Europe*, gives details of how both USAID and NED pretended to be the 'good guys' who were helping other countries become more democratic and enlightened. Both funded media outlets that spread American propaganda, supported political opposition factions that were US-friendly, as well as NGOs working for regime change. They helped the CIA plot coups systematically, relying on local forces to agitate and take over the country. The list is long but leaders overthrown in this manner include Guyana's Cheddi Jagan, Congo's Patrice Lumumba, Chile's Salvador Allende, Libya's Muammar Gaddafi, Serbia's Slobodan Milošević, Ukraine's Viktor Yanukovych, Georgia's Eduard Shevardnadze and others. Both these organizations were the CIA's sock puppets in these countries. To quote Horton, 'The colour coded revolutions were US coups d'etat dressed as local "uprisings" primarily against Russian-leaning states in the near abroad.'[18] Several other agencies have been involved in other locations – like the Omidyar Network, Soros's International Renaissance Foundation in Ukraine, the Soros Foundation, the Atlantic Foundation Open Society Foundation. These operations and activities have not only been Euro-centric, but have taken place in Asia too, including India.

At the beginning of his second term as US President, Donald Trump's decision to freeze both NED and USAID meant an automatic withdrawal of American influence and abilities globally. China has already shown interest in replacing them for similar humanitarian efforts.

Closer home, there have been leaked reports that expose the US role in destabilizing Bangladesh and the ouster of Prime Minister Sheikh Hasina in 2024. The US government-funded and Republican Party-run subsidiary of NED, the International Republican Institute, trained an army of activists to achieve a power shift to destabilize Bangladesh politics.[19] Sheikh Hasina reportedly accused the US government of removing her from power because she refused to allow a US military base on St. Martin's Island, a small coral island in the Bay of Bengal.[20]

Muhammad Yunus, a Nobel Laureate (2006), winner of the United States Presidential Medal for Freedom (2009) and the Congressional Gold Medal (2010), took over as the Interim Government's Chief Adviser in August 2024. He has also been invited to the Clinton Global Citizen Award (2012). The Americans have cultivated Yunus for nearly 20 years. In his new incarnation, Yunus described the ouster as 'meticulously designed' at the Clinton Global Initiative's annual meeting in September 2024.[21] Quite obviously he has been accepted by Washington as their 'Man in Dhaka'.

Superspy Versus Superspy

The Cold War between American and Russian spies was fought with extreme intensity and suspicion. It was a continuation of the old British–Russian imperial rivalry that preceded the Bolshevik takeover of Russia. Tradecraft of the most strenuous and innovative kind was used to defeat surveillance and collect intelligence from human sources. Spies of all kinds – idealistic, mercenary – and equally devoted professional handlers, were the Cold Warriors who put their lives on the line. Deceit, deception and manipulation remain some of the sterling qualities of spies, and there cannot be any moral judgement in the world of espionage. Both sides realized while spying on each other that blind hatred for a regime was not a good enough reason to expect sound intelligence.[22] The best sources would be from within the adversary's establishment. As a result, the Russians always took espionage and counterespionage seriously.

In spy fiction, the Americans have had their Jason Bourne, and the British their James Bond, with all their glamour and gadgetry. The best-known fictional Soviet spy is probably Max Otto von Stierlitz (his German cover name) who was tasked to penetrate the Nazi high command during the Second World War and after it to hunt for Nazi war criminals. Stierlitz shunned all the gadgets that subsequent spy-fiction heroes possessed. In real life, more spies are of the George Smiley (John Le Carré's famous creation) kind than the Bond or Bourne kind.

In the world of classical espionage, the best spies are those that perform their tasks, deliver the goods, are never caught and, therefore, we do not get to read about them. A very productive spy may end up getting caught by the opposition either by betrayal, or because of out-of-the-ordinary behaviour that attracts questions.

There could be four broad categorizations of spies. One is the spy who is first spotted by a talent spotter, and recruited and trained according to his or her abilities. Examples are Klaus Fuchs, of German descent but a British national, the Rosenbergs and the physicist Nunn May, all of whom helped the Russians unravel the Manhattan Project and enabled them to develop the bomb much sooner than they would have otherwise.

The second category of spy is a 'walk-in', the spy who manages to establish contact with the right person in a foreign intelligence agency and can deliver results, at times for years. Many American and Soviet spies during the Cold War were in this category. The motive is usually mercenary, occasionally revenge. Robert Hanssen of the FBI was one such spy for the Soviet Union. Hanssen began spying for the Russians in 1979 and, over a period of 22 years, he first spied for the GRU and then for the KGB. He was able to identify Soviet General Dmitri Polyakov as a long-term agent of American intelligence. Polyakov was arrested and executed in 1988. Until his arrest in 1990, Hanssen supplied about 6,000 pages of classified documents to his KGB handlers. These included nuclear deployment plans, satellite positions, the complete contents of classified FBI computers and other valuable intelligence.[23]

The hard-drinking, frequent security regulations violator with a troubled marriage, Aldrich Ames, worked in the CIA's Soviet Division from 1972. In debt, with mounting expenses because of his girlfriend and an impending divorce, Ames walked into the Soviet embassy in April 1985, offering valuable intelligence in exchange for money. On him was an envelope containing information about two Soviet military officers who had offered their services to the CIA. Between 1985 and 1986, about 30 Soviet operations of the CIA were compromised as a result. Ultimately the CIA, having ignored his alcoholic transgressions for years, began to investigate Ames. He was sentenced to a life term in October 1994, but only after he had done incalculable harm to the CIA. Hanssen and Ames were two major American security embarrassments at roughly the same time, their downfall brought on by greed and carelessness.[24]

Perhaps the most audacious approach was by Chief Warrant Officer John Walker, who drove his red MG sports car to the Soviet embassy in October 1967 and asked to meet the Intelligence chief. The KGB station chief intuitively agreed to meet Walker, a deal was made, and Walker was soon feeding the KGB vital intelligence about cryptographic secrets and navy submarine warfare. Eventually betrayed by his wife when he confided in her, his 16-year career ended in the usual manner.[25]

The CIA also had their successes against the Soviets. Electronics engineer Adolf Tolkachev made several attempts to establish contact with the CIA in Moscow with the motive to escape from the Soviet Union. Eventually, Langley relaxed its self-imposed stand down and allowed a meeting with Tolkachev, who quickly blossomed into the CIA's 'Billion Dollar Spy'. In June 1980, he provided the CIA's Moscow station chief, Gardner Hathaway, 179 rolls of 35-mm film of valuable intelligence on

Soviet airborne radars and armament control systems. Dispatching this, the director of CIA, Stansfield Turner, pointed out that this documentary evidence was double of what CKSPHERE (pseudonym for Tolkachev) had provided in the eighteen months he had worked for the CIA.[26] Eventually, the KGB began to suspect leakages and pinned them on Tolkachev. In June 1985, he was arrested from his dacha north of Moscow. It was Ames, the CIA mole with the Soviets, who provided information about Tolkachev to the KGB.[27]

The CIA along with the British SIS had another notable success in operating the Soviet system. In 1960, Colonel Oleg Penkovsky was a 'walk-in' in Moscow offering intelligence to the Americans. Penkovsky would be operated through a British businessman Greville Wynne, who frequently visited Moscow. When this system was changed, an alternative 'cut-out', Janet Chisholm, wife of Ruari Chisholm who was an official in the British Embassy, would meet Penkovsky and collect the documents. The KGB had learnt from their spy in Berlin, George Blake at the British Embassy, that Ruari Chisholm was from the SIS. Chisholm was under KGB watch from the day he arrived.

Penkovsky was a productive source, but it was not long before the KGB closed in and arrested him along with Wynne in 1962. Penkovsky was 'terminated with extreme prejudice' (in intelligence world terminology). There were some who believed that Penkovsky was a KGB plant to convince the West that the Soviet ICBM programme was far less developed than assumed. The British on the other had were keen to seek rehabilitation with the Americans after the Cambridge Five disaster and were thus taking unnecessary risks in how they ran the Penkovsky operation. Besides, the Anglo–American project in 1953 to dig a tunnel from West Berlin to the Soviet military headquarters (Operation Gold) would have been truly gold, but Blake had shared this intelligence with the KGB from the very beginning. The KGB let it run for three years, feeding false, incorrect and sometimes accurate information. They blew the operation in 1956 about the time the Cambridge Five were making headlines.

These events led the already paranoid American chief of counter-intelligence at that time, James Jesus Angleton, to freeze operations in Europe. He had probably been led into this by a Soviet defector, Anatoliy Golitsyn. There was a KGB masterplan to place defectors in the path of American or British counter-intelligence to pick up.

The third category of spy is the long-term ideologue, who is usually spotted by the agency, which spends time grooming him and then waits patiently till he becomes productive. The famous Cambridge Five – Kim Philby, Donald MacLean, Guy Burgess, Anthony Blunt and John Cairncross – who had successful careers in British government, began spying for the Soviets because of their belief in the dream of a Marxist-communist heaven. There were others too.

The fourth category is the spy who works for an intelligence agency, but his handler makes him believe he is working for a newspaper, a private corporation or a financial corporation.

Soviet Russia began to send 'illegals' to America in 1921 after using this strategy first in Europe in 1919. These were/are persons who live in America or Europe under false identities. Col. Rudolf Abel in America and Richard Sorge in Japan were the more famous ones in the early years of the Cold War.

The US and the Soviet Union also fought their spy wars in India with great zeal. This was particularly sharp after India and the Soviet Union signed the Treaty of Peace, Friendship and Cooperation in August 1971, when East Pakistan was rebelling against Pakistan's rule and which had resulted in a massive flow of refugees to India. The CIA report for Nixon, based on an Indian source, was that the Soviets had signed the treaty to prevent India from recognizing an independent Bangladesh. The gist of the report was leaked to the *New York Times*, apparently by the White House.

A startled CIA Director Richard Helms protested that this release had endangered the life of their source. Yet the Indian source continued to report and when the India–Pakistan war was about to break out in December 1971, the same source informed his handler that India would launch an attack on Pakistan on 7 December. Nixon appreciated this timely intelligence report but someone in the White House leaked it to the famous columnist Jack Anderson, who naturally carried the story. The Indian source was considered exposed by the CIA.[28] Indira Gandhi presumably suspected one of her ministers in the cabinet but did not pursue the matter. In July 2010, A.G. Noorani wrote about this in a review of Anuj Dhar's book, *CIA's Eye on South Asia*, in *The Hindu* but by then the issue aroused little interest.[29]

Technology, Communications and Security

Spying for one's country is a noble and dangerous task. It involves breaking the laws of another country, which might also be a friendly country. Real intelligence officers, those who handle and run spies – do not pick locks, steal cars, break safe codes, carry a Walther as a weapon or speed around in an Aston Martin. Among fictional spies, only Ian Fleming's James Bond did this; John le Carré's George Smiley did not. It was le Carré who took the reader into the spy world as it is, in a complicated, slow way. Graham Greene's two novels, among the many he wrote, *Our Man in Havana* and *The Quiet American*, were about espionage in a long-gone age, but they continue to haunt. The spy war between the erstwhile two superpowers was an endless war – in time and space with no holds barred. It attracted the most attention, in fiction and on screen, even at the time of the American elections in 2020, when the Russians were accused of interference.

A good spy must have a good memory so that he or she does not have to write down addresses, dates and venues, and is able to recall car number plates, phone numbers and passwords at will. He or she must be able to deceive, cheat and manipulate people. It is a job for the inquisitive and the devious. Even so, it is a noble profession. Spies need to be adept at fending off uncomfortable questions and concealing real intent – it means a life of practised duplicity.

Spying on allies and friends is not considered out of bounds. The five-nation ECHELON operation was run by the NSA of the US and GCHQ of the UK along with the intelligence services of Canada, Australia and New Zealand. Essentially an anti-communist operation with listening towers all over the world, it was not averse to listening to what friends and allies were saying. For instance, the Brazilian president and the German chancellor discovered that their conversations were also being listened into.

In the context of present-day communications systems and the internet along with the dark web, ECHELON was succeeded by various other more powerful eavesdropping and surveillance operations. Satellite-based intelligence collection overtook earlier means of intelligence collection. Edward Snowden, a former NSA contractor, leaked classified information about the PRISM surveillance program in 2013. This program allowed the NSA access to data from global tech corporations like Microsoft, Yahoo, Google, Facebook and Apple. It was declared that PRISM was designed to target non-Americans, but it did collect a large amount of information from and about Americans. DISHFIRE was an NSA program that collected SMS messages at the rate of about 200 million messages a day.[30]

The CIA even resorted to privatizing intelligence collection and analysis. It began during Reagan's presidency but became massive during the Clinton era. In the 1990s the Clinton administration privatized even high-risk military operations and intelligence functions. By the time Clinton's term ended, more than 100,000 Pentagon jobs, including thousands of intelligence jobs, had been transferred to the private sector. Clinton's successor, George W. Bush, carried this forward and the main corporations that gained were Booz Allen Hamilton, Halliburton (Vice President Dick Cheney's former employer) and several others working for the NSA. There were also jobs to be swung around for ex-CIA and NSA officers, a common pattern of the revolving-door practice. Booz Allen was considered a valuable part of the shadow intelligence community.

While the CIA expanded, so did the NSA and, alongside, also rose its authority to download communications both within the US and externally. It became a massive behemoth covering all American citizens in all modes of communication, from social media to emails and data collection. About ten years ago the NSA admitted to 'touch' only 1.6 per cent of daily internet traffic out of the 1,826 petabytes of information transmitted per day at the time. In other words, the NSA only 'touched' about 29 petabytes a day. The exact meaning of 'touched' was not defined. (One petabyte is equal to 1 quadrillion bytes, which is 1 million gigabytes, or 1,000 terabytes. A petabyte is conceivably equivalent of 20 million tall filing cabinets or 500 billion pages of standard printed text.) This figure would only have risen in the last 10 years but is a clear indication of the kind of work the NSA performs and the speed at which this would have to be done could only be possible with superfast computers and AI. A good percentage of this work has been outsourced to private contractors.

Mike McConnell was appointed director National Intelligence (DNI) in 2007 by George Bush. Ten years before that, McConnell was vice chairman of Booz Allen, one of America's premier intelligence contractors, and this was the first time that an individual from a top spot in the industry was appointed as head of intelligence. McConnell did have considerable intelligence experience, but he was Cheney's man as DNI and had come to this new assignment at a time when 70 per cent of the US intelligence budget had been spent on contracts with the corporate world.[31]

When Intelligence Fails . . . or Does It?

A truly successful espionage operation passes by without a flutter. It is the failed or exposed ones that get attention. A successful intelligence operation is an invisible operation; behind it lie pedantic planning, patience and precautions,[32] and it is not necessarily the one everyone talks about because there was a flaw or it failed due to sheer bad luck. While operating in hostile countries, for a spy the most difficult aspect is communication, safe meetings with the source, receiving documents and transferring funds. These must be swift, safe and inconspicuous.

A country's power is reflected in its military and economic strength, with an ability to run its own narrative about itself and the world, and to reach parts of the globe in pursuance to ensure its writ. Intelligence agencies, their professionalism and abilities often act as the first line of offence and defence. This in turn is dependent on the attitude and policies of a democratically elected government or an autocratic dictatorial regime – military or political. Dictatorships are usually paranoid and narcissistic, and prefer to lean heavily on intelligence agencies for protection of their domestic interests and external goals. Intelligence agencies thus are a dictator's favourite weapon, where loyalty to the leader is of paramount importance. Relationships between the head of government and the head of intelligence in a closed society can be enduring and functionally useful in preserving the leadership and, maybe, the party. In a democracy this is dependent on how seriously the democratically elected government views the utility of the intelligence service to country.

At the time of writing this, the Israel versus Hamas, Hezbollah and Iran War is still on. It is well documented, but two aspects stand out, unanswered. One is the apparent total surprise of the massive Hamas attack on Israel, which provided the initial trigger. One had assumed, quite fairly, that Israel, facing an existential threat to its existence at all times, would have physical barriers on its frontiers that would immediately react in case of an attack. Second, Israel's intelligence services – Mossad, Shin Beth and Aman – have attained a degree of professionalism that makes its intelligence capabilities rated among the world's best. It is not unusual for political masters not to accept intelligence that does not suit their plan of action. They tend to ignore the intelligence or in some cases, seek doctored intelligence as the Bush administration did preceding the US attack on Iraq in March 2003.

What happened on the morning of 7 October 2023 was surreal. Hamas did not carry out a stealth attack; it was a massive, hours-long attack, the deadliest on Jews since the Holocaust. The border was considered virtually impregnable and geared for instant reaction. None of that happened. Well-equipped Hamas terrorists with vehicular support rolled in, slaughtered civilians and babies, committed sexual violence, burnt whole families alive and took 240 hostages. More than 1,200 Israelis were killed during the attack. There was none of the famed, immediate and massive Israeli reaction.

The utter brutality and scale of the attack was bound to create the perception of a total Israeli intelligence failure. While the former was true, it was difficult to accept that the Israelis completely missed out on what the Hamas was planning. When the Israelis did begin their counter-response, they besieged the Al-Shifa hospital in November 2023, knowing that beneath it lay a network of tunnels that was an arsenal and Hamas command headquarters. There had to be a justification for destroying these tunnels and arsenal. The brutal Hamas attack probably provided the justification needed for retaliation in this manner.

The Israelis had other very specific real-time intelligence as they went about successfully targeting the Hamas leadership not only in Gaza but also in Iran. Surely, the US intelligence behemoth that spends billions every year to keep America and its allies safe, must have had some intelligence about Hamas movement. In contrast, the Americans had intelligence that ISIS-K was going to attack in Moscow in March 2024, and they sent out a public travel Advisory to American citizens not to travel there. Americans were present where Hamas attacked Israel on 7 October. There was no alert sounded.[33]

Questions remain.

3

Philanthropy for Profit

To make a contented slave, it is necessary to make a thoughtless one. It is necessary to darken his moral and mental vision, and, as far as possible, to annihilate the power of reason.

— CARL SAGAN[1]

In the corporate world, there is nothing bigger in size, resources, influence and power than the American corporation, its wealth is measured not in billions but in trillions of dollars. This is only relative; even 60 years ago when the US federal government spent around $70 billion, one or two of the world's richest could have provided the funds.[2] And nothing is 'free' in the corporate world, much less charity and philanthropy. Corporate power equations go beyond wealth and profits that seek, and at times direct, government approval or participation; they are equally about influence and control. Philanthropy has undoubtedly played a crucial part in the growth of American society, but it has done so while benefiting the philanthropist.

Philanthropic giving is usually neither democratic nor transparent. It is used as a form of private political power, a means to use wealth to dictate policy without regulation or accountability. It is no replacement for an equitable tax system or robust, publicly funded programmes to eliminate poverty.[3] Hence there is need for caution while evaluating the intent and effects of philanthropy.

Corporate Beginnings

John D. Rockefeller was perhaps the single most important figure to shape both the American oil industry and its philanthropy. Rockefeller's nineteenth-century Standard Oil Company operated ruthlessly in a milieu of full-throated capitalism. It was the first multinational, and at one stage its revenue of $900 million exceeded the US federal budget of $185 million; at its peak, it was 2 per cent of US GDP.[4] Eventually, it was broken into seven companies, but by the end of the 1880s, Rockefeller had begun to donate to his church, committed to creating a great Baptist University and had provided the endowment for the University of Chicago.[5] He gave away most of his wealth, establishing the Rockefeller Institute of Medical Research and the Rockefeller Foundation. The Rockefellers retained tremendous influence in American society that by all counts will continue till posterity.

David, a grandson, became chairman of the Chase Manhattan Bank. Nelson, another grandson, became vice president of America, yet another grandson was governor of Arkansas, while Jay, a great-grandson, became Governor of West Virginia. At least one member of the Rockefeller family remains a member of the powerful Council on Foreign Relations (CFR). David Rockefeller helped bankroll the Trilateral Commission to share European, Japanese and American views of the world. National Security Adviser Zbigniew Brzeziński's association with it generated conspiracy theories but many also began to think of the Commission as a pastime for retired gentlemen.[6]

Andrew Carnegie, a self-made Scotsman, like Rockefeller epitomized ruthless and competitive American capitalism. The total production of Carnegie Steel, the largest steel company in the world at the time, was equal to half that of Great Britain and supplied a quarter of the American demand. Known to treat his employees shabbily and underpaying them, his philanthropic generosity stood out in sharp contrast; the former helped him increase his profits and the latter gave him fame. He gave away $350 million in his lifetime including to trusts for universities in Scotland and various institutes that carried his name, like the Carnegie Endowment for International Peace. He also contributed to the building of about 2,500 libraries in the English-speaking world.[7]

Rockefeller and Carnegie were forerunners among the super elites; their rules and practice of business were ruthless, though we can say that their philanthropy came from the wealth they earned and was not in itself an instrument for earning more wealth. This is in sharp contrast to the twentieth and twenty-first centuries, where corporate leaders often use philanthropy both for creating wealth and for acquiring control.

With new-age billionaires like Warren Buffet giving away more than $56 billion by 2024 to fellow billionaire Bill Gates's Gates Foundation, it is possible that the global elite are in a mutual admiration society and frequently discuss their own generosity. This sudden surge of charity was clearly noticeable early in this century and could have been related to aging internet and hedge fund millionaires and billionaires looking to leave an everlasting legacy beyond their businesses. It could also be associated with the cyclical rise and fall of elites: elites of an age who had led a breathtaking growth in inequity wanted to do some damage control to pre-empt the inevitable backlash against them, which almost did come with the economic crisis in 2008.[8]

The Sackler Model

Take the story of the Sackler brothers and the dynasty they built. Arthur, Mortimer and Raymond Sackler were born of immigrant parents and were all physicians. The Metropolitan Museum of Art has a Sackler Wing which is a monument to one of America's great philanthropic dynasties. There is a Sackler Gallery in Washington, a Sackler Museum at Harvard, the Sackler Centre for Arts Education at the Guggenheim Museum and a Sackler Wing at the Louvre. The three brothers died by 2010 and their tradition of benevolence was taken up by their next generation. Their philanthropy had presumably bought them immortality of a different kind, and by the middle of the second decade of this century they had become one of America's richest families.[9]

While the Sackler philanthropy was well known, the source of their wealth from their family business, Purdue Pharma, was scarcely ever mentioned. Quite evidently, the Sacklers had thrown the Hippocratic oath out of the window and were leery about too close an association with their most profitable product, OxyContin, the prescription painkiller. It was hailed as a medical breakthrough, providing relief to patients suffering from moderate to unbearable pain. The drug generated a fabulous fortune of $35 billion for Purdue.

Investigative journalist Patrick Radden Keefe in *The Empire of Pain: The Secret History of the Sackler Dynasty* has detailed how the Sacklers got wealthy and unscrupulous. OxyContin, it was later discovered, had an active ingredient, oxycodone – a chemical related to heroin and twice as powerful as morphine. Purdue launched an effective and aggressive campaign to convince doctors who had reservations about prescribing such an addictive medicine. Their campaign was to make doctors say that concerns about opioids were exaggerated and that OxyContin was safe to use across a range of maladies. [10]

Instead, since 1999, 200,000 Americans have died from overdoses related to OxyContin. Those who found the medicine too expensive turned to heroin, and in fact, four out of five heroin addicts have been found to have first tried OxyContin. Soon it became the highest selling drug, surpassing Viagra and leaving trails of drug addiction and abuse. Inevitably, court proceedings demanding damages followed. In March 2022, Purdue and the Sacklers agreed to a $6 billion deal with state attorneys general.

In the afterword to his book, Keefe commented that his intention was 'to tell a different kind of story, however, a saga of about three generations of a family dynasty and the ways in which it changed world, a story about ambition, philanthropy, crime and impunity, the corruption of institutions, power and greed'.[11]

Apparently, the pharmaceutical world is today an industry that helps detect a disease and then provide its cure. For some, both detection and cure can be frightfully expensive, particularly for those in the middle- and lower-income groups and in poor countries where even food is a luxury. The latter also end up becoming guinea pigs for pharmaceutical research.

The capitalistic ecozystem enabled by big pharma is one of competition between sellers and buyers, and repayment for items purchased on commercial loan or treatment originally paid for by personal credit cards. Advertisements for hospitals and treatments, and lobbying with the medical profession, medical experts, politicians and bureaucrats, have become part of the routine. Then there are insurance companies that work alongside pharma companies.

Philanthropy for Capitalism

About 100 years ago, Rockefeller and Carnegie were trendsetters when they established foundations in their names, and Ford followed in 1936. Since then, private philanthropy has played a vital global role in ensuring that the hegemony of neoliberal institutions remained intact and the ideologies and interests of the Western ruling classes were secured. There was interconnectivity of foundations, NGOs sponsored by the foundations and US government institutions like the National Endowment for Democracy whose patron was the CIA.

It is interesting to note that America's philanthropy, and perhaps that of most Western imperialist nations of the last century, viewed the fight against infectious diseases in the colonies in the context of keeping labour healthy and productive. Schools for tropical medicine were established in the US late in the nineteenth century with the intention of safeguarding the productivity of colonized labour and protecting their white masters. As always, interests and goals determined attitudes. This was the underlying interest in the formation of the Rockefeller Foundation in 1913, whose initial goal was to eradicate hookworm, malaria and yellow fever. A healthier worker worked harder and longer for less cost per unit of work and still earned more money. This in turn led to increased profits for the owners. The understanding of and cures for tropical diseases would also help US military adventures in the underdeveloped world without being hamstrung by sick troops.

Rockefeller expanded his international health programmes in consultation with US agencies and other organizations. There were additional advantages to the corporate world. Modern medicine reflected the benefits of capitalism to 'backward' people, which in turn undermined their resistance to domination by imperialist powers. It also helped create a native professional class increasingly receptive to neocolonialism and dependent on foreign beneficence.[12]

Philanthropy became a policy weapon during the Cold War, closely aligned to US foreign policy goals. Privately funded foundations began to collaborate with USAID. They supported interventions that were designed to increase production of raw material required by the West and create new markets for Western products. The aim of these philanthropies was to increase productivity through investments in public health and social causes – a noble function of private foundations and NGOs.

Mid-twentieth century onwards, new nation states with doubtful security and unknown alliances in the developing world were seen as incubators of infections like AIDS, SARS and so on, leading to demands for global health governance. Even the influential Council on Foreign Relations came to agree that state-sponsored national healthcare systems were out of date. Healthcare required greater involvement of NGOs, philanthropic foundations and multinational corporations who could perform this task better and quicker. This meant new international rules, joint public–private efforts and innovative financial arrangements. All this translated to a greater involvement of US government, multinationals and other organizations in global healthcare.

The reliance on corporate charity to support public projects came to be known as 'philanthrocapitalism'. The golden age of philanthropy is not just about benefits that accrue to individual givers. More broadly, philanthropy serves to legitimize capitalism, as well as help extend it into all domains of social, cultural and political activity.

Philanthrocapitalism has many goals beyond the simple act of generosity. It seeks the inculcation of neoliberal values personified by billionaire CEOs who have led its charge. Philanthropy is now recast in the same terms in which a CEO would consider a business venture. Charity is run on a business model that employs market-based solutions characterized by efficiency, costs and benefits. Super-rich businesspeople fund the process, and experienced executives manage the business. The result, at a practical level, is that philanthropy is undertaken by CEOs the way they would run businesses. It is the true privatization of charity and philanthropy, where standard capitalist procedures and goals are invoked.

Philanthrocapitalism has become the new muscular, even neo-imperialist, terminology that sees the world as full of problems that can only be solved with the skills of (mostly) American billionaires. Their philanthropy, therefore, has to be strategic, market-conscious, impact-oriented, knowledge-based, often requiring high engagement and motivated by maximizing the leverage of the donor's money.[13] It is as if the billionaires were going to solve their crises in the West by meddling in the East, and use their considerable power to reshape nations according to what they considered suitable for their own interests.

In early twenty-first century, traditional bureaucratic foundations were making space for philanthrocapitalism. The Bill and Melinda Gates

Foundation (BMGF or the Gates Foundation), founded in 2000 with an endowment of $38 billion, left others like Ford ($10 billion), Rockefeller ($3 billion) and Carnegie ($2.7 billion), far behind.[14] Gates, prescient about the future, knew that he had to change course from Microsoft to newer activities that would have an equally universal scope and effect. He quit being a full-time executive at Microsoft in 2008 while retaining substantial shares in the company; Gates was moving on to other, nobler pastures and eventually left the Microsoft board in 2020.

Lately, more and more wealthy CEOs have been pledging to give away parts of their fortunes – often to help fix the very problems that their companies caused. In this sense, philanthrocapitalism might just as well be called corporate hypocrisy. In 2010, Warren Buffet and Bill Gates institutionalized the Giving Pledge. The campaign encourages billionaires to give away most of their wealth. Joining it is more than a one-time act. It means becoming part of an energized community. Some of the world's most engaged philanthropists meet to discuss challenges, successes and failures, and share ideas to get smarter about giving. The Giving Pledge team provides opportunities to learn from experts and from one another how to best leverage philanthropy to address some of the world's biggest challenges. A signatory must have at least $1 billion in personal net worth and be ready to make a public pledge to donate most of it to philanthropy. The pledge does not require specifics about the destination, purpose or the timing of donations; it is a public commitment to use private wealth, ostensibly for public good. It is a moral commitment and not legally binding.

In 2018, Melinda and Bill Gates were named the most generous philanthropists in America after they gave away $4.8 billion to their own foundation.[15] Others like Mark Zuckerberg gave away $2 billion in 2017, and Michael and Susan Dell gave $1 billion to their own charities. This was a smart move and Peter Isackson, in his March 2020 article in the *Fair Observer*, quotes from Ambrose Bierce's *The Devil's Dictionary*: 'An attribute reserved for very rich people who can impress the media and the poverty-stricken public by giving away massive amounts of money that in no way diminishes the much more massive amount of wealth they possess. This turns out to be a very painless way of qualifying such persons for secular sainthood, free of the traditional obligation to practice some spectacular form of personal asceticism and penitence.'

The Chan Zuckerberg Initiative (CZI), started by Mark Zuckerberg and his wife Priscilla Chan in December 2015, donated over $3 million to aid the housing crisis in the Silicon Valley area. The CZI has committed billions of dollars for philanthropic projects to address social problems, with a special focus on solutions driven by science, medical research and education. Zuckerberg and Chan said that over the course of their lives they would donate 99 per cent of their shares in Facebook (at the time valued at $45 billion) to the 'mission' of 'advancing human potential and promoting equality'.[16] This was immediate stardom in the world of philanthrocapitalism.

The CZI, through which this money was to be funnelled, is a limited liability company and not a not-for-profit charitable foundation. This legal status has significant practical implications, especially when it comes to tax. As a company, the initiative can do much more than charitable activity: its legal status gives it rights to invest in other companies and to make political donations. Effectively the company does not restrict Zuckerberg's decision-making as to what he wants to do with his money; he is very much the boss. Moreover, as Pulitzer Prize-winning journalist Jesse Eisinger described it, Zuckerberg's move yielded a huge return on investment in terms of public relations for Facebook, even though it appeared that he simply 'moved money from one pocket to the other' while being 'likely never to pay any taxes on it'.[17]

Apart from the Zuckerbergs, as of June 2022, the pledge had 236 signatories from 28 countries. Most of them were billionaires, and include household names such as Richard and Joan Branson, Michael Bloomberg, Barron Hilton and David Rockefeller. Anil Agarwal, Rohini and Nandan Nilekani, P.N.C. and Sobha Menon, Azim Premji, and Kiran Mazumdar-Shaw are some of the Indians who have taken the pledge. As of 2016, their pledges are estimated at a total of $600 billion.

An Unequal Society

The US is a highly unequal society. This inequality has only increased despite the changes ushered in by technology and globalization. From the 1980s to about 2015, the average pre-tax income of the top tenth of Americans doubled, that of the top 1 per cent more than tripled and that of the top 0.001 per cent went up seven-fold. During these decades, the lives of those at the bottom (about 117 million Americans) remained unchanged. Upper-class Americans have a 70 per cent chance of realizing their American Dream, while the rest have about 30 per cent chance of improving on their parents' status.[18]

While rich Americans continue to live better with more money and progress, which they monopolize to ensure longer lifespans, those at the bottom of the rung have longevity equal to those living in the Global South. Obviously, there is something that is broken in the machine. Many Americans feel that it is a game that is fixed against them; they condemn 'the system' where all the gains from innovation are seen to have been cornered by billionaires. The top 10 per cent of humanity holds about 90 per cent of the planet's wealth. It is not surprising that the American voting public has become increasingly resentful and suspicious. Simultaneously, populist movements are becoming attractive. This has created a fertile ground where conspiracy theories and fake news abound.

The reaction of wealthy and powerful Americans, and indeed others globally, has been to preserve their status quo. Some shut themselves away from the world while others felt they could do something by taking ownership of the problem, laudable but ultimately self-serving. Elite networking forums like the Aspen Institute and the Clinton Global Initiative groomed the rich to become self-appointed leaders of social change and try to solve problems which they created in the first place. The route for this had to be the private sector and its charitable spoils, the market's way of doing things by bypassing the government.

This was going to be achieved by 'market world', a concept Anand Giridharadas in his 2019 book, *Winner Takes All*, described as 'an ascendant power elite that is defined by the concurrent drives to do well and to do good to change the world while also profiting from the status quo'.[19] This world would include enlightened businessmen and their collaborators in charity, academia, media, government and think tanks, with their own thinkers or thought leaders and their own jargon. 'Market world' was to be a community and a network but also a culture and state of mind. Seemingly, it did not go beyond noble intents.[20]

Today, the elite might have apparently become more socially concerned, but they have also become more predatory, which is reflected in their philanthropy.

The Hand of Gates

Bill Gates made his billions as the joint innovator at Microsoft along with his friend, Paul Allen. Gates has clearly redefined philanthropy in the post-Cold War era. By 2015, he was the richest in the world with an estimated worth of $80 billion even after having given away about $30 billion. In his 2011 annual letter, posted on the Foundation's website, he invoked 'the rich world's enlightened self-interest to continue investing in foreign aid' and warned that if societies were unable to provide for people's basic needs, their populations and problems would grow, making the world an unsafe place. By making this connection between the needs of the poor and instability that might result if these were not met, he essentially stated that the aim of his philanthropy was to make the world safe *for his kind*.[21]

According to a 2016 report by Global Justice Now, a UK-based social justice organization, 'The Gates Foundation has rapidly become the most influential actor in the world of global health and agricultural policies, but there's no oversight or accountability in how that influence is managed nor a clear definition of its end-goals. This huge concentration of power and influence is even more problematic when you consider that the philanthropic vision of the Gates Foundation seems to be largely based on the values of corporate America. The foundation is relentlessly promoting big business-based initiatives such as industrial agriculture, private healthcare and education,' and seems to be left largely self-regulated.[22] The Gates Foundation's focus areas extend beyond agriculture and health to poverty alleviation, gender equality, education, global policy development and media partnerships.[23]

The foundation was not alleviating problems of poverty and lack of access to basic resources, asserted Polly Jones, head of campaign and policy at Global Justice Now. Their report also said that Bill Gates had regular access to the world's leaders, bankrolling hundreds of universities, NGOs and media outlets. This made Gates the single most influential voice in international development. Independent researcher Colin Todhunter published an article in 2016, saying, 'The foundation's strategy is a major challenge to progressive development actors and activists around the world who want to see the influence of multinational corporations in global markets reduced or eliminated.'[24] He also pointed out that most of the foundation's senior staff were from corporate America; consequently the question was, whose interests were being served – those of corporate America or those of ordinary people who were seeking social and economic justice rather than charity?[25]

In the first few months of 2020, Gates saw his popularity soar through the roof. According to YouGov, 58 per cent of Americans polled about Gates had a positive opinion of him; he was equally liked by men and women and adored by both Boomers and Millennials. This might have been due to a viral Netflix documentary about his life that was released in late 2019. Combine that positive press with a wave of media interviews seeking the guidance of the man who 'predicted' the next major pandemic, and voila – Bill Gates almost appeared to be a superhero who would save the planet from impending doom.

Sometime early in 2000, having achieved his goal in Microsoft, Gates had begun to move away from his aggressive monopolistic style where he would devour or destroy new competition, or battle with antitrust prosecutors. The inspiration for the way to soothe his moral conscience and ego came from Warren Buffet, and Gates began to focus on health, education and poverty. As part of his new adventures, sometimes he dealt with food and agriculture, sometimes health and pharma, sometimes vaccines, sometimes malaria and polio in Africa and South Asia; at other times it was education and population control. His extensive network of NGOs and organizations, his access and control of the media and extensive use of America's revolving doors that exist between every profession, the professional systems and the government, ensured Bill Gates remained among the top 15 richest persons in the world – the thirteenth-richest man in the world today with a net worth having fallen from $120 billion in 2018 to $108 billion in 2025.[26]

In 2009, in the backdrop of the great financial crisis of 2008, a few of America's richest, such as Buffet, George Soros, David Rockefeller and others met on the initiative of Gates in a closed-door meeting that was dubbed the 'Good Club'. Among other issues like education, emergency relief, government reform, and the impact of the economic crisis, they also discussed overpopulation – an obsession of the rich. Overpopulation is often seen as a potential disaster for the environment, society, industry and the way of life of rich nations.[27] The intentions of the Good Club sounded noble but it also meant the coming together of enormous wealth and power in private hands with which they could reshape nations.[28] The very fact that this was a closed-door meeting even though the declared purpose was altruistic and noble, shrouded it with a mysterious air, not unlike secret societies like the Bilderberg Group, with the undercurrent of the effect of philanthropy on global politics.

Big Money and Big Pharma

In May 2020, Trump, then in his first term as US president, withdrew American support from the World Health Organization (WHO), an act he repeated soon after being sworn in for his second term in 2025. This left the Gates Foundation, already the second-highest donor to WHO since 2018, as the prime donor and, therefore, the owner of WHO. Health policy was a means to corporate dominance.[29] The Gates Foundation effectively privatized WHO, which was traditionally charged with creating health policy, and transformed it into an instrument for corporate dominance. According to a 2020 report in independent news website The Grayzone, 'It has facilitated the dumping of toxic products onto the people of the Global South, and even used the world's poor as guinea pigs for drug experiments.'[30]

The Gates Foundation's influence over public health policy is dependent on ensuring that safety regulations and other government functions are weak enough to be circumvented. Therefore, it operates against the independence of nation states and as a vehicle for Western capital. 'Because of the Gates Foundation, I have watched government after government fall in its sovereignty,' Dr Vandana Shiva, a scholar and founder of the India-based Research Foundation for Science, Technology and Ecology, told The Grayzone.[31]

Even before the US withdrawal from WHO, Gates and his foundation exercised considerable influence over the Organization's funding and activities. The Gates Foundation also funded the Global Alliance for Vaccines and Immunization (GAVI) created by Gates with the seed money of $570 million in the 2000s, growing to $4 billion by 2020. GAVI was meant to facilitate bulk sales of vaccines to poor countries. At WHO, part of its strategy was to play both a financial and technical role in shaping vaccine markets. Robert F. Kennedy Jr., who in 2025 joined the Trump administration as health secretary, called GAVI in February

2021 'a faux governmental agency that he created to push his diabolical chemical, medical and food concoctions, and conduct villainous vaccine experiments on Africans and Indians'.³²

In 2017, Tedros A. Ghebreyesus became director-general of WHO, before The Gates Foundation took control as its main donors. Ghebreyesus was very much Gates's man, having been on the boards of GAVI and the Global Fund where he was the chair. He became the first individual without a medical background to lead the WHO and often tweeted commendations of Gates's opinion pieces. It is important to note that half of the 15-member SAGE (Strategic Advisery Group of Experts) board, WHO's primary Advisery group, listed Gates Foundation connections as possible conflicts of interest. In 2017, out of 23 global health partnerships, seven depended entirely on the foundation while another nine admitted that the Gates Foundation was their main donor.

Fear Is the Key

In February 2017, Bill Gates addressed the Munich Security Conference, considered the world's primary security conference and therefore the most prestigious. Gates cautioned the high priests of security that ignoring the link between health security and international security would be perilous. He warned his audience that a highly lethal pandemic could occur any time, and it could be a natural disaster or one created by a bio-terrorist.³³ A scare scenario was being created among powerful men and women who were working to shape the global future to their satisfaction.

Then, at a malaria conference in London on 18 April 2018, Gates ominously declared that a deadly new disease would hit the world by surprise within a decade, killing tens of millions. He advised that the world needed to prepare for pandemics the same way as countries prepared for wars. A week later, Gates warned President Trump that there was an increasing risk of a bio-terrorist attack. Later in the same month, Gates told listeners at the Massachusetts Medical Society and the *New England Journal of Medicine* that America was not ready for the next pandemic. Gates described himself as the optimist in the room, reminding the audience that Americans were helping children around the globe and getting better at eliminating diseases like polio and malaria. However, there was lack of progress about pandemic preparedness.

He said he feared that new pathogens emerged all the time as the world population increased and humanity encroached on wild environments. He warned that a small non-state actor could build an even deadlier form of smallpox in a laboratory and that this could spread like wildfire around the globe. He referred to a simulation by the Institute of Disease Modelling, which found that the new flu-like epidemic that killed 50 million people in 1918 could happen again and kill 30 million people in six months.[34]

A few weeks later, the Rockefeller Foundation and intelligence agencies passed on the task of primary funder to Bill Gates for the intelligence/military communities' increasingly alarming pandemic simulations. In May that year, representatives from G20 nations gathered in Berlin to participate in a joint exercise which imagined that China was responding to a contagion codenamed MARS – 'Mountain Associated Respiratory Virus'. Mars is the Roman god of war, but that was a coincidence, surely.

German institutions collaborated in the production of the simulation with the Gates Foundation, the Rockefeller Foundation, the World Bank, the WHO and the Robert Koch Institution. The two-day exercise depicted the timeline for the pandemic, and how it would spread rapidly and could only be controlled with draconian clampdowns in the country and neighbourhood, with centrally controlled and tightly choreographed responses to prevent a 'chaotic dystopian apocalypse'.[35]

The next halt for Gates was the Johns Hopkins Centre for Health Security, the global biosecurity command centre, in October; Gates Foundation, Anthony Fauci's National Institute of Allergy and Infectious Diseases (NIAID) and the National Institutes of Health (NIH) were the main funders. Also participating in the simulation codenamed SPARS2017 for an imaginary coronavirus in 2025–2028 were representatives from the intelligence community. Prominent among the participants were Luciana Borio, vice president at CIA's In-Q-Tel, and Joseph Buccina, director of intelligence at In-Q-Tel. The narrative about an inevitable pandemic and what American companies would be required to do to keep control, was being carefully crafted.[36]

According to a 2003 article, 'In-Q-Tel is an interesting company. It was formed as a Central Intelligence Agency (CIA)-chartered and first government-sponsored venture capital firm. This was in February 1999. The company represents twenty-first century fusion of US espionage efforts with the venture capital industry. It was designed to expand the research and development (R&D) efforts of the CIA into the private sector. In-Q-Tel has access to CIA funds to make strategic investments in startup companies which develop commercially focused technologies that are of interest to the CIA and the larger intelligence community.'[37]

It is not surprising that US intelligence would have interests in the pharma and chemical industries.

The Media and Bill Gates

Narrative-building and creating perceptions need time and communication, as does the broadcast of good and noble deeds done in the service of humanity and to save the world. Bill Gates has woven this aspect into his schemes in a masterly manner.

Bill Gates decided to invest some $319 million with different media outlets and related projects. It includes those that have usually talked the loudest about propriety and morality yet figure at the top of the list of recipients of millions of dollars. This does suggest conflict of interest. If not, at least some agenda-driven compassionate identification, beyond professional ideals, with the donor. The highest being the radio organization NPR at $24.6 million, *The Guardian* $12.9 million, *Der Spiegel* $5.4 million, Project Syndicate $5.3 million, *Le Monde* $4.01 million, BBC $3.6 million, CNN $3.6 million, the *Daily Telegraph* $3.4 million, *Financial Times* $2.3 million. Al Jazeera is also on the list but there is no Indian media outlet on the Bill Gates rolls, or the amount was too small to be mentioned.[38]

In addition, the Gates Foundation donates to charities which are closely aligned with big media outlets. They assist investigative journalism, like $20 million to the International Centre for Journalists out of a total allocation of $38 million. The destination of a substantial amount is declared to be for helping develop African media; funds are also available for press and journalism associations, for their training all over the world with scholarships, courses and workshops. Training reporters from the Gates grants, helping find them a job at a Gates-funded outlet, and then having them belong to a Gates-funded association – that is how a friendly journalist is born. Some of this money finds its way to Johns Hopkins University, Columbia and Berkeley Universities, Tsinghua University in China and Ashoka University[39] in India (one of its founders, Ashish Dhawan, has joined the Foundation's board). Many of Ashoka's projects are funded by the Gates Foundation, which also supports media projects with about $75 million.[40] Journalist Alan Macleod, in his article on the Gates Foundation's grants to media organizations, also refers to some skillful accounting that keeps payments under the radar, like grants for academic articles, and includes a $13.8 million grant to *The Lancet*, the prestigious British medical journal.

It is often forgotten that the MS in MSNBC stands for Microsoft. Microsoft-owned products for communication are Skype (retired in May 2025) and Hotmail (now Outlook.com). LinkedIn is also a Microsoft product, and the Microsoft Xbox is for entertainment. All these are useful instruments for creating a narrative and perception. It is inevitable that a low but extensive profile does seriously affect media objectivity; but perhaps that is the essential idea. Way back in 2008, Rob Flynn, the communications chief of PBS NewsHour, said that 'there are not a heck of a lot of things you could touch in global health these days that would not have some kind of a Gates tentacle'.[41] This was the time when the foundation gave NewsHour $3.5 million to establish a dedicated production unit for reporting on important global health issues. The dollars had worked.

Besides, Gates also used the American revolving-door system and attracted drug manufacturers like Merck, Novartis, Pfizer and GlaxoSmithKline (GSK), among others, to work for the foundation. In its turn, the foundation invested sums in these and other companies.

Gates's campaign prophesying a pandemic continued into 2019 and became louder as the year progressed. The famous Event 201 – a pandemic simulation exercise, jointly organized by the World Economic Forum, the Johns Hopkins Centre for Health Security and the Gates Foundation, was held at the Pierre Hotel in New York in October 2019.[42] The simulation was an eerie precursor to events that unfolded in 2020. The world was not ready for this, but Bill Gates was.

The Gates–Fauci Duet

Several years ago, early in this century, Bill Gates met Dr Anthony Fauci, director of the National Institute of Allergy and Infectious Diseases

(NIAID), and both saw mutual benefit in keeping this contact alive. Robert F. Kennedy, in his 2021 book, *The Real Anthony Fauci*, makes some startling personal disclosures about Fauci and Gates, some of which appear conspiratorial and may not be based on sound evidence. The fact that the book has not been withdrawn and there are no legal challenges to it means that there may be some truth in Kennedy's statements and perhaps they would need more investigation. The book is heavily researched, and obliterates a great deal of the media spin about Fauci.

In his commentary about the book, philosopher Elliot Benjamin[43] commented that it would indeed be appalling if it were true that Fauci had suppressed and mischaracterized two potentially beneficial drugs to treat Covid: ivermectin and hydroxychloroquine, while promoting a detrimental Covid treatment drug: Remdesivir, as Kennedy maintains. Benjamin considered some of Kennedy's portrayals to have enough merit to warrant serious investigation. Kennedy had made a compelling case to show a strong unethical connection of Fauci, supported by billionaire Bill Gates, to Big Pharma.

Another concern was that Fauci continually promoted vaccines that had detrimental consequences, while taking punitive action against reputable researchers who criticized these vaccines. He did not address the dangers to the health of millions of people in Third World countries who were used as guinea pigs in vaccine drug trials. According to Kennedy, Fauci's promotion of use of vaccines in Africa and other Third World countries was buttressed by the immense financial and promotional support of Bill Gates. This had nothing to do with the improvement of the day-to-day health and living conditions of people in these countries.

Fauci was still head of NIAID when the Wuhan Virus (renamed Covid-19 in deference to Chinese objections) hit the world. Fear of the unknown, the greatest of all fears, had gripped the world. The first move was to numb the world into total isolation. New York was declared an epidemic epicentre in March 2020 and India imposed a three-week lockdown on 22 March 2020, by when it had hit all 50 states of the US. The WHO declared a public health emergency for the sixth time in history.

Despite claims in the US pharma world, the world did not have an answer to the epidemic. Three months was far too early to find a response as the fatalities mounted; schools, colleges and working establishments shut down. Work From Home (WFH) soon took over. International travel was prohibited except for evacuations in strict conditions. The pall of gloom refused to lift as doctors struggled to save human lives and many governments faced logistical problems to handle this mega-crisis.

In April 2020, with the US locked down and hospitals full of patients, Dr Fauci, at that time also a member of the President's Coronavirus Task Force, was asked at a White House briefing about the possibility of the virus having originated in a laboratory in Wuhan. Fauci's reply was evasive and interesting. 'There was a study recently that we can make available to you, where a group of highly qualified evolutionary virologists looked at the sequences there and the sequences in bats as they evolve. And the mutations that it took to get to the point where it is now is totally consistent with a jump of a species from an animal to a human.'[44] In everyday English, Fauci was saying the virus had jumped from animal to human, and had not been engineered in a Wuhan laboratory. This would be the tenor of the argument from that day.

No one really could pinpoint the origin of the Covid-19 pandemic. Theories varied in 2020 from zoonotic origins in a bat cave that infected meat in Wuhan's wet market to a leak from a Chinese laboratory, the latter being what Trump wanted to go with more as an election gambit rather than on scientific evidence. However, it seems that later, scientists too began to accept that one way or the other – the lab or the wet market hypothesis might be the correct one. It was politically expedient to keep that opinion under cover in the initial phase.[45]

Fauci continued to push the narrative that this was a natural occurrence. He steadfastly stuck to this theory and insisted that it was unlikely that the virus had its origins in the Wuhan Institute of Virology (WIV). However, in July 2023, the United States House Select Subcommittee on the coronavirus pandemic revealed documents which gave evidence of Fauci's and other officials 'involvement with scientists and journalists trying to quash the lab leak theory'.[46] The private communications disclosed extensive uncertainty that the virus was the result of a natural event as claimed by Fauci. Doubts will always remain about the origins of the virus because the Wuhan Institute, which received funds from US taxpayers, had deleted data about the virus, and given the extent of secrecy in the Chinese Communist party, it was unlikely that the truth would ever come out. That US Department of Health and Human Services cut off funds to WIV, despite Fauci's protestations that they could be trusted, is testimony to the fact that there was something deeply troubling about the origins of the pandemic.

At the onset of the pandemic, there were many dire televised speculations about India by a little-known expert from the US.[47] Mercifully the Indian state held its nerve and the people rose to the occasion. In the end, India, with its own vaccine and systems, did a lot better than many advanced countries, including the US.

'Saint Bill'

In February 2010, Bill Gates spoke at a TED talk about a rising global population of 9 billion people that the earth could not endure. In March 2015, he spoke at another TED talk, where he prophesied that a pandemic larger than a nuclear attack was coming, and the world was not prepared for this calamity. Yet again in 2018, Gates spoke with *Barron's* magazine, referring to the extensive links he had with pharma companies for vaccine development.[48]

In America, Bill Gates was quite the hero. The man who would save Americans with his vaccines. The *Washington Post* called him a champion of science-backed solutions, the *New York Times* described him as the most interesting man in the world. Netflix ran a docuseries, *Pandemic: How to Prevent an Outbreak,* where Gates was the star.[49] It was perhaps no coincidence that the producer was Sheri Fink, a *New York Times* correspondent, who had previously worked with three Gates-funded organizations: Pro Publica, the New America Foundation and the International Medical Corps.[50]

The Netflix documentary, *Inside Bill's Brain: Decoding Bill Gates,* failed to acknowledge conflicts of interest which might portray the film – and Bill Gates – in a different light. In a recent investigation examining the reach of Gates's money, *The Nation* observed that 'in the first episode, director Davis Guggenheim underlines Gates's expansive intellect by interviewing Bernie Noe, described as a friend of Gates's. Noe spoke of Gates's ability to read 150 pages an hour with 90 per cent retention. However, *The Nation* reported, 'Guggenheim doesn't tell audiences that Noe is the principal of Lakeside School, a private institution to which the Bill & Melinda Gates Foundation has given $80 million.' Coincidentally, this is the same school that the Gates children have attended.[51]

Using the foundation's wealth to influence media coverage is not new for Bill Gates. Considering his investments in media outlets (mentioned earlier in the chapter), it is easy to understand how Gates could quickly organize a speaking tour of his favourite media outlets.

Corporate media outlets have not been the only beneficiaries of the Gates Foundation. It has also invested in technologies and companies, including Monsanto, geo-engineering, 5G technology and vaccines. For the last two decades, the foundation has invested in a range of controversial companies and projects while pursuing its stated goal of improving global health and access to vaccines and reproductive care. This has all been done as part of Gates's plan to reshape his public image as that of a friendly and kind billionaire whose only aim is to help the world. The reality is much more suspect. Gates was hosted by CNN, CNBC, Fox, PBS, BBC and MSNBC, he was the most familiar face in America and the hope of many. That Gates described himself as a health expert on BBC though he had no medical degree, helped too.[52]

With the media singing his praises, and Fauci and Ghebreyesus on his side, Gates felt he would have a free run of winning the vaccine battle. Besides, Gates held corporate stocks and bonds in drug manufacturers while $2 billion in tax-deductible charitable donations were given to private companies. These included donations to GSK. *The Nation* found close to $250 million in charitable grants from the Gates Foundation were given to companies in which the foundation holds corporate stocks and bonds: Merck, Novartis, GSK, Sanofi and Pfizer that were at one point the frontrunners in the race to develop the vaccine.[53] The Gates Foundation had co-founded and funded the Coalition for Epidemic Preparedness (CEPI), besides GAVI, as a vehicle for interaction and development.[54] GAVI routed Gates Foundation funds to WHO, over which the Foundation had tightened its hold.

Encouraged by this huge fan following, Gates declared that creating and distributing a Covid-19 vaccine to everyone on earth was the ultimate solution to tackle the pandemic. His CEO reiterated that a successful vaccine had to be made available to all seven billion people. The barely hidden hope was that America or American companies where Gates had a hold would supply these, and there would thereafter be second doses and booster doses.

Most governments, including those considered powerful and orderly, were overwhelmed by the ferocity of the pandemic. Both the US and the UK were floundering and more concerned about what happened within their territorial limits, although the pandemic recognized no borders. This meant that this task shifted to four NGOs in the corporate world and governments had no control. There was no accountability and no time to worry about it either. These organizations were: the Gates Foundation; GAVI, the global vaccine organization that Gates helped to found to inoculate people in low-income nations; the Wellcome Trust, a British research foundation with a multi-billion-dollar endowment that had worked with the Gates Foundation in previous years; and the Coalition for Epidemic Preparedness Innovations (CEPI), the international vaccine research and development group that Gates and Wellcome both helped create in 2017.

These four organizations spent almost $10 billion from 2020 to 2022, gave $1.4 billion to the WHO to create a critical initiative to distribute Covid-19 tools but were not successful.[55] The four had extremely easy access to the highest levels of governments and spent millions lobbying in US and Europe. This was an indication that the West was getting preferential access, and it became clear with time that low-income countries were without life-saving vaccines. Leaders of three of the four organizations insisted that lifting intellectual property protections was not needed to increase vaccine supplies but activists believed it would have helped save lives. It was India which came to the aid of the Global South by sharing vaccines at a time when the West was restricting access to vaccine producing equipment and prioritizing profits and power over others.

Doctors Without Borders, active in poorer nations, expressed discomfort 'with the notion that Western-dominated groups, staffed by elite teams of experts, would be helping guide life-and-death decisions affecting people in poorer nations'. Those tensions only increased when the Gates Foundation opposed efforts to waive intellectual property rights, a move that critics saw as protecting the interests of pharmaceutical giants over those of people living in poorer nations.[56] Private activists began to ask what qualified Gates to give such advice or tell the US government where it should put its funds.

The summer of 2020 was one of confusion and uncertainty as Western governments and pharma companies remained unsure about the vaccine itself and how it would be distributed. Originally, President Trump had pushed for chloroquine/hydroxychloroquine, an anti-malaria drug, for treatment. Gates had his contacts in the medical world, media support for his campaign and a multi-million-dollar arrangement with Dr Fauci, who began asserting Gates's line that mass vaccinations could save the world.[57] The only problem was that they did not have the vaccine.

The Gates Foundation was shopping for a vaccine when it backed Inovio Pharmaceuticals with a $9 million grant, followed by Moderna. In its eagerness to find a vaccine, it also funded the Institute of Health Metrics and Evaluation and Imperial College London, who between the two of them gave wildly scary models of the coronavirus that caused mass panic and led to government lockdowns. Gates was a proponent of lengthy lockdowns.[58]

Mid-summer 2020, the Trump administration began expanding its vaccine development portfolio by investing $1.6 billion in Novavax's manufacturing and an initial $1.95 billion to Pfizer for large-scale manufacturing and nationwide distribution of 100 million doses. It pledged $2.1 billion to support the development of Sanofi and GSK's vaccine. Representatives from the Gates Foundation got into the act as they pushed US officials to share the immune correlates of protection (measurement of the efficacy of a vaccine) from Covid vaccines for the low-income countries and granted funds to organizations working on Covid vaccine development across the world.[59] Gates wanted to be in on every project.

The Dealer

Bill Gates and Anthony Fauci worked as a pair. Both succeeded in an upward transfer of wealth. In 2020, the working class lost $3.7 trillion because of layoffs and the downward spiral of all economic activity. In the same year, billionaires gained $3.9 trillion. Nearly 500 people became billionaires that year while an additional 8 million Americans dropped below the poverty line. The biggest winners were the companies that cheered Dr Fauci's lockdown and criticized Fauci's critics. These were representatives of 'Big Technology, Big Data, Big Telecom, Big Finance, Big Media behemoths (Michael Bloomberg, Rupert Murdoch, Viacom and Disney) and Silicon Valley Internet titans like Jeff Bezos, Bill Gates, Mark Zuckerberg, Eric Schmidt, Sergey Brin, Larry Page, Larry Ellison and Jack Dorsey.'[60] While millions went below the poverty line and applied for unemployment benefits in the US, Bill and Melinda Gates purchased a $43 million mansion. According to Forbes, Gates's net worth increased by $10 billion during this Covid period.[61]

As the pandemic gathered momentum, the Gates Foundation's media presence and political influence seemed to far outstrip its actual philanthropy. The Gates Foundation reported only $1.75 billion in charitable grants for the pandemic till about mid-2020. Compare this to the charity's endowment in 2020, $50 billion, and Bill and Melinda French Gates's private wealth that was estimated at around $130 billion. The Gates couple had $180 billion at their disposal but gave only 1 per cent of that enormous wealth – $1.75 billion – to tackle the greatest public health crisis in generations.[62] The story line in the mainstream media was not about the Gates pair's miserly grant, but about their giving away their fortune to save the world.

Alexander Zaitchik, in his researched paper published in April 2021 in the *New Republic*, says that the person most to blame for America's failure to respond effectively to Covid-19 was neither a scientist nor a politician. It was Bill Gates. He had the WHO under his belt and their credo was to coordinate a research and innovation forum to mobilize international action. Gates would have none of this. Gates had invested $1.75 billion in the development and distribution of a Covid-19 vaccine; so, he was calling the shots, and few could compete with his cash reserves.[63] The entire effort was to prevent any watering down of the intellectual property rights of drug manufacturers supplying vital drugs to Africa. Bill Gates, the most powerful defender of drug companies, would not allow any dilution of the rights of the private behemoths. He believed in monopolistic practices and was not concerned if this would adversely affect poorer countries.

By early April 2021, the inequity in the supply of vaccines was visible. Less than 600 million people had been vaccinated globally, three-quarters of those in just 10 mostly high-income countries. As many as 130 countries, containing 2.5 billion people, had not received even the first dose. When India and South Africa, supported by more than 100 low- and middle-income-group countries, called for relaxation of certain aspects of intellectual property relating to Covid-19 vaccines, Gates again backed the drug companies. The companies who most feared loss of their monopoly were AstraZeneca, GSK, Johnson & Johnson and Pfizer, led by Bill Gates's shadow, Thomas Cueni, director-general of the International Federation of Pharmaceutical Manufacturers and Associations. The Pfizer CEO Albert Bourla openly denounced the idea of pooling or sharing of intellectual property as 'dangerous' and 'nonsense'.[64]

Years earlier, in December 1997, when South Africa faced a 22 per cent HIV rate that threatened a whole generation, the Nelson Mandela government passed a law authorizing government production, purchase and import of low-cost drugs, 'including unbranded versions of combination therapies priced by Western drug companies at $10,000 and more. In response, 39 drug multinationals filed a suit against South Africa alleging violations of the country's constitution and its obligations under the World Trade Organization (WTO's) Agreement on Trade-Related Aspects of Intellectual Property Rights, or TRIPS.'[65] This action had the support of the Clinton administration. In his 2012 documentary, *Fire in the Blood*, Dylan Mohan Gray pointed out that it took Washington 40 years to threaten apartheid South Africa with sanctions and less than four to threaten the post-apartheid Mandela government over AIDS drugs. Altruism was never the goal of medicine men; it was profit.

Big Ag, Big Chemical, Big Food

'How much land does a man need?' is a short story by Leo Tolstoy, whose moral is that greed might lead a man to endless acquisition but ultimately, he needs only six feet of earth to be buried in. Somewhat like the story's protagonist, Bill Gates has made himself one of the largest owners of farmland in the US. It is estimated that by 2021, Gates had acquired 242,000 acres of farmland across America and 27,000 acres of other land in Louisiana, Arkansas, Nebraska, Arizona, Florida and several other states.[66] Some of these acquisitions in California, Illinois, Iowa, Louisiana and other states took place in or soon after 1994, when Gates was not even 40 years old. He was already working on a plan.

The Gates Foundation also has links to Big Ag[67] (Cargill, a Big Ag giant received $10 million from it to build supply chains for South African soya), Big Chemical[68] and Big Food.[69] Combine this with financial behemoths BlackRock, Vanguard and State Street, and what is apparent is a huge canopy of controlling interests centred in the US, whose goal is to control global supplies of food, seeds, fertilizers and pesticides. This is portrayed as helping the world's starving billions but is also an exercise in population control. Gates has put technology at the centre of all solutions to convince his chemical, pharmaceutical and oil industry partners.

The strategy for food production was to force GMO-, chemical- and fossil fuel-based agriculture on African farmers who had farmed differently for 10,000 years and were unable to comprehend the new methods. The Gates and Rockefeller Foundations together put in $424 million for an Alliance for a Green Revolution in Africa (AGRA), promising to double crop productivity by 2020 and reduce food insecurity by half.

Gates spent $4.9 billion to dismantle Africa's farming systems to be replaced by high-tech, corporatized, industrialized agriculture, chemically dependent monocultures and extreme centralization with top-down control. Gates forced small African farms to shift to imported commercial seeds, fertilizers and pesticides. Extreme hunger increased by 30 per cent in the 18 countries that were Gates's unfortunate targets. Rural poverty spread rapidly and there were 131 million people facing starvation by 2019.[70] The experiment failed, as was expected.

The only success was Monsanto in which Gates Foundation had in 2010 purchased 500,000 shares worth $23 million. The Africans described this Gates endeavour as neocolonialism or corporate colonialism. A spokesperson for AGRA Watch, a group that challenges AGRA, described it as a 'trojan horse for corporate kleptocracy' and that the two foundations 'take advantage of food and global climate crises to promote high-tech, centralized, industrial agriculture that generate profits for Gates' corporate partners while degrading the environment and disempowering farmers. Their programs are a dark form of philanthrocapitalism based on biopiracy and corporate biopiracy.'[71]

The Gates Foundation, through AGRA, is one of the world's largest promoters of chemical fertilizers. Some grants from BMGF to AGRA were intended to help AGRA build supply chains for fertilizers in Africa. AGRA in its turn sought to build dealer networks so that the fertilizer could reach the farmer. Over a period, African famers began to prefer chemical fertilizers to traditional methods. It is not about the fertilizer alone; genetically modified (GM) seeds can be used only once and do not reproduce. The entire cycle is built on fertilizers, pesticides and seeds based on modern technology. A farmer is easily caught in the vicious circle. From times immemorial, farmers have passed on their knowledge about seeds and sowing or harvesting down the generations. Their experience with the rains, irrigation, nutrition or improving seed quality helped them retain biodiversity and innovation.

The Rockefeller Foundation had proposed in 1970 that a worldwide network of agricultural research centres under a permanent secretariat should be established to develop high-yielding, disease-resistant varieties of the kind that had been developed in India. Supported and developed by the World Bank, Food and Agriculture Organization (FAO) and United Nations Development Programme (UNDP), a consortium called the Consultative Group on International Agricultural Research (CGIAR) was established in May 1971. The stated goals were to collect primary seeds from across the globe, to coordinate international agricultural research efforts to reduce poverty and achieve food security in developing countries, and preserve biodiversity for the future.

In 1990, Gates contrived to take control of 768,578 seeds with the CGIAR and establish his monopoly in global agriculture. He hijacked the system after pumping in $720 million along with Rockefeller and then claiming ownership, literally. He merged all the 15 subsidiary units of the seed banks under Gates Ag One and then transferred the seeds to his partner corporations, like Bayer and Cargill. Gates AG One's director is a former executive of Monsanto and then of Bayer Crops Science.

Seed and biodiversity piracy began not only by corporations that, through mergers, became bigger and fewer, but also had the interest of billionaires like Gates. CGIAR today holds the largest and most widely used collection of crop diversity in the world.[72] There has been criticism about attempts to centralize and monopolize agriculture with management consisting mainly of the Global North, whereas it is agriculture of the Global South that needs sympathetic support. It is pertinent to mention that the Gates Foundation project under AGRA since 2006 has not been successful. Fifteen years is too long a period for trial and error.

Gates's faith in technology as a problem solver is close to being messianic. He is not known to listen to contrary opinion. Due to his idolizing of GMOs (genetically modified organisms) and gene-editing technologies, Gates spent billions to prevent GMO and other gene-editing laws in countries that wanted to ensure safety standards. Documents show that the Gates Foundation paid a private agriculture and biotechnology PR firm $1.6 million for activities on Gene Drives, a highly controversial new genetic extinction technology, a form of genetic engineering, that was being developed. This included running a covert 'advocacy coalition' meant to skew the only UN expert process dealing with it. Other documents also showed similar covert coordination by an established biotech lobby group coordinating with government representatives of Canada, UK, Brazil, US and Netherlands in the same process.[73]

Acquisition of gene-editing technology would help Gates's schemes to create and patent new and improved species of plants and animals, or to exterminate species. In an interview with Dr Joseph Mercola in 2021, Vandana Shiva, the Indian environmentalist, physicist and activist, said, 'In the next decade, if we don't protect what has to be protected . . . and take away the sainthood from this criminal, they will leave nothing much to be saved.'[74]

The Gates Foundation, considered the world's largest foundation with assets worth $43.5 billion (2021),[75] has an arrangement with Monsanto, the world's leader since 1980 in genetic modification of seeds which had by 2008 won 674 biotechnology patents. The company spends $2 million per day on research to identify, test, develop and market new seeds and technologies that are advertised to benefit farmers. It is paranoid about others stealing its patents since the stakes are so high. Farmers once entrapped, are required to buy Monsanto's Roundup Ready seeds every year along with Roundup weed killer,[76] which are Monsanto's chief money-spinners.

In the seventeen years up to 2020, Gates Foundation had spent about $6 billion, ostensibly to improve agriculture in Africa. More than half of the funds went back to institutions and organizations in the West, that is, to the Global North for the problems of the Global South, while totally ignoring the existing knowledge and technologies of the farmers of the Global South. The route was familiar – the contracts/donations/grants went to four big groupings: CGIAR, AGRA, the African Technology Foundation which was promoting GMOs in Africa and other organizations such as the World Bank. The rest of the money was sprayed over hundreds of researches, development and policy agencies. This amounted to about 80 per cent of the total funds to groups in North America and Europe. Africans got less than 10 per cent of the allocations. The Gates Foundation also follows a similar pattern with 90 per cent of the funds going to North American and European organizations and institutes.[77]

Gates's other dream has been to transform agriculture by using artificial intelligence (AI). Speaking at a conference in 2018, Gates predicted, 'We used to all have to go out and farm. We barely got enough food, when the weather got bad, people would starve. Now through better seeds, fertilizer, lots of things, most people are not farmers. And so AI will bring us immense new productivity.'[78]

The Gates Foundation, with its significant investment in Alphabet, the mothership of Google, probably influenced Alphabet to launch a project, Mineral, and invent 'crop sniffing robots' meant to replace farmers and ranchers.[79] Gates also had a significant investment in Amazon and within one year of purchasing Whole Foods, Jeff Bezos was investing in robot-controlled vertical farms.[80]

While ostensibly promoting artificial meats to combat climate change (raising livestock is considered a major cause of greenhouse gas emissions), Gates ironically decided to team up with BlackRock and make a $3 billion offer to buy a private British aviation company. According to an academic study at the Lund University, Sweden, Gates is one of the world's biggest 'super-emitters'. He took 59 flights on his private jet in one year, travelling more than 200,000 miles, and the report estimated that Gates's private jet travel emitted about 1,600 tonnes of carbon dioxide. The global average is less than five tonnes per person. Researchers have found that private jets emit up to 40 times as much carbon dioxide per passenger than commercial jets. In the foreword to his book, Gates loftily declared that he had spent a decade studying the causes and effects of climate change, and presumably he had found the answers.[81] He is not perturbed by such minor issues and he does not have to contend with any major issues. The pontificating rich have never been overly concerned about dichotomies of high ideals and low practices.

Bill Gates is a twenty-first-century phenomenon. A brilliant mind, he sits astride the pharma world and the worlds of food and agriculture, energy and technology. With so many arrows in his quiver and so many varied and massive financial interests, there will be some arrows that could go astray or even turn rogue. At times he gives the impression of a Colossus striding the globe. Surely, he is not a Lone Ranger; he has a whole team of elite wise men and women who help him and themselves in preserving their elite status forever. Gates is the front man, the icon, the opening batsman, but he is not alone. He symbolizes the New Order. Gates has a whole ecozystem supporting him, or the system is using him to strengthen itself.

These efforts must be backed by a kind of Deep State, where wealthy and powerful men and women dream of the Great Reset so that they will continue to rule. It is almost like Robert Ludlum's novel, *The Chancellor Manuscript*, where powerful men meet in secret to discuss what they should do with the world. Perhaps fiction imitates reality. But with Trump at the helm, it is difficult to predict which way the tide will turn.

And the reality looks grim.

4

Decline of an Empire

An old world is collapsing and a new world arising; we have better eyes for the collapse than for the rise, for the old one is the world we know.

— JOHN UPDIKE

As far back as 1966, a worried J. William Fulbright wrote in his book, *The Arrogance of Power*: 'Gradually but unmistakably, America is showing signs of that arrogance of power that has afflicted, weakened, and in some cases destroyed nations in the past. In so doing, we are not living up to our capacity and promise as a civilized example for the world.'[1]

Prophetic, one might say.

No country has the right to endanger the rest of the world just because it can do so, in what it calls the pursuit of its national security interests. This happens because, over time, powerful states convince themselves about their invincibility and the permanence of their status on earth. Intoxicated by their own propaganda and surrounded by fawning courtiers, they live in their own world, till the ugly truth begins to unfold.

The powerful and wealthy Western world has lived far too long in its echo chamber, unwilling to listen to the rest, secure in the belief that its decisions and actions are for the good of the less fortunate. At one point the US was indeed the mightiest power that history has known. It is a pity that it exercised its self-ordained responsibility as the protector of the free world rather poorly. The Americans went all over the Middle East like Ninja soldiers, attacking Iraq soon after the collapse of the

Soviet Union and splitting Yugoslavia with NATO's help with Big Brother in Washington watching closely. If the first Iraq War was Bush Sr.'s war, the Balkans were Clinton's, the second Iraq War was Bush Jr.'s and Iraq, Syria and Afghanistan were hand-me-downs for Obama. Ukraine was Biden's war, and the world now awaits Donald Trump's war. America has invested greatly in Israel in its interminable conflicts with Iran and Qatar-backed Hamas and Hezbollah, while keeping a foot inside the Arab door.

Lessons of the past have not been learnt. The Korean War (1950–1953) was a stalemate between the world's strongest army and the then comparatively ragtag People's Liberation Army (PLA) of the fledgling People's Republic of China. Vietnam, which went on for 20 years, from 1955 to 1975, was an unmitigated disaster. The photograph of some Vietnamese clinging to an American helicopter leaving Saigon became the iconic image of the debacle. The venue shifted to the Afghanistan–Pakistan region in the 1980s. The Americans created the Afghan Mujahedeen to fight an Islamic religious war, on their behalf, against the Soviet Union. This venture created in effect a sense of united Muslim identity globally, or ummah, which has since set out to conquer the world, beginning with the Middle East and spreading to Europe.

Wars were easier begun and invariably ended in a stalemate at best or in an entangled mess. The US was able to retain its global hegemony through its enormous wealth, its industry, its control over vital resources and the strength of the dollar.

This story has a long beginning.

American Exceptionalism

American Exceptionalism – that we are different, the Chosen People, with a city on a hill and a manifest destiny – set in very early in American history along with an ability to ignore or misremember inconvenient facts. As the novelist Herman Neville would claim, 'We Americans are the Peculiar Chosen People – the Israel of our time. We bear the ark of the liberties of the world.'[2] In 1776, political philosopher Thomas Paine said, 'We have it within our power to begin the world over again.'[3] More than 230 years after Thomas Paine's remark, in 2009, Obama's secretary of state Hillary Clinton echoed this sentiment when she said, 'We are called upon to use this power.'[4]

This self-adulation became the essence of America's global leadership. 'To question American Exceptionalism and oppose the American Empire was to become persona non grata wherever members of the foreign policy establishment congregate.'[5] Linked to this has been the rule that entry into the sanctum sanctorum where insiders formulate American statecraft required an individual to forfeit or suppress any inclination for genuine independent thought. This meant accepting the worldview of the American political class. Americans have long held the belief that that the rest of the world wanted to be like America and Americans, but did not know how. It was, therefore, America's noble task to create American clones, which would then ensure peace. Meanwhile, realism demanded that America always be ready to fight wars with the greatest lethality as a way to maintain American Exceptionalism.

On 19 February 1998, on NBC's *Today* show, Secretary of State Madeleine Albright said, 'But if we have to use force, it is because we are America; we are the indispensable nation. We stand tall and we see further than other countries into the future, and we see the danger here to all of us.'[6] This was in preparation to President Bill Clinton's decision to target Iraq with another round of air strikes recommended by policy hawks in Washington, DC, who had persuaded themselves that Saddam Hussein was an existential threat to the United States.

Four days after Albright's remarks, Osama bin Laden, sitting somewhere in the caves of Afghanistan, called for an 'international jihad' against Jews and Crusaders. He was speaking on behalf of what was then an obscure Al Qaeda, formed in Peshawar in 1988, whose primary goal was to seek the expulsion of US forces from the Arabian Peninsula. Osama was seeking support from Muslims all over the world and several Islamist terror organizations joined in, including the Pakistan-sponsored and -based Hizbul Mujahideen, active in Jammu and Kashmir.

In September 2001, when the World Trade Center towers were struck, the first call of sympathy to President George W. Bush came from his primary adversary, Vladimir Putin, followed by President Jiang Zemin of China; President Jacques Chirac of France flew in that night to be at the site of the tragedy. Here was an opportunity for global powers to make common cause against the several dangers that lurked from poverty, economic disparity to climate change to terrorism in a genuinely new world order. However, in less than two years, when the

Americans attacked Iraq in 2023, all three leaders – Russian, Chinese and French – who had supported the US war on terror, opposed the invasion.

Soon after the launch of Operation Iraqi Freedom in 2003, *New York Times* correspondent Gregg Easterbrook declared that the extent of American military superiority was impossible to overstate. US forces were the strongest the world had ever known, stronger than the Wehrmacht in 1940, stronger than the legions at the height of Roman empire, and for years no other power would rival American power.[7] The commentator Max Boot declared that America's military performance had been so outstanding that it made German generals like Erwin Rommel look positively incompetent. The world knows what transpired in George W. Bush's Iraq War, which eventually became Obama's war and Trump's war. It was all about American Exceptionalism, American Invincibility and American Righteousness, tragically based on concocted evidence against Saddam Hussein.

'America First' has been an oft-heard slogan in America. Recall what presidential candidate John F. Kennedy said in his debate with his rival Richard Nixon on 1 October 1960. 'I think we have to demonstrate to the people of the world that we're determined in this free country of ours to be first – not first if, and not first but, and not first when – but first. And when we are strong and when we are first, then freedom gains; then the prospects for peace increase; then the prospects for our society gain.'[8] The theme has not changed over time. But it has not worked, either. America has spent trillions of dollars at the cost of millions of lives to try and prove, unsuccessfully, that American actions are noble.

Critics of American Exceptionalism have long argued that this needed to change. In his 2021 book, *After the Apocalypse: America's Role in a World Transformed*, American historian Andrew J. Bacevich cautioned that regardless of whether America's self-inflicted contemporary apocalypse led to its renewal or further decline, it would have to revise its long-held belief in its role in the world. Basic US policy would have to change. He argued that even before the COVID-19 pandemic swept the nation, cumulative policy failures clearly meant that a national security paradigm, which was centred on military supremacy, global power projection, decades-old formal alliances and wars that never seemed to end, was at best obsolete, if not itself a principal source of self-inflicted wounds. The costs, approximating a trillion dollars annually, were just too high.⁹ The outcomes, ranging from disappointing to abysmal, came nowhere near to making good on promises issued from the White House, the State Department or the Pentagon and repeated in the echo chamber of the establishment media. The bug of American Exceptionalism, a kind of entitlement, has become toxic, but from this belief has flown a great deal of American global action.

Others have also worried about America or where it might be headed. Carl Sagan said in the early 1990s: 'I have a foreboding of an America in my children's or grandchildren's time – when the United States is a service and information economy; when nearly all the key manufacturing industries have slipped away to other countries; when awesome technological powers are in the hands of a very few, and no one representing the public interest can even grasp the issues; when the people have lost the ability to set their agendas or knowledgeably question those in authority; when, clutching our crystals and nervously consulting our horoscopes, our critical faculties in decline, unable to distinguish what feels good and what's true, we slide, almost without noticing, back into superstition and darkness.'¹⁰ This prophecy that applies to other powerful countries as well – China, for instance – was made amid a Cold War and underscores the perspicuity of Sagan.

Cold War's Long Shadow

At the end of World War II, the Allies were ready with post-victory measures. One of them was the Nuremberg Trials against Nazis, even as the useful scientists were smuggled out to America. Speaking at the Nuremberg Tribunal, US Supreme Court Justice and Chief US Prosecutor Robert L. Jackson said, 'We must make clear to the Germans that the wrong for which their fallen leaders are on trial is not that that they lost the war, but that they started it. And we must not allow ourselves to be drawn into a trial of the causes of war, for our position is that no grievances or policies will justify resorting to aggressive war. It is utterly renounced and condemned as an instrument of policy.'

How utterly noble and magnificent a statement and how utterly impractical it proved in the years that followed. Germany had been replaced by the Soviet Union as the arch-enemy and plans were already being made to counter its influence. The Cold War had begun and in the decades that followed, one would increasingly witness declarations from the 'free world' of public nobility while pursuing national interest through control and dominance.

Soon after Prosecutor Jackson's statement, George Kennan, whom we encountered in Chapter 2 as one of the foremost US strategic planners of the Cold War, briefed US ambassadors in Latin America. He advised on the need to be guided by a realistic concern for the protection of raw materials required by the US. America would need to preserve its self-proclaimed inherent right of access, by conquest if necessary. There was also agreement among planners that it was better to have a strong autocratic regime in power than a liberal government that is indulgent, relaxed and penetrated by communists.[11] It was the same George Kennan who had said that the less the US was hampered by slogans the better.[12] This was shorthand for interventions and regime change.

In keeping with Kennan's real politick precepts, in 1950 Winston Churchill wrote in his book, *The Second World War,* that the governing of the world had to be entrusted to satisfied nations who wished nothing more for themselves than what they had. On the other hand, if it were in the hands of hungry nations, they would always be in danger. In other words, the rich, comfortable in their reserved places, had the right and abiding duty to rule. This belief lingers among cozy, invested interests in many capitals of the world, including New Delhi.

Thomas Jefferson had commented on the world situation of his time, in the nineteenth century, from an American point of view. 'We believe no more in Bonaparte's fighting merely for the liberation of the seas, than in Great Britain's fighting for the liberties of mankind. The object is the same, to draw to themselves the power, the wealth, and the resources of other nations.' A century later, after the formation of the League of Nations, Woodrow Wilson's secretary of state, Robert Lansing, with little faith in Wilson's idealism, commented sarcastically about policies. The British, French and Italians, he said, were eager to accept a mandate from the League of Nations if there were mines, oil fields, rich grain fields or railroads that would make it a profitable undertaking.[13] The false air of nobility of the Europeans was not lost on the Americans who would soon adopt the same principles wholeheartedly.

After the Yalta conference in February 1945, which was essentially about post-war reorganization of Europe and Germany, the Americans and Russians had begun to revert to their pre-war status as enemies, with each battling for global influence and space. The Soviets moved into Eastern Europe and threatened Italy and Greece with communism, while the US got involved in the Korean War to stem the communist tide. The US acquired allies, many of them ruthless dictators, to fight their battle for democracy and created a series of military alliances, with NATO as the most powerful. Spies in both camps had begun their lonely and dangerous spy games across the Iron Curtain while vile surrogates with allegiance to either camp battled for territory, resources and influence across the Third World in Africa and Asia.

The frantic race to amass WMDs led to a cold peace in the Global North, but there were several proxy wars in the Global South. American leadership did not spare even its most favoured ally, as it eased out Great Britain from the Middle East and established a comfortable relationship with oil-rich Iran, Iraq and Saudi Arabia, as well as Israel. Regime change crafted by the CIA in Iran was an early warning that those who opposed the US would have shortened career paths. The CIA has been a valiant secret (sometimes not-so-secret) fighting force for preserving, strengthening or creating interests for its country. Perceived national interests were always rated far higher than principles of democracy. This would appear to hold good to an indefinite date.

One of the fears the Americans had was that a reunified Europe with a rich history stretching millennia could well declare itself independent of the hold of the US, which sought a new global order that was subordinated to the needs of its economy and which remained under its political control. Britain was thus required to terminate or hand over its imperial controls. Henry Kissinger made the global status quite clear when he spoke at the Year of Europe address in 1973. The world system should be based on the recognition that 'the United States has global interest and responsibilities' while America's allies had only 'regional interests'.[14] This speech was in the background of the famous OPEC energy crisis of 1973 and the fact that American wealth declined from being 50 per cent of global wealth in 1945 to nearly half of that, with new economic power centres in North America, Europe and a Japan-led Asia. America had to shore up its position at the top.

The 'Schwarzenegger of International Politics'

The Cold War lasted till the collapse of the Soviet Union in 1991, which further strengthened American perceptions about its global power and invincibility. Vietnam was forgotten and the Afghanistan debacle was yet to happen. Victory in the surreal Iraq War of 1991 was enough reason for President George H.W. Bush to exult, 'A world once divided into two armed camps now recognizes one sole and pre-eminent power, the United States of America. And they regard this with no dread. For the world trusts us with power, and the world is right. They trust us to be fair and restrained, they trust us to be on the side of decency. They trust us to do what's right.'[15] Clearly a case of masterly self-adulation.

Bush's successor, Bill Clinton, grandly announced in 1996, 'When I came into office, I was determined that our country would go into the 21st century still the world's greatest force for peace and freedom and security and prosperity.'[16] Even as this drumbeat continued, there were others who were sceptical about American abilities and attitudes. Germany's well-known news magazine[17] commented in its 1 September 1997, issue: 'Never before in modern history has a country dominated the earth so totally as the United States does today ... America is now the Schwarzenegger of international politics: showing off muscles, obtrusive, intimidating ... The Americans, in the absence of limits put to them by anybody or anything, own a kind of blank check in their "McWorld".'[18] No one in America listened or cared; they were in their own happy world.

The Pentagon's National Defence Strategy released in 2022 called for fighting and winning wars against Russia or China, engaging in military action in Iran and North Korea, and deploying 200,000 American troops globally for participating in counterterrorism operations in eighty-five countries. Fighting such massive wars needs massive funds and massive armament production. These need Congressional approvals. There is a neat way that this is done in America. The House Armed Services Committee chief from 2021 to 2023, Mike Rogers, a Republican, received more than $444,000 from weapons manufacturers, while Ken Calvert, also a Republican and head of the Defence Appropriations Committee, received $390,000. Key Democrats like Adam Smith, former House Armed Services Committee chairman, received $276,000. This is not corruption; it is for services rendered.[19]

This status has come at a price in real terms. The Pentagon's star project touted as the most futuristic fighter jet, Lockheed Martin's F-35 jet fighter aircraft, will cost Americans about $1.7 trillion to produce or about $5,000 per American. From the time of the Biden presidency, Americans have been asking India to buy the F-35, considered by many experts to be an expensive white elephant. As of now, the aircraft has 845 design flaws, with more being discovered regularly.[20] Overpriced and underperforming, but this has not deterred the powers-that-be. The Pentagon's budget ask in 2025 is $849.8 billion, half of which is likely (as always) to go to private manufacturers. In 2023, the top five alone – Lockheed Martin, Raytheon, Boeing, General Dynamics and Northrop Grumman — made $150 to $200 billion from Pentagon contracts. It is precisely this kind of profligacy that makes the rest of the world wonder about the amount of money being squandered to perfect the art of killing and often aimed at nations without the ability to retaliate.

Interestingly, between 2014 and 2019, 1,700 Pentagon officials left their government jobs to work for the arms industry, all with fourteen of the top weapons manufacturers. In addition, there are cost overruns, price fixing by manufacturers or unnecessary programmes. These wastages apart, American counterterrorism operations since 11 September 2001 have cost the country more than $8 trillion.

After the end of the Cold War, American strategic experts considered that peace could be achieved through interdependent ties of commerce, culture and shared values among the democracies of North America, Western Europe and Japan. No other country in Asia, Africa and Latin America was considered relevant. For this, it was necessary that the US remained the world's leading military power, engaging wherever its interests lay. This happened frequently. A corollary to this was that the US, while acting cooperatively with others, should retain the option of unilateral action. The other aspect was that the world's resources devoted to military forces and equipment should be cut down substantially, reducing weapons of mass destruction and strengthening efforts to block proliferation. None of this happened. The Congressional Budget Office (CBO) estimates that the US is set to spend some $756 billion on nuclear weapons modernization programmes in the fiscal period 2023–2032, which averages to $75 billion a year on nuclear weapons. That is more than two Manhattan projects every year.[21]

Americans relished the title of 'Sole Superpower' and were consumed by the 'end of history' illusion. Inevitably hubris took over. The US's actions globally, beginning with the Balkan Wars, leading on to the twenty-first century with its much-proclaimed Global War on Terror, the Iraq War and the Middle Eastern imbroglio with the mess in Afghanistan, the Ukrainian stalemate, and the battle between Israel and Islamic terrorists, became an indication of what a unipolar world would look like. Schwarzenegger was alive and well.

The New Emperor

From the beginning of his second term, President Trump began to execute all the schemes he promised in his election campaign as part of his plan to 'Make America Great Again'. He threatened to occupy the Panama Canal and Greenland for security but also for economic reasons. The Canadians weren't amused at being declared America's fifty-first state. Greenland rebuffed Trump as he threatened to take over that country. Internationally this meant legitimizing Putin's action in Ukraine, even though Putin acted after grave provocation by the US and after giving ample warning to the West. Trump also launched his policy on tariffs, thereby violating WTO regulations, which validated President Xi Jinping's global strategy seeking domination by weaponizing trade, diplomacy and technology.[22]

Trump upended many relations with the EU by asking them to fend for themselves and by seeking a resolution with Russia on Ukraine without involving the EU. The old norms of Second Cold War were being discarded. His sharp actions domestically and across the board left the country sharply divided between those who favoured his moves and those who did not. Some even gloomily forecast a civil war. Perhaps, Trump sees that the old order has changed and he needs to make adjustments, or perhaps chaos would lead to a new world order restoring America's superiority.[23]

Trump's ability to fulfil his campaign promise about bringing peace to Ukraine will not depend on Putin and Zelenskyy accepting a ceasefire but on his ability to exert an authority of the kind President Eisenhower had in Korea, which ended the killing, prevented further war and allowed the Koreans to rebuild.[24] The question is, does Trump have the kind of authority Eisenhower had in 1952? Probably not.

When Trump and his vice president, J.D. Vance, met Volodymyr Zelenskyy in the Oval Office on 28 February 2025, they gave a new definition to diplomacy.[25] It was quite evident that Trump and Vance were looking for transactional deals from Ukraine and felt they could be openly rough with a country America was aiding. This left their other allies angry and apprehensive about their long association with America.

Wealth as Source of Power

It is difficult to define or measure power, but it is true that wealth is a source of power and the ability to project violent force adds to that power. Jean Anouilh, the French playwright, famously remarked, 'God is on everyone's side . . . and in the last analysis, he is on the side with plenty of money and large armies.' When an indefensible argument succeeds in asserting itself, it indicates the power of the system. It is this power, to assert itself and have its way, that the US possessed in the previous century, that is shrinking, as reflected in its inability to translate military power into success despite its great wealth and technological prowess.

State power – military and economic – are hard command powers, and if a state has the power to set the agenda, determine the framework of a debate along with the ability to make another state do what it, the powerful state, wants done, then the weaker state remains obedient. For some years after the Second World War, the US did have this power. Even so, the ability to make others do what it wanted, through coercion, rewards and by attraction, did not always work. Strangely its strength began to fade away rather rapidly after the collapse of the Soviet Union, unable to capably handle a unipolar world where it did not have a definable enemy. The overemphasis on military power as a dimension of American power was one of the strongest reasons for this decline.[26]

The influential American political scientist, Joseph Samuel Nye Jr., wrote in 2002, 'Power in the 21st century will rest on a mix of hard and soft resources. No country is better endowed than the United States in all three dimensions – military, economic, and soft power. Our greatest mistake in such a world would be to fall into one-dimensional analysis and to believe that investing in military power alone will ensure our strength.'[27] This is precisely what happened. In a later book, Nye argues that the US did not control the largest countries of the world, which included the former Soviet bloc, China, India and Indonesia, among others; the American world order covered less than half the world.[28] Nye prefers to describe American power as that of primacy or pre-eminence, rather than hegemony. Sanctions – military, nuclear or economic – against countries who stepped out on American redlines or were even reluctant supporters – became a favourite tool of American policy, even though the results were not always as successful as was hoped.

For most Americans, wars took place at a remote distance and seemed almost surreal on their screens. The sound of screaming missiles was only on the screen; there have been no Daisy Cutter bombs exploding in American neighbourhoods, or children running with their bodies aflame with napalm, or sudden death from Hellfire missiles. Brave American troops were out fighting against Evil Empires or members of the Axis of Evil, to make America and the world safe. There was never any call on the American public for austerity or for sacrifices; no war taxes or war bonds.[29]

This made it easier for the US under successive administrations to indulge in adventurism, which was seen as a profitable venture with trillion-dollar wars in faraway countries. Wars were good for American business. Wars were economic opportunities, with all the support that accompanied the American soldier the world over. It is often said that if American food chains and bars suddenly appear in a certain country of interest, American troops are about to land. It is a good intelligence report about battle indicators.

An intense fear of losing control can drive rich, powerful nations to first criticize, then micromanage and finally manipulate others. All three can in fact happen simultaneously. A state's power declines not just in terms of what it is unable to do to its external adversaries. A decline internally can be hidden for longer but when it rolls out, it gathers speed very fast. The decline and fall of the Roman Empire took place not because of a series of defeats but also out of boredom, even as the elite organized wrestling bouts among slaves who would fight to the death. The rich placed bets and presumably fixed some bouts while the commoners sat in the stalls and applauded the pantomime. Staying on top requires constant endeavour.

The last time Americans fought on their soil for their mainland, not counting Pearl Harbour that was miles offshore, was during the Civil War in the nineteenth century. The only other time there was violence from external sources was the attacks on 11 September 2001. The American Global War on Terror was fought entirely outside the US. Death was long distance. Americans have not had to fight for their own land like people in Europe, the Middle East, Asia and Africa. External violence therefore comes easily to the American establishment, especially in these times of remote targeting where death is a blip on the screen. Better to fight distant wars than have wars come home or even the neighbourhood.

The two world wars had been good for the American economy, leaving it at the top of the table in 1945. This had to be preserved. Roosevelt met the Saudi King Abdul Aziz ibn Saud in a secret meeting on February 14 aboard the USS *Quincy* in the Suez Canal, laying the foundation of a long-standing friendship and a dependable source of oil. It was a treaty of blood and oil that has survived all these decades.[30]

Soon after the Second World War, the US graduated from being the accepted hegemon of the West to being an empire, almost without much effort. Playing its imperial role, the US was busy keeping Western Europe free from communism and handling communists in Italy and Greece. It battled Soviet-aided North Koreans in the Korean Peninsula, handled the Suez crisis of 1956, nearly hit a nuclear flash point with the Soviets, averted by some hasty behind-the-scenes negotiations, in the Cuban missile crisis of 1962, then on to its biggest blunder till then in Vietnam, which ended when the Americans scampered home in 1975. The Indo–Pak War of 1971 was seen as a serious impediment to American overtures to Mao Zedong, and the US played favourites quite blatantly, something it would repeatedly do in the decades that followed, culminating in the disasters of Iraq and Afghanistan. US–Saudi relations in the twenty-first century are a far cry from earlier days, as China seems to be moving in. In March 2023, it brokered a peace deal between Saudi Arabia and Iran, a clear indication of its influence over the two oil-rich countries.[31] After the initial nervous flutter in Washington DC and its think tanks, following the China sponsored peace deal, the situation has more or less subsided at a new level. Diplomatic relations were resumed but Saudi suspicions over Iranian assistance to terrorists in the region will take some time to abate.[32] The US bombardment of Iran as punishment and the US willingness for a realignment of US-Saudi relations was evident as the two began cooperation Saudi Arabia's transformation in the era of AI.[33] China may have receded into the background but perhaps temporarily.

To maintain international peace, which task the US assumed for itself, it needed global military presence to be able to project power and counter existing or anticipated threats through a policy of intervention.[34] American leaders presumed that the world had to be organized to prevent chaos and only the US possessed that capacity to enforce a global order. American principles would decide the nature of that global order, and barring a few mavericks who would oppose this, all the other countries would accept this.[35] In effect, the US anointed itself the Global Good Cop.

There is a long list of American interventionism globally in the twentieth century. In the first half of the century, there was Italy (1948), Albania (1949–1954), Iran (1953), Guatemala (1954), and one of the most vicious ones on the Marshall Islands in the South Pacific from 1946 to 1958 during which the US conducted 67 nuclear tests. Some of these tests were 1,000 times more powerful than the Nagasaki bomb with lingering and devastating effects on the population and the ecology. America had a twelve-year involvement in Indonesia, which had become a battleground between the communists and the Americans from 1958 to 1980. The Afghan Jihad (1979–1990) was America's comeback story against the Soviet Union, ending in the collapse of the communist regime in Moscow. The first Iraq War followed soon afterwards. The longest American war of the twenty-first century was the twenty-year war in Afghanistan (2001–2021) that ended in ignominy for the mighty power. The Bush administration's plans to establish a direct presence in the Central Asian Republics, and look for supremacy in the Caspian and Black Seas regions for strategic value and energy resources, collapsed with the quagmire in Iraq.[36]

The Cold War was mostly a serious ideological battle between the US and USSR, which often led to vicious proxy wars in the Third World. There were few rules and both sides played dirty. Subversion, regime change, stealing elections or preventing them, human rights violations and friendship with friendly or amenable dictators while ostensibly fighting for democracy, were all part of the arsenal. Democracy was the slogan on one side and socialist equality on the other, but the real goal was, and still is, total domination.

During the Cold War, US intelligence played a stellar role for its country. They had to initially deal with a paranoid Stalin who would not hesitate to destroy the messenger from NKVD (predecessor of KGB) if his intelligence information did not agree with his own thinking. Underestimation of the enemy's capabilities and overestimation of its intentions and one's own capabilities is a major stumbling block, especially in tyrannical regimes, because then there is no reliable fallback.

A New World Order

The protests in Myanmar in August 1988 were an opportunity to rally the world for democracy since they happened soon after the beginning of the Soviet departure from Afghanistan in May that year. The US was sensing victory and the need for a new narrative for domination. When the Berlin Wall fell in 1989, the American Deep State did not know how to treat the Russians, and instead of downsizing and trying to woo the Russians away from the Chinese, they unwisely began to commit themselves to maintaining and strengthening their global empire. The fall of the Soviet Empire led to unreal times and wild dreams. The first batch of newly minted Russian elite looked at American institutions and way of life in unconcealed awe and were more than eager to replicate them in Russia, but the romantic dream died young. Russia was too old a country and too proud to adopt other models.

The Americans were perhaps not prepared for this sudden change in the course of history and perhaps are not ready even today. They were geared for a longer conflict against a worthy enemy. They could not afford the loss of that enemy, but the Soviet Union fell ahead of any anticipated date and without any warning from the CIA. Life suddenly without such a stupendous enemy, who was evil incarnate and always menacing, was unthinkable for the US.

The Soviet Union had given nine American presidents a raison d'état, a free pass to do whatever they pleased. It had helped boost the GDP based on prodigious defence spending and helped silence domestic political dissent.[37] Its downfall meant an economic loss and livelihood for many defence and ancillary industries.

Myanmar's 1988 protests were small change compared to the Tiananmen Square massacre in Beijing that followed in 1989. This was a huge scoring point for democracy and American leadership. Yet this had its limitations too, because massive American business interests were involved in a rapidly growing China. High ideals and national interest clashed again, and national interest won.

The quest and establishment of a new world order in the 1990s was to be led by Western democracies with the US in a commanding position. This new world order was going to adopt the recommendations of the powerful, elitist Council on Foreign Relations to safeguard American interests. It was to have an international structure that would be imperialistic but would not be described as one.[38]

To achieve this goal, America would use military, economic and, later, technological power. This would ensure the establishment of like-minded regimes in countries which were then expected to show good governance and respect for human rights, and follow democratic principles. If regimes did not follow such pristine principles domestically but were in general acquiescence of US policy objectives, the US had no problem aligning with them, either. The economic arrangements were to be based on free market trade principles, except that it was the Western world that would fix the prices of everything.

The new world trade order was a culmination of this goal to enable free access to the Western powers to energy and natural resources. For this, terrorism and religious fundamentalism had to be eliminated, especially that which threatened the Western way of life, its security and stability. Other essential things in the rest of the world would have to wait. Generosity and bonhomie do not lead to empires. Fixity of purpose in the name of national interest must be accompanied by perfidy, dishonesty and an adequate amount of cruelty. Boy Scouts had no role here.

To begin with, the idea perhaps was to transform the entire Islamic world, from Morocco all the way through to Pakistan, Central Asia on to Indonesia, and southern Philippines. The proclaimed strategy devised by the Bush administration in response to 9/11 was that for all evils of terror to be defeated, most of the countries in the Islamic world or at least in the Greater Middle East would have to be reconfigured. The Arab Spring Revolutions and the Eastern European Colour Revolutions were designed to strengthen the Western/American hold on these regions. This great desire to deconstruct and reconstruct 'evil nations' is partly a reflection of what the sociologist C. Wright Mills described as 'military metaphysics' – a tendency to see all international problems in military terms and seek only military solutions, discounting all other possibilities of solution.[39]

That is what happened in the first twenty years of this century. In the process, humanitarian crises in the Middle East, Africa and Afghanistan sharpened and allowed Russia and China to make inroads into Syria, Iran and Iraq. This would also be the inevitable fate of the various undeclared wars that America is currently waging in Africa. America's own image has been indelibly soiled for it allowed or encouraged the growth of newer forms of Islamic terror – and when it came home, they turned around and wondered why.

The nature of the global Islamic threat was such that the military and political campaigns against it could only be led by countries with technological, military and economic might, along with the political will (generally exhibited by the United States), to engage the enemy. The West (read the US) needed to assert its presence across the globe; directly if required or indirectly through arrangements with local regimes for bases of operations against target countries, regimes, and organizations. Thus, there was increased military presence in the Central Asian Republics, and the Afghanistan–Pakistan region. The US Navy was in Diego Garcia and the Mediterranean, off the ports of Hormuz, Gwadar and Pasni; there was US Air Force presence in Dal Badin, Afghanistan and Kyrgyzstan; there was increased military establishment in areas close to Russia and China and also other member states of the Shanghai Cooperation Organization. At one stage it looked as if the US had approximately 800 bases of different kinds all over the globe.[40] US military and diplomatic presence in countries from Türkiye (formerly Turkey) to the Philippines ensured access to vital resources, important shipping lanes and markets. Countries like Russia, China and India acquiesced in this arrangement as the Great Global War on Terror was being fought. There was no choice at that time even as this war extended American ambitions to remain the global hegemon.

The American version of the New World Order was tested in September 1991, as George H.W. Bush prepared to lead his country into a coalition war in Iraq after its invasion of Kuwait in August 1990, commonly known as the First Gulf War (1990–1991). Victory was preordained, and chest thumping was in order. This war was short but should have warned the Americans that all was not well in the Muslim world, and organizations like Al Qaeda were gaining momentum, with attacks against US interests in Saudi Arabia, Kenya, Somalia and Yemen.

In a similar attempt to portray the US as sole superpower through an exhibition of strength, the Republican leader Bush's Democrat successor Bill Clinton did the same in the Balkans in the 1990s by using NATO to divide Yugoslavia.

Exactly ten years after Bush Sr.'s New World Order speech, terrorists struck America in September 2001 when Bush Jr. was president. The American reaction was typical of a rich and powerful person who had been attacked in his own home by a bunch of hoodlums. At one level, the sheer audacity was unacceptable. It was embarrassing that despite all its intelligence capabilities and security measures, the fortress had been breached. At another level, it was an opportunity to strike in the Middle East. So, retribution, heavy and immediate, was the war cry.

Yet when the massive military machine blazed into Afghanistan in October 2001, America's destiny was manifest. It was going to lose because it had chosen Pakistan as its ally. The rest is history, where the world saw the globe's strongest nation, after twenty years and spending $2 trillion, had to negotiate with an insurgent group for safe passage out, leaving behind a tattered and torn nation that it had sworn to protect.

Forever Wars

This new global empire was fired by dreams of Pax Americana and a designation of the US's self-assigned role as indispensable keeper of the peace. This came with a background of countless invasions and interventions all over the globe, ostensibly for democracy but actually for preservation of national and economic interests. The credo written by a narcissistic elite was that Washington alone would lead, save, liberate and ultimately transform the world. What the United States, and indeed most of the rest of the world, did not realize was that in the twenty-first century there would be a new competitor for a global role. When the United States proclaimed it had defeated an 'Evil Empire' as Soviet forces left Afghanistan, there was an Islamic group in Afghanistan that claimed it owed its success to faith and Islam in its victory over the Godless one. Both would seek dominance, one using market forces and military power and the other using its creed to conquer the world.

Over the years, wars launched by the US, from the Middle East to Africa, have had the support of both the Democrats and the Republicans.[41]

At home, Washington had interlocking institutions of powerful people from the higher echelons of the executive, legislative and judicial branches of government. This included the principal components of the national security state, that is, the Departments of State, Defence and now Homeland Security,[42] along with intelligence agencies like the CIA and NSA, and the federal law enforcement community. 'Washington' also meant select think tanks and interest groups 'lawyers, lobbyists, fixers, former officials and retired military officers'[43] who always enjoy access. 'Washington' goes beyond the Beltway and includes big banks and other financial institutions, military contractors and major media corporations including television networks and publications like the *New York Times* and quasi-academic institutions like the Council on Foreign Relations and Harvard's Kennedy School of Government.

Post the Cold War, the geostrategic consensus in America had four elements. The first was globalization or globalized neoliberalism and its main feature was unconstrained corporate capitalism. This operated universally in a new world that was open to the free movement of goods, capital, ideas and people. It helped create wealth at a scale that had never been imagined and solutions to the problems were also on a global scale. The second element was global leadership which was a euphemism for hegemony, or quite simply, empire. Global leadership implied order attained through the unchallengeable military might of the United States, which would manage and police in a post-colonial, but imperial, order that favoured American interests and values. This would enable it to enforce globalization in a way that order and abundance would work together.

The third element was freedom with traditional moral prohibitions declared obsolete and constraints removed to maximize choice. Order and abundance would ensure freedom and would relieve Americans from concerns regarding safety and survival, which the less privileged would handle on their own. This is where America went seriously wrong with its woke-ism, political correctness and gender wisdom – all carried to absurd limits, and against which we now see a backlash. The fourth element was presidential supremacy. This translated into a glossy monarchical status, which in turn meant a revision of the political order. While the Constitution continued to be treated as a holy text, the other two branches of government, the Congress and the Supreme Court, were no longer on the same pedestal as the executive.[44] Ultimately, the American post-Cold War moment was extremely short and nowhere near an American Century, lasting only till the end of the Balkan Wars in 1999.

It seems that although the US had been more powerful or was perceived as more powerful in the bipolar world, it did not handle its single superpower status well. Despite the Gulf War in 1991 that brought victory for it in a highly publicized Nintendo-style war in Iraq, things seemed to be going awry but only the most perceptive or sensitive saw this. Carl Sagan, the eminent astronomer, expressed his foreboding about the future in his book, *The Demon-Haunted World: Science as a Candle in the Dark*, published in 1995, just four years after the Gulf War.

Carl Sagan commented that, 'The dumbing down of the American is most evident in the slow decay of substantive content in the enormously influential media, the 30-second sound bites (now down to 10 seconds or less), lowest common denominator programming, credulous presentations on serious science and superstition, but especially a kind of celebration of ignorance.'[45]

Regardless, about a decade after the Gulf War, the United States was back in another of its interminable, forever wars. Hubris had again led them there. Its invasion of Iraq in 2003 was an exercise in empire-building driven by hardline right-wing neoconservatives in the Bush government. It was a dream since the preceding decade of a group of out-of-work hardliners looking for greatness for their empire and themselves. They were led by Donald Rumsfeld and Dick Cheney.[46] The region has known no peace in these last thirty years, Americans have not been able to reorder the region to suit their strategic comfort and the Islamist threat continues to mount. It is difficult to say that American security interests have been ensured. Any ideology that has a global mission backed by military power accompanied by an increasing propensity to use force as a first option is dangerous.

The 'permanent wars' in the Greater Middle East, parts of Africa and Afghanistan have achieved nothing despite huge budgets, equipment and lethality exhibited through brand-new bases in the Middle East for the launch of massively destructive airpower, including drones. This is partly the result of an assessment that permanent wars translate into permanent power, and partly motivated by the military–industrial complex seeking bases and selling hardware to oil-rich countries to ensure enduring US presence in energy- and mineral-rich regions. The old military–industrial complex of the Cold War days has evolved into a much larger conglomerate of self-interests, which includes technology, communications and intelligence.

It is nobody's case that a perfect weapon has been found to counter the threats. If that were to happen it would be the end of the defence industry. The logic of the industry requires that the search for new weapons and new wars must continue. Besides the manufacture of multirole F-35 aircraft manufactured by Lockheed Martin, is estimated to cost over a trillion dollars over their lifetime. Apart from this, Lockheed Martin are manufacturing F35A, a single-seater single engine stealth supersonic aircraft along with Northrop Grumman. The US government has already made a down payment of $55 billion to Northrop Grumman and also set aside funds for a trillion-dollar upgradation of its nuclear strike force. Contrast this with the generally accepted estimate that Osama bin Laden's Al Qaeda spent roughly about $400,000 to $500,000 for 9/11. It is obvious to all that the cost–benefit analysis shows that Al Qaeda has been an overwhelming success. The United States today has the world's most advanced and extensive security surveillance systems to defend democracy and freedoms, for which there is a trillion-dollar budget.

Costs of War

At the turn of this century, George W. Bush's electoral victory brought the neocons back to power. American leadership felt it would continue to exercise global domination through its ententes with major powers, its leadership in international organizations and its fifty formal military alliances with other nations. There was an aura of imperial power with its 800-odd military bases strewn across the Middle East, Europe, Southeast Asia and Africa. It built permanent bases in Kosovo, Kyrgyzstan and Uzbekistan between 1999 and 2001. Some of the bases were luxurious like the ski and vacation resort at Garmisch in the Bavarian Alps, a resort hotel in downtown Tokyo and 234 military golf courses operated worldwide, all of which were some of the luxuries of war and security. Seventy-one Learjets, thirteen Gulfstream IIIs and seventeen Cessna Citation luxury jets were used to fly the military top brass to such locations.[47]

Like other empires, the Americans also protected their own by enforcing what they called the Status of Forces Agreement (SOFA) on host governments. These agreements ensured that American troops were not held responsible for crimes they might commit against residents. Clearly a part of the problem was also imperial overreach. With military bases in thirty-six countries as far back as 2010, and several overseas territories, the cost of running these operations was estimated to be around $900 billion per year or 5 per cent of US national income. Besides, with its long history of using covert and overt means of regime change, in Latin America alone there were forty-one cases of successful US-led coups/regime changes between 1898 and 1994 at the rate of one overthrow every twenty-eight months in a 100-year period. Such attempts were extremely costly, and also counterproductive, as America found out in Iraq and Afghanistan. In 2008 Columbia scholar Joseph Stiglitz and Harvard scholar Linda Bilmes calculated the cost to be $3 trillion,[48] and today the cost is estimated to be $5 trillion from just its Iraq and Afghanistan misadventures.

The Cost of War Project at Brown University's Watson Institute calculated that the War on Terror, beginning 12 September 2001, had cost $5.6 trillion by the end of 2018.[49] These costs and casualties would have naturally increased since then. There was a price to be paid for extravagant lies and exaggerations, which cannot be measured in dollars. Over twenty years, from 2001 to 2020, the Iraq body count among civilians was between 185,454 to 208,493, and even the second figure may have been an undercount according to the Cost of War project, which also calculated that at least 800,000 people were killed by direct war violence in Iraq, Afghanistan, Syria, Yemen and Pakistan.[50] In these twenty years, US presidents repeatedly used Congressional Authorization for the Use of Military Force. Meant to be used only in 9/11-related cases, they went ahead and used it against eighteen different countries.

There is also the cost for the countries and the people attacked; but there is no estimate available for the destruction of towns like Ramadi and Mosul in Iraq, Raqqa and Aleppo in Syria, Sirte in Libya or even Marawi in the Philippines where America engaged in battles with Islamic terrorists. No one paid attention to the warning from Amr Moussa, the then head of the Arab League, when he said that an invasion of Iraq would open the gates of hell. Two years after the invasion and the US occupation of Iraq, Amr Moussa confirmed in 2004, 'The gates of hell are open in Iraq.'[51]

American hyperbolic reaction in Afghanistan and globally would have been applauded had the US wiped out Al Qaeda and the Taliban. It did neither. In that first decade of the twenty-first century, it seemed to have lost considerable ground with new powers making inroads into American domains. The costly and futile warfare and its own economic uncertainties were indications of a waning power. Historian Alfred McCoy cautioned in 2017, 'While rising empires are often judicious, even rational in their application of armed force for conquest and control of overseas dominions, fading empires are inclined to ill-considered displays of power, dreaming of bold military masterstrokes that would somehow recoup lost prestige and power.'[52]

When the Americans loftily declared Operation Infinite Justice had been launched to invade Iraq in 2003, Muslim sensitivities forced a change in the name to Operation Enduring Freedom, which then became Operation Freedom Sentinel. None of the changes helped. Meanwhile it is often forgotten that America's 'forever wars' continued elsewhere around the same time. The battlefields stretched all the way from Libya to the Philippines, including Iraq, Yemen, Somalia, Syria, Yemen, Burkina Faso and more. About $6.4 trillion have been spent at a human loss of at least 335,000 civilians killed and 37 million displaced from their homes. There were 201 air strikes in Somalia during Trump's first presidency, up from 42 during the presidencies of Bush and Obama.

Limitations of Power

Limitations of power were visible to the discerning. Dreams of managing history through a selective recall of events were the result of a peculiar combination of arrogance and narcissism that was potentially a mortal threat to the United States.[53] Bacevich cites theologian Reinhold Niebuhr's perspective in his book *The Irony of American History*, where he says that the global economic crisis, total war, genocide, totalitarianism and nuclear arsenals capable of destroying civilization were the real problems and reflected the nature of man. Instead of humility accompanying realism, narcissistic realism had taken over and found expression 'in an outsized confidence in the efficacy of American power as an instrument to reshape the global order'.

The opposite of humility, according to Niebuhr, was sanctimony, giving rise to the conviction that American values and beliefs were universal. This led to the assumption that it was necessary to remake the world in America's image, where hubris and sanctimony became paramount expressions of American statecraft, and all this was evident since 11 September 2001. According to Niebuhr, the most significant moral characteristic of the nation was its hypocrisy. The chief danger of hypocrisy in international politics was that it inhibited self-understanding, and the hypocrite ended up fooling mainly himself.[54] The reality was that a long, unending war might be ruinous for local populations but was needed to preserve the American way of life, to extend the American empire and remake the world in its own image. That hope has hardly abated. Neither in the Middle East, nor in Latin America or Africa.

The Cold War era produced its own tensions of mutually assured destruction, where two superpowers ensured that their battles for supremacy through surrogates were fought far away from Europe and North America. There was a certain cold comfort in the Cold War and there were difficulties adjusting to the new order. Its end did not lead to peace; instead, it led to an open exhibition of hubris and triumphalism. This was going to be short-lived, as the US decided to treat Russia as its main enemy, which encouraged a Russian resurgence and its amity with China against the US. The Helsinki Commission, a bipartisan body of the US Congress, in the context of the Ukraine war, designated Russia as the principal adversary in its September 2024 report, and pressed for Russia being designated as a persistent threat to global security.[55]

The idea that the US, having defeated its arch-rival, the Soviet Union, was the sole superpower on the globe, prevented the US from making use of this opportunity to shore up its former adversary instead of trying to crush it completely. This was a repeat of the attitude of the victorious powers who had forced an extremely unfair deal on the Germans after the First World War. After the collapse of the Soviet Union, the West moved in for the kill, the Warsaw Pact was wound down and NATO expanded. It was a misreading of the Russian character. A people who had fought off the Nazi war machine on their own in the historic 872-day Siege of Leningrad were not going to give in to external pressures. It was a matter of time before its nationalism surged. By the end of the 1990s Russia was beginning to find its way back from the brink, not to the same extent as before, but substantially so.

Dissatisfaction among Muslims in the Middle East against their despotic rulers supported by the US and Western powers, sectarian rivalries among Shias and Sunnis, the Shia revolution in Iran and the presence of US forces in Saudi Arabia angered puritanical Saudis enough for them to launch terror attacks against US interests in Africa, culminating in 9/11. With the Taliban in Afghanistan, the entire region from Pakistan to Libya was in ferment. US attacks into Afghanistan, ostensibly to wipe out terror, were a massive display of hurt pride. The attack on Iraq under false pretexts left the entire area engulfed in an arc of instability. Pakistan, with its abilities in running jihadi battles suddenly sharpened after the Afghan Jihad, continued its terrorist violence against both its neighbours, Afghanistan and India. But the US had lost interest in the region in 1988 after the withdrawal of Soviet forces from Afghanistan in 1986. It would close shop in Afghanistan again in 2021 after having been there for twenty years fighting the much-touted Global War on Terror but with nothing to show for itself in the end. The Americans left in such haste that they abandoned $5 billion worth of military equipment. It could have been just an escape or with a purpose for the future – perhaps for another 'forever war' against China.

The rise of the American Empire has been described by American authors and commentators at different times. The late historian and playwright Howard Zinn, for instance, said, 'More and more it seemed that World War Two had been waged by a government whose chief beneficiary was a wealthy elite.'[56] Zinn went on to add that the day there was widespread support for the war there was also widespread profiteering; wages rose but profits skyrocketed. Earlier, World War One had been a boon for US goods and loans and enormous profits were divided among American business interests in a British victory against Germany. This was an outgrowth of attitudes and policies that had become prevalent in America after President McKinley issued the rather pompous Benevolent Assimilation Proclamation in December 1898. This outlined his colonizing policies in the Philippines. Politics and business interests ensured the establishment of empire underlaid with paternalism and racism while every conquest of empire was seen as a reward for the Christian zeal of the new Crusaders.

Profitability and war have been a constant feature in this game of empire. Although some American commentators often describe their country as a reluctant empire or an accidental empire, the relentless ambition to acquire a global Pax Americana has meant that continuous wars helped shape the character of the country.[57] America emerged on top after the Second World War, which had accounted for 50 million killed but none on American soil. This made it easier for it to pursue military adventurism. This was no accident, and American leaders were not reluctant; they systematically and deliberately sought Empire. It was profitable to do so. In its essentials, nothing had changed over the centuries. The powerful sought more power and wealth through the means that they had then. In the twenty-first century it is not military power or even economic power that is paramount; it is the power of the narrative and of technology that work in tandem with traditional sources of coercion to achieve goals.

Some feared that if the United States were to retreat from global hegemony the planet would plunge into an anarchic Dark Age of waning empires, religious revivals, incipient anarchy and a retreat into fortified cities.[58] Historian Niall Ferguson forecasts a grim world where there are too many people while technology upgrades destruction and violence. This would be a world without a hyper-power and there would be no coming back. Some lauded America and said it must emulate the British Empire but be more devious and secretive about it;[59] others described it as an attractive empire sought after by troubled lands like Afghanistan.[60]

Author and military historian Max Boot's description in 2002 of American military prowess took the meaning of euphoria to another level when he said this level of martial excellence far surpassed 'the capabilities of such previous would-be hegemons as Rome, Britain and Napoleonic France'.[61] Soon after the US invasion of Afghanistan in 2001, there were many who happily and prematurely agreed with the notion that the US would be the world's sole military superpower until the end of time.[62] Boot recommended that the US establish a colonial office to administer the Middle East.[63] Quite clearly, right-wing jingoism and imperial arrogance dictated this kind of misplaced optimism and events would begin to reveal the reality in merely a few years. The Americans were not only borrowing tactics including headlines from their British friends' imperial past to secure their empire, but also using their tactics at creating narratives.

The Bush White House had an air of infallibility about itself and a powerful set of people in a team that believed it could really move mountains; a feeling that permeated it after 9/11. Many who met Bush during that time left with an uneasy feeling about the president's lack of curiosity about complex issues. Those were the days when many of Bush's White House aides looked beyond reality-based solutions. Karl Rove, Bush's strategist, was quoted by Ron Suskind in the *New York Times* as having said, 'We're an empire now and when we act, we create our own reality. And while you're studying that reality – judicially, as you will – we'll act again creating other new realities . . . And that's how things will sort out. We are history's actors . . . and you, all of you, will be left to just study what we do.'[64] It was faith-based arrogance that led the Americans into Afghanistan and then into Iraq. Most of the neocons were driven by faith-based apocalyptic tasks.

Some believed that the world needed an effective liberal empire, and the United States had the best credentials to play this role, both from the point of view of its own security and its altruism.[65] Richard Haass, who served in the Bush Jr. administration, favoured an informal American empire with a doctrine of integration, which meant arrangements that would sustain a world consistent with US interests.[66] Thomas Donnelly from the Project for the New American Century, a Washington-based neocon think tank, said that many people would not talk about an empire openly and preferred to use code phrases like 'America is the sole superpower'. Max Boot vigorously made 'The Case for an American Empire' in his article for the neocon weekly, the *Weekly Standard*. William Kristol, another neocon, declared that the US needed to err on the side of being strong. 'And if people want to say we're an imperial power, fine.'

There is the school of thought that believes America's share of the global economy has been intact for the past several decades and its military strength remains unmatched and that American primacy is resilient.[67] There are other commentators who think differently. They argue that the West as an entity will lose ground to other rising or resurging powers. While in 2010, four of the top five economies were the US, Japan, Germany and France, by 2050, Goldman Sachs predicted that the top four would be China, India, Brazil and Russia. China would be threatening US interests, and it is possible that other powers may not necessarily be American partners.[68]

Michael Lind, a former professor at Harvard and Johns Hopkins, in his 2014 essay 'The American Century is Over: How our Country Went Down in a Blaze of Shame', was sure even then that the American century was over because of 'having lost two wars in a decade, a stalled economy choked by parasitic lobbies and a political system dominated by billionaires'. No one was willing to acknowledge the severity of America's problems, or even think about the radical structural changes required.[69]

The two Trump presidencies have made the situation even more difficult for the US.

'How Did We Get Here?'

In answering the question 'How did we get here?' like Carl Sagan had asked fifteen years earlier, David Graeber in 2011 said he suspected what the world looking at were the final effects of the militarization of American capitalism itself. '... it could well be said that the last thirty years have seen the construction of a vast bureaucratic apparatus for the creation and maintenance of hopelessness, a giant machine designed, first and foremost, to destroy any sense of possible alternative futures.' Adding that it 'is a veritable obsession among the rulers of the world ... In response to social movements – in response to the upheavals of the 1960s and 1970s ... [they] cannot be seen to grow, flourish or propose alternatives; that those who challenge existing power arrangements can never, under any circumstances, be perceived to win'.[70]

There was considerable debate in the United States about the 'American Empire' in the decade following the establishment of Bush's New World Order. As John Kerry readied himself to be nominated as Democratic candidate for the presidential elections in 2004, there was a national security consensus which presumed that American military supremacy was an unqualified good and evidence of a larger American superiority. Armed might was presumed to be the key for creating an international order that would accommodate American values. One result of this thought process has been that in the past twenty years, US policy has become increasingly militarized, with tendencies suggesting America was enamoured with its self-image as the prime military power.[71]

Other comments were equally grim. Howard Zinn, the author of *A People's History of the United States*, pointed out that the American Empire had always been a bipartisan project with both parties lauding and justifying it. 'For the people of the United States, and indeed for people all over the world, those claims sooner or later are revealed to be false. The rhetoric, often persuasive on first hearing, soon becomes overwhelmed by horrors that can no longer be concealed: the bloody corpses of Iraq, the torn limbs of American GIs, the millions of families driven from their homes – in the Middle East and in the Mississippi Delta.'[72]

This mood was reflected in the 2012 National Intelligence Council (NIC) report on Global Trends 2030. It referred to a few game changers that could undermine the US-dominated world order or even end US domination. In its projections for 2030, the NIC considered an evolving world order, economic decline, military misadventure and even World War III.[73] It concluded that while it was true that American global reach would recede and that there would be a possible challenger to the top spot, there was still no power which could give the world an appealing ideology, the kind of technological and educational resources that the US has, or one that had comparable military power to replace the US.

Every empire created some universal appeal for its subjects. The Spaniards promoted Christianity with considerable fervour. The British claimed they gave the world fair play and free markets and the US portrayed itself as a champion of democracy, human rights and the rule of law.

Not all empires behaved nobly but sold a narrative that was so. Some might see the US as an empire on the wane, but it is also true that there is no replacement in sight. China with all its sources of power – military, economic and technological – does not look as if it can replace the US. Both China and Russia are inwards-looking, they have 'self-referential cultures, recondite non-Roman scripts, non-democratic political structures and underdeveloped legal systems that will deny them key instruments for global dominion'.[74]

The NIC in its 2021 Global Trends report gave projections up to 2040. It is interesting that terrorism is mentioned in it only peripherally. Presumably after twenty years of fighting terrorists in Africa, the Middle East and Afghanistan, the Pentagon had reduced the threat from a rampaging monster to an annoying mosquito cloud. Future threats would be China and Russia. This is even though China has only one overseas military base and Russia is economically rickety but with ambitions. In his first term, the more significant aspect of Trump's military legacy was to prepare the US military to move away from a global counterterror force into one meant to fight an all-out, cataclysmic, potentially nuclear, war with China and/or Russia.[75] This is unlikely to have changed in the second Trump presidency, given his approach to Ukraine; the same fear of a nuclear war does not exist in Trump's calculations while supporting Israel.

The biggest change in the twenty-first century for the US is not China's rise; it is that the rest of the world is no longer willing to stand and wait for the US to acquire what it wants for itself and be happy with the crumbs it leaves in its wake. If the US seriously believes in global democracy, it should cease to renege on agreements when they no longer suit America or enforce its domestic laws on the rest of the world. It must not try subterfuge to ensure regime change in countries that do not obey it. That is not how democratic arrangements function. Despite being the world's strongest military and economic power, for the last thirty-plus years, it has been misled by subterfuge or allowed itself to be misled owing to preconceived notions, for instance by Pakistan in its Global War on Terror. The US may still be the world's most powerful and richest nation, but it has not won any war after 1945, and other nations have been able to defy it and survive.

While its foreign policy might be awry or in decline, average American individual income is still seven times that of the Chinese, whose country is the world's largest exporter goods and services and food. American entrepreneurial skills and technology ensured that in 2025, eight of the largest technology companies of the world by market capitalization were based in the US.[76]

If it wishes to still be the 'go-to nation' it must become a country others wish to emulate. But it is no longer exceptional nor indispensable; nor is it always right. That empire has begun to recede.

Traditionally, there has been a bipartisan agreement that America must remain the strongest military in the world. This would be in keeping with the belief held by many Americans in all seriousness that the US was required by history to create a global order in its own image. Barely 250 years after the country came into being, its military is active in more than 150 countries, and it has about 800 or so military bases strewn all over the globe. This makes the US a neighbour to most countries. As a result, local and regional conflicts make consistent policy decisions difficult, as quite often the US is friendly to both parties in the conflict.

Principal global threats – for instance like those posed by climate change, enduring conflict and turmoil in the Islamic world, China's emergence as a potential rival, and how the Americans have mortgaged their prosperity – do not get the same attention as they should. Peace, justice, growth and freedom are laudable objectives, but the economic reality is that the US has always needed a strong adversary along with frequent wars to be able to run many of its industries to replenish supplies. The US never had the aura of a monarch and dynasty like the Europeans and Asians did. Its grandeur was different, and the world was controlled ostensibly through the United Nations Security Council (UNSC) but it was actually by the US backed by the best universities and research, manufacturing capability which included the best military hardware and streets-ahead technology, as also its financial controls and the dollar. Leverage was exercised through the World Bank and IMF, controlled by Western nations. That aura has begun to fade.

The first decline was an inability to win a war in the sense that stated goals were never achieved in Vietnam, Iraq, Afghanistan and, as looks likely, in Ukraine. The second was that from being a manufacturing nation, the US had become a goods and services nation. The earlier dreams of neocons Dick Cheney and Paul Wolfowitz for global dominance, were at a time when the US accounted for 22 per cent of global production. By 2016 this had declined to around 16 per cent, with China ahead at 18 per cent; by 2021 according to IMF, US produce was about 15 per cent compared to China's global output at 20 per cent. In 2024, China's manufacturing output was significantly larger than that of the United States, accounting for roughly 31.6 per cent of global manufacturing output, while the US accounted for 15.9 per cent, according to Safeguard Global.[77]

With the dollar under pressure, there are now increasing demands from leaders in Latin America, Asia and Africa that a new financial management system was needed to replace the IMF and World Bank. The P-5 (five permanent members) of the UNSC were based on archaic principles and were a Cold War construct. They did not represent the true strength and relevance of nations. The expansion of BRICS (Brazil, Russia, India, China, South Africa) ruffled feathers in Washington because BRICS now holds greater GDP strength than the G7.

American reluctance to seriously solve the global environmental crisis seemed to be because of pressure from its corporate world's anti-environmental stance. Consequently, many multilateral environmental agreements like the Montreal Protocol to control the production of CFCs were sacrificed at the altar of the WTO agreement, which placed trade above environment. US mega-corporations like Monsanto, Dow and Syngenta among others, produce genetically modified food. However, the introduction of GM food was resisted by Europeans. More than fifteen European countries opted out of the GM crop scheme that required signing of territorial exclusion requests with Monsanto, Dow and Syngenta. In 2015, 140,000 hectares of Europe's land were being cultivated with GM products compared to 181 million hectares in the rest of the world.[78] These figures hold till today.

European resistance was seen as a conspiracy to deny US its high-tech edge in global competition. Global warming remained an issue and the Bush administration refused to ratify and sign the much-weakened Kyoto Protocol on climate change. Several attempts to address climate change failed to deliver any meaningful progress.

With the military disaster in Afghanistan, the US lost ground in real terms and in terms of perception globally. As the Soviet Union learnt, a country may hold long-range nuclear missiles, yet unless its economy is sound, power cannot be retained. To become a Great Power – that is, a state that can hold its own against any other country, it must have a strong, flourishing economic base. Wars, continuous or frequent, may be essential in some situations and good for short-term financial gains, but the diversion of massive amounts of economic resources to unproductive pursuits erodes the economic base of a country.[79] That is what happened in the US: it gave up its manufacturing base in favour of creating a system that relied on external sources to satisfy consumption patterns at home.

The stealthy manner of the US Army's departure from Afghanistan in the dead of the night, leaving behind billions of dollars' worth of military equipment, has dented not just US dependability but also its credibility. The US conduct of its war in Iraq had already dented its image considerably, with the infamous Abu Ghraib and Guantanamo Bay prisons becoming symbols of American atrocities, even as the false pretext that Saddam possessed WMDs damaged its credibility. It was not because of failure of intelligence that the US retreated; it was a failure of imagination. It was a case of imperial overstretch, where it was becoming difficult to distinguish between religious fanatics and market fanatics, where a global free market on the loose with profit as the sole motive had made money power the newest weapon.

Alongside Iraq and Afghanistan, US activities in Syria inflamed Muslim sentiments in the Arab world and in South and Southeast Asia. These were massive ideological gains for the Islamic radicals. As the Americans battled for control in the Middle East, there were anti-US movements in Latin America – Brazil, Venezuela and Ecuador voted for distinctly anti-US leadership.

As the years went by, American proxy adventures in Ukraine led to the Ukrainians being pushed to take on Russia, while the US provoked Russia to invade Ukraine. The expectation was a short, sharp conflict with Russia that would end in Ukrainian victory with Russia reduced to nothing – clearly a case of overestimating your own abilities and underestimating that of the adversary. No lessons had been learnt from recent history. America has begun to lose control and direction as it abdicated responsibility as the global guarantor of peace and security. These adventures reflect a sense of entitlement and self-proclaimed superiority. Realism and understanding the limitations of power take time. American leaders will not stop trying to remain in control.

It is not only lost wars, wars in stalemate or unnecessary wars that have hurt America internationally. Today, it seems to be bleeding from within from what Washington-based Atul Singh, founder of the media platform Fair Observer, calls 'a very modern feudalism',[80] where income disparities between the financial elite and ordinary Americans are massive. Depending on how this is calculated, the top 10 per cent of Americans own 84 per cent of all shares in the US, with the top 1 per cent owning half.[81] About half the American population owns no stocks at all and may not have savings beyond $500. Meanwhile, over the years, American high technology has created the Big Five – or the Frightful Five – Amazon, Apple, Facebook, Microsoft and Alphabet (Google's parent company)[82] – who control the internet and huge sections of the economy, strangulating small-sized and medium-sized business houses. Thousands of working-class jobs have disappeared, while some highly paid ones have been created. Singh also alludes to Big Tech's algorithms, filter bubbles and echo chambers, which have created a post-truth world of fake news and conspiracy theories, where the deluge makes it difficult to distinguish between fact and fiction. The irony, Singh says, is that the leaders of these mega-companies are 'self-proclaimed liberals, avowed philanthropists and cheerleaders for progress. Yet they have unleashed Frankensteinian monsters that have wrecked journalism, destroyed discourse and damaged democracy'.

Singh presents a dire prognosis.[83] An increasingly unequal America with declining social mobility is seething with rage. The rich have turned into rentiers, profiting from rising asset prices with a stock market that is a bubble about to burst while those without capital have no upward mobility. A significant portion of the over 73 million, who voted for Trump in 2024, have lost faith in the system. And many of them have guns. Without bold political and economic reform, the situation will not mend itself. Adventures abroad that tend to become misadventures only add to the problem.

Empires do not rise or die overnight, or even in a decade. Sometimes it takes generations. The American Empire has been the cleverest of all its predecessors. It ran its empire by remote control. It is inevitable that an empire that has risen will fall, eventually; change is eternal and there could be different reasons for this. A great deal also depends on perceptions about the empire, regardless of its wealth and power. Credibility, dependability and intentions matter. Once these perceptions plunge, a return journey is very difficult.

Despite the challenges outlined in this chapter, the US is not going to give up so easily. Military might may overcome the enemy but to restrain it and rule it, the victor needs other levers. It means pursuit of a ruthless foreign policy. No friends; allies maybe, but preferably vassal nations. The US will remain an empire so long as it controls money and banks, mega-corporations that span the globe, the latest technology, military bases and the media. It does not occupy territory like the Europeans did; it controls the mind in a rather Orwellian fashion. It controls what the world eats by peddling its GM crops and seeds to developing countries, dominates the imagination and the aspirational quotient with its movie and media industries, regulates global health through gigantic pharma companies and controls the cyberspace with its protocols, companies and root servers.

Most of all, it relishes proxy wars and conflicts; Afghanistan was a proxy war. In Europe, Ukraine was the ostensible cause but other outcomes would work in its favour as well – the collapse of Ukraine through deliberately induced conflict, the economic collapse of the EU and a weakened Russia. This will provide opportunities for American companies to reconstruct their economies. What the Pentagon had helped destroy, the State Department will help rebuild. Winner takes all.

The US relishes regional conflicts where it can intervene in keeping with state policy that no regional power should become so strong as to hurt American interests. 'Total dominance' and 'accept no rivals' have long been the credo but it is beginning to look increasingly tenuous.

India–China tensions may create an Indian military dependence on the Americans, given the Russian situation today. Even so, US influence will inevitably decline, more because other countries like China, India, Brazil and possibly one of the Arab nations, are learning to stand up to it. This does not mean that the US is about to surrender its primacy or hegemonic status. In the twenty-first century, empire is not just about controlling or possessing territory; it is about controlling every aspect of life, whether it is technology, pharma, food, money or arms.

US foreign policy has always had continuity regardless of the incumbent in the White House, despite sharp differences at times between the Democrats and Republicans. It operates within a band, and it appears as if there were a mysterious power that guides it. President Trump may appear to have gone out on a limb and changed policy but it is mostly a matter of tactics and style – it is still a decisive pursuit of American national interest first. In fact this is being expressed more forcefully now in the trade sector, currency and immigration, and displays a readiness to impose sanctions. This is an advantage that other post-1945 democracies could not acquire or were not allowed to. The US had the strength to maintain continuity. Nevertheless, the most strident and scathing criticism came in 2005 from Harold Pinter in his acceptance speech for the Nobel Prize for Literature.

'Low intensity conflict means that thousands of people die but slower than if you dropped a bomb on them in one fell swoop. It means that you infect the heart of the country, that you establish a malignant growth and watch the gangrene bloom. When the populace has been subdued – or beaten to death – the same thing – and your own friends, the military and the great corporations, sit comfortably in power, you go before the camera and say that democracy has prevailed.'[84]

Other empires have thrived on the gun which helped control cheap local labour, transport labour from one colony to another or arrange outright sales of slave labour. More recently, Europe had acute labour shortages after World War II, so the solution was extensive import of labour from former colonies into Europe. Immigration has been an important component of Western capitalism.

As the West became prosperous, greater profits and cheap products needed some amount of cheap labour so cyber technology provided cyber coolies who operated in their own countries at hours that suited the West for salaries that were higher than normal in their countries but still lower than Western standards. Operating on a similar principle, sweat shops in Southeast Asia provided cheap goods. There were no problems with trade unions, and everything was impersonal. Soon this period was over as supplier countries started employing these skilled personnel themselves. The decision now is that manufacturing must be brought back to America. All this needs labour, lots of it and cheap, to keep the prices down. Acquiring this is not easy or straightforward.

There has been a steadily rising illegal migration into America from Mexico,[85] and into Europe from North Africa across the Mediterranean, or into Britain from across the English Channel.[86] According to another report,[87] study visa enrolments were growing mainly for Indian and Nigerian students, with Indian figures surpassing the Chinese. These were not for studies but for employment, once again in sweat shops to keep inflation in control.

Undoubtedly, in the US entrepreneurship is highly rewarding and attracts young immigrants with all kinds of skills and without skills as well. Yet there is a certain amorality in the US brand of capitalism. It is financially lucrative but ruthless. The deliberately decrepit or otherwise expensive healthcare system for medical care or social security system for old age pensions hurt the underprivileged the most. At present, any treatment of illness in the hands of Big Pharma is unaffordable for most. This has capped life expectancy at around mid-seventies in a prosperous country like America. The weak and the poor are left by the wayside, which is tantamount to population control. The gap is sought to be filled by allowing immigration – legal or illegal.

Also operating along the borders and in the corridors of power are powerful gangs that operate human trafficking operations. They have held sway for a long while but the current Trump administration seems determined to curb them.

It cannot be said with any certainty whether there has been an increase in street violence, robberies in supermarkets, racist and religious attacks in the West, US included, with the police either helpless or even conniving, or if access to social media leads to that conclusion. The 'woke' dialogue and endless contorted discussions about gender choices has added to social insecurities. The blurring of age-old gender identities have led to further fraught social narratives.

Worse, it is quite possible that the violence with which debates are being settled could lead to civil war. One in three adults in the US believe that political violence is necessary to advance certain political goals. According to data analysed by the Federal Emergency Management Agency (FEMA), about 20 million Americans – double from 2017, are preparing for a cataclysm. In May 2024, Ray Dalio, who founded one of the largest hedge funds in the world, Bridgewater Associates, believed that there was a 35 per cent chance of a civil war breaking out in America.[88] In June, Dalio raised the chances to 50 per cent. No one really knows why, but many expect this to happen in the next few years.

The Return of Trump

Donald Trump achieved what was considered at one stage unthinkable and unattainable. His victory in the 2024 presidential elections was against the received wisdom from well-known commentators like Fareed Zakaria who, just weeks before, was supremely confident of Kamala Harris winning. Winning the elections when he was considered the underdog was impossible according to the Democratic party sages, but he did, despite being an outsider, a capitalist billionaire but 'not the right kind', and facing charges of felony. The Democrats had failed to read the people of America. Trump came across as what he was – at times rough, with an ego, with misogynist remarks against his opponents this time and the last (Hillary Clinton), both of whom he defeated.

Harris's self-portrayal as belonging to the working class was false and everyone knew that. This narrative did not hold with her declared assets of $8 million, $850,000 in cash, book royalties worth over $400,000 and being married to a millionaire. A Trump victory had been predicted a few months prior, for good reasons that others refused to read.[89] Trump declared a tough To-Do list soon after taking over as president. He controlled the Senate, the House of Representatives and the Supreme Court too.

No president in recent times has had this level of control. He is in the process of making good on his promises to roll back illegal immigration, cut down the power and size of the bureaucracy – military and civil, impose trade tariffs and take on Russia and China. He stressed free speech and abolition of censorship, reordering the social media. In 2022, Trump had declared, 'When I'm president, this whole rotten system of censorship and information control will be ripped out of the system at large. There won't be anything left.'[90] The revolving door for security and intelligence services would be far stricter, he said.

He has revamped the security apparatus, downsized other departments like the State Department and has been taking, what appear to be, snap decisions.

Trump's method of governance is autocratic, and his ego makes it self-centred. Nothing has been more apparent than his eagerness to take credit on the India–Pakistan conflict in April 2025 when he insisted that he had brought about the ceasefire. This despite several Indian denials. Trump has officially claimed he ended conflicts between Thailand and Cambodia, Israel and Iran, Rwanda and the Democratic Republic of Congo, India and Pakistan, Serbia and Kosovo and Egypt and Ethiopia. According to him, this qualifies him for the Nobel Peace Prize. Pakistan was the first one to sponsor his name, and this is one of the reasons Pakistan is his current favourite. Unable to face criticism he has also been harsh on the media.[91] As a result, India–US relations are at their lowest ebb after decades.

Trump's tariff wars against the rest of the globe have been another destabilizing factor not only for the US but the rest of the world. Only three countries have so far stood out – India, China and Russia – members of BRICS which makes Trump even more nervous. At home he has shown an ability to somersault on issues notably the case of the Epstein files where after the initial bravado the issue has been swept under the carpet the moment it was revealed in the media that his name figures in those files.

Never before in its history has the United States repudiated or rebuked its allies or devalued its friends like Trump has done. In his second term he has described some of America's closest allies as cheaters and freeloaders; Japan and other Asian traders were passed off as being very spoiled. America's democratic partners are has-beens, weak or dishonest. On the other hand, autocrats such as Viktor Orbán is a very great Hungarian leader, the North Korean Kim Jong Un is a smart guy and Putin is a genius and so on.[92] There are three and half years still to go.

While there is talk of World War III, Trump will have to give up America's incessant chauvinism and triumphalism with China and Russia. The reality is that China is far stronger now than a few decades ago, in every aspect – military, economics, trade and technology. Chinese exports to the Global South and BRICS countries were nearly four times its exports to the United States and more than the combined total of Chinese exports to the United States, Europe and Japan, which reached a seasonally adjusted annual rate of $1.38 trillion in March 2024.[93] Quite clearly China had moved on, expanded, adjusted and is prepared to deal with America on more equal terms. Various American experts like Prof. Jeffrey Sachs, Col. Douglas Macgregor and Prof. John Mearsheimer have consistently warned about the decline of American power.[94] These three are only samples of the prevailing opinion in America.

Asked to comment on US–China relations, political scientist and a leading geopolitical scholar John Mearsheimer said recently, 'The US cannot do much at this point to slow down Chinese economic growth' and that he 'would bet that the Chinese will overcome the American effort to damage the Chinese economy more than the American economy is damaged as a result of these sanctions and tariffs'. The implication being that the US now hurts itself more by trying to contain China than it hurts China.[95]

Russia was a country that the US thought it would one day destroy and break up through its military and economic superiority. That is what Ukraine was all about. But that is not how it has turned out. The claim that Russia wanted to conquer Europe was only a narrative – a storyline for the consumption of the masses. Meanwhile, Ukraine has lost 600,000 soldiers, 1.2–1.5 million are wounded and the country is as good as ruined. The US has lost hundreds of billions of dollars, while the Russian economy has improved: sanctions have hurt it marginally. A Russia–China coalition could be Trump's nightmare.

Externally, Trump must sort out the messy and violent but energy-rich Middle East, which goes beyond Israel, Hamas, Hezbollah and Iran. It is no longer simple being a superpower and wanting to remain at the top of the table. In addition he has to sort out rather quickly the domestic issues of racial divide, of gender and of economic inequality or unfairness that existed before he took over and the new ones that have been created by his seemingly autocratic actions.

It is amazing and worrying how much power and control America has lost after the Cold War ended in 1990. Incessant unsuccessful external wars have only left the hubris intact but a country cannot go on forever with this and its $36 trillion debt, an outsourced manufacturing capability and a growing rate of unemployment. US government diktats about sanctions have been ignored as countries make their political and economic adjustments in their own interests.

Nothing reflects the present US situation as in Donald Trump's post in the Social Media 'Looks like we've lost India and Russia to deepest, darkest, China. May they have a long and prosperous future together!' Trump wrote this on Truth Social.[96]

It was a mixture of helplessness, accusation and threats that did not go down well with many Americans who value US-India friendship. The adverse reaction in America and India led Trump to quickly attempt to try and make amends for his rant by saying, 'I'll always be friends with (Narendra) Modi… He's a great prime minister. He's great. But I just don't like what he's doing at this particular moment. But India and the United States have a special relationship. There's nothing to worry about …'[97]

India's response has been correct and diplomatic. The important aspect is that Trump's remarks indicate a helplessness and frustration of the United States and Trump unable to have his way. In yet another move, President Trump has threatened to impose a tariff on Indian IT software exports to the US. Proposed to be known as the Hire Bill, but financial experts say this is going to affect US corporates first and may also have WTO implications. The earlier impression that Trump was going to be soft on India after his initial outburst, was premature.[98]

This depicts the fickleness and desperation of a President. It may be best not to react to his pronouncements; knee-jerk reactions to knee-jerk statements are best avoided.

In today's world, a superpower would have to learn to live with lesser powers, India included, and understand that a difference of opinion or interests does not mean enmity. Hopefully, the US leadership would have learnt by now that the old Cold War rhetoric and the belief that the world owes everything to the US were wrong anyway.

5

Provocation of an Old Rival

If the leadership of a country has any views but the following, it's not going to be the leadership of that country for very long. And that is: We do what we can in our own interest.

STROBE TALBOTT,
Bill Clinton's deputy secretary of state, 1994–2001[1]

The Cold War never really ended. If at all it did, a new Cold War started the day the Soviet Union collapsed.

The dramatic and aggressive events in the last phases of the twentieth century changed several global calculations. The Soviet withdrawal from Afghanistan in February 1989 marked the defeat of a superpower in a US-led Islamic jihad that set in motion a chain of events elsewhere. The Tiananmen Square massacre took place in Beijing in June 1989, the German Democratic Republic in faraway Europe collapsed when the Berlin Wall came down in November 1989, Iraq was hammered into submission by February 1991, and heralding the coming New Age of a sole superpower, the Soviet Union wound down in December 1991 and soon began to unravel. It was at this time in history that China began to open up, seriously.

Suddenly, the New World Order had arrived, yet no one really knew how to adjust to it. Old enemies and old friends were gone; new enemies, threats and friends had to be created – for a state, to survive, would need all three. It was with the background of this victory for the Western way of life, the arch-enemy Soviet Union rendered ineffective and a ray of hope that China could also be won over, that American strategists produced their National Security Doctrine, also known as the Wolfowitz Doctrine.

US strategists have consistently favoured global military supremacy. The Defence Planning Guidance of 1992, prepared by then under secretary for defence, Paul Wolfowitz, merely stated the obvious – that the first objective was to prevent the re-emergence of a new rival who would pose the kind of threat the former Soviet Union had done. Therefore, the US would have 'to prevent any hostile power from dominating a region whose resources would, under consolidated control, be sufficient to generate global power'.[2]

This desire for global supremacy was not a neocon mindset alone; it has been mainstream American – Republican and Democrat – and remains immutable. Clinton's Pentagon talked of 'full-spectrum dominance',[3] his successor talked of pre-emptive unilateralism[4] and his might-have-been-successor, John Kerry spoke of 'muscular internationalism'.[5]

Cold War: Season One

In August 1945, an American DC-3 assigned to Gen. Bedell Smith, who was Gen. Eisenhower's chief of staff, took off from Germany carrying a precious cargo of several Nazi generals who had abandoned their loyalty to Hitler. Also on board was General Reinhard Gehlen, Hitler's former intelligence chief for the Eastern Front against the Soviet Union. He was going to help the Americans spy on Stalin's Russia with all his human assets, which included those from the Gestapo, SS and Wehrmacht. There was to be no Nuremberg trial for them; all sins had been forgiven because they were going to serve a higher cause of freedom and democracy.

The Americans were thrilled, although they did not know that Soviet intelligence had already suborned Gehlen's boys rather extensively. Even so, Gehlen was sent to West Germany to head its newly created external intelligence agency, the BND. Realpolitik, oriented towards self-interest, demanded that yesterday's enemy was today's collaborator, and yesterday's ally of convenience was today's enemy of choice. The rest was all narratives, perceptions and advertisements. Hot wars as part of Cold War Season I also began, which were fought all over the world, except in Europe or North America, and would play out for the next forty-five years.

In a magical moment in December 1991, the Soviet Union collapsed without warning to the CIA, who were caught napping. Mikhail Gorbachev, with his glasnost and perestroika in 1989–1991, had allowed the winding down of the Soviet system. He had accepted the bringing down of the Berlin Wall, which effectively ended the Cold War. The steps were epochal, but America missed the opportunity to become a responsible and sole global superpower; instead of magnanimity, there was more hostility. It converted the Cold War against communism into a Cold War against Russia, and the Russian people, who had in effect conducted a bloodless revolt against communism, became the enemy.

The Fukuyama 'End of History' moment was an optimistic overreaction and the flavour of the season, even as the Huntington prophecy of a 'Clash of Civilizations' began building into a sombre reality. The idea of perpetual peace among great powers after the end of the Cold War was stillborn. Since 1991, the US has fought six major wars along with various minor ones, and every president, except Trump, has owned a war. All these wars were against minor opponents. The world remained a dangerous place.

After the collapse of the Soviet Union, the West succeeded in persuading the gullible and eager-for-acceptance former Russian apparatchiks to wind down the Warsaw Pact. The West also promised that NATO would not expand eastward and would not be a threat to the Russians. This was a ruse, obviously. In the practice of realpolitik, the West was not going to cease being a threat to the Russians because it would mean world peace, which would be unacceptable to the thriving US military industry.

The US ecosystem could not afford post-Cold War amity; it needed a healthy war. While in 1914 the world led by Europeans sleepwalked into war over events in Serbia, in 2022 Ukraine presented a similar blind spot, which put the West in a predicament. More than a 100 years after the assassination of Archduke Franz Ferdinand in Sarajevo that set in motion the First World War, the Americans and Europeans refused to see the implications of trying to meddle and change when they no longer had the ability and capacity to do so; nor did they understand, much less appreciate, the other side's, in this case Russia's, security compulsions. It was all about domination and control through armed might, and economic and financial strength. This was the storyline then and this is the storyline today. The people did not matter then, they do not matter today.

Hot War in Europe

The Ukraine conflict, ongoing at the time of writing this book, is the result of Russian fears of a continued push by the West against Russian ambitions to sit at the same table as the US and China. It also indicates an American desire to hold on to its following and its fading primary position by encouraging Russia's neighbours to stand up to Moscow. Having provoked the Ukrainians to die and the Europeans into taking a hostile stand, all the US could do was enforce sanctions, which seemed to hurt its European allies as well. No country, European or North American, was willing to fight the war with its troops. Ukraine, as America's friend and obeying American interests, will eventually pay the highest price, in terms of people that die or live in a war that is being fought to the last Ukrainian. Ukraine's leaders might want to stop glamourizing war and outcomes of victory if they recall what happened to three of America's one-time friends of convenience – the Shah of Iran, Saddam Hussein and Muammar Gaddafi. The Shah was abandoned, and the lives of the other two were brutally terminated.

Ukraine could well be the culmination, or the continuation, of a 100-year war that started in 1917 with the Bolshevik takeover in Moscow. World War I saw the mobilization of 65 million troops, the decline of three empires, 20 million civilian and military deaths and 21 million wounded. It was a catastrophe from which Europe never really recovered. The American historian Fritz Stern described it as the first calamity of the twentieth century, a calamity which led to other calamities.[6]

The US has since led several global wars in the name of freedom and democracy. Soviet leaders had similar global ambitions but lost out initially – now the world is seeing a Russian resurgence. The Ukraine crisis was simply waiting to happen; it was not created by the Russians but was a reaction to decades of provocations since the dissolution of the USSR. Unfortunately, with all means of communication monopolized by the West, the voices the world hears are of those who control the airwaves.

One of the earliest assurances given by US Secretary of State James Baker in his discussions with President Mikhail Gorbachev in February 1990 was that 'not an inch of NATO's present military jurisdiction will spread in an eastern direction'.[7] This was designed to reassure or beguile

Russia into believing in a peaceful future by claiming that the US had no intention of striving for full-spectrum global dominance.

The Russians would have recalled what the French president in the 1960s and national hero General Charles de Gaulle had warned about US intentions and NATO's purpose. De Gaulle wanted an independent (of US) Europe and viewed dimly any thought of leaving the defence of Europe to NATO. He was not willing to let the US be in charge of Europe's defence, nuclear and conventional. De Gaulle was prophetic.

De Gaulle elucidated 'subterfuge' and said this meant submitting themselves to a so-called military command structure which was answerable only to the US president and that in 'giving up the state and the country, it is losing our soul'. And further, 'The Anglo-Americans wanted the ability to use force as they pleased and didn't want us for that reason. What they want is to dominate.'

Cries in the Wilderness

Some of America's best-known strategic thinkers and practitioners, such as George Kennan and later Henry Kissinger, had warned about the grave consequences of NATO's expansion eastward, particularly into Ukraine. The thrust of the advice, collectively and at different times, was that Ukraine was important to Russia and that importance by itself did not make it a threat to the West. Despite this, American leadership continued with a policy that would end in bloodletting in Ukraine. The real motive was an ambition to cut down and weaken Russian influence and then maybe take on China.

When there were whispers in Washington in 1996 that the US had decided to expand NATO to the Russian border, George Kennan, whose blueprint had defined America's cold war strategies, warned that doing so would inflame nationalistic, anti-Western and militaristic tendencies and push Russian foreign policy in directions decidedly not to American liking.[8] Kennan later added that this decision was the beginning of a new cold war and a tragic mistake.[9]

Jack F. Matlock Jr., US ambassador to the Soviet Union from 1987 to 1991, in his testimony to the Senate Foreign Relations Committee in 1997 described NATO's expansion as the most profound strategic blunder and the most serious security threat since the collapse of the

Soviet Union.[10] William Perry, Clinton's defence secretary, explained in his memoir that NATO enlargement was the cause of 'the rupture in relations with Russia' and he had considered resigning on this issue.[11] In June 1997, fifty prominent foreign policy experts, including former senators, retired military officers, diplomats and academicians, sent an open letter to President Bill Clinton opposing NATO's expansion. This group included former defence secretary Robert McNamara and senators Bill Bradley and Gary Hart. The letter warned that any US-led effort to expand NATO would be a policy error of historic proportions and could destabilize Europe.[12] William Burns, later to be CIA director (2021–2025) and a former ambassador to Russia, argued similarly in 2008 that Ukrain's entry into NATO would be the brightest of all redlines for Russia, and almost everyone agreed that it would directly challenge Russian interests.[13] He also asserted that NATO's expansion to Ukraine would force Russia to intervene.[14]

Henry Kissinger cautioned in 2014 that the West needed a reconciliatory policy but was also convinced that 'Ukraine should not join NATO'.[15] Prof. John Mearsheimer, has repeatedly said that the West was misleading Ukraine and that ultimately Ukraine would be wrecked. In an interview in 2015, he said, 'What we're doing is in fact encouraging that outcome.'[16]

Despite all the warnings, NATO led by the US moved to turn Ukraine into a Western pro-American liberal democracy on Russia's border, which, from a Russian perspective, was an existential threat.[17] There were US concerns not only about Russia in general but Ukraine in particular, even in the 1990s. Former President Richard Nixon, fresh from his last visit to Russia, decided to write to President Clinton in March 1994, expressing his concerns about the way the situation in Russia was evolving. He foresaw that relations between Russia and Ukraine would worsen; the situation could get explosive and if allowed to get out of control, 'it will make Bosnia look like a PTA garden party'.[18] Nixon urged Clinton to strengthen the American embassy in Kyiv and send his best officers to the country. The situation did dissolve but not in the manner Nixon predicted. A far worse situation than Bosnia prevails in Ukraine today, but that was deliberately made to happen by Western powers eager to cut Russia to size.

US policy of trampling all over the globe after its unipolar moment and trying to create liberal democracies led to disastrous results, as seen in the Middle East. Soon after the current war started in Ukraine, Mearsheimer repeated his fears and asserted that US–Russia relations started to go downhill following the April 2008 summit in Bucharest, when NATO declared that Ukraine and Georgia would become a part of NATO. Even though by then most Eastern European members of the Warsaw Pact and ex-Soviet states – Estonia, Lithuania and Latvia – had become members of NATO, Georgia and Ukraine were definitely Putin's redlines. Washington created the crisis in Ukraine, hoping to surround and fragment Russia through NATO expansion and its neo-Nazi allies in Ukraine. In retaliation Russia would dismantle Ukraine, Mearsheimer warned. An America in decline could only resort to using financial assets and networks to subvert most of the world.[19]

In his book, *War with Russia? From Putin and Ukraine to Trump and Russiagate*, Stephen F. Cohen, a well-known American scholar of Russian studies, warned that if the US moved NATO forces toward Russia's borders, it would militarize the situation and Russia woulds not back off. A new and far more dangerous cold war, with its vicious Russophobia that demonizes not just Putin but all Russians, has begun. Hawkish policies towards Russia became fashionable but may change course during Trump's presidency so long as he and the US retain some primacy.

The first Soviet American Cold War was a struggle between capitalism and communism – there were many mainstream advocates of detente with the USSR. The new Cold War is being fought directly along Russia's borders, most dangerously as a proxy 'hot war' between the US and Russia in Ukraine.[20] One of America's well-known economists and commentators, Jeffrey Sachs, warned in 2021 that any NATO enlargement was utterly misguided and risky and there was need for a compromise with Russia.[21] Patrick Buchanan, a former White House communications director and now a conservative journalist, politician and commentator, has been consistently criticizing American policy on Russia and Ukraine. His argument is that the US had neither any obligation nor any interest in Ukraine.[22] Did America provoke Putin, push Ukrainians in but stay out of the war itself?[23]

A month ahead of the Russian invasion of Ukraine, the United States National Security Council warned Joe Biden that Putin would view steps to bring Ukraine and Georgia closer to NATO as a provocative move that could result in pre-emptive Russian military action. Ultimately, these warnings were not heeded.[24] A former British ambassador to Russia, Sir Roderic Lyne, also warned in 2021 that pushing Ukraine into NATO was 'stupid at every level' and would be 'the best way to start a war with Russia'.[25]

The NATO expansion in Ukraine was always unacceptable to the Russians who were looking for a compromise where Ukraine would guarantee that it would not become a member of NATO,[26] and if that were not possible, an invasion was inevitable.[27] Maybe that is the war the US in its wisdom wanted. And that is the war it got.

Cold War: Season Two

Cold Warrior Zbigniew Brzeziński was President Jimmy Carter's NSA and of Polish origin, therefore likely to be rabidly anti-Russian by nature. Just as a Polish Pope helped the revival of democracy in Poland, Brzeziński pushed for drawing Ukraine away from Russia. For the Americans in the 1990s, it was a question of extending their control and dominance, from Vladivostok to Lisbon. They saw the possibility of having a free run of all the markets, control on technology in Western Europe and Russia and access to all the energy and gas of Russia and the newly independent Central Asian Republics (CARs).

Brzeziński in his book, *The Grand Chessboard*, published in 1997, wrote at length on Ukraine. Brzeziński assigned Ukraine a new and geopolitically pivotal space on the Eurasian chessboard. He argued that Ukraine's very existence as an independent country would transform Russia, and without Ukraine, Russia would cease to be a Eurasian empire. If Russia became a predominantly Asian imperial state, then resentful of the loss of its vassal states and their recent independence, it would be sucked into never-ending conflicts with the Central Asian republics, who would be supported by their fellow Islamic states to the south. China would also be likely to oppose any restoration of Russian domination over Central Asia, given its increasing interest in the newly independent states there. The US too has heavily invested towards the five Central Asian states in terms of attention and resources since its unilateral withdrawal from Afghanistan.

However, if Moscow were to regain control over Ukraine, with its 52 million people and major resources as well as its access to the

Black Sea, Russia would automatically regain the ability to become a powerful imperial state that spans Europe and Asia. Ukraine's loss of independence would thus have immediate consequences for Central Europe, transforming Poland into the geopolitical pivot on the eastern frontier of a united Europe.

That is precisely how the situation of rearming Poland feverishly is developing. The sudden surge in the Polish defence budget to 3.9 per cent of GDP is almost double since 2022 when the Ukraine War began, and assistance from the US is flowing into Poland and could possibly make it the next lynchpin of US strategy in the region.[28] Poland is well on its way to becoming the Germany of the twenty-first century – a frontier state against Russia, which is industrial and prosperous too.

Ukraine's determination to preserve its newfound independence was encouraged by external support. Although initially the West, especially the US, had been tardy in recognizing the geopolitical importance of a separate Ukrainian state, by the mid-1990s both America and Germany had become strong backers of Kyiv's separate identity. In July 1996, the US secretary of defence declared, 'I cannot overestimate the importance of Ukraine as an independent country to the security and stability of all of Europe,' while in September the same year, the German chancellor – notwithstanding his strong support for then Russian President Boris Yeltsin – went even further to declare that 'Ukraine's firm place in Europe can no longer be challenged by anyone ... No one will be able any more to dispute Ukraine's independence and territorial integrity.' It is interesting that the chief of BND was airlifted out of Ukraine soon after the Russians launched their attack in February 2022.[29]

American policymakers also came to describe the American–Ukrainian relationship as 'a strategic partnership', deliberately invoking the same phrase used to describe the American–Russian relationship. Without Ukraine, as already noted, an imperial restoration based either on the Commonwealth of Independent States (CIS) or on Eurasianism was not a viable option. An empire without Ukraine would eventually mean a Russia that would become more 'Asianized' and more remote from Europe, stuck in the quagmire of Central Asian problems.[30]

There was thus considerable well-informed opinion about Ukraine, NATO and the Russian reaction – and previous US presidents somehow evaded taking a decision as the hardliners clamoured for an eastward expansion of NATO. Joe Biden became that president, and came to own a war like all his recent predecessors. There has been undisputed information that Putin had spelt out his redlines: that he would react; there was also an assessment that Ukraine did not matter to the US in the same way as it did to Russia. A NATO without Ukraine in it would not reduce its efficacy but could in some way be reaching out to Putin and Russia as it would set to rest Putin's basic fears about Ukraine in NATO. Yet Americans, with an eager Britain and some reluctant Europeans, a belligerently anti-Russia media and think-tank intellectuals, saw an opportunity to 'fix' Putin and Russia. Perhaps, the US strategically calculated Putin would get provoked. They were quite sure they could start a war and keep it going, but they were not sure how to end it.

The current conflict did not, however, begin in February 2022. It has been brewing since the mid-1990s. Condoleezza Rice, former secretary of state and national security Adviser with George W. Bush, explained the hidden motives. Speaking to a German TV channel (NTV) in the immediate aftermath of Russia's Crimean annexation in 2014 and the expulsion of Russia from G8, she said, 'The Russian economy is weak, 80 per cent of Russian exports are oil, gas and minerals. People will say, okay, Europe will run out of energy, yes, but Russians will run out of cash before they run out of energy [in] Europe ...'[31] In March 2006, Senator John McCain could not hide his arrogance and frustration with Russia when he describe it as a 'gas station pretending to be a country' in a speech in the US Senate.[32]

Even without its East European allies, a truncated Russia was still too big to be conquered or ignored. Its abundant natural resources made it into an Alaska–Texas and much more. There were huge corporate strategic interests involved; control and domination of that country or its marginalization remained important. The country possessed lethal nuclear weapons and possibly chemical and biological weapons (CBWs) as well. This interested the Pentagon immensely.

All this also meant a larger role for intelligence – human, technical and special tasks. Since conquest was ruled out, the alternative was to chisel away at the periphery, invite former Soviet Republics into NATO and EU, keep the Western bloc intact and under control in Washington/New York, destroy Yugoslavia and ensure the Middle East boiled.

The wages of war and profits would come first from destruction and then from reconstruction. This meant great corporate delight. It is interesting that the conversation about costs in Ukraine is now shifting from the cost of war to the cost of reconstruction. Both mean American private–public participation. The Clinton Global Initiative (CGI) has offered assistance to rebuild Ukraine and provide humanitarian support. The CGI Ukraine Action Network was announced at the Clinton Global Initiative 2023 as part of its theme of 'Keep Going'.[33]

James Baker's promise to Gorbachev was thus openly disregarded and even denied despite constant Russian objections. By the end of the 1990s, the NATO powers had discarded previous assurances; they assumed Russia had become too flabby and disorganized to prevent NATO's moves. From twelve NATO countries in 1949 there were thirty facing Russia by 2004 with virtually no buffer between Russia and 'the free world'. At that time President Yeltsin, who was often incoherent and sometimes absent, could not protest strongly enough, and was soon replaced by the aggressive and clearheaded Vladimir Putin who had his own ideas about making Russia great again. Putin's Russia kept warning about redlines but the West, led by the Anglo–Americans, kept intriguing and conspiring to install pro-Western regimes in Kyiv. This automatically made him a dire threat to the West, and they have been diligently working on dislodging Putin ever since.

Covert Ops in Ukraine

The crisis did not erupt suddenly on 24 February 2022, when 'evil' Putin attacked a helpless country. There were no Russian troops in Ukraine before that date. The truth is that the crisis began the day after the Soviet Union collapsed. And America, the victorious, planned total control. As NATO moved eastward enticing and embracing all the former Soviet republics, the only two remaining were Belarus and Ukraine.

Ukraine's large Russian-speaking population in its eastern region had moved there mostly during the Stalin era. Western Ukrainians were always pro-German and had supported Hitler's Nazi troops as they invaded Stalin's Soviet Union. On other hand, Eastern Ukraine with its large Russian-speaking population opposed this Nazi onslaught. The extreme-right wing in Ukraine is now represented in the Ukraine Army, after the Azov Battalion of volunteer right-wingers was converted into the Azov Regiment. Stepan Bandera, now a symbol of resistance and heroism for those fighting the Russians, was a Nazi collaborator. After the end of the Second World War, many of Bandera's followers were reorganized by the British and Americans to fight the Soviets.

The US began arming and training far-right militants, probably since 2015, the ideological descendants of Nazi war criminals described as the 'most vicious and malignant combatants' that America has ever used to push its foreign policy agenda.[34] President Vladimir Putin alluded to the Nazi problem in Ukraine when he spoke about the need for 'denazification'.[35]

In 2003, the Rose Revolution broke out in Georgia, and then President Eduard Shevardnadze was forced to step down. In this colour revolution, America's National Endowment for Democracy (NED), funded by the US government and commonly alluded to as a CIA creation, had planned and participated in the entire process from 'selecting' opposition leaders, training the opposition, to providing huge funds. After the revolution succeeded, NED continued to offer 'generous funds'. In 2004 alone, NED provided nearly $540,000 to twelve NGOs in Georgia. NED funded as many as sixty-five NGOs in Ukraine during the Orange Revolution in 2004 and the United States offered $65 million to the Ukrainian opposition through NED and other organizations.

As soon as the invasion of Ukraine started, the NED removed details of its funding from its site but details of financial assistance given by NED to various institutes on Ukraine is accessible.[36] The idea behind its foundation was that the NED would overtly perform the same acts of promoting democracy and liberty while preserving US interests that the CIA had been doing covertly for decades.[37] Over time NED became active globally, presumably in all the colour revolutions and Arab Spring adventures that preceded Ukraine.

Between 2000 and 2005, Russia-allied governments in Serbia, Georgia, Ukraine and Kyrgyzstan were overthrown through bloodless upheavals. Though Western media generally portrayed these colour revolutions as spontaneous, indigenous and popular uprisings, they were the result of extensive planning, mostly in the West. There were Advisory pressures, finance and campaign strategies for pushing the democracy agenda.

Organizations like the USAID, the NED and its funded institutes, George Soros's Open Society Institute, Freedom House and others were participants in spreading the message. The plan was to free the Eastern European region for commercial, strategic, military, cultural and political domination by the West. Radio Free Europe/Radio Liberty, and its propaganda channel and website, were aimed at Central and Eastern Europe and Russia.

In 2004 alone, the US spent about $34 million on regime-change initiatives in Ukraine while Soros Open Societies Institute pitched in about $1.6 million in support of a local 'Freedom of Choice' NGO coalition and Ukraine's 'New Choice 2004'. The German Marshall Fund of the United States, Freedom House and the Canadian International Development Agency together provided $130,000 for activist training. The broad public relations strategy was to aid a youth protest movement, transport out-of-town protesters into Kyiv, create an online TV protest station, create agitation paraphernalia and provide offshore training to the anti-Yanukovych, (an elected pro-Russian president of Ukraine) student leadership based on a template 'revolutionary' strategy. The movement towards provoking Russia or forcing it to submit, was gathering momentum.[38]

Russian conditions for allowing German reunification – no NATO expansion eastward – accepted by the US, were highlighted once again in an American alt-news service but mainline news avoided any reference to this.[39] However, the German magazine *Der Spiegel*'s disclosures after extensive research confirmed this promise by the Americans. Titled 'Is Vladimir Putin Right?' the investigation was an extensive historical reconstruction of the negotiations between NATO and Moscow that accompanied the end of the Cold War.[40] The Italian *Start* magazine, while reporting the *Der Spiegel* disclosure, quoted the NATO Secretary General Jens Stoltenberg denying this: 'No one, ever, on any date and nowhere, made such promises to the Soviet Union.'[41] This was a repeat of what for years has been Washington's defensive or mendacious line on NATO's eastward expansion.

In 2014 several commentators spoke about Washington's path to war, its recklessness and the Ukraine gambit, as Americans had begun to seriously mess around in Ukraine, with its Orange Revolution, and elsewhere in former Soviet territories. It was not just about expanding

NATO but with regime change as a goal. The CIA had begun training right-wing dissidents from Ukraine in 2015. Putin assessed that the West would not stop at what they had started in Europe many decades ago. Seeing this inevitability, it was better for him to take on the West in Ukraine now or face the possibility of having to defend Russia against the West in the future.[42]

Ukraine as the deciding theatre for the US–Russian rivalry could spill over into mainland Europe, where the US wants to destroy Russia for complete global control and dominance, while Russia is fighting to regain its stature as a world power that it lost in 1991. Without Ukraine on its side, if not part of it, Russia is an incomplete power. Neither is fighting for Ukrainian interests. It would be difficult to accept that Ukraine decided on a policy of open hostility against a powerful neighbour without support and suggestions from powerful, but distant, friends. It is too early to predict victory for any one side, but for the present it looks as if there will be no victors, only losers.

Aware that the Ukrainian Army would not be able to prevail against the Russian Army, the Americans concentrated on developing Ukrainian capabilities to provoke and draw the Russians into a Chechnya-type quagmire with its built-up urban centres. This was a dangerous proposition, considering that the Americans themselves had come out of one such quagmire a few months prior to the start of the war. The next one would be theirs too, being the distant power with restricted logistic support against the neighbour, the Russians.[43] Quite clearly, the Ukraine theatre was carefully choreographed high drama. At one stage, the Russians seemed content in seeking control oblast by oblast at their own pace rather than a blitzkrieg as the Americans had hoped.

The euphoria that was manufactured in the West in the early days of the conflict dissipated a long time ago. As always, the Americans overestimated their prowess and the ability of their friends and allies, and underestimated the enemy's capabilities and resilience. Global support was missing, the sanctions did not quite work and Ukraine has been taking a beating. The Russians had not rushed in to declare war and attack Ukraine, instead concentrating on special operations using the Wagner Militias. Army generals and officers along with conscripts launched assaults in the initial days. This saved the army for another day to clear the country and avoided urban centres while taking highways. The Russians had a plan; the Americans only had an objective.

A second stalemate for the US after the great escape from Afghanistan does not make for a happy picture.

Putin's Long Game

It was after 2021, a six-year hiatus during the Trump presidency and the economic slowdown during the pandemic, that American defence and security establishments returned to discover new enemies and new battlefields. In November 2021, the Americans began to warn of a Russian invasion after the Ukrainian Air Force conducted drone strikes in Donetsk in October. No one condemned these violations of the Minsk Agreements of 2014 and 2015; apparently the Ukrainians were under pressure from the Americans to violate the agreement. The Minsk Agreements referred to self-determination/autonomy in the state of Ukraine, not independence or much less merger with Russia. A narrative was being created. Quite obviously the Americans were spoiling for a war and on 17 February 2022, Biden rather mysteriously announced that Russia would attack Ukraine in the next few days.

Biden used his own intense personal dislike for Putin and the Russians to support Ukraine's nationalists. This further soured relations between the US and Russia and between Ukraine and Russia. The Second Cold War was warming up. Biden's conflict of interest in Ukraine could also be a factor.[44] As vice president, Biden had visited Ukraine six times,[45] suggesting a special interest in the country. From 2013 through 2018, his son, Hunter Biden, and his company brought in about $11 million via his roles as an attorney and a board member with a Ukrainian firm accused of bribery.[46]

The prospect of a broken-down Soviet Union then and a weakened Russia now was a source of immense satisfaction and even delight for the West. Their adversary, Vladimir Putin, a former colonel of the KGB, was quite different from his predecessor Boris Yeltsin as president. In 1996, Yeltsin relocated Putin to Moscow from St. Petersburg, making him the head of the Federal Security Service (FSB) in 1998, the agency that was the successor to the Soviet KGB. The purpose was to let Putin steady the ship of state. Soon after, Putin became prime minister and eventually took over as president in August 1999. His rise was meteoric and he was probably someone the Russians wanted.

Putin had been tough on Chechen terrorists and soon turned his attention on annihilating the oligarchs who were running Russia as a private fiefdom. It was at that time that Britain showed a keenness to play a role in Russia. Maybe it was Prime Minister Tony Blair's dream to play that grand role. British intelligence had an interest relating to the oil company BP's oil interests in Chechnya and had recommended an interaction between Putin and Blair, according to declassified documents.[47] Putin was Russia's man of the hour, and the Russians approved of his handling of the Chechen issue.

Putin became prime minister in August 1999, and suddenly Yeltsin resigned in December the same year. Two weeks before Putin was formally elected president in March 2000, Tony Blair flew into St. Petersburg to meet him. According to the UK Foreign Office briefing notes, obtained by British journalist Matt Kennard in 2021 and published in *Declassified UK,* this trip was devised as a way to extend support to Putin, who they hoped would win. The head of MI6 at the time, Sir Richard Dearlove, had been approached by a senior Russian intelligence official in London, asking for help to get Putin elected. The same official asked if Blair would attend the opera alongside Putin on the visit, which MI6 made happen. The reason was clearly the belief that when elected, Putin would in turn help protect and advance British interests, specifically BP's interests. Clearly the shopkeeper was pushing for a closer relationship with Russia while publicly condemning Russian action in Chechnya and hoping Putin would not notice.

The year 1999 was when NATO, led by the US, conducted a seventy-eight-day bombing campaign on Serbia, the Balkan nation that had historically been a protectorate of Mother Russia even before the Soviet Union came into existence. The same year, three former Warsaw Pact nations, the Czech Republic, Hungary and Poland, were inducted into the NATO alliance. More followed and in 2004 NATO admitted Lithuania, Latvia, Estonia, Slovakia, Romania and Bulgaria, along with Slovenia but excluded the Serbs. Then, in 2008, came the Bucharest declaration and the news that NATO would invite Ukraine and Georgia, both bordering Russia, to join and give coverage under Article 5 of the treaty under which an attack on any one member is an attack on all.[48]

The crisis that surfaced more than a decade prior, finally blew up on 24 February 2023. There were arguments in the US on whether the

Cold War ever ended,[49] and that Washington should think twice despite billions already committed to the war.[50] On the other hand, there was advocacy for a trillion-dollar military[51] while other commentators wanted America to prepare and win simultaneous wars against Russia and China.[52] A lead singer for this theme song of war was former Reagan-era State Department official Elliott Abrams, arguing that a larger percentage of GDP needed to be spent on defence.[53] Similarly, former defence secretary Robert Gates insisted in a *Washington Post* op-ed that America needed a larger, more advanced military taking full advantage of new technologies to fight in new ways. The fact that America is already outspending China on military expenditure by a three-to-one margin and Russia by ten-to-one seemed immaterial.[54]

The war in Ukraine is not about Ukrainian sovereignty or its desire to join NATO. That is the Western narrative. But for both, Russia and the West, 'It's all about energy – oil gas, coal, uranium, hydroelectric power. Today, when you are talking about energy you are talking about Putin and vice versa.'[55] Global investor Marin Katusa wrote this in his book, *The Colder War*, in 2015, much before the present crisis. Canadian geopolitical risk firm SecDev's analysis indicates that at least $12.4 trillion worth of Ukraine's energy deposits, metals and minerals are under Russian control as of August 2022.[56] Today the war is also about control and hegemony.

For most of the past sixty years, the US had prospered because it dominated the energy market, and all energy trade was conducted in US dollars. This was a vital monopoly for the US, which had begun to slip away even before the present crisis. In the US, the energy market is an immensely lucrative industry controlled by seven American companies, commonly referred to as the 'Seven Sisters', former Rockefeller companies Chevron, Exxon Mobil and Esso, along with BP and two others, Gulf Oil and Texaco, that had merged with Chevron.

Germany and Japan lost the Second World War partly because they ran out of oil, whereas the US had it in abundance. The booming post-war US economy became a huge oil-guzzler and by 1949, it had become a net importer of oil. This was of some concern to the US in the Cold War days. The Yom Kippur War of 1973 and the OPEC clampdown was a huge lesson for America, and it quickly succeeded in making the US dollar the currency for oil transactions.

There has been a consistency in Western approaches. Economic interests were paramount then; they are paramount today. The grand act of IMF's harsh sanctions on Russia that hurt the Russian people provided an opportunity for Putin to surface on the national scene as a prospective saviour. Putin's principles were quite simple. He wanted Russia to be secure from attack and intimidation. The only country that had the ability to do this was the US. For Russian security, its neighbours were the buffers, and Putin could not see them aligned to the West. Prosperity was a desirable goal, for which the development of natural resources, especially energy, was necessary. Export of vital energy resources would draw consumers, especially the neighbours, who would then become quasi-dependent on Russia. This gave power to Russia, as it could withhold the supply of essentials – oil, uranium or gas – at will.

Speedy development of energy resources needed foreign capital and technology. Foreign partners were encouraged, but since the energy industry was a matter of security, it would be kept under Russian government control. Having established its credentials as major supplier of energy, Russia would then have the capacity in times of turmoil, like in West Asia, to play the game to its advantage. Since the US had the greatest ability to intimidate or even attack Russia, that country had to be weakened and the best way to undermine was by subverting the petrodollar which would subvert the dollar.[57] Putin had presumably assessed that over time US strength and interest would ebb, while he would be ready for the push. He was in for the long game, beyond presidential or congressional elections.

US 'Annual Threat Assessment' Gets It Wrong

A declassified version of the 'Annual Threat Assessment (ATI) of the U.S. Intelligence Community' was released on 7 February 2022, just a fortnight before Russia moved into Ukraine. It had some interesting comments about Russian threat perceptions. The assessment had considered information available up to 21 January 2022, by which time there would have been enough indications of Putin's plans.

According to the ATI, the US intelligence community expected Moscow to remain an influential power and a formidable challenge amidst the changing geopolitical landscape during the next decade. Russia would pursue its interests in competitive and sometimes confrontational and provocative ways, including pressing to dominate Ukraine and other countries in its 'near-abroad', while exploring possibilities to achieve a more stable relationship with Washington. Further, it said that Russia did not want a direct conflict with US forces but sought an accommodation on mutual non-interference in both countries' domestic affairs and US recognition of Russia's claimed sphere of influence over much of the former Soviet Union.[58]

The ATI assessed that Russian officials believed that the US was trying to undermine Russia, weaken President Putin and install Western-friendly regimes in the former Soviet states and elsewhere, which gave Russia a reason to retaliate. This is part-prophecy – that Russia would attack, and part guilt – that the Russian act would be in retaliation against US actions in its neighbourhood. America was taking on an enemy it felt it could handle (Russia) and ignoring an enemy (China) that it could not afford to tackle and succeed. The Chinese were presumably happy with these American priorities. A weak anti-West Russia would make Russia subservient to the Chinese. A strong anti-West Russia will be an equal partner in China's campaign against the West. Either way, it would benefit China and signal a lose–lose situation for the West.

The ATI assessed that Moscow would continue to employ an array of tools, mainly intelligence services, proxies and wide-ranging influence tools to try to advance its own interests or undermine the interests of the US and its allies in the Middle East, North Africa and elsewhere. It would seek to increase its influence, present itself as an indispensable mediator and gain military access rights and economic opportunities. This assessment was clearly a Pentagon-driven narrative to play up the Russia–US rivalry globally, as well as Russian capabilities. This kind of a wide prediction indicates a predetermined mindset suggesting the kind of action desired.

Russia's invasion of Ukraine was accompanied by a massive unrelenting information war against Russia in the West. It was also a time when the US policymakers was seeking to bring in legislation to curb the power of Big Tech. This prompted an open letter in April 2022 from former senior intelligence officers, including James R. Clapper, former director of National Intelligence, Michael J. Morell, former acting director and deputy director, CIA, Leon E. Panetta, former secretary of defence and former director, CIA, to warn the US government against introducing any law to restrict or break the power of Big Tech corporates like Google, Facebook and Amazon. The argument was that action against them would jeopardize national security at a time of Russian invasion. Centralized power and the ability of these companies was essential at a time when Putin and the Kremlin were on the rampage.[59] In other words, Big Tech's monopoly had to be preserved in America's national interest, as it gave them power to handle (censor) information when combatting information attacks.

The US security establishment proved yet again that free speech is a convenient slogan the US deploys in the rest of the world. The American sociologist C. Wright Mills observed more than sixty years ago in his 1956 masterpiece, *The Power Elite*, that America was ruled by those who controlled the 'strategic command posts' of society, which were the big corporations, the machinery of the state and the military establishment. These dominant cliques had a deep mutual stake in a 'permanent war economy' that had emerged during the Cold War.[60]

The Rand Corporation study, 'Overextending and Unbalancing Russia: Assessing the Impact of Cost-Imposing Options' dated 24 April 2019,[61] is an eye-opener about American intentions and how Russia could be checkmated since Rand is considered a Pentagon think tank. This is a clear indication of the thought processes that remain at work in the US. The report is a detailed examination of 'nonviolent, cost-imposing options that the United States and its allies could pursue across economic, political, and military areas to stress – overextend and unbalance – Russia's economy and armed forces and the regime's political standing at home and abroad. Some of the options examined are clearly more promising than others, but any would need to be evaluated in terms of the overall US strategy for dealing with Russia . . .' For instance, it recommends breaking the Russian economy through sanctions and by forcing Russia to consume its own resources, and there could be immense and relatively risk-free investment opportunities, mainly in Russia-specific strategic bombers and long-range attack missiles directed against Russia. This indicates a new arms race as well.

Both these reports would have been read by the Russians. The Rand report listed six possibilities to undermine Russia – arming Ukraine with lethal weapons, increasing support for Syrian jihadists, promoting regime change in Belarus, exploiting tensions in the South Caucasus, reducing Russian influence in Central Asia and rivalling Russian presence in Transnistria (a small tract of unrecognized independent territory in Moldova).[62] The Pentagon had begun with the first four items listed – Ukraine, Syria, Belarus and South Caucasus, even though Rand seemed to favour only the first option, Ukraine.

The world has begun to change, in fact this has been happening for some time. The Chinese have grown in strength, economically and militarily, for some years; the rapid growth of the Indian economy in recent years, the slowdown in Europe, a restive Africa and a perennially unsettled Middle East are the main factors that alter global equations. This was adequately exhibited by the lack of global support for US policies on Ukraine–Russia. The Global South has begun to resist the US hegemony that was accepted so far. The new thinking is that while the Global South needs US and Western support, it would not automatically accept US policies on Russia. Indeed, a strategic defeat of Russia would increase the hegemonic strength of the West and reduce chances of a multipolar world.[63]

6

Retaliation, Pushback

What we are against will unite us, while what we are for divides us. Therefore, we should emphasise what we oppose. The common enemy unites us, while the positive values each of us are defending actually divides us. Therefore, we must create strategic alliances to overthrow the present order of things.

— ALEXANDER DUGIN

The Russians watched American-led manoeuvres carefully since the end of the Cold War, read them right and under Putin's rule, made their own plans. The territory and coastline from the western Black Sea coast of Ukraine all the way across to the eastern Black Sea coast is the geopolitical reason for Moscow to seek control of the region and not let it fall into 'enemy' hands. It has been an important sea route for Russia into the Mediterranean Sea and beyond. At best, Moscow would agree to certified neutrality but Western tactics did nothing to reassure the Russians, as we discussed in the last chapter. In conjunction (or jointly) with Türkiye, Moscow has controlled access to Black Sea in accordance with the 1936 Montreux Convention, which allowed safe passage for vessels of littoral states. There were restrictions for non-Black Sea vessels.

Russia has come a long way from its internal chaos and external irrelevance of the 1990s. American strategic planners would not have missed this, but political compulsions might have forced them to acquire another unnecessary war. On the other hand, wars have been good for the

American economy, or parts of industrial groups, in the past; so maybe this was one of those exercises.

Alexander Dugin, a Dostoevsky lookalike who is popularly known as 'Putin's philosopher', wrote his treatise, *The Foundations of Geopolitics: The Geopolitical Future of Russia,* in 1997 where he said, 'The absolute imperative of Russian geopolitics in the Black Sea coast is total and unrestricted control of Moscow all the way from Ukrainian to Abkhazian territory.' It is possible the West has not read this or disregarded Moscow's commitment to the treatise. According to Sir Roderic Lyne, a former British diplomat, it was possible that 'there were people, particularly in America, in the neoconservative circles, the "John Bolton Brigade", who simply didn't understand that, because they had very little understanding of Russia.'[1] Dugin, who has been described as 'Putin's brain' because of his ideological influence on Russian politics, endorsed Donald Trump in a CNN interview aired on 30 March 2025. He based his support on the philosophy of Russian greatness, cultural superiority and the perception of Russian unity. He energizes voters behind Putin, and his influence has been felt throughout Russian government and society.[2]

The West was running out of options on how to handle Putin. Aware that the West had few options, and also of the ability and resilience of his own people, Putin took advantage of the evolving situation. It became a 'Russia versus the rest' issue and not 'democracy versus communism' or any other ideology. This meant it became an issue of Russian nationalism and Russian pride. A people who could defeat Napoleon and Hitler were made of sterner stuff, more than anyone in the West could have imagined. The war could become a long-drawn-out affair with the Russians awaiting a change of American focus.

Sergey Karaganov, a former presidential adviser to both Yeltsin and Putin, has been associated with many key decisions of the Putin government in the past and is close to both Putin and Foreign Minister Sergey Lavrov. Karaganov has been associated with the Ukraine issue for many years. In an interview on 28 March 2022, he stated explicitly that for twenty-five years – as far back as 1997 – people like him had been saying that 'if NATO and Western alliances expand beyond certain redlines, especially into Ukraine, there will be a war.'[3]

According to Karaganov, Russia had two main objectives in Ukraine. One was to demilitarize the country, and second, to denazify Ukraine.

Russians were concerned with the rise of ultra-nationalism there to the extent that, to them, it was beginning to look like Germany in the 1930s. This was ominous, and the Russians would have to free the Donbass region after eight years of bombardment by the Ukrainian government. Karaganov went on to explain that if the Russians had waited for a few more years, the problem would have reached the Russian mainland. It had to be stopped now. Predicting the future, Karaganov said the biggest loser would be Ukraine; Europe would be a great loser, and Russia would lose somewhat, and so would the US, but it would survive like a giant island surrounded by two oceans, while China would be the actual winner.

Action Man Putin

Putin is a former KGB officer who has gone to war having worked out his options. He is seen in Russia as a nationalist, a patriot and a ruthless realist who wants to restore Russia to the great and respected power it once was. His actions, both in Georgia and Ukraine, were warlike and unfortunate, but established his credibility as a leader who could deliver strong messages. On the other hand, the US comes out looking weak in Ukraine, especially after its credibility and ability were damaged successively in the Middle East and Afghanistan. Putin will not give in or give up. He will stay the course till he overcomes all resistance; should some things not work out according to plan, as it often happens, he will not settle for a less-than-compliant Ukraine. At some time in the future, he will make another attempt.[4] He has the past record of receiving popular support from Russians for his action in controlling the Chechnya insurrection.

Putin's goal has been that Russia should regain its superpower status. He is not a reckless gambler nor a blind risk-taker. He is a cold, careful calculator of strengths, weaknesses, vulnerabilities and abilities, intentions, and even timing; he would believe in a total SWOT analysis. Unemotional in his decision-making, he learnt how to manipulate the ropes of political power and used them to climb to the top during his days in St. Petersburg, where he rose to be the mayor, outsmarting both political and mafia opponents. He brought that experience to Moscow, where he showed a certain ruthlessness in eliminating opposition and punishing disloyalty.

In Moscow, Putin began to take steps to improve Russia's status, having seen the precarious position his country was brought to by naïve and incompetent leaders misled by conniving foreigners. He set about improving the military, with its budgets enhanced by 30 per cent in real terms between 2010 and 2019 and by 175 per cent between 2000 and 2019,[5] introduced military reforms and emphasized the development of new weapons systems.

The results were visible when the Russians conducted their operations in Georgia in 2008, Crimea in 2014 and incursions into the predominantly Russian region of Donbass in Ukraine. After this came a particularly striking intervention in Syria in 2015. Putin began to strengthen Russia's nuclear capability with the acquisition of additional Intercontinental Ballistic Missiles (ICBMs) in 2015, followed by the deployment of more nuclear attack submarines the next year and the testing of new ground-launched cruise missiles in 2017.[6] Putin also concentrated on strategic weaponry modernization – the Western media described the new weapons as his 'superweapons'. In his presidential campaign address in March 2018, Putin announced the introduction of a variety of cutting-edge weapons, including five new types of delivery systems.[7] He was clearly preparing for the future.

Putin had learnt his lesson from the Western sanctions following his annexation of Crimea in 2014. He had begun to bolster his foreign currency and gold reserves which were at $630 billion in 2022. Russian financial advisers developed an independent financial infrastructure where they reduced dollar holdings and switched energy transactions to euros and yuans; simultaneously, imports from the West were reduced and trade with China, India and other parts of Asia increased. Putin remembered that Europeans were reluctant to impose sanctions on Russia because of their dependence on Russian gas and oil. He began to increase their dependency on Russia while at the same time finalizing long-term energy deals with China. He had also hoped that the Russia–Germany Nord Stream 2 pipeline of natural gas in the Baltic Sea would create fissures in Western Europe's unity with Poland and Ukraine, who had been excluded from this pipeline deal. The US was also opposed to it. Ultimately, Germany suspended certification of Nord Stream 2 on 22 February 2022, because Russia had recognized the Donetsk and Luhansk republics and deployed troops in these territories. The scene was set. Putin had done his homework and he was ready.

There was another lesson – that superpowers will have little hesitation in dumping allies and friends should that need be felt. Germany did not expect it when its lifeline of the future, Nord Stream 2 was blown up in September 2022. It took a veteran journalist, Seymour Hersh, to determine that the pipeline had been blown through a clandestine operation by US and Norwegian forces. Seymour Hersh's earlier exposés, including the My Lai massacre in Vietnam and torture at Abu Ghraib, had been widely published, but not his Nord Stream 2 story. It was too much of a potential embarrassment. Ultimately, Hersh published 'How America Took Out the Nord Stream Pipeline' on his blog on 8 February 2023.[8]

Quite clearly, America was pursuing its national interest. Calculated leaks from the White House were meant to show Russia as the culprit in the Nord Stream 2 case, without showing why Russia would want to damage its own geo-economic asset. Hersh pointed out that the US State Department could not hide its glee at this. Secretary of State Antony Blinken described it as a tremendous opportunity to once and for all remove dependence on Russian energy and Putin's capability to weaponize it. America will ensure that citizens of 'our countries' do not suffer, Blinken assured the Europeans.

Victoria Nuland, the State Department's hardline point person on Ukraine, exulted at a Senate Foreign Relations Committee hearing in January 2023. She told Senator Ted Cruz, 'Like you, I am, and I think the administration is, very gratified to know that Nord Stream 2 is now, as you like to say, a hunk of metal at the bottom of the sea.'[9] Reading between the lines: *We have damaged the Russian economy and the gains will go to American companies to sell energy to Europe in the time to come. The US will also look after Europe and help it recover.*

What is not said is that this will benefit the American economy the most. And Ukraine? Who cares? No wonder Henry Kissinger was absolutely accurate when he once quipped, 'To be an enemy of America is dangerous, but to be a friend is fatal.' Old friend Western Europe is learning this lesson the hard way. Maybe other, newer friends need to be that much more cautious.

Putin's goals in Ukraine are simple. One, Ukraine should allow free passage of Russian natural gas through its territory on to Europe (half of Russian gas meant for Europe passed through Ukraine, which got cheap gas in the bargain). Two, the Russian Navy should be secure in its Crimean naval base at Sebastopol. Three, the Russian government should be seen as the protector of all Russian people. Eight million Russians live in eastern Ukraine, which makes them about 18 per cent of the Ukrainian population. Four, Ukraine should remain a buffer that keeps NATO at a distance.[10]

The 2014 Ukraine ban on the Russian language in a country where 40 per cent of the population speaks the language made for a very bad start. This was followed by the deployment of the avowedly anti-Russian (some say pro-Nazi) Azov Battalion in Donbass to attack the pro-Russian Ukrainians. They also cut off the water to Crimea. Anti-Russian sentiment had been aroused and the West did not realize or did not seem to care. No wonder Putin reacted; he was not going to abandon people of his ethnicity in the region.

Putin's China Connection

Prior to invading Ukraine, Vladimir Putin, in a move that amounted to covering his flanks, met Xi Jinping in Beijing in early February 2022 at the start of the Winter Olympics. In this meeting, Putin was the supplicant in a complete reversal of roles to when Stalin and Mao met seventy years ago, in December 1949. While Russia's economy remains small and over-dependent on petroleum exports, China has become the world's industrial powerhouse. Even militarily, China has overtaken Russia with its large navy and assertive presence in the western Pacific and its hypersonic missiles, leading to a tremendous missile armada accompanied by an extremely secure global satellite system. Its military capabilities are immense but untested in battle.[11] Aware that US economic sanctions were inevitable, Putin desperately needed Beijing's diplomatic support. He had been wooing China by offering shared petroleum and natural gas pipelines and joint military manoeuvres in the Pacific, and was now looking to cash in his political chips.

At their 4 February 2022 meeting, Putin and Xi drew on thirty-seven previous meetings to announce the foundation of their new 'global governance system', where they promised to 'enhance transport infrastructure connectivity to keep logistics on the Eurasian continent smooth and . . . make steady progress on major oil and gas cooperation projects'.[12] These words gained weight with the announcement that Russia would spend another $118 billion on new oil and gas pipelines to China. The result: an integrated Sino–Russian oil and gas infrastructure is being built from the North Sea to the South China Sea. In a landmark 5,300-word statement, Xi and Putin proclaimed that the 'world is going through momentous changes', which would lead to 'redistribution of power' and 'a growing demand for . . . leadership' (which Beijing and Moscow clearly intend to provide).[13] The two leaders denounced Washington's ill-concealed 'attempts at hegemony', and agreed to 'oppose interference in the internal affairs of sovereign states under the pretext of protecting democracy and human rights'.

Putin's projected 'Eurasian Economic Union' would be merged with Xi's ongoing trillion-dollar Belt and Road Initiative (BRI) to promote greater interconnectedness and build an alternative system for global economic growth. Proclaiming their relations 'superior to political and military alliances of the Cold War era', the two leaders asserted that their entente had 'no limits . . . no "forbidden" areas of cooperation'. On strategic issues, the two parties were adamantly opposed to the expansion of NATO, any move towards independence for Taiwan, and 'colour revolutions' such as the one that had ousted Moscow's client president of Ukraine in 2014.

Putin had secured what he so desperately needed ahead of the invasion. In exchange for feeding China's voracious appetite for energy (on a planet already in a climate crisis of the first order), Putin got a condemnation of US interference in 'his' sphere. In addition, he won Beijing's diplomatic support.[14]

View from France

One of the most forthright interviews on the current crisis was what Alain Juillet, former head of French external intelligence, DGSE, told political commentator Greg Tabibian on 3 April 2022.[15] Speaking on the origins of the Ukraine War, Juillet said invasions were unacceptable 'but we are co-responsible for it'. Since 2014, the West had simply never asked the Ukrainians to respect the Minsk agreements of 2014 and 2015 even though the French, Germans, Russians and Ukrainians were all signatories. The Russians complained, others did nothing. Juillet agreed that two former French foreign ministers, Dominique de Villepin and Hubert Védrine, had blamed the Americans for the crisis.

Commenting on the promise made to Russia in the early 1990s that NATO would not expand eastward, Juillet affirmed that former French Foreign Minister Roland Dumas, who participated in the negotiations, along with US Secretary of State James Baker and German Chancellor Helmut Kohl agreed that NATO would not expand East of a reunified Germany. The Americans had not kept their word and pushed for the eastern expansion of NATO 'in total contradiction with what was said [to Russia]', Juillet said.

Asked to comment on whether the Maidan Revolution in February 2014 was organized by the Americans, Juillet characteristically replied, 'One thing that particularly caught my attention is Victoria Nuland, who is currently the US Under Secretary of State for Political Affairs, saying that ... it cost the US $5 billion to get into Ukraine and that they weren't going to leave now after that. What does that mean, Madame Nuland? She is by the way the same one who, when told the Europeans weren't happy, said, "[expletive deleted] the EU". So, it's pretty clear ...' He was referring to the leaked tapes of a conversation between US Assistant Secretary of State for European and Eurasian Affairs Victoria Nuland and US Ambassador Geoffrey Pyatt in 2014, which clearly indicated American involvement in government formation in Ukraine that year.[16]

Juillet was understandably being circumspect here but there have been detailed reports about US interest in and assistance to anti-Yanukovych groups in Ukraine.[17] In his 2022 article, Washington-based geopolitical analyst Mike Whitney details that 'In March 2015, Ukrainian Interior Minister Arsen Avakov had announced that the Azov Battalion would be one of the first units to be trained by US Army troops, and that their training programme could have a serious impact.' Apparently, the US had been providing combat training to Ukrainian Nazis and other far-right groups in secret camps since 2015.

Later, President Biden promised a much larger sum, $33 billion, as part of military aid to Ukraine – raised to $40 billion, of which $14 billion was disbursed, but the gravy train has been considerably reduced by Trump. Till June 2025, the size of US military aid to Ukraine is an estimated $60 billion.[18] It is more than likely that large sums went to weapons manufacturers such as Raytheon, Lockheed Martin, Boeing and the usual suspects and to the CIA for unspecified reasons.[19]

The main aid givers in the year after February 2022 have been the US and EU, with €71 billion including €43 billion for military assistance; EU institutions gave €35.5 billion including €3.6 billion for military assistance; other good friends of the US gave assistance in single-digit billions. It is worth noting that in 2008 the GDP of the EU was 30.2 per cent of the global GDP whereas the US GDP was 23.1 per cent, despite the economic crisis of 2008. In 2021 US GDP was 23.9 per cent against the EU GDP which was 17.7 per cent, while the Chinese were at 17.8 per cent. In the years ahead, the EU GDP, less UK, will become even smaller. With the US withdrawing aid, EU will need to pick up the shortfall.

Retired French General Jean-Bernard Pinatel, vice president of Geopragma and author of *Histoire de l'Islam radical et de ceux qui s'enservent* (*History of Radical Islam and Those Who Use It*), 2017, commented on the situation in Ukraine a month after the Russian attack.[20] Pinatel was concerned that after two murderous wars, Europe could not allow the situation to deteriorate into civil wars at a time when there were already ecological disasters staring at the world amid continuing challenges from radical Islam. An arms race for ultimate supremacy between the US and China would be unacceptable to Europeans; and a second front in Europe, in addition to the Pacific, the designated battlefield of the Sino–American confrontation, must be prevented. The risk was an American and NATO provocation against Russia which would lead to a Russian–Chinese alliance. The fear was that the French would lose their strategic autonomy by aligning with the Anglo-Saxon camp and be dragged against their will into what might escalate into another world war.

The war in Ukraine and the voting pattern in the UN indicate the end of US domination of the world which it has exercised since the end of World War II. The West, which represents less than one-seventh of the world's population, failed to convince more than half of the planet's inhabitants to condemn the Russians, with China and India taking the lead in refusing to do so. Pinatel warned that the Ukrainian crisis would hasten instability in Europe, and if France did not want to go down with it, it needed to regain its strategic autonomy and no longer entrust its destiny to anyone else. It seems Pinatel's assessment was prophetic.

One of the clearest and most detailed accounts of what has been happening in Ukraine is by Jacques Baud, a former colonel of the General Staff, ex-member of the Swiss strategic intelligence, and trained by American and British intelligence. As a UN representative he had considerable experience in Africa and from Mali to Afghanistan, and had opposed NATO plans to proliferate small arms in the African continent. Within NATO he has followed the Ukraine crisis since 2014. Three of his recent commentaries on the current crisis provide thorough accounts normally lost in the din of Western propaganda.[21] Baud's opinion is that what appeared in media outlets, globally, was dubious information leading to all sorts of hypotheses. The Ukrainian Army was suffering from chronic corruption, its morale was low, as also its training and professionalism, and people were reluctant to join the armed forces. Yet despite these strong opinions from outside the Anglo–Saxon world, Europe is involved in the Ukraine War minus the manpower but with its economy hugely dented.

The Economic War

The dollar has been the globe's hegemonic currency that has given Washington the ability to artificially increase military budgets, sustain prolonged fiscal and trade deficits, monitor international transactions, implement sanctions, block transactions, freeze foreign assets, strengthen the influence of Wall Street heavyweights in global financial markets, manipulate the prices of strategic commodities and accumulate stratospheric levels of debt with no meaningful consequences.[22] The dollar as the fiat currency is ultimately backed by massive multispectrum military firepower, ranging from aircraft carriers to drones. Those who challenged the dollar (like Saddam Hussein when he switched from the petrodollar to the euro) have paid a heavy price. The dollar is a formidable pillar of US national strength, but it is also vulnerable as its downfall unravels the unipolarity coveted by the US since the end of Cold War I. Today the US dollar is under threat.

Putin's counterattack away from the battlefield into currency and energy wars has widened the game, which it seems the Americans did not factor in. The Russian strategy of accepting payments for energy only in roubles has led even Goldman Sachs to warn that America's weaponization of the dollar and Russia's response could encourage many countries to move away from the dollar and diversify their transactions and holdings. Consequently, the dollar will be under pressure, leading to a decline in its value in the years ahead. Even though rouble payment for oil made headlines, payment through roubles or other currencies has been going on for a while now.

There is no way to find out if American strategists had anticipated this Russian response. The fear is that the dollar's decline could be like what the sterling had in the early twentieth century, even without a substitute readily available. The IMF claims that the emergence of a new world order that reorders geopolitical forces could mean that the structure of international payment networks and the nature of reserve holdings might also alter. The Biden administration would have surely thought this through as a collateral fallout of waging an all-out economic war by freezing Russian reserves, seizing gold reserves and suspending Russia from the SWIFT payment system. There are other doubts. For instance, to what extent, including a military confrontation with Russia, would the US be willing to pursue a combative line to protect the dollar as the world's hard currency? Whether the US government has a fallback option is another question that must be explored.[23]

America resorted to its favourite weapon of statecraft – economic sanctions and currency wars – against a militarily powerful Russia, and for a while it did succeed. Quite apparently, the Americans were not looking for a hot war with the Russians; instead they were looking at a hybrid war that concentrated on economically throttling and isolating Russia. After their Cold War success, the Americans consider unilateral sanctions to be the safer option. However, as the American share in global GDP declines, so does the efficacy of its sanctions.

The rouble had fallen from thirty-six to a dollar at the time of the annexation of Crimea by Russia in March 2014, to sixty-six in February 2015 after the Minsk II conference. Putin reacted by taking advantage of falling gold prices and in February 2022, Russia became the sixth-largest holder of gold stockpiles in the world. The West responded to the Russian invasion by freezing the assets of the Russian Central Bank held in places like the US, the UK, the EU and Switzerland, which amounted to about $400 billion. The Western bloc, led by the US, froze more than €200 billion in Russian assets in addition to €30 billion of Russian oligarchs. The Belgian prime minister proposed in June 2023 that the $3 billion of the windfall profits annually from the frozen assets should be used to rebuild Ukraine.[24] Russia's suspension from the SWIFT payments system within a fortnight of the war alarmed the Global South as a message primarily aimed at China to prevent any Chinese adventure in Taiwan. This has led to the Global South resorting to payments in currency swaps or in each other's currencies as in the case of Russian oil and gas. This might not lead to an immediate collapse of the dollar but it will mean alternative payment systems that are not under the control of SWIFT.

The economic sanctions were intended to diminish Moscow's ability to fund its campaign in Ukraine, disrupt the economy in a major way, trigger hyperinflation, prompt the collapse of the Russian banking system and evaporate savings. The West is 'waging a total economic and financial war against Russia' hoping this would lead to a total collapse of the Russian economy, triggering civil unrest, widespread turmoil and a destabilizing power struggle in Moscow led by those not satisfied with Putin's strategic gamble.[25]

It was hoped that all this would lead to regime change in Moscow. After all, this has been a favourite strategic goal of US policy. Regime-change enthusiasts would presumably ignore past failures. The most consistent outcome of foreign-imposed regime change is an increased likelihood of civil war. This is because regime change missions weaken existing state institutions and create a power vacuum, leading to rebel movements. In about 40 per cent of cases of covert regime change undertaken during the Cold War, a civil war occurred within ten years of the operation.[26]

This overconfidence partly stems from the way Western media projects developments – one-sided, optimistic and as exaggerated successes, along with a sense of righteousness and an emphasis on the nobility of the cause. This is unlike autocratic societies, where the population is cynical and disbelieving of media handouts. When the truth eventually emerges, as in the Ukraine story, it is the free world that is the most disappointed. In the US, the main power behind the Ukraine defence, most of the accepted reporting has been by the *New York Times*, *Washington Post* and *Wall Street Journal*. The extent of influence and reach of these papers in circles that matter is immense. This elite media has relied mostly on one think tank for their information. In the first week of June 2022, ten articles in one newspaper cited the Washington-based Institute for the Study of War (ISW). This institute has neoconservative roots and is run and staffed by hawks. 'Over the years it has gotten funding from various corners of the arms industry – General Dynamics, Raytheon, lesser-known defence contractors and big companies, like General Motors, that aren't known as defence contractors but do get Pentagon contracts.'[27]

The history of the formation of ISW and its political leanings will explain why the US has been so generous with funding the war effort in Ukraine. It is a window into the way America works. Kimberly Kagan, a military historian, is the president and founder of the ISW. She is married to Frederick Kagan, who is also a military historian and works for the ISW. Frederick is a well-known neoconservative, but not as well-known as his brother, Robert Kagan, who along with Bill Kristol (who is on ISW's board), founded the Project for a New American Century (PNAC) in the 1990s, and is believed to have played an important role in convincing George W. Bush to invade Iraq.

The Kagan couple cultivated Pentagon and were considered close to General Petraeus, and this proximity helped ISW obtain funds from defence contractors. Robert Kagan's wife, Victoria Nuland, is the state department official who very publicly supported Ukraine's 2014 Maidan Revolution – the overthrow of pro-Russia President Viktor Yanukovych – which led Russia to seize Crimea and give military support to secessionist rebels in the Donbass. Nuland also played a role in this transition of power.

The Kagan–Kristol Project for a New American Century was funded by arms makers, thanks largely to the work of Lockheed Martin executive Bruce P. Jackson who later became a director of PNAC. 'Some people think NATO expansion – in particular George W. Bush's 2008 addition of Ukraine to the list of future members – helped cause the Ukraine war, but in any event NATO expansion has over the past quarter century made lots and lots of money for Lockheed Martin and other arms makers.'[28] As an immediate fallout of the Ukraine war, European arms imports rose by 92 per cent in 2022, which is the largest year-over-year increase seen since the fall of the Berlin Wall. Ukraine became the world's third largest arms importer in 2022.[29]

The Ukraine War was never just about territory; it is no longer a military engagement because it now includes currency, trade, energy embargoes, food shortages, health issues and migrations, with the idea that Russia must be economically ruined never mind the suffering involved. At the same time the earlier shrill campaigns about how the Ukrainians were winning with massive Western assistance comprising American armament worth billions of dollars has been replaced with statements about negotiated settlements. This was a clear indication that the war was not going America's way. There was comment to the effect that America, once described as the arsenal of democracy because of its ability to provide enough weapons not only for itself but also allies, now had a shrunken base and was unable to provide munitions and missiles to meet US military requirements let alone those of its allies.[30]

In its 19 December 2022 report, the *Wall Street Journal* also alludes to stocks dwindling to 850 Javelin missiles after nine years' worth of supplies to Ukraine in nine months. Production needed to be doubled but there was a shortage of 250 semiconductor chips. There was similarly a shortage of Guided Multiple Rocket Systems (GMLRS) and High Mobility Artillery Rocket Systems (HIMARS).[31] There have been calls for increased production, assuming that this will be a very long war. It also means that US supplies would run out before Russian resilience wears out. For defence contractors, this is a golden opportunity for increased sales. Lockheed Martin received orders for 950 missiles to refill depleted stockpiles. Raytheon needed to manufacture $2 billion worth of missiles to replenish the 1,600 Stingers given to Ukraine. There were other smaller manufacturers in the market, but the other problem was procuring key components like missile warheads and microelectronics.[32] The Ukraine war, like other wars, has also become a testing ground for US arms manufacturers to innovate and implement new battlefield strategies and techniques.[33]

This even as the Russians got down to their battle fatigues and exhibited a new resolve not seen anywhere in recent years. After decades of fighting between the former Soviet republics of Armenia and Azerbaijan, Russia had deployed thousands of 'peacekeeping' forces to resolve the conflict in favour of the loyal, pro-Moscow regime in Azerbaijan.[34] Subsequently, some Russian peacekeeping troops were withdrawn from the Nagorno–Karabakh region. The post-Soviet Union regional security organization, Collective Security Treaty Organization (CSTO), consisting of six members – Russia, Belarus, Kazakhstan, Armenia, Tajikistan and Kyrgyzstan – which had been scoffed at for being dormant for so long, was used by Russia to intervene in Kazakhstan to quell the mobs and restore order in January 2022.[35]

The China Factor

Much before the Ukraine crisis, and as far back as 2010, both Russia and China had begun developing international trade in roubles and renminbi, without touching the dollar, and countries like India were later willing to buy oil from Russia in roubles. In 2012, China and Japan agreed to direct reciprocal transactions in renminbi and yen. And in 2013, China announced that it was ready to transact sale and purchase of oil in renminbi. The petrodollar was further threatened because of the Ukraine conflict and subsequent sanctions. Unlike the decline of the British pound, which took over thirty years and two world wars, the decline of the dollar could be sudden and disturbing and sooner than anticipated. Inevitably, the Ukraine conflict has hastened the need for alternative payment mechanisms or further revitalizing direct payments.

It is not that Putin was watching the world go by. Even before the invasion of Ukraine, Russia and China were pursuing a strategy of ratcheting up slow, relentless pressure at both ends of Eurasia, hoping the US military and naval presence surrounding them would collapse. Washington probably concluded that Putin might be getting ambitious by trying to reclaim significant parts of the old Soviet sphere of influence in East Europe, Central Asia and the Middle East. Putin had become extremely wary after the colour revolutions in Georgia (2003), Ukraine (2004) and Kyrgyzstan (2005) at a time when NATO and EU had expanded eastward despite Russian objections. To Putin it appeared like a synchronized Western campaign which, if not checked, could reach Moscow.

At the eastern end of Eurasia, China has pursued a somewhat similar, if subtler strategy, that has avoided war but the punch is yet to come. Starting in 2014, Beijing began dredging a half-dozen military bases from atolls in the South China Sea, slowly ramping them up from fishing ports to full-fledged military bases that now challenge any passing US naval patrol. Then came swarming fighter squadrons over the Taiwan Strait and East China Sea, followed in October 2023 by a joint Chinese–Russian fleet of ten ships that sailed provocatively around Japan in what had previously been considered unchallenged US-controlled waters.

If Xi follows Putin's playbook, then all the push could indeed lead to a shove – possibly an invasion of Taiwan to reclaim lands Beijing sees as integral to China, much as Putin considers parts of Eastern Europe.[36] Should Beijing attack Taiwan, Washington might find itself expressing great admiration for the island's heroic resistance, but little else. Should Washington send its aircraft carriers into the Taiwan Straits, they would be sunk within hours by China's formidable DF-21D 'carrier killer' missiles or its unstoppable hypersonic ones. And once Taiwan is gone and the first island chain breached, the Chinese Navy will be able to move freely in Pacific. Washington's position on the Pacific littoral could be effectively broken and a retreat to the mid-Pacific preordained.

Joe Biden armed Taiwan in a limited way and provoked the Chinese and Russians, which had little effect. Sanctions on Russia too had little effect; in fact the Russian economy became stronger and was expected to grow at 3.2 per cent in 2024, according to the IMF in its latest World Economic Outlook published in April 2024, exceeding the forecast growth rates for the US (2.7 per cent), the U.K. (0.5 per cent), Germany (0.2 per cent) and France (0.7 per cent).[37] However, in 2025, the Russian economy is slowing down and showing signs of fatigue.[38]'

In the Middle East, where Washington had backed without success the ill-fated Arab rebels who tried to topple Syria's ruler, Bashar al-Assad, Moscow had a massive air base at Latakia in that country's northwest. Russian aircraft flying out of Latakia reduced rebel cities like Aleppo to rubble, while serving as a strategic counterweight to US bases in the Persian Gulf. Eventually the Americans succeeded in their efforts in getting rid of Bashar and replaced him by Ahmed al-Sharaa formerly a trusted lieutenant of ISIS commander, Abu Bakr al-Baghdadi. Sharaa has been described as someone who is 'refreshingly pragmatic or profoundly untrustworthy' and who has worn many hats in his insurgent career.[39] This is the sort of leader the Americans are comfortable with so long as the Russians were removed. Meanwhile, the Druze and Alawite communities are under constant attack from the Sunni militia. The Druze who are predominantly in southern Syria have Israeli support. Sharaa's government has not gone out of its way to protect the Druze or Alawites.[40] In Eastern Europe, Putin helped Belarus's strongman, Alexander Lukashenko, crush pro-democratic opposition after the 2020 elections and made it a virtual client state.

Russia's presence in Africa has continued to increase and threatens French influence in the Sahel region. Algeria, Angola, Burkina Faso, Egypt, Ethiopia, Mali, Morocco, Rwanda and Uganda are some of the countries who have imported arms from Russia and have done so since Soviet times. This amounts to 49 per cent of Africa's total military equipment.[41]

Africa is another front that the Russians opened, as it were, by suddenly enhancing their profile in the continent when American and European stock was low due to American arrogance and historical exploitation by the Europeans. Apparently, the Russians were trying to take advantage of the situation in Niger that it would not supply uranium to France. The Americans sided with France and threatened sanctions, which did not seem to frighten Niger. Countries have seen how sanctions can be evaded. In actual fact, it was Europe that was caught in an energy pincer by the Russians – no gas from Russia and no uranium for French nuclear plants from Niger.

Putin did not think of this overnight. He had war-gamed it for at least eight or nine years, ever since the Americans started being aggressive on extending the NATO to Ukraine. Putin's move into Niger and other French colonies at this juncture is a challenge to America as well. Wagner and other Russian private military companies are now furthering Russian interests in Africa and South America. The Russian private militia, the Wagner Group, is said to have become active, for instance interacting with the Chinese in Mali and helping them with their mining companies.

Denouement Forewarned

In the early days of the Ukraine conflict, a manufactured euphoria about a war already won and Russia's imminent collapse had gripped the West. It was a conscious media creation, along with loud claims from official sources. Theoretically well-rehearsed, well-coordinated with official statements, dire threats of sanctions were broadcast on editorial and television networks controlled by the West. The naïve, the gullible and the agenda artists accepted these stories, as did sections of the Indian media, without any of their own assets in place to confirm the claims. The Russians were shown to be incompetent soldiers, ill-equipped with weapons and equipment, ready to lose. Their economy was creaking, and they were heading for a collapse. The propaganda was that the Russians were going to be defeated by the valiant Ukrainians.

Putin had watched how NATO's increased unilateralism and infringement of international law, especially in Libya during the Arab Spring period 2011–2013, led to demonstrations even in Russia. He had observed how the Americans were leading from behind to bring about regime change in the Middle East and North Africa. He had watched how US President Barack Obama dragged his feet in and about Syria and his feckless ally Britain too could not win parliamentary approval for crossing the much-touted redline in Syria.[42] Putin apparently concluded that the US was still affected by the Vietnam Syndrome, which had prevented it from launching any major military intervention for seventeen years till 1990 in Iraq. The massive failure in Iraq – the second since Vietnam, and the botched withdrawal from Afghanistan, the third since Vietnam – assured Putin that 'starting with Obama, the United States has mostly resorted to cowardly remote warfare, mostly waged under the radar'.[43] Putin was suitably emboldened to act in Crimea and Ukraine.

The Russians were not in for a blitzkrieg. Actually, they were playing the long game of attrition, and no one knows how to do it better than them. Putin probably came to the war with a worst-case scenario, like all intelligence agencies do to start their preparations for an operation, and then worked backwards. Thus, he was in for a long war with huge casualties, and knew how unsure NATO countries might be. The US egged on the Ukrainians, assuming they would win, overestimating itself and its allies and underestimating the opposition. This is because high-tech weapons do not ensure victory; nor do air-supported battles. It is ultimately the people on the ground and their grit that matter. The war has gone on for much longer than was expected by either combatant. US commentators and analysts have spoken of the fact that the Ukrainians have been fulfilling American goals, while the Europeans have applauded Ukrainian efforts to keep Russia away from Western Europe. However, a prolonged war also means that the US could lose allies for various other reasons too.

Andrei Martynov, a Russian-born naturalized American, has written a trilogy on US supremacy and power in relation to Russian strengths: *Losing Military Supremacy* (2018), *Disintegration* (2021) and *America's Final War* (2024). Martynov's argument in his latest book, *America's Final*

War, is that the West, led by the US, has never understood Russia. They have been misled by their own propaganda about Russia, the Russophobia of leading US thinkers like Zbigniew Brzeziński and over-optimistic presumptions about their own prowess along with downplaying Russian capabilities in military technology and R&D. Further, many American strategists do not have military backgrounds and have little understanding of these matters.[44]

Russia had been talking about Ukraine from a position of strength, with the world's largest nuclear arsenal and the strongest conventional forces in Europe. Putin also had access to intelligence from the finest global intelligence services – the Russian General Staff, Service of Foreign Intelligence (SVR), FSB and the Foreign Office. The West cannot bring themselves to accept this reality. The US did not realize that starting a war in Vietnam or Iraq had a different meaning for them as opposed to the Russians starting a war in Ukraine. The Biden administration failed to realize that Russia was still a formidable military power backed by sophisticated and advanced intelligence, surveillance and reconnaissance systems.[45] As it happens, the Americans have also been running out of military equipment and the Europeans have no stomach for a war to save Ukraine despite all the political bravado. Martynov predicts a collapse of the Western war machine in Europe[46] and an impact on 'America's fortunes in a manner that will surpass that of the first American civil war'.[47]

The Russian economy did not collapse, the entire world did not turn against Russia, the Ukrainians could not take on the Russians who were just too powerful and well equipped for the long haul, and Ukraine's Western friends could only give lip service to their cause. Worse, they are now beginning to blame Ukraine and Zelenskyy for an impending debacle. The European economy took a beating, NATO was unsuccessful and the domestic audience in the US and Europe is gradually becoming anti-war as more and more military experts begin to tell the truth. Meanwhile, Trump has his own ideas. The quid pro quo that Trump asked of Ukraine, rare minerals in exchange for military support, has been the American way. Trump is perhaps doing it more openly than anyone else. Possibly Trump is not looking for an extension of the conflict but some kind of a deal with Putin.

Commentaries by Scot Ritter, a former UN weapons inspector and a Marine Corps intelligence officer, who was a part of the team in Iraq,[48] and Col. Douglas Macgregor, a military expert, have been unequivocal that the Ukraine War is going Russia's way, albeit slowly.[49] No wonder there were slogans in Germany calling for America to leave and seeking peace with Russia and TV visuals or social media displayed these. This should not surprise those who know how harsh a European winter could be without Russian gas. This led US Secretary of State, Antony Blinken, to comment in September 2024 that Putin was 'weaponizing winter, weaponizing the weather and using energy as a weapon to subjugate Ukraine'.[50]

There is a Ukraine fatigue in the West. Ukraine's counteroffensive floundered, despite the West pumping it with tens of billions of dollars' worth of new weapons. It seemed Biden was running out of ideas beyond throwing more money and weapons at the war.[51]

US actions in 2014 suggested that America had no intention of allowing an early resolution of the Ukraine crisis.[52] This was more than a decade ago after American interference in the Ukraine elections, and Biden's actions did not suggest that there was any change in US policy, only it had been more violently active before. It was a continuation of what the Wolfowitz Doctrine stated in 1992 in the Defence Planning Guidance paper: 'Our first objective is to prevent the reemergence of a new rival, either on the territory of the former Soviet Union or elsewhere, that poses a threat on the order of that posed formerly by the Soviet Union. This is a dominant consideration underlying the new regional defence strategy and requires that we endeavour to prevent any hostile power from dominating a region whose resources would, under consolidated control, be sufficient to generate global power.'[53] This message, it should be noted, was in the context of Russia and China, but in today's world it can realistically apply to other states, allies, friends or adversaries.

The context of the ongoing war also meant that this could lead to an indirect US–Russia shutdown. This is unlikely so long as both the Russians and the Americans observe the understanding that has been in place since 1945 that they would not attack each other's forces or assets directly. Putin clarified that in the draft document on nuclear deterrence in September 2024, that any aggression against Russia by a non-nuclear state, if supported or backed by a nuclear state, would be treated as a joint attack. Belarus under a nuclear shield has been explicitly mentioned.[54]

In a poll conducted in August 2023 by the CNN, most Americans opposed more US aid for Ukraine in its war with Russia. Politically there was a divide among the Republicans and Democrats on this issue. The Republicans were opposed to the Congress giving more funds to Ukraine while the Democrats favoured it.[55] American mainstream newspapers were also reluctant to publish any setbacks that the Ukrainians faced and would rather highlight or exaggerate setbacks for the Russians. Contrary news was available in non-mainstream media and via social media.

The fog of war had begun to lift a bit, and it was becoming apparent that Ukraine was not going to win – not that there was ever any hope. Mere animosity towards another nation does not assure victory; perhaps the Ukrainians were discovering this somewhat late in the war. Friends promising military aid and money may be inadequate against a determined enemy. Europe had lost ground politically and economically while obeying US commands. The Americans had lost the plot, and their image had taken yet another knock. There was no easy exit, because as usual the Americans did not think it might be needed.

Is it possible that Washington could be caught in a Moscow–Beijing hunter's trap?

Washington and some of its allies had been heating Second Cold War but so far it has not boiled over to the rest of the world. It is time to remind ourselves of the global consequences of First Cold War. It was a period of US-led coups and regime changes in Latin America and the Middle East; brutal wars in Vietnam, Cambodia and Laos, havoc in Afghanistan twice over, in Iraq twice and endless wars in the rest of the Middle East, North Africa and the Balkans. In all, there were more than fifty wars involving USA.

This display of endless belligerence extended to global sanctions on allies and enemies and were usually counterproductive. The other part of the current policy to arm Ukrainians to the hilt and make them fight America's war against Russia is a replay of earlier policy. The recent international voting pattern on various aspects indicates that the world is no longer willing to toe America's line despite all the high-decibel information campaigning. This was because the world no longer believed in American proclamations, and US credibility and capability to deliver was considered very low, after the dismal outcomes in Iraq, Syria and Afghanistan. As political scientists Alexander Downes and Lindsey

O'Rourke observed, of the twenty-eight cases of American-engineered regime change, only three had proved successful in building a lasting democracy.[56] Instead, most Cold War policies outlined above, even though carried out under the rubric of promoting 'freedom' in 'the free world', actually undermined democracy in a disastrous fashion.

The days of 'us versus them' rhetoric and global military manoeuvrings may be over. A drastic switch of resources to military adventure will divert attention and resources from the biggest risks to humanity, which include climate change. America, already stretched at the seams, is not going to escape the consequences. A new Cold War should be considered a folly of the first order and evidence of an inability to learn from history.[57] It sounds ominous.

Anyone who thinks that the Ukraine War is about Ukraine is incredibly naïve; that is just the narrative. Everything that America does is for America – that is the ultimate intention. Up until a few years ago, America had the power to push its agenda quite successfully, but after a series of defeats, this power has weakened. Its narrative lost its sheen when America tried to achieve greatness by killing a million Iraqis or thousands of innocent Afghans or, more recently, putting Ukrainians on the frontline to settle scores with arch-enemy Russia.

The attempts to cripple Russia economically and financially have succeeded only partially but will leave the globe in a horrible mess with no winners, only losers. The initial euphoria, self-generated with the help of a powerful global media, is beginning to tire. A glorious victory accompanied by marching bands and cheering crowds is not happening. What is going to happen is a broken country where others come for the pickings. As it appears, today sanctions are going badly for Western Europe because of Russian retaliation. Countries have quickly adopted alternative ways of transacting international business. Psychological warfare to undermine Russian resilience has boomeranged.

America has ICBMs, a global navy, numerous bases, some of the most lethal military aircraft, the best-equipped ground troops and reputedly the widest all-encompassing intelligence system. Yet, in the end, all these put together do not seem to deliver much. At the same time, America remains the most powerful country on the globe. It is the technology and the dollar that is its true power. It is possible that the dollar in the near future may suffer, and that would lead to a whole new world order.

Western powers need to realize that the rest of the world will no longer blindly accept rules and laws passed in the West outside the UN; more so when they are selective and exclude those sanctions that would hurt the West. Duplicity of intentions aimed at enemies of convenience while pretending to help a newly found friend, will not work. India will remain a friend of the West but will not follow Western domestic regulations by jeopardizing its own national interest. In this globalized world, India needs friends, but it is not a one-way street anymore; the West too needs a growing democratic prosperous India that trades with them, buys their products, and provides resources as well. The West also needs a friend and ally in the Indo–Pacific region.

Six months into the conflict, some American observers were concerned that the US narrative that described themselves and the West as noble heroes ranged against the Russians and Chinese was faltering. In a conversation with Democracy Now, Jeffrey Sachs was explicit about US intentions when he said, 'I have seen, in my own experience, over the last 30 years working extensively in Russia, in Central Europe, in China and in other parts of the world, how the U.S. approach is a military-first, and often a military-only, approach. We arm who we want. We call for NATO enlargement, no matter what other countries say may be harmful to their security interests. We brush aside anyone else's security interests. And when they complain, we ship more armaments to our allies in that region ... And we end up in terrible confrontations.'[58]

As any war would, the Ukraine war has had an impact on the nuclear sphere. Putin put his nuclear forces on high alert before the Ukraine venture in February 2022.[59] This was reminiscent of the Cold War era of high alerts. NATO realized that the Russians might be serious about their nuclear options should the Ukraine war turn adverse.[60] Exchange of verbal threats and nuclear blackmail between the Russians and Americans were a constant feature as the war dragged on. Both conducted drills for tactical nuclear weapon deployment. Russians claimed that their nuclear arsenal had stopped the Americans from participating in the Ukraine War.[61]

Ukrainian drones targeting the Russian strategic early warning radar system was the first real escalation of the war in probing and testing Russia's early warning capabilities.[62] Russia responded in kind by selectively leaking in August 2024 the nuclear dossier showing thirty-two NATO targets. One of the largest ammunitions dumps in Russia was destroyed by drone swarms in September 2024, which was attributed to Ukraine.[63] Meanwhile, the world is living dangerously, with both the US and Russia testing and revalidating their doctrines and machines in a live environment. There seemed to be stalemate developing.

When Vladimir Trumped Donald

All this changed as President Trump, anxious about the Nobel Peace prize, raised the tempo of events. Eight months into his presidency and Donald Trump could not live up to his claim that he would solve Ukraine crisis in a day. It was never going to be that easy because it is a war that had its origins in American NATO plans for Eastern Europe since the fall of the Soviet Union and in the Russian determination not to let Ukraine become a member of NATO. That was more than 30 years ago. All American Presidents pursued this policy for Ukraine. Ultimately, it was a Deep State war conducted by the CIA, Pentagon and the military intelligence complex.[64]

Unable to push back the Russians for the simple reason that, as usual the adversary's capabilities and resilience were underestimated and realizing that the great Euro–American alliance was running out of choices, President Trump invited President Putin for a bilateral dialogue in Alaska on 15 August 2025. It was a mini-Yalta. Zbigniew Brzeziński's dream that expansion of NATO eastward could reduce Russia to a second or even a third-rate power had soured by this invitation as it signified that Russia was still a first-rate power.

It seems that Putin had his way with Trump and insisted on the basic conditions of peace, not ceasefire and that Russia would retain territory captured. The Zelenskyy model, supported by Europeans that there should be a ceasefire and return of territory, has not worked. This was not acceptable to the Russians knowing fully well that ceasefire was meaningless if it is going to be violated a few years down the line once the rest of Europe had rearmed Ukraine. The Russians were not going to surrender what they won on the battlefield. Trump has stopped talking about the ceasefire.[65] US Secretary of State Marco Rubio admitted that the best way to solve the problem was through a peace deal: 'Best way to end' Russia-Ukraine war 'is through a full peace deal'.[66] The US will now go through the usual ritual of bilateralism, followed by a multinational

(European) assent and pretend they have won, and leave their proxy to carry on.

Meanwhile, Zelenskyy has offered to buy $100 billion dollars' worth of arms from the Americans, who do not have the weapons, by borrowing from Europeans who do not have the money and Ukraine does not have the manpower to fight – given the conscription that has been going on. All Europe is left with is the absurd self-created narrative that Russia will attack Europe, if Ukraine is not armed.[67]

India's Position

There are some who still believe that in a China–India confrontation, the world led by the US would come to India's aid and rescue. We should therefore jump on to their bandwagon now and live in the blissful comfort of a Quad, perhaps. This is living in cloud cuckoo land. Besides, the US corporate world has too much at stake in China to jeopardize its gigantic profits. The US will never come to our rescue. Each country must fight its own battles. This is also the lesson for EU and Ukraine. American weapons in billions, sympathy by the hour and minute, and sustained disinformation is available, but there will be no troops on the ground; America will not take on Russian troops on battlefields far from home. Previous attempts against much lesser powers have been dismal failures. It is also a war that in the long term has no winners. Ukraine, Europe and Russia – in that order will suffer the most; the US will only be a marginal gainer as its word will no longer be the last word and its dollar is not going to be the only currency.

The pressure on India to support the Ukrainian war effort has been immense, with the US pretending to be highly moralistic while the campaign was highly amoral. There was insistence that it was in India's interest to be on America's side and that this was probably India's last chance. A prime ministerial visit to Russia was criticized officially and in the media, and the warmth of the Putin–Modi meeting frowned upon. When it really mattered that India's voice be considered, as our security was of great concern during the Afghan troubles, India was consistently and deliberately sidelined by the US. The Indian stand on the crisis, our relationship with Russia and on the issue of abiding by US-led sanctions, is purely for our national interest and not for a war that we have not been involved in and have no intention of getting involved in.

Americans are bad losers, and anything seen to be going against their way must be the fault of others. As also is Ukraine. India is blamed for buying crude oil from Russia despite American sanctions which provides the Russians money to continue the war.[68] India is not going to do that.

The global economy, already imperilled with even countries like China on a downward trajectory amidst US-led sanction wars, is going to hurt Europe very hard every winter. As of now, the most widely held independent assessment is that the US plan has collapsed, taking Ukraine and the EU along with it, while Russia has been able to hold out even though not as a complete victor. In fact, this war leaves no winner, only losers, but the highest economic price is being paid by Europe; the US loses prestige, and Ukraine loses everything. The Russians may be left exhausted but undefeated.

The future looks grim.

7

Challenge from a Would-Be Global Power

> *The United States brags about its political system, but the President says one thing during the election, something else when he takes office, something else at midterm and something else when he leaves.*[1]
>
> — DENG XIAOPING

Xi Jinping and Joe Biden met in Bali in November 2022 during the G20 summit. This was their first meeting after Biden became president in January 2021, which reflects the state of relations between the two world powers. The two had met after the China–US stand-off following Speaker Nancy Pelosi's visit to Taiwan. The meeting had the usual Chinese theatre when Xi arrived outside the conference room, planted himself firmly in front of the Chinese flag and waited. Then Xi watched Biden trundle across a long hotel lobby and the two shook hands vigorously. The Chinese leader was enacting 'li', which is Chinese decorum in the emperor's court – the implication was that Biden was coming to him as a supplicant. China had for decades followed Deng Xiaoping's famous advice, to 'hide your strength and bide your time'. No longer so, for the China of today is far more confident, even arrogant, with the US than ever before.

After the Bali meet, in October 2023, Majority leader Chuck Schumer was in Beijing trying to reset ties. Biden and Xi eventually met again in San Francisco in November that year; military ties were opened a bit but the trade ties had deteriorated. Americans resorted to their favourite technique and imposed sanctions on high-end technologies and semiconductors supposedly in an attempt to prevent industrial espionage and Chinese firms rapidly developing dual use technology capabilities. Tariffs were raised on electric vehicles (EVs), solar cells, steel and aluminium products, medical devices and semiconductor chips, against a China grappling with industrial overcapacity. The effectiveness of the sanctions was mixed, as always, and relations remained tepid, at best.

Chinese surveillance of American business visitors has increased, which has contributed to extreme caution in investing in Chinese firms. The Chinese economy is facing a deep economic downturn owing to an over-leveraged real-estate market and relatively weak domestic consumption at a time when foreign direct investment has collapsed. The Chinese have stepped up their efforts to hack US infrastructure, of which there have been frequent incidents. Chinese academics and researchers are increasingly under the scanner for potential R&D intellectual property (IP) theft.

From Mao to Deng

Mao was a great leader who led his people to a famous guerilla victory but thereafter became a complete autocrat, who had to face the Korean War almost as soon as he had declared victory over his rivals. Mao's reign was marked by the convulsions of the bizarre experiment of the Great Leap Forward and the purge that was the Great Proletariat Cultural Revolution. The wily Stalin had led Mao into Korea, and thereafter China got embroiled in the never-ending Vietnam War too, which ended just months before Mao died.

The Vietnam War ended in American ignominy but did not bring Vietnam into the Chinese camp. Mao's China had also been involved in a short but bloody war with Nehru's India in 1962, which left the two countries permanent enemies with little possibility of a solution. Indians like to think that China views India as a threat to its hegemony in Asia, while the Chinese are convinced that India is a pretentious power which is no rival to them in any manner.

Very early in the Cold War, in the 1950s, the two communist powers, the USSR and the PRC, fell out after Stalin's death. This preceded the famous Kennedy–Khrushchev nuclear showdown over missiles in Cuba in 1962 and the two neighbours' military clash across the Ussuri river in Siberia in 1969. In this falling out, the Americans saw an opportunity to divide the communist bloc. Richard Nixon made his famous journey to meet Mao in Beijing in 1972, after Henry Kissinger had broken the ice with a clandestine journey to Beijing, kind courtesy the Pakistanis. Kissinger described this as a 'tacit alliance' between the US and China.

Nothing substantial happened with the US–China bilateral relationship for some years, as America remained involved in Vietnam till 1975. Both Mao Zedong and Zhou Enlai died in 1976, and Deng Xiaoping became the new paramount leader. In early 1979, after the US and China established diplomatic relations, Deng was on his way to America. On board, Deng remarked, 'As we look back, we find that all those countries that were with the United States have been rich whereas all of those against the United States have remained poor. We shall be with the United States.'[2] It was a clever remark, as it would have pleased his hosts in Washington and was in line with his own belief in reform and opening the economy.

Progress, however, was slow in the years of hope till 1989, when the Tiananmen Uprising in Beijing caused another slump in the US–China relationship. It revived thereafter, and China witnessed an overwhelming transformation as a result of its cooperative relationship with America. It would be an error to underestimate this.

Deng Xiaoping set China on an upward path with his 'Four Modernizations' – in agriculture, industry, science and technology, and defence. Deng saw virtue in capitalism for economic progress. He had to find his way gingerly to keep the Politburo purists at bay as he resorted to pragmatic communism where the state held political power but allowed economic decentralization. The 1980s featured gradual dismantling of heavy industry and a move to consumer-related industries with foreign trade and investment; state farms and communes disappeared and agriculture was privatized. This and a great many other steps marked the beginning of Deng's Great Transformation of China.

Deng's three goals were to double China's GDP by 1990 and double it again by 2000, with the intention of becoming a mid-level global power by 2050. This was a methodical approach to build Comprehensive National Power – the American concept of national power with Chinese characteristics – from the 1980s onwards. The reforms and opening up that Deng wanted had run into trouble with the hardliners. It was Deng who ordered the Tiananmen Square crackdown in June 1989.

There were political casualties to this and Deng, the de facto paramount leader, stepped back from the power centre and resigned as Chairman of the Central Military Commission in 1989. The reforms received a setback, the West reacted with the usual sanctions and irked the Chinese by awarding the Dalai Lama the Nobel Peace Prize in 1989. The last date for submission of nominations for the Nobel prize is midnight of 31 January of the year but Tiananmen Square incidents took place in June 1989; it is not known whether the nomination was received by the due date or it was the outcome of a rethink. This is not discrediting the prize or the recipient, but the timing was uncanny. It was an unmistakable message to China.

In early 1992, Deng returned from his retirement and went on a tour of southern China, ostensibly in a private capacity, as he held no official position. During his tour of Shanghai, Shenzhen and Guangzhou, Deng's homilies like 'be bolder, more quickly', were described by the media as nanxun jianghua, or speeches from the emperor's southern journey. Soon afterwards, Deng's remarks became a 7,000-word speech on the country's economy and what needed to be done.

The result was electric. Deng Zhifang, Deng Xiaoping's youngest son, soon struck multi-million dollar deals with the Hong Kong billionaire Li Ka-shing, while another 'princeling', Larry Yong, son of Vice President Rong Yiren, had acquired enough wealth in 1993 to buy Birch Grove, a 700-acre estate in England once owned by the late British Prime Minister Harold Macmillan. Nothing worked better in China than guanxi, a typically Chinese system of networks based on trust and a strong family connection with the powerful.[3] This was capitalism working overtime.

In the twenty years from 1990 to 2010, China made steady and silent progress. There was a continuity in the efforts of the leadership, following Deng's line, when they demonstrated a determination and vision to pursue a path to lay the foundations of a global power. It was this effort that enabled Xi Jinping to launch his policies of global initiatives like the Belt and Road Initiative and seek global hegemony for China, from Latin America though Africa to the Western Pacific.[4]

China Begins to Rise

The West needed economies of scale that only an autocratic China could offer through its centrally controlled real estate.[5] A democratic China would have been of little value to the US when one of the latter's main objectives was to reduce inflation. Since 1990, inflation in large part was under control, as the US increasingly imported volumes of finished goods across the value chain from China. This gave the Federal Reserve greater flexibility to reduce interest rates, increase lending to corporates and spur domestic growth.

Human rights advocates, and labour unions and representatives of American manufacturing industries already feeling the pressure of competition from Chinese imports, protested these concessions, but US Congress voted in favour of them. The impact was immediate. A joyous US corporate world saw its trans-Pacific commerce grow faster than ever before. Within weeks, companies like Caterpillar, Apple, Owens-Corning and Kentucky Fried Chicken all announced plans for major new investments in China.[6]

After the massacre at Tiananmen Square in June 1989, China's growth rate had fallen to 4.2 per cent, and then to 3.9 per cent in 1990. The future looked gloomy. Human rights and democracy in China were never an issue that troubled the Americans much, except when their economic interests were adversely affected. Otherwise, it could be business as usual. China, or particularly the CCP, was rescued by US President George H.W. Bush, backed by CEOs of powerful American corporations who revealed their huge economic trade interests in China. Bush made the customary lament about the use of excessive force by the PLA but urged that America must 'keep open relations with that very important country' and avoid alienating or isolating it.[7]

Post-Tiananmen, Bush declined to recall the US ambassador in Beijing, and instead persuaded the US Congress not to withdraw the Most Favoured Nation (MFN) status for China and sent his National Security Adviser Brent Scowcroft to assure Deng that the US would not break relations with China. This was not geopolitics at work but geo-economics, with vital US prospects at stake in China. China received the same consideration about its exports to the US market as were available to Britain, Japan, Germany, France and other allies.

Bush could not punish or reprimand China because corporate interests would not let him. Of China's total exports, share by foreign-owned companies rose from 10 per cent in 1990 to nearly 50 per cent in 1998, largely because numerous companies – largely American, European and Japanese – outsourced their production to China. Foreign direct investment, which was virtually non-existent in 1990, shot up to $20 billion in 1992 and doubled by 1995.[8]

Every corporate group wanted a share in the China dream, and they garbed their greed in convenient stories like trade would bring liberal ideas and democracy to China or that communism would not survive Deng. That was the narrative; short-sighted and dangerous, as it turned out. In these frenzied American investments in China, exports from China rose, and the US goods trade deficit with China stood at $295.4 billion in 2024, a 5.8 per cent increase from the previous year, according to data published by the US Trade Representative.[9]

The impact of globalization began to sink home in America as US companies cut 5 million jobs. Cheaper products came at significant domestic cost. China's trade surplus grew, and China accumulated about $1 trillion of US currency reserves.[10] The Americans helped the CCP, the owner of everything in China, become the richest political party in the world. A remarkable comment on the strategy employed by a country that wanted to stay the strongest power on earth forever.

'Hide Your Strength, Bide Your Time'

By the end of the twentieth century, China was already the third-largest economy, behind the US and Japan. Hopes that a capitalist China would inevitably become a democratic China had already begun to fade, leading to fears in the West about the implications of this explosion of wealth in an autocratic and still-communist China.

Globalization had taken root, and the West did not wish to miss out on the opportunity to help their own economies with cost-cutting practices through cheap labour offshore. China became rich and powerful economically and militarily but there were no signs of democracy, nor are there any signs of this happening in the future. There were apprehensions also of China becoming a powerful military power, but no one anticipated that in the first two decades of the twenty-first century, China would become a leading nation globally in state-of-the-art technology, ahead even of the US in some cases.

As anticipated, access to the markets, resources, technology, educational systems and managerial know-how of the advanced industrial nations of

Western Europe, North America and East Asia helped China grow richer more rapidly than would otherwise have been possible. Trade and societal interaction with China did not yield either the anticipated benefits of political liberalization or a move away from a state-led economy. Instead of a liberal and cooperative partner, China became an increasingly wealthy and powerful competitor who was repressive at home and aggressive abroad.[11] This was probably the fastest transformation ever recorded in history; ironically it was ill-advisedly given to an adversary for short-term gains based on long-term hopes.

The West had opened out to China eagerly, but Document Number 9 (Communiqué on the Current State of the Ideological Sphere), a political directive issued during the early years of Xi Jinping's presidency clearly showed that the CCP saw a liberal world order as inherently threatening to it. The Chinese military predicted endless conflicts over different ideologies, social systems and foreign policies with the US, which would make it impossible to fundamentally improve Sino–US relations. For decades the Chinese narrative has been that Washington 'was waging a deliberate well-orchestrated campaign – a smokeless World War III, in Deng Xiaoping's words – to weaken and finally subvert the CCP'.[12]

America's beliefs and policies in engaging China turned out to be largely mistaken. One hope was that China was a fragile power on the road to democracy, and wanted to be like the Americans but did not know how to get there. So, the Americans should engage with it and help it along this path. This partly reflected America's misplaced optimism and an overestimation of its own strength, but was also essentially a cynical use of the argument for engagement. In the American mind, hope had become synonymous with reality. China, on its part, never retreated from its territorial claims, or gave any indication that Chinese nationalism was a fringe belief. Its dream has always been to replace the US as the foremost global power, ruled by a strong leader. As Confucius said, 'There cannot be two suns in the sky.'[13]

No one paid attention to the fact that Mao read only one book repeatedly during the Long Marches in the 1930s, as did his followers, like Deng. It was an eleventh-century history of China, *Zizhi Tongjian* (*The General Mirror for the Aid of Government*). It includes sections on the use of deception, avoiding encirclement by opponents and how a rising power should induce complacency in the old hegemon until the right moment when it strikes.[14] That is what Deng advised when he gave the dictum, 'Hide your strength, bide your time.'

The West dismissed these goals of dominating the world as delusions of grandeur. They laughed off suggestions that Mao had been reluctant to play second fiddle to Stalin, something the Soviets understood early enough. US intelligence failed to read the signs and were misled by their own biases. This overestimation of one's own strengths and underestimating that of the adversary has been a common US failing and has led to situations where the adversary has shown far greater resilience than expected, and the US has been inadequate or ill-prepared.

While the West pursued a policy of engaging China, the Chinese suspected these efforts to be a clever Western conspiracy to weaken it. The West sought to expose Chinese people to liberal ideas, which the Chinese perceived as dangerous and which would release societal forces that would pressurise the CCP for political change. They viewed it as a Western containment policy through alliances and forward military bases, which aimed to prevent China from assuming its rightful place not only in Asia but in the world.[15] The Chinese firmly believe in the value of what is best described as 'the alignment of forces' or the 'propensity of things to happen'. They tried it with the Soviets and failed but succeeded with the US. They found a way 'to coax the United States into providing American technology, foreign investment, political support and access to America's domestic market for Chinese products – without tipping off the Americans to China's larger ambitions'.[16]

The Chinese were smart enough not to alert American intelligence to the dangers of strengthening China. Instead, they sought assistance from American conservatives to partner with them in opposing the Soviet Union. This happened openly during the Afghan War of the 1980s. In 1979, Deng Xiaoping had observed that the Soviet invasion was by no means an isolated case but a component of the global strategy of Soviet hegemonism. He even claimed that the Soviet Union was closer to the Indian Ocean than ever before and would be able to interfere with oil supplies to Japan and Europe. The Chinese supported the US-led diplomatic campaign in the UN against Soviet presence in Afghanistan.

The Chinese were soon secretly involved in the arming of the Afghan Mujahedeen, as their anti-Soviet policy began to pay rich dividends. National Security Adviser Zbigniew Brzeziński convinced President

Jimmy Carter to expand defence sales to China. The initial supply was thirty types of defence support equipment, which were licensed for export to China, expanded on 1 September 1980, to 400 items, ranging from transport aircraft, long-distance communication and military helicopters, among others, leading to an increase in Chinese conventional capabilities.[17]

Despite the White House Office of Science and Technology Policy raising red flags as early as 1987 in an official report discussing the transfer of technology to China, the US government pressed on. The report described China as a 'potential adversary with an alien ideology and unstable, unpredictable political system'. Technology was seen as potentially dual use, for industrial modernization and possibly to enhance military capabilities. It also noted that China preferred to import technology instead of equipment, a rationale particularly compelling for the military. However, at the same time, in the context of the Cold War with the Soviet Union, the report pointed out that many dual-use technologies were being transferred because any Chinese gain in defence capability would be of concern to the Soviets. The report was clearly myopic when it stated that 'China will not have the strategic strength for serious threats for several decades'. Technology transfers were seen as explicit 'bargaining chips' and tools for 'enhancing trade'.

Short-term economic benefits combined with poor geostrategy resulted in the US steadily transferring technology to China for the next three decades, a move which ultimately paved the way for a new Cold War.[18] The CCP that owns China, rather like how the Pakistan Army owns Pakistan, has never deviated from its central goal, which is to recast the international order with China at the centre. It hopes to achieve this without firing a shot – at least not against America. Instead, it seeks to erode resistance from within, by winning supporters in the enemy camp, silencing critics and subverting institutions.[19]

The American policy of engaging China clearly failed to achieve its objective of developing a democratic, liberal China, simply because the US and other Western policy makers never clearly understood the character of China's domestic political regime. The West overvalued its own systems and underestimated the resilience, resourcefulness and ruthlessness of the CCP; it also misjudged the strength of the CCP's resolve to retain domestic political power and failed to recognize the extent and seriousness of its international ambitions. China has now begun to pose an explicit challenge to the efficacy, moral authority and supposed universality of the principles of Western political systems.

Historically, expansion and imperial assertion were accompanied by rapid industrialization and economic growth – by Britain and France in the nineteenth century, followed by Germany and Japan as well as the US and the Soviet Union in the twentieth.[20] Ever since China began its reform in 1978, successive Chinese leaders focused on the task of modernization. As China progressed along this road, it became less constrained by the imperatives of development and more confident about what it was, where it came from and where it was headed. It eventually became less anxious about being accepted internationally and more at ease with being what it is.[21]

The Chinese, like the Russians and the Indians, watched the Americans occupy centre stage after the collapse of the Soviet Union. Post Cold War, the US felt it was free to take on smaller powers militarily for whatever reason, but essentially to assert its supremacy and discipline those it considered recalcitrant. So it was Iraq (1991), Bosnia (1995), Kosovo (1999), Afghanistan (2001–2021), Iraq again (2003–2011), Libya (2011) and Ukraine (2022 onwards), even as staunch ally Israel battled terrorist organizations, the Hamas and the Hezbollah. Seven wars with nothing to show for these tragedies.

Any realistic assessment would conclude that, given Chinese history and attitude, it would seek to dominate Asia first much in the same way the US dominated the Western hemisphere after World War II. It was not important how China reacted in the first decade of the twenty-first century. It had not acquired the capability to provoke the US to a war and hope to win. The global balance of power was in America's favour then, but by the beginning of the second decade, Chinese military, economic, political and technological capabilities had vastly improved.[22] The US is now in a position to be concerned about going to war with China – over Taiwan for instance – or militarily come to the assistance of another democracy – India, for another instance.

The problem with Western analyses or opinions in the case of China, Russia and possibly India too, is that these countries' views are not taken seriously if they are contrary to the Western ones. This might be a colonial hangover that equates modernity with 'Westernization'. Language, spoken or written, has much to do with this too. Till some years ago, the Chinese language had the most speakers in the world, followed by English and Hindi, but it is English that became universal across various international transactions, particularly in technology and in globalized culture.[23]

The West has viewed the world from a position of hubris – a conviction of the superiority of its own values and practices.[24] Consequently, it has evaluated events, situations and outcomes through heavily tinted glasses, rather than see them for what they are. Over time and with the success of China, the meanings of the words 'advanced', 'developed' or 'civilized' will cease to be synonymous with the West. The definitions of modernity and of good governance will be contested by China and possibly India. Historically, Chinese leaders have believed that a strong central authority is essential to good government and culturally, too, this was acceptable to the people. The urge to modernize and become liberals in the Western sense is perhaps not as strong as the West would like to believe. China, with its economic and military power, will not be ignored by other nations; they will deal with it, but many will also have concerns about Chinese behaviour and attitude.[25]

The other problem that the West has in their handling of international relations is their inability to see others, Chinese or Indians, as they see themselves. For instance, the developed West misses out on the rural life-systems of India and China, of resilience despite poverty, inequalities, shortages and uncertainties. Henry Kissinger once observed that the US and China each assumes 'its national values to be both unique and of a kind to which other people naturally aspire, and reconciling the two versions of exceptionalism is the deepest challenge of the Sino–American relationship'.[26]

After the global economic crisis of 2008, the Chinese felt that they had navigated it well, probably swayed by their own propaganda about their superiority. Then, the endless turmoil in the Middle East, the fallout of the Arab Spring and the economic turmoil of the Trumpian era left the US weakened. The China–US relationship changed, perhaps forever, as the American economy contracted and the Chinese economy, which had already been growing rapidly, surged at an astonishing speed. A new world order was taking shape, something that the West did not see or refused to see.[27] There was a new self-confidence as Xi Jinping ascended the throne; economic success meant political success and geopolitical alterations.

In a *Washington Post* article in October 2008, Henry Kissinger, along with George P. Shultz, was advising that the drift towards a confrontation with Russia must be ended. In January 2009, he was advising the new American president-elect Barack Obama how important it was that Sino–American relations be taken to a new level, as a new generation of leaders could shape relations for a common destiny, like in the case of trans-Atlantic relations after the end of World War II. The challenges were not military but political and economic. It was during Obama's presidency that Xi Jinping rose to power. Xi had other ideas, as did Trump who succeeded Obama.

China began to look beyond attaining merely regional primacy, with its long and proud past that had suffered from domination and humiliation by the West and Japan. It sought more than to just return to being the centre of Eastern civilization. The well-known Chinese view of their position in the world is that they are the centre of the region, surrounded by barbarians who must acknowledge the superiority of Chinese power and status, and that one day the Chinese will attain their rightful position. For China, a multilateral world is one in which there are only two powers – the US and China – with China as the paramount power in Asia.

Apart from America's historical security fixation with Czarist Russia, the Soviet Union and now Russia, it also fears fierce economic competition from China, the very country it helped grow, hoping it would democratize with wealth and help counter the then Soviet Union. The US succeeded in helping China grow but failed to get it on its side. It was a classic case of a failure of imagination and policy. Today, US policy seems to want to get ahead of China economically, so they want to move supply chains out of China, but European demand has begun to shrink and with NATO activity in Ukraine, the long-term economic prospects for Europe look bleak. This aspect of market demand is not available with countries like India seeking to indigenize as much as possible, so it would be only America that can import Chinese goods at higher prices.

However, China's economy itself seems to be in trouble now. There were indications in 2022 that China might be fudging its GDP figures, as it decided to hide many economic indicators. In October 2022, the

Chinese government decided to delay indefinitely the publication of main indicators, including its gross domestic product. Obviously, the high rate of growth had slid to a more modest figure – a case of burnout and over-capacity.[28] China has mastered the art of concealing the state of its economy and its growth figures for years, and anybody who questions official economic figures faces consequences.[29] In 2024, the economist Zhu Hengpeng, who worked for an influential government think tank, reportedly 'disappeared' or was not seen in public since making disparaging remarks about the economy and Xi Jinping in April that year on WeChat.[30]

The property sector in China crashed beginning 2021, when the China Evergrande Group, the world's most heavily indebted property developer, filed for protection under Chapter 15 of the US Bankruptcy Code to protect its US assets. Other companies in China have also begun to discontinue construction before completion. The real estate market continued its decline even in 2024; the sales were down across the country and millions of homes that had been paid for but were not delivered [31] and ASEAN markets had become cautious.

The main problem seems to be an inability to pay building costs, a problem shared by property developers in the country. An 18 August 2023 report in *Nikkei* said: 'The problem is dampening consumers' willingness to buy homes and aggravating sluggish home sales. Now that China's population has begun to decrease, many experts forecast that a long-term recovery in demand for homes is unlikely. Chinese property developers are successively releasing huge red-ink results. Country Garden Holdings, the biggest private developer in China, said it may have fallen into a net loss of 45 billion to 55 billion yuan in the January–June period of 2023.'[32] An estimated 233 home developers in China filed for bankruptcy in 2023 according to the China Real Estate Association. The highest number of applications came from Zhejiang province, followed by Hunan and Guangdong provinces.[33]

In 2022, Xi Jinping had admonished his party leaders for insisting on construction activity financed by borrowed capital and scaling up investments (already at a high of 44 per cent of GDP). The CCP remains wary of allowing individuals to decide where to invest thereby weakening central control. That being so, Xi has pushed for greater state intervention to make China an even bigger industrial power, strong in state-run or favoured projects like semiconductors and artificial intelligence. This alone will not help create enough jobs for the millions of college graduates entering the work force. This is a circular problem that India has too; if there are not enough jobs then there is less money to spend. And unless there is more money to spend the industry cannot grow fast enough. With supply lines being altered and challenged, domestic consumption is a major factor for overall growth.

In 2023 there was more dismal news about China drowning in debt with millions of apartments unoccupied, underused bridges, stalled highways and empty airports. Economists believe that China's economy is slowing down at a time of adverse demographics and worsening relations with the US and its allies. This has hurt foreign investment and trade. Meanwhile, the government spent millions of dollars to construct new Covid-19 quarantine mega-facilities to put money in the market and stimulate demand. It is not just economic weakness, it could be the 'dimming of a long era', according to the *Wall Street Journal*.[34] This massive overcapacity in the industrial sector was created with borrowed money, and if the present trend of shifting supply chains out of China gathers momentum, then the factories and manufacturing companies will have to close down, with money to the banks unpaid.

Prime Enemies

In the present context, Michael Pillsbury's prediction in his 2015 book, *The Hundred-Year Marathon*, that by 2050 Chinese values will replace American values, seems a little dire. 'It is time to start imagining that world. By 2050, China's economy will be much larger than America's – perhaps three times larger, according to some projections – and the world could then be a unipolar one, with China as the global leader. Other scenarios project China and the United States as dual superpowers, and still others predict a tripolar world of China, India and the United States. A factor common to all these scenarios is that China will be the most economically dominant nation. The US dollar will no longer be the leading currency . . .'[35] Perhaps a bit premature currently, as one sees a massive global economic and political churn, with militaries involved in battles for supremacy, and the decline of many European powers and the US as well.

China's goal has been to project power globally, and especially in Asia. Its deep dependency on West Asian energy resources will increase steadily over time, which in turn would bring it into a serious security competition with the US. China would want to restrict the US as far as possible to the Western hemisphere, also to safeguard its major economic and political interests in Africa. The Chinese pushback against Western interests in Africa has been quite remarkable. Namibia, Eritrea and Tanzania received enhanced allocations by 457 per cent, 359 per cent and 347 per cent during a time when twenty-seven other countries (Russia included) did not receive anything.[36]

The US is not dependent on the Persian Gulf for its energy resources but wishes to control it. The sea lanes between the Persian Gulf and the South China Sea remain important for China. The pipeline and railroad supply of oil and gas via Myanmar and Pakistan is inadequate, so China would like to secure the sea lanes from the South China Sea into the Indian Ocean. A Chinese naval presence in the Indian Ocean region is inevitable.

A great deal would depend on how the China–US battle of economies works out. If China is somehow able to sustain its rapid economic growth, which at the moment looks unlikely, and the US is able to recover its economic power, which also looks unlikely, the future of who remains a superpower is also indeterminate. It was easy to predict in 2014 that China would eventually become a superpower with power projection capabilities necessary to compete with the US across the globe. It does not suit China to get into a conflict, nor would the US want to enter a direct clash with it, but the Chinese could create trouble in Africa against Western interests and in Latin America or even in north America through Canada and Mexico.[37] Pakistan will remain China's cat's paw against India.

The year 2025 was the Year of the Snake in China and was supposed to bring with it wisdom, transformation, calmness and creativity, something that would give its leaders hope in their tariff battles with President Trump. American efforts to decouple from China, disengage after forty years of economic entanglements, which the US defines as building resilient supply chains, is seen by the Chinese as another means to try and contain China. These measures will become stringent with time with the powerful American military–industrial complex continuing to sell the China threat theory. Chinese scholars and commentators are convinced that the US will try to prevent China from becoming the world's supreme economic power and the US–China mistrust will lead to deglobalization. The American China Competition Act 2.0 is aimed at strengthening export controls and curbing investment to cut off China's access to sophisticated technology. Similarly, the American Creating Helpful Initiatives to Produce Semiconductors (CHIPS) and Science Act allocated $52 billion for boosting innovation and competitiveness in the semiconductor market.

Image Building

The 2008 Summer Olympics in Beijing ended in August that year and the Chinese leadership was basking in the sunshine of a rising China. In an unrelated development, the fourth-largest investment bank in the US, Lehman Brothers, went bankrupt triggering a global financial crisis in September. This did not deter a group of Chinese executives from the State Administration of Radio, Film and Television from landing in Los Angeles for a crash course on the functioning of Hollywood.

Apparently hardly anyone noticed that the Chinese were quietly learning the ropes of narrative-building and image creation as they began laying the foundations to become a credible rival to the US. They needed their voice to be heard, in their way, the world over. They had obviously studied the impact and reach of Hollywood as the embodiment of virtues of American culture and were seeking to apply these to Chinese culture. The mandate of these students was to learn how the American film industry had achieved its status as a leader in global culture – and how China could recreate that achievement back home.

Inside the UCLA classroom of film professor Robert Rosen, a galaxy of Hollywood executives from Universal Pictures, Metro-Goldwyn-Mayer and the William Morris Endeavor agency conducted a series of lectures on how America's entertainment industry functioned and was managed. They delivered lectures on financial management, lobbying and advertising, along with other intricacies.

This kind of a move would have been unthinkable decades earlier when China had not recovered from the imagery of the Cultural Revolution and the Tiananmen Square massacre, yet the fact that here they were, in the heart of capitalism and free speech, indicated a new level of self-confidence and aspirations. Earlier on, in 1997, Hollywood became alert to Chinese redlines on Tibet and the Dalai Lama. By 2008 China was ascendant, but unnoticed by many Americans, and within a decade after the first meeting between the Chinese and representatives of Hollywood, the roles were reversed. The Chinese were in control, and Hollywood had begun to become dependent on Chinese money and understanding.

Soon Chinese stars were being given roles, even as Americans and Paramount rushed to edit scenes from a 2013 film, *World War Z*, which 'implied a zombie outbreak had occurred in China', fearing Chinese anger and retaliation.[38] Most filmgoers did not know that 'studios were removing scenes and dialogue from scripts and finished movies to appease Chinese censors – scrubbing any production of plot points that brushed up against sensitive Chinese history or made the country look anything less than a modern, sophisticated world power'.[39] The fear of angering Chinese officials also resulted in some films not getting made. Hollywood had become the willing commercial arm of a politically ascendant China that wished to rewrite the global order in the twenty-first century.

In a manner of speaking, Beijing had considerably suborned America's most powerful medium of spreading its cultural superiority. This experience also became an example for other industries to follow. Circumspection became the rule, almost like paying homage to the Middle Kingdom. The route to global power does not lie solely via the military, economic or technology routes; it lies through the ability to build narratives and create perceptions. American Hollywood had helped its country's emerging rival blossom into an even greater threat.

Crisis as Opportunity

The collapse of Lehman Brothers sent the world financial system into a tailspin and shook the established capitalist system. The Chinese saw this economic crisis as both a challenge and an opportunity. Their greatest expectation perhaps was that it would hasten the decline of US power. The danger was that there could be tension arising from disagreements over trade imbalances and exchange rates. China therefore needed to stand up for itself without getting involved in disputes because of the American tendency to let nationalism and differences in 'ideology, philosophy and values influence (in) handling trade issues'.[40] Chinese policy had in the past been to avoid matching its strength to America's in the international economic order and to continue to conceal its strength for a more appropriate time. This was early in the second decade of this century. The Chinese knew that although the Americans were dependent on them for managing the global economy, they had not abandoned their 'two-faced policies' against them, where they would try to guard against, contain and even hold back China. This was also the time when the ambitious Xi Jinping was readying the ground for his eventual paramountcy.

The global churn – economic, political, military and technological – that is currently underway adds to uncertainties. China's rise and the US's relatively reduced ability to have things its way reflect a changing equation.

The tariff war unleashed by President Trump at the beginning of his second term in 2025 was widely considered to be aimed at curbing China, correct trade imbalances and penalize it for stealing American technology and manufacturing capabilities that, according to Trump, caused unemployment in the US. Xi Jinping, unimpressed by the US escalation on tariff rates on Chinese goods up to 245 per cent, responded by raising tariff rates on American goods by 125 per cent.[41] It is unlikely that these rates will finally prevail but a tariff war was launched. China shifted its import of soybeans to Brazil from the US. It also announced that its airlines will not accept any further delivery of Boeing aircraft. The European luxury goods industry was shaken by revelations that the price differential between the manufacturing cost and the price charged by luxury goods was enormous.

The US is one of the biggest trading partners of China and, according to data from Beijing's customs authorities, Chinese exports to the US exceeded $500 billion, accounting for 16.4 per cent of the country's total exports in 2024. This may sound huge, but China's GDP was more than $18 trillion, therefore the tariffs are unlikely to affect China to the magnitude expected by many. China imports $143.5 billion worth of goods from the US, with much of that trade centred around agricultural products – particularly oilseeds and grains – according to the US Trade Representative's office.[42]

The total Chinese exports in 2024 were valued at about $3.5 trillion. As long as these are safe, the effect of American restrictions on China will be limited. However, as some commentators argue, ultimately it is the size of the economy that matters and the US holds the upper hand. Others assert that the Chinese would be forced to come to the negotiating table because their economy is dependent on exports to the US and the West and they are dealing with a man who will not get coerced.

The Chinese government has also made use of their nation's near monopoly as source of supply of rare earths, some of them critical for the manufacture of products ranging from missiles to wind turbines to electric vehicles, by announcing a ban on their export. China holds 90 per cent of global refining capacity at 44 million metric tonnes with the US a bare 2.3 million tonnes. No wonder the Americans are looking for rare earths in Ukraine and Greenland and had earlier in 2025 lifted decades-old sanctions on India's state-owned Indian Rare Earths Ltd. After the recent visit of Prime Minister Modi to the US, the two leaders announced US–India Strategic Mineral Recovery programme.[43]

Some consider Trump a master strategist and insist that he has caught China on the backfoot. Trump's tariff war against China has not really taken off in its full fury following Chinese threat to raise tariff rates as well. However, the argument that Scott Bessent, the US Treasury secretary, gave, that 'We export one-fifth to them of what they export to us, so that is a losing hand for them,' is flawed. Since China exports far more to the US than the US does to China that becomes a leverage with the Chinese – not a weakness.

Once these products become much more expensive on American shelves because of the tariffs – or disappear from the shelves altogether, Americans will suffer. More than half the smartphones sold in America are iPhones and 80 per cent of those are made in China. Americans will complain loudly if they more than double in price. Phones and computer equipment are the most obvious candidates for a Trump climbdown. Further, about 80 per cent of the world's air conditioners are made in China; as are three-quarters of the electric fans that America imports. Of course these can be made in America but it will take time and will be expensive.[44]

There are other several American critics of Trump's tariff policy. Notable among them are three American professors – Jeffrey Sachs, John Mearsheimer and Richard Wolff. It is doubtful if Trump is in any mood to listen to them. Perhaps, according to both Trump and Xi

Jinping, trade wars are the best way to win a bloodless war. The fate of the underprivileged is not of any consequence to the elite and the powerful. One of the results has been that US allies are being encouraged to loosen or break their security alliance with the US. If that happens, in the long run, dependence on defence purchases from American companies will also decline.

A bipartisan US congressional poll in April 2025 showed support for a bill to place a legislative 'check' on presidential tariff orders. The legislation, co-sponsored by Senators Maria Cantwell, a Democrat from Washington, and Chuck Grassley, a Republican from Iowa, proposes that presidents who want to institute new tariffs be required to issue a statement justifying such an action, after which Congress would have two months to decide whether or not to overturn the new tariffs.[45] Certainly Democrats and a few Republicans are understood to be in favour of this. This is clearly a case of closing the stable door after the horse has bolted.

Another aspect of the China–US turf war was highlighted recently by the Republican right-wing quarterly, the *National Interest*, which has been associated with Nixon and Kissinger in the past. It pointed out that the US economy had lost as much $600 billion annually on intellectual property because of Chinese espionage.[46] By December 2024, Chinese state-sponsored hacks had breached the US Treasury Department's systems, after which they had access to the Committee on Foreign Investment in the United States. Another Chinese state-sponsored group had hacked into US critical infrastructure networks and aimed at disrupting communications during a crisis. The Chinese were executing a well-laid-out campaign to develop China's own capabilities while undermining American economic strengths. These acts have a heavy cost for American business and will become costlier unless the Americans evolve a system to shield US businesses and secure their leadership in global innovation.[47]

China had initially grown by producing cheap state-subsidized goods produced by a workforce that did not have fair working conditions. China used its neighbouring countries in Southeast Asia to dump cheap consumer goods, which has hurt domestic manufacturing industry in these countries. China also exploited geopolitical and security crises and periods of global financial uncertainty to advance its interests. The Asian financial crisis of 1997 exposed the weaknesses in emerging economies, and Thailand, Indonesia and South Korea saw large-scale devaluation of their currencies as the quick exit of speculative money wreaked havoc on their economies. China, with its tight regulatory set-up that limited exposure to external shocks, emerged stronger from it, and its exports grew steadily. Domestic demand also rose as GDP growth remained between 7 and 10 per cent. China did not have to devalue its currency despite the financial crisis in the region.

The message to the developed world was clear – China provided stability at a time of turmoil. The 1998 Tokyo G7 Summit explicitly recognized[48] the international responsibility that China shouldered. A closed, centralized system run by an authoritarian regime was perceived in Western capitals to provide value at a time when the world needed it the most. As demand for labour export to emerging economies increased, countries with open financial systems and limited domestic demand were considered risky places for investment. China had successfully sold its economic model to the West. Four years later, in 2001, China was admitted into the WTO. As China opened its financial system gradually, it insisted on strict controls that foreign investors had to adhere to.

By the time the global financial crisis came in 2008, China had reaped the benefits of joining the WTO, disrupting established free-market rules and undercutting global competition. While the US was preoccupied with its War on Terror in Iraq and Afghanistan, China increased its trade and the size of its economy by subverting the free market. Between 2001 and 2008, the country's economy grew threefold, reaching $4.6 trillion. From being 13 per cent the size of the US economy at the turn of the century, it had reached 31 per cent in eight years.

Reckless American lending and speculation had created the great financial bubble of 2008. When the bubble burst, it sent shockwaves through the globe. As Washington deployed financial tools to shore up the economy, China with a manufacturing- and export-driven economy, took a knock from the slowdown in the US economy but responded with a stimulus programme of its own, aimed at boosting infrastructure. China's GDP grew rapidly even as the American recovery was slow. The gap between the two economies began to shrink rapidly.

In 2009, Fred Bergsten from the US National Security Council put forward the idea of dividing the world into two spheres of influence – the Chinese and the American – in what he termed 'Group of Two', or

'G2'.⁴⁹ The concept was predicated on the idea that China and the US were the two most consequential countries in the world. This was seen as necessary to find a stable working relationship that addressed regional and international issues, ranging from trade to climate change.

China envisioned a more formalized G2 dialogue to claim shared global power with the US. Leading US think tanks like the Center for Strategic and International Studies elaborated on the value of a G2 summit of sorts on the sidelines of the 2009 G20.⁵⁰ A weakened America was less capable and interested in managing the risks posed by a rising, authoritarian China that refused to follow international laws and free-market rules. An emboldened Beijing was able to have its comprehensive national power grow to the point that it materially challenged the unipolarity enjoyed by Washington.

It was during Donald Trump's first presidency that the US woke up to the reality of China breathing down its neck. Washington claimed that China's theft of technology intellectual property, aggressive state subsidies and an artificially depressed currency left it with no other option to but to demand fairer terms of trade. Trump wanted China to open its markets to US products. Xi agreed to open some segments in exchange for a formal recognition of his BRI. But the economic fallout of the trade war fell disproportionately on the US. The agricultural industry struggled, as did manufacturing and logistics. American consumers continued to purchase Chinese goods at higher prices because of a lack of alternatives. As a result of this, the economic gap between the two countries narrowed further.

In October 2022, at the end of the Twentieth Party Congress, Xi Jinping, re-elected for a third term, exhibited to the world, in a carefully choreographed televised event, his power and ruthless control when he had his predecessor bundled out from the front benches. Xi Jinping as China's paramount leader with complete unfettered command, expected to push Chinese ambitions towards world hegemony much faster. Once attained, this would affect the West the most.

There is a cautionary tale here, though. Mao too attained total control of the party at the Ninth Party Congress in 1969. The Politburo and its Standing Committee was filled with Mao loyalists, but in the absence of a defined line of succession, aspirants fought brutal battles among themselves, and soon after his death in 1976, Mao's legacy was in tatters.

It was left to Deng Xiaoping to manage succession when he chose Jiang Zemin and then Hu Jintao as successors. Both were cautious technocrats who pursued reform and opening as laid down in Deng's playbook.

The Chinese frequently talk of 2049, the hundredth anniversary of their independence, as the year when everything will come together for China's global ascendance. Xi may not be around then, but a continuity of policy for goals determined long ago will make the task easier. Xi may have won the top spot and fortified his position, but he will need to carefully draw a line of succession to determine whether he will leave a legacy of continuity or of chaos.

The 2008 US National Intelligence Council report, 'Global Trends 2025: A Transformed World' predicted, 'By 2025, the United States will find itself as one of a number of important actors on the world stage albeit still the most powerful one.'[51] Martin Jacques, author of *When China Rules the World*, added that the US would have to accept the emergence of a new multipolarity and may have to share power with China and India, but only a minority inside the Washington Beltway recognized the impending change.

Cut to the beginning of the Covid-19 pandemic in December 2019. Beijing reacted harshly to serious concerns from the international community over the origins and mishandling of the infection. China's coercive and confrontational method was termed 'wolf warrior diplomacy', with the involved officials making controversial, often unparliamentary, statements in public, targeting individuals and countries across the world. The aim was to deflect blame, engage in whataboutism and openly discuss power differentials with partners and foes alike. While the aggressive stance became more evident post-Covid, it was another assertion of a muscular, nationalist communications policy under Xi Jinping.[52]

Trump, in his first presidential term, called out China's trade malpractices – and Xi in particular – as bad faith actors. While Trump had pushed the boundaries of common diplomatic protocol with allies and adversaries, Xi saw it imperative to 'correct' his country's image, both at home and abroad. China's diplomats and media outlets seemed to try and outcompete one another in the sharpness of their attacks. At one point in 2020, Chinese state media outlet, *Global Times*, stated, '[Australia is] always there, making trouble. It is a bit like chewing gum stuck to the sole of China's shoes. Sometimes you have to find a stone to rub it off.'

This was in response to Canberra asking a tough question on the origins of Covid-19. As an aside, Australia is deeply dependent on exporting natural resources to China.

Chinese diplomats in Germany derided the German auto industry, suggesting that China could replace it within years. This was in response to Berlin cracking down on Huawei products, which were known to be part of Beijing's global electronics surveillance architecture. In another incident that sparked media outrage, the Chinese ambassador to France was quoted as saying that the Taiwanese population would be re-educated.[53] The term 're-education' had been known until then in the context of China's incarceration of millions of Uyghurs, a move that had received the harshest of criticisms from the global community. The success of wolf warrior diplomacy was largely muted. If anything, it was counterproductive. Beijing partially course-corrected but the damage to China's reputation had already been inflicted.

China's Position in the World

The US may have reasons to fear China's rise, and the Thucydides trap – the inevitability of a conflict between an established power and a rising one. For other Western countries, anti-China rhetoric was based on years of indoctrination by their own governments through the patronage of the media, think tanks, China experts and agencies. China is now ahead in the developing world where about 62 per cent of people view China favourably in comparison to the US. Of the 4.5 billion people living in areas supported by China's BRI, two-thirds hold positive views about China as compared to about just a quarter in non-participating countries.[54] Meanwhile, Chinese standing in Muslim countries has improved in recent years and the Organisation of Islamic Cooperation (OIC) commended China for its treatment of Muslims. Whether this was the result of deep pockets or genuine conviction is immaterial, as a pro-Chinese perception has been created. The Muslim world is willing to adjust to Chinese predilections. The US narrative now sits well only in the West; elsewhere, it is counterproductive, as such narratives are seen to have been created to justify hostile action against China and as a weaponization of human rights issues.

A shift in attitudes began in 2017 with Trump's trade war in his first term and the anti-China tirade that emanated from the US; by

2018, a new-age McCarthyism began with America's Attorney General Jeff Sessions and FBI Director Christopher Wray leading a campaign against anyone of Chinese origin and prosecuting perceived Chinese spies. Possibly the provocation was the new Chinese laws promulgated between 2014 and 2017. One of them, National Intelligence Law (NIL) adopted on 27 June 2017, was enough to send alarm bells ringing. Any country that is aware of it cannot afford to allow Chinese companies in its critical infrastructure. Article 7 of the Law is explicit about what the Chinese government expects from its citizens: All Chinese organizations and citizens shall support, assist and cooperate with national intelligence efforts in accordance with law, and shall protect national intelligence work secrets they are aware of. The obvious interpretation is that all Chinese companies and individuals are bound by law to support China's intelligence activity.

In the first decade of the twenty-first century, there was a firm belief among many American China watchers that China was in a dangerous corner, and that China's challenges would be from within China.[55] This was the Hu Jintao era. But by 2012, Xi Jinping had begun to change the atmospherics, which would be noticeable in many ways by the end of the decade. It was also thought that preventing war with China would be America's biggest foreign policy challenge.[56] Two years after assuming charge, President Xi had reeled out his new security concept in 2014 – the comprehensive national security which was to be managed through the Central National Security Commission. It was tempting to assume that this was like the US National Security Council, but the Chinese version was essentially meant to deal with domestic security issues – trouble in Xinjiang or Tibet, and then Covid-19. The definition of its role was wide and covered almost every issue: political, economic, activity over ground or beneath the high seas, from space, cyber, nuclear and biological to homeland security.

The scope clearly showed the mindset of a totalitarian ruler, where the greater the imagined fear, the greater the recourse to countermeasures, beginning with an ever-tightening ring of security procedures and penalties, and harsh punishment for violations, real or imagined. Xi had introduced the all-powerful National Security Law in June 2017 as the culmination of a series of security laws meant to strengthen the legal basis for the CCP's security activities, with enterprises and organizations made to cooperate. Xi was re-elected in March 2018 with even more stringent security provisions in place. Chinese surveillance capacities were enhanced rapidly, along with harsh repression in Xinjiang and Hong Kong – two places where the Chinese feared the most Western interest. By the end of 2021, party leaders were expressing fears of a global churn against which they did not have adequate safeguards. The danger they perceived was not just internal but also external.

It is possible this was one of the aspects that spurred Xi to deliver his April 2022 lecture to world leaders and corporate executives at the annual Biao Forum for Asia in Hainan province. Xi proposed a Global Security Initiative (GSI) to 'promote common security of the world'.[57] The significance of Xi's speech was lost in the din of the Ukraine War. Clearly, Xi's intent was to challenge US-led alliances and replace them with systems that would be more compatible with Chinese security interests. The GSI was intended to provide an external dimension to Chinese internal security concepts. The Chinese were seeking a reform of the global security architecture because they thought that the US-led system was destabilizing and pursued group security only for its own at the expense of those who were not members of their exclusivist clubs. The second issue the Chinese pressed for was that there should be new ways to handle non-traditional security threats; they were in effect seeking greater Chinese involvement in policing and security activity globally.

The rise of China is sure to threaten Western universalism – values and institutions, currency and language. The notion of a Western civilization ruling the world will change. For the first time in a few hundred years, the West will be forced to engage with other cultures (or culture) on an equal basis. The world will no longer be Western, but its centre will lie elsewhere – in Asia. Possibly unable to deal with this new phenomenon, the West will begin to fragment. Many European countries have been pursuing a greater interaction with China and are bound to China via their sovereign debt. It is unlikely this process will happen peacefully and without any resistance from the West.

The Defence Planning Guidance document, which sought to protect US interests globally, was first issued in 1992, drafted by the neocons of the Bush era. Rather than collective action through the United Nations, including on nuclear matters, it recommended US-led collective action. The paper dwelt at length on Russia and the former Warsaw Pact countries, but the rest of Asia apart from the Middle East did not figure very prominently. However, by the first two decades of the twenty-first century, power had diffused after several failed ventures in the Middle East, and US hegemony was increasingly under threat from aggressive (China), reckless (Saudi Arabia, North Korea, Turkey) and ambitious (India) states. This hegemony had to be restored or reaffirmed for the good of the world because only a liberal democratic hegemon can best shape evolving trends in its favour and that of the free world. This move by the US to reinvest in protecting its military, economic and technology status was also the best hope to limit dangers emanating from Chinese ambitions for Taiwan.

A China–US competition would certainly dominate the global scene in the years ahead, and a powerful US willing to be a hegemon was best suited for the globe; it was a far more effective way than retreating into isolation or opting for multipolarity. China was certain to play a big role in international affairs and the long meetings President Xi had with President Biden in November 2022 at the G20 summit in Bali is a clear indication that Xi was talking to Biden as an equal. The November 2023 summit in San Francisco also left the same impression.

The Next Few Decades

After twenty years of relentless pursuit of terrorist threats, the CIA opened a new China Mission Center (CMC) in October 2021. William Burns, the CIA director, announcing this in a statement, 'CMC will further strengthen our collective work on the most important geopolitical threat we face in the twenty-first century, an increasingly adversarial Chinese government.'[58] China was described as a sophisticated global threat to American interests and had to be handled with priority in all spheres.

The next few years were dominated by US–China rivalries and the US hoped that it would be able to sustain hegemony in comparison to alternatives like isolationism, multipolarity or emerging security arrangements. This was to be achieved with America's unique assets, such as alliances that added to its capabilities abroad. This enabled it to further its own interests, and its institutional dominance allowed it to decide outcomes, ideational attractiveness of political values, national culture and global engagement. America's massive military capabilities always enabled it to enforce its will.

Some of these qualities are clearly exaggerated. While the US has immense power to destroy, it has significantly less ability to restore what it destroyed. America is the self-proclaimed beacon of liberal democracy and upholder of the values of global free trade that benefit not only it but also its trading partners, also the one who can take care of its own physical security and that of its partners. This aspect of being a beacon of liberal democracy is a fervent appeal for status quo as China rises, which is seen as the main danger in the years ahead. In the December 2022 edition of *The Atlantic* magazine, George Packer, author of *The Assassins' Gate*, argued that the United States is the only country that can and must lead the world.[59] Prior to this, there were frequent comments by American experts on China such as David Shambaugh (in 2016) that unless there was political reform in China, its economic progress would stall, even stagnate, although it might not collapse. Shambaugh said this in an interview with *Wall Street Journal*'s Andrew Browne.[60]

The Chinese economy may have slowed down – it is impossible to sprint for too long, and it happened in the context of a post-Covid global slowdown. It is also true that its political apparatus has become even more authoritarian with complete concentration of political power in the hands of one man – Xi Jinping. This marks a watershed moment in China's contemporary history and the beginning of a new phase.[61]

There is also the argument that to make China behave better and to respond to Beijing's increasingly assertiveness, the US must impose limited conduct-based sanctions, which could make China alter its behaviour at an acceptable cost to it. There is also caution that unlike sanctions on Iran and Russia, sanctions on China run the risk of political and economic retaliation. Therefore, they would have to be calibrated, which does not leave much scope for very stern sanctions.[62] At the same time, China also faces major challenges – an aging population, stress on the pension system, real estate crisis, loss of confidence from foreign investors due to political uncertainty, realignment of supply chains away from China – and the impact of these on an export-dependent economy. This economic stress will have a bearing on the political and social situation, which an authoritarian system will not be able to handle except by force.

For over thirty years, the US kept its inflation under control by offshoring the production of goods to China. Decoupling from China today would be an expensive process. Geopolitical compulsions to remain a global hegemon led the US to take the economically painful decision to reduce dependence on China and diversify supply chains into more stable regions. Countries like India, Vietnam and Indonesia seek to replace China in some export domains but have been unable to develop the economies of scale that China has built. The alternative to China has not always been a competitive one. The ultimate cost is borne by the American consumer in the form of structurally higher baseline inflation. The cascading effect of this will be felt by the global economy for years, in what the World Bank suggested in 2023 could be a lost decade ahead as the manufacturing in China is sought to be reduced but alternative manufacturing capabilities are not in position.[63] This is what Trump is trying to effect with his tariff policy.

More than the US, it is Europe that will struggle to decouple from China. The Ukraine War and the loss of Russian piped gas have caused significant economic troubles and deindustrialization in Europe. Inflation, demographic aging, rising social security contributions, growing defence spending and shrinking tax revenues have pushed Europe into terminal decline. In this environment, dependence on cheap Chinese goods has grown. China aims to supplant the region's automotive industry by flooding countries with state-subsidized, low-cost electric vehicles. Importantly, China controls a vast majority of the world's critical metals and minerals used in batteries. Meanwhile, as European consumers become increasingly price-sensitive, the EU is finding it difficult to prevent further deindustrialization triggered by Chinese dumping. Given that 7 per cent of all European jobs are in some way related to the automotive industry, the effect on the economy is set to be significant.

While the US and much of the Western world may face economic headwinds because of a concerted geopolitical pivot away from China, Xi's great gambit of challenging the US as the dominant global power may unravel unfavourably. Structural weaknesses in the Chinese economy have also crept up quickly. The country has hit a demographic wall. The working-age population is shrinking. Much of the infrastructure boom that generated economic growth over the last two decades was financed by a healthy trade surplus. As supply chains move out, Beijing's policymakers will have to tighten their belts. While China still seeks investments in its economy, a surge in hostility towards foreign investors has only accentuated the risks of running manufacturing operations in China. Muscular control over supply chains is largely a function of China's own hubris. But this could change over the next decade should India get its act together.

An aging population tends to save for the future than spend on mass consumption. A consistent one-child policy has meant that a generation of Chinese lack siblings to share the social and financial responsibility of aging parents. Entrepreneurship and risk-taking in general become casualties in such a situation, as does kick-starting a new consumption cycle. The average Chinese is now parking savings in long-term bank deposits to secure their future. The People's Bank of China has tried on multiple occasions in 2023 to disincentivize this behaviour by cutting interest rates on these deposits. However, consumption has not risen much in response. This points at a balance sheet recession similar to what Japan experienced in the 1990s, as its population aged and total fertility rate dropped. Inevitably, economic stagnation is the result.[64]

The CCP faces twin crises of lethargic domestic consumption and declining exports, likely to put pressure on an authoritarian regime that delivered rapid economic growth in exchange for public support for a one-party system. Xi is growing intolerant to any written or other media content that could be perceived as critical of his emperor-like stature. In late 2023, a historical biography of the Ming dynasty's last ruler, Chongzhen, was withdrawn from bookstores and the internet. The account described how Chonghzen centralized and misused power, eliminated opposition figures and mishandled the kingdom, ultimately leading to his suicide in the Forbidden City surrounded by a public in revolt. Apparently, the book cover had the following text: 'The diligent ruler of a failed dynasty, Chongzhen's repeated mistakes were the result of his own ineptitude. His "diligent" efforts hastened the nation's destruction.' A blurb on the cover asked the reader to 'read about how, misstep by misstep, the Chongzhen Emperor brought about his own demise.'[65]

The CCP is using technology for surveillance and propaganda to counter growing discontent and simultaneously spending heavily on AI R&D to create new artificial 'workers' to make up for a shrinking workforce in the future. Both objectives can be attained only if Beijing gets access to or develops its own high-end chips. Export controls by the US are aimed at countering both Chinese technology authoritarianism and economic competitiveness.

The Biden administration's National Security Strategy paper, released in October 2022, described China as the only competitor with an intent to reshape the world order that had the diplomatic, military, economic and technological capability of doing so. After decades of policy that sought to help China integrate into the US-led international order and which failed to lead Beijing to an open market–oriented system, the Americans have begun to find ways of limiting China's rise and constrain its international behaviour. This by itself will be a cause for conflict. One of the reasons for China's economic success has been that the party and its successive leadership retained the 'One China' policy with nuances. There could be more pressure on Taiwan coming from a confident Xi Jinping who has total control on the levers of power in his country. He can be expected to make economic, political and even military moves to influence Taiwan.[66]

While hardliners may want aggression against China, all the annual war games conducted by American think tanks over the past few years have shown the US losing to the PLA in simulated battles over Taiwan and the South China Sea. In a similar war game conducted by the Center for Strategic and International Studies, US intervention in Taiwan ended with considerable losses in ships, aircraft and personnel in fighting Chinese forces to a standstill.[67] Even though war game simulations have rarely gone right, they do provide an overall perspective.

Taiwan as the Hotspot

It appeared bizarre that during the Ukraine crisis, in August 2022, the US would send Speaker Nancy Pelosi for an otherwise pointless visit to Taiwan unless it was a deliberate attempt to provoke the Chinese. Quite obviously, the US felt it had to show that it could wage a two-front war, and the world would be impressed. Ultimately after considerable heavy breathing by the Chinese, nothing transpired. By October, think tanks like the Carnegie Endowment were actively discussing the possibility of China invading Taiwan by 2027, a date ostensibly given by Xi Jinping.[68] China made more than the expected noises and military mobilization; the theatrics showed that modern-day leaders are prepared to put the world at risk for domestic political compulsions. It suited US President Biden to show himself as tough and willing to open a second front in the name of freedom and liberty, and it suited President Xi to appear similarly tough ahead of the CCP's Twentieth Party Congress. Backed by strong anti-China sentiment on Capitol Hill, Biden erased the ambiguity over US policy to defend Taiwan, announced a sale of $1.1 billion worth of weapons to Taiwan and a proposal for another $10 billion. Obviously, this would provoke China.

After years of sluggish US arms sales to Taiwan, prospects became brighter in 2022 when the Senate passed a defence authorization bill which approved $10 billion in military aid, but where sales would be under the Foreign Military Financing programme meant for sovereign countries, with the US government as the principal financier.[69] The political signalling was not lost on Beijing, which responded with appropriate dissatisfaction. While the initial tranche of $80 million in weapons may seem small, especially in relation to the hundreds of billions spent in Ukraine, it opens another avenue to speedily support Taiwan when needed. A $14 billion backlog of Taiwanese arms deliveries (outside of the $10 billion in military aid) must be cleared, and this means that the military–industrial complex would be pleased.[70]

Europe's dependence on China and its alliance with the US have made France and Germany cautious in their dealings with Taiwan. Macron stated in 2023 that France should refrain from getting entangled in the US–China rivalry. President Macron seeks to position France as a more balanced power as it navigates carefully the complexities of its relations with China.[71]

By omitting references to Taiwan in a public press statement in Beijing during Macron's visit to China in April 2023, France was indicating that it was taking a line different from the US, suggested foreign policy observers. Later upon return to France, Macron went on to say that he wanted the 'status quo' on Taiwan to be preserved while in the same breath stating that France was an ally of the US, and not a 'vassal'.[72] In June 2003, Germany's Chancellor Olaf Scholz said he had 'warned China on using force against Taiwan'.[73] But with the rise of right-wing politics against the backdrop of a worsening economic conditions and and a migration crisis,

European governments may seek to position themselves differently in the years ahead. China is likely to seek greater influence over these political parties, some of which seek a lot more independence from centralized EU policymaking.

Potentially the most steadfast ally of the US in dealing with the Chinese threat to Taiwan is Japan. Tokyo is spending a record amount on its defence as it seeks to grow its capabilities.[74] As China, Russia and North Korea begin to work more closely, Japan's threat perception of a broader conflict has grown. Higher military budgets are coming at a cost, economic growth has slowed and an aging demographic dampens prospects. Consequently, social spending is likely to make way for higher defence spending.

India needs the West for its economic growth and Taiwan for specific technology; it also needs peace on its borders with China. India's increased tilt Westwards and the Indian tri-services chiefs' visit to Taiwan might have raised concerns in China. At this stage the situation remains delicately poised – India needs to maintain border vigil and any move towards Taiwan could well translate into conflict on India's borders. If such a thing were to happen, would the US intervene? *Should* it intervene, possibly enlarging the conflict? It is doubtful if a larger conflict is in any country's interest. India would have to be prepared to handle any sudden policy reversals, as Trump is prone to do, although so far he does not seem to favour a prolonged hot war.

Roll Back or Drums of War

In the first instance, the goals of a new strategy must be defensive. Having tried and failed to transform China by drawing it into an inclusive and globe-spanning liberal international order, the democracies must once again band together to strengthen and protect the core of what American planners described in 1950 as a 'successfully functioning political and economic system in the free world'. In other words, a 'rules-based world order'. It would be delusional for the US to presume that removing Xi Jinping, to enable a more comforting arrangement, would be easy.

In practical terms, this means that in the future, the US and its partners must mobilize their societies for a protracted rivalry with China and harden themselves against CCP's influence operations of the kind that they have successfully carried out in Hollywood and even Bollywood (for instance, the success of movies like Aamir Khan's *Dangal* dubbed in Chinese makes China a money-spinner for Bollywood). They must also partially disengage their economies from China's while strengthening ties among themselves. They must intensify military preparations and diplomatic measures to deter coercion or aggression. Finally, they must actively challenge Beijing's ideological narratives, both in the developing world and, to the extent possible, inside China itself.[75]

Deterrence and defence also mean reducing collective economic reliance on China, both as a market and as a source of supplies. Since complete decoupling from China is neither feasible nor desirable, it would be better to distance American and Taiwanese economies from China. Several moves should take place simultaneously or in a synchronized manner. America's allies in Europe and East Asia should fall in line and Taiwan's biggest trading partner should not be Xi Jinping's China. Considering that the US and NATO have not fared too well in Ukraine, there may be reluctance in Europe to follow the do-as-I-say model of the US.

The goal should be to avoid war, needless provocation, not make Taiwan's independence a key issue and reassure China on the 'One China' policy. From the American point of view, the China–US–Taiwan triangle is more about managing a situation rather than solving a problem; and it's about avoiding unilateral action. This leaves many confused about American goals and how they will be achieved. This may be US policy but what if China does decide to take unilateral action in the years ahead?

There are four non-military aspects of US policy in dealing with China: mobilization, counterbalancing, partial disengagement and discursive struggle or the struggle of narratives. The leadership of democratic countries must be mobilized to speak more openly about the nature of the Chinese regime and the threats it poses to their way of life. This has begun to happen and there is a change in attitudes and opinions, but the free world is still uncomfortable about speaking to China bluntly. China cannot be contained nor should it be by the US; the goal should be to sufficiently deter China and raise the cost of coercion quickly. Given the existing economic, financial and trade arrangements, the US cannot completely decouple its economy from China. Instead, the economic relationship has to be restructured through imposing restrictions on Chinese companies' activities in the US, especially the high-tech companies. America sources many if its material requirements from China. The Covid epidemic was an eye-opener for the US as it did not even have the capacity to manufacture masks.

In Xi Jinping's leadership team, 'globalists' have been replaced with Xi loyalists and nationalists who are able to take unpopular decisions at a time when the US and China are in 'a trade war, a technology war, a geopolitical influence war, a capital/economic war, and . . . are now dangerously close to a military war'.[76] Xi spoke of a 'dangerous storm' in his opening speech at the Twentieth Party Congress in October 2022. Perhaps it is this, along with other commentariat emerging from US think tanks to discuss possibilities of war, that has led the American corporate sector to also express concern. Billionaire investor Ray Dalio remarked that the US and China were dangerously close to going to war and Xi's remarks at the Party Congress were scary and paralysed activity.[77] Others like investor Kyle Bass have also warned that Xi's statement at the Party Congress should be taken seriously, and in the event of an attack on Taiwan, the semiconductor business would immediately be in a high-risk area where fighting might take place.[78]

The rise of China and the decline of the US at the same time has led to apprehensions that this tension might spill over one day. Speculative dates when this might happen vary.[79] There was also an intelligence assessment about the state of Chinese capabilities by 2027 to 2034.[80] The former arises from a deadline attributed to Xi Jinping, and the latter from a chilling novel, *2034: A Novel About the Next World War* (2021) where the authors describe how a naval battle with China unleashes the next world war. It might be a cautionary tale but there are many who fear that war with China is a scary possibility that can come to pass. The two authors, ex-Marine and novelist, Elliot Ackerman, and former NATO commander, Admiral James Stavridis, said that they feared that the war would most probably start in the South China Sea, of which the contentious Taiwan Straits are a part. They predicted that this might happen at a time when the Chinese Navy becomes the largest navy in the world even as the Americans fight their wars in Iraq, Syria and Afghanistan. Iran remained a flashpoint in the region, and this was another advantage for the Chinese.[81] In 2022, Henry Kissinger commented to the *Wall Street Journal* that the US is 'at the edge of war with Russia and China on issues which we partly created, without any concept of how this is going to end or what it's supposed to lead to'.[82]

China's need for unrestricted access to the Pacific despite the ambitious BRI that seeks access to continental Europe through China's Eurasian links, is seen a destabilizng factor by the West, notably the US, mostly because the BRI seeks to replace Western overlordship. China's amazing growth in the last two decades has been helped by access to the Pacific for its exports, and the US has been the biggest market; going forward, China would need this and access to adjacent waters. This brings China into conflict with US strategic interests in the western Pacific; China sees itself restricted by Japan, Taiwan, the Philippines and Indonesia, and to a certain extent by India, Australia and Vietnam. China wants a breakthrough while the US seeks status quo. The opening of the resource-rich Arctic will change big power priorities; a joint Russian–Chinese navigation vessel is already a-sailing. It is unlikely that China will go to war with the US on this but might resort to salami-slicing its areas of influence in the region.

The battle for supremacy will spread into the Indian Ocean, through which a million ships pass each year carrying trade and energy. The future will be about energy supplies to India, China and Japan, along with the western Pacific and Southeast Asia. The India–China competition will be more on sea than on land, and the Chinese will keep India diverted to land battles across an undemarcated land boundary as it strengthens its naval presence. Zhao Nanqi, a former director of the general staff logistics department of the Chinese Navy, once remarked, 'We can no longer accept the Indian Ocean as an ocean only of the Indians.'[83] It is important to remember that globalization was dependent on shipping containers and the Indian Ocean accounted for half of the world's container traffic.

The Indian Ocean rimland from the Middle East to the Pacific accounts for about 70 per cent of global traffic of petroleum products for the entire world. This figure may have altered since 2010 but only slightly. It is estimated that by 2030, the world's energy needs will rise by 50 per cent and half of this will be in India and China.[84] The competition will become fierce. One is not sure if China will ever go for a conventional war with India; their preference would be to win without fighting, through cyber and telecommunications attacks. The last war the Chinese Army fought, and in which it did not do too well, was in 1979 when China took on its former ally, Vietnam. The Indian Armed Forces have fought more wars successfully and one could infer that Indian troops are better equipped to handle hot conflict.

Aware of the results of US-led sanctions on Russia following the outbreak of war in Ukraine, China has been buying gold. This has fundamentally altered the global precious metals landscape, positioning China as a central player in reshaping monetary power dynamics. 'Since 2022, the People's Bank of China has reportedly acquired 280 tons of gold per quarter through covert methods, leveraging London-based transactions and sovereign wealth fund vehicles to obscure its true reserves. Industry analysts estimate China's actual holdings exceed 5,065 tons as of late 2024, rapidly closing the gap with the United States' official 8,133 tons reserves.'[85] It is speculated that China might have bought a substantial amount of gold from Russia (estimated to be about 300 tons). These are the highest purchases of gold by any country since the 1960s. Apparently China is shoring itself for the future and helping Russia along the way.

Once China attains meaningful presence in the western Pacific, countries of Southeast Asia will quietly acquiesce to the new power. The US is just too far-off and hot wars will be disastrous. Besides, the US and Chinese economies are closely interlinked. Weapons like sanctions and restrictions are double-edged swords. For the US to try and hurt the very economy on which it relies for markets, resources and manufacture, would hurt its own economy too. Depending upon how strong the US Navy remains in the area, China would fix its sights on the Indian Ocean and Taiwan. The Quad – the grouping of India, Australia, Japan and the US to counter Chinese influence in the Indian Ocean – does not have a military component and it is unlikely that it would be an effective means to stall China. India would prefer to deal with this bilaterally, unless more nations with interests in the Indian Ocean region, which is the route for energy and other trade both ways, join in.

The near hysteria generated in the US about China is worrying, given US proclivities to start wars for less-than-convincing reasons and then find itself unable to end them. The US position on Taiwan has always been one of strategic ambiguity, where the Americans are obliged to help Taiwan defend itself but not go to war to defend it militarily. Taiwan is an existential issue of legitimacy for the CCP and since Mao's time, the party is committed to its reunification with mainland China. On various issues like trade, Xinjiang, Hong Kong, Tibet and the Line of Actual Control with India, China seems to be happy dealing in the short term – event by event, with its own long-term perspective. But about reclaiming Taiwan, the Chinese will act one day, decisively. American ambiguity will not deter them.

It is difficult to predict very accurately what the world might look like halfway through this century as Chinese leaders have set 2049 – the centenary of the founding of PRC – as the year when they will attain their appointed place on the globe as the 'super hegemon'. Whether this happens in a way that leaves China as the undisputed global leader is still debatable, but a few aspects of Chinese power should be quite apparent. Given the rate at which the Chinese economy has grown, it is possible that it will be considerably larger than the American economy. A counterview that places caveats on this prediction, articulated by author and fund manager Ruchir Sharma in a 2022 article in the *Financial Times*, argues that China will not overtake the US by 2060, if ever.[86] The world will be unipolar, and the pole will be Chinese, some insist.

Western prognostications in the media, by think tanks and strategic commentators or the Pentagon about their adversaries tend to be maximalist. They fear the worst for their adversaries' economies and fear the most from their military prowess. Consequently, when China is described as failing or rising at a fantastic speed, it is prudent to look for alternative, non-Western sources to understand the real situation.

Water Hegemony

Apart from geopolitical factors, there are other issues of concern. There is an enormous difference in the scale of China's industrial revolution and the one that began in the West in the nineteenth century. Naturally the former's potential success is larger and quicker, and in that lies the problem of potential damage. China is a water-shortage country with 55 per cent of its groundwater unfit for drinking. Add to this the industrial waste that is dumped in water bodies. China's massive economy with all its adverse health and climatic effects will continue to seek fossil fuels, toxic chemicals, unsafe antibiotics, pesticides and hormones for rapid agricultural and livestock growth.[87]

Yet China seeks to establish a kind of water hegemony and its river map explains its centrality as the upper riparian to other nations in mainland Asia. After 1949, Chinese communists acquired control over Xinjiang and annexed the Tibetan plateau. This was largely because of its own subterfuge and India's inability to understand the implications of surrendering Tibet without a strategic quid pro quo. Consequently, China today sits on the source of the world's largest repository of fresh water after the Arctic and Antarctica. Asia's ten main rivers, fed by thousands of Himalayan and Tibetan glaciers and mountain springs, provide the water that flows down into South Asia, the Indian subcontinent, Central Asia, and Russia. In addition, numerous lakes on the Tibetan plateau store about 608 billion cubic metres of fresh water, according to the Chinese Ministry of Water Resources.[88]

China controls the headwaters of more than a dozen major rivers and about half of the global population depends on the water supply from these rivers. Yet China does not consider it necessary to discuss the concept of water sharing or cooperation with downstream countries. It does not have a single water-sharing treaty with any riparian country on its borders. Disputes with all its neighbours do not seem to have led to any change in its behaviour. China also voted against a new international water law – the 1997 United Nations Convention, which laid down rules on the shared resources of international water courses.

China has built one dam per day since 1949 (when it had only 22 dams) and by 2014 had far outpaced the US which has 5,500 large dams, with 90,000 dams with reservoirs and those with run of the water for power generation. Chinese leaders from the days of Mao paid great attention to this, although most dams were built after Mao. There were huge human losses in 1975 (estimated 83,000 killed) when some of the dams in Henan collapsed; epidemics followed, and the total fatality was 230,000. There were other human costs too. About 22.9 million Chinese were relocated to allow dam construction.[89] All this was kept under wraps by a totalitarian regime. China formed large hydropower equipment companies and exported dam construction to other nations. Its company, SinoHydro, eclipsed major Western companies like ABB, Alstom General Electric and Simmons, and began taking on projects by offering low-interest loans to countries while not being too bothered about environmental or humanitarian concerns.[90]

China is a water-starved country, and it seeks to make good the shortage by accessing all the rivers that flow through it on their way to Southeast Asia and India. It observes no international or bilateral responsibility as the upper riparian. It has dammed the Mekong to the extent that the river has virtually dried up. China has refused to give hydrological data about the Brahmaputra, on which it proposes construct a dam. There have also been schemes to divert the Tibetan rivers to the arid north.

Technology by Stealth

It is no secret that China's phenomenal growth was aided by its large-scale theft of foreign science and technology. Its national industrial policy goals encourage intellectual property rights even as China is the world's largest perpetrator of intellectual property theft. Allowed by the WTO to get away unchecked with these transgressions over decades, it is possible that by 2050, China, backed by others in the Shanghai Cooperation Organisation, will become the global rule-maker on this front, although there are indications that other countries are pushing back in the telecommunications, AI and cyber sectors. The Chinese attitude to international agreements has been cavalier to the point of being irresponsible. China is not a member of the thirty-five-country Missile Technology Control Regime (MTCR) but pledged to abide by it. Despite this, it has supplied forbidden items related to missile technology to nations like Pakistan and North Korea, or given design information to Pakistan and earlier to Libya.

Three unrelated activities seem to have given the Chinese an opportunity to think their chance had come. China exhibited its ability to destroy satellites in 2007. Soon after came the global economic crisis of 2008, and the Russian intervention in Georgia the same year where the US and its NATO allies looked on helplessly. These were interpreted as a decline in Western abilities. Chinese policy-makers concluded that it was the time of *Xi* (best described as 'the alignment of forces' or 'propensity of things to happen'). The time and need to keep a low profile were over. The Chinese scuttled the Copenhagen Climate Conference in 2009, when Prime Minister Wen Jiabao snubbed officials by refusing to attend the negotiation meeting, instead working at separate agreements with some countries. In effect, the conference had been torpedoed, a clear indication of how China might behave once it assumes near-supremacy.

A December 2021 paper by the American Rice University's Baker Institute makes for interesting reading. The title of the paper, 'US–China Competition Enters the Decade of Maximum Danger: Policy Ideas to Avoid Losing the 2020s' is self-explanatory.[91] It begins by saying that America and its allies faced a decade of danger with Xi Jinping now in charge of all aspects of governance and control in the country at a time when it would experience the 'S-curved slowdown' common to great powers. This was even before Xi got himself elected for an unprecedented third term. Having achieved a phenomenal rise in the last two decades, China had begun to exercise coercion in the region but should attain its peak comprehensive national power between 2030 and 2035.

The paper suggests that by about 2025, Chinese leaders would conclude that its worsening demographic profile, growing structural economic problems and technological isolation from centres of innovation across the globe, would erode its leverage vis-à-vis Taiwan. Faced with these challenges and internal disturbances all over the country, Xi could become risk-embracing.

The paper says that his two-decade rule has given enough indications, with his harsh repression in Xinjiang, coercion in Hong Kong, grabbing of Bhutanese territory and provoking India in Ladakh, apart from forays into the South China Sea and sabre-rattling across the Taiwan Straits. For China, the biggest prize would be Taiwan. The paper argues that unless deterred, Xi Jinping could well be tempted to leave his mark on history, and it is necessary for the US to maximize capacity to deter Chinese aggression in the current decade.

The exclusive and secretive Western power elite group belonging to the Trilateral Commission[92] met in Japan in November 2022. This time three reporters from *Nikkei Asia* were invited to the discussions, which had in the past been held in camera. The Asia–Pacific countries were worried that unless China was engaged, its neighbouring countries would be forced to choose sides and they could choose China. In Washington, however, the idea of engaging Beijing by inviting it to the WTO is now considered mistaken. Biden's National Security Strategy paper, as mentioned before, said that China would simply exploit the opportunity without meeting US expectations. The US has begun to tighten arrangements with China by imposing restrictions to prevent it from having access to advanced computing chips and chip-making equipment. The Indian delegate also spoke of keeping China engaged while a South Korean academic remarked India could no longer continue to be on the sidelines of international institutions. 'Otherwise, India will be the next China. Imposing their own values on the rest of the world.'[93] The inclusion of an Indian representative at the Trilateral's inner core discussions was a message to India to join the camp to isolate China.

Meanwhile, Chinese strategists had suddenly brought out centuries-old maps to justify their claims that China had historical links with islands in the East and South China Sea. The South China Sea became a flashpoint with the US, with China asserting ownership of the Spratly Islands, as Chinese strategists continued to discuss the implications of an American decline, but how much or where the decline might be was not answered.

According to a 2011 study by the US National Defence University, *The Paradox of Power: Sino–American Strategic Restraint in an Age of Vulnerability* by David C. Gompert and Phillip C. Saunders, the US–China military balance had shifted in favour of the Chinese. The Chinese did not accept that the study only reflected a personal assessment but insisted China's moment of *xi* had arrived. More important, the ambitious and aggressive Xi Jinping took over control of the CCP in 2012 to begin what has now become autocratic rule with complete control vested in one person. Even with Xi's aggressiveness, China's basic tenets of diplomatic strategy remain. These would be to induce complacency so as not alert the enemy, manipulate the enemy's advisers, be patient for decades or even more if necessary, steal your opponent's ideas and technology, recognize that an existing hegemon will take extreme even reckless action to preserve its hegemony, develop and employ yardsticks to measure challenge, be vigilant to avoid being encircled and, finally, never ever forget the power of *Xi*.

Democracies have the richness of debate and discussion unlike opinion in autocratic China, which is only a top-down phenomenon. This diversity of opinion has its drawbacks, and arguments and counterarguments are endless. In July 2019, *Washington Post* published a letter to President Trump written by four China-watchers and endorsed by a host of well-known American foreign policy experts, businessmen, military experts and academicians. The thrust of the letter was that despite irresponsible and troubling behaviour, China was not an enemy of the United States. It was neither an economic enemy nor an existential security threat to be confronted at every opportunity. American efforts to treat it as an enemy and decouple it from the global economy would be counterproductive for America. The letter mentions that China was becoming militarily stronger, but confrontations would not help; that China's goal was to weaken Western democratic norms, but it was not 'seeking to overturn vital economic and other components of the international order from which China itself had benefited for decades'.[94] The authors did not mention that the US had also benefited immensely from the same order and there was continued American corporate interest in dealing with China commercially. Interestingly, as a footnote, *Washington Post* also cited links to alternative opinion describing China as a threat and saying that compromise with it would be futile.

There has been considerable anguish in the US about decoupling with China. It has been considered the brainchild of a few disgruntled hawks, but few Americans in power saw that China had begun decoupling itself much earlier. In fact, China never allowed any foreign company a free run in China; it had to have a Chinese partner to whom technology would be transferred. Foreign executives, like those from GE and Intel, were told very clearly that if they wanted to sell in China they had to produce in China. Long before China joined the WTO that the West had graciously offered it, the Chinese started tightening surveillance on the internet and built the 'Great Firewall of China' between itself and the world. Google, Amazon and Facebook had no role or presence in China. This was decoupling, Chinese style. A WTO membership did nothing; if at all, the Great Firewall became greater as China's technology and economy became stronger.[95]

A realization of Xi Jinping's plan for the 'Great Rejuvenation of the Chinese People' would mean a high degree of self-sufficiency or even exclusivity of critical industrial, scientific and conceptual areas.[96] Labour Economist Clyde Prestowitz explains that the CCP is not really a communist party but a Leninist party whose primary purpose is to hold absolute power, leaving no room for human rights, religion and law. The basic condition of any Leninist party is to be at war permanently: against internal dissidence and against any external institution or country that has the power to prevent it from attaining is goals. These wars may not be hot wars but indicative of a state of permanent hostile mistrust.[97] China's main adversary has controlled its own neighbourhood to ensure that neither of its immediate neighbours, Canada or Mexico, are a threat to it while oceans protect it on both its flanks. In contrast, China is in a permanent state of conflict or at best a non-war status with its numerous neighbours on its long land frontiers. This state may also be a result of geography.

America needs to recognize and accept the degree of challenge posed by a rising China. It will have to change its 'structures, coordination and alliances to meet whatever comes'.[98] America cannot count on China facing daunting tasks and suffering like the Soviet Union did. The world, America included, is not aware of the full dimensions of the Chinese challenge.

An instance of the power of the Chinese can be gauged from American responses to Chinese anger or even unhappiness. In 2021, American papers carried a story about Daryl Morey, the general manager of the basketball team, Houston Rockets. He had to withdraw his tweet, 'Right for Freedom, stand with Hong Kong', as the National Basketball Association feared its lucrative business in China would be damaged by this tweet. Apple's CEO happily deleted the company's app that was being used in Hong Kong by protestors to track the police, simply on a mild suggestion from the Chinese. Google deleted from its Play Store a game called 'The Revolution of Our Times' which dealt with the Hong Kong protests.[99] Giants like Mercedes-Benz, Delta Airlines, the Gap, Marriott and others became similarly circumspect about their product lines, staff behaviour and commercial messaging to align them with the CCP line.

The main declared act, in the drama, according to the US, is free speech, rule of law and democracy pitted against authoritarianism, and this conflict is reflected through competition in trade, globalization and IT practices, technology theft, investment and, of course, the military. Instead of China becoming liberal with economic progress, as the US anticipated, it has become more authoritarian and more centralized; liberalism is not in China's DNA. Corporate America thinks of China as a source of inexpensive products, but not as an entity that threatens the American way of life.

There is another aspect that is often overlooked. Most of the so-called Chinese manufacturing has been by foreign companies based in China, and Chinese technological progress has relied on collaboration with American companies. In both these, there is apparently some impatience and disillusionment with the Chinese way of working. China's growth is based on heavy infrastructure, property development and urbanization. All three will face a decline in the current decade. Also, the working-age population will decline. Meanwhile under Xi, China will continue to be increasingly centralized and under stricter autocratic control.

There is a growing consensus in Washington which favours a move to treat China as an adversary. According to it, the US must challenge and confront China across issues, isolate China on technology and follow policies to retain American pre-eminence. What the backers of this kind of thinking do not realize is that a war over Taiwan, for instance, will not be restricted to Taiwan; it will spread. The Pentagon brass would continue to testify that China was arming to attack Taiwan while intelligence assessment would be that China has no such intention.[100] Capabilities do not necessarily translate into execution, but the storyline remains that the attack could come anytime in the next five years.

The CCP sees the US as a dangerous and permanent foe that stands in the way of China acquiring its rightful place on the globe. The US therefore must be constantly watched, not necessarily to try and destroy it, but to surround it with the help of allies and to keep it distracted and weakened. A mixture of hubris, exceptionalism, feigned paranoia and collective greed has created the present situation where the US, with all its might, has not been successful militarily in most of the wars it began or supported. On the other side is similar hubris about China's own importance, of being the centre of the world, surrounded by barbarians. Both the US and China feel they are ordained for hegemony. In the process they follow no rules or only those that suit them, and show few signs of behaving as a responsible power even towards their own citizens. In their greed they have jeopardized sustainable growth and together have contributed to climate disasters.

Xi's China Dream may have soured a bit already with a slowing economy, rising cost of living, growing unemployment and graduate unemployment burgeoning to 20 per cent. Salaries have been cut, bonuses paid have been recovered and foreign investors have begun pulling out.

To add to Xi's worries, there is restlessness within the political set up, with the Jiang Zemin faction resentful of Xi's autocracy and his forcing the introduction of new laws – to resolutely safeguard the CCP and Xi Jinping.[101] There were fears of a purge of Jiang's supporters and this did happen, when the defence minister and a few generals went missing in December 2023.

China is unlikely to take on the US Navy in the Pacific despite being perhaps the strongest navy in the region. No dictator can take on an adversary, lose and hope to survive. Chinese action in the South China Sea and the Pacific will have ripples in the Indian Ocean region, which transports 70 per cent of global trade on its waters. Any disruption in this region is something that China cannot accept or survive. The US knows of only one weapon – sanctions – but as has been apparent in the Ukraine case, these sanctions work both ways. Huge Western financial tie-ups with China would preclude any major financial restriction on China. A Chinese loss of face must be avoided by the Chinese leadership.

Chinese Manoeuvres

Chinese strategy would be to continue to push diplomatically against the Americans and try its military tactics against neighbours to assert superiority. Generally, the attempt with the latter would be to force them to make concessions. Repeated statements by Xi Jinping and aggressive actions do suggest that the China Dream of 2049 is a very real one. For India, the attempt will be to demand that the Dalai Lama be sequestered, insist on naming his successor, or force India, the EU and the US to stop aiding Tibetan exiles. It will continue aggression on the Line of Actual Control with India, push America on Taiwan and become more strident about its territorial claims in the neighbourhood, particularly where valuable natural resources are involved. Over time and with rising power, China will become increasingly bellicose. Sooner or later, there will be a call to the ramparts.

Despite domestic setbacks, China has continued to move into spaces that its leadership assesses the US has vacated. On his visit to Saudi Arabia in 2022, Xi Jinping was received personally by the king. There is now a strong mutuality of interests between the Saudi and Chinese governments. The Americans, in their short-sightedness or arrogance, have pushed the Saudis and the Chinese together as they did with the Russians after 1991. The West Atlanticist alliance of which NATO and EU were a great part relied mostly on controlling issues like energy scarcity. These were handled by Western corporate giants backed by Western, chiefly US, military power.

Consumption of energy was payable only in dollars. Deviations or attempts to do so were punished by the West, as in Iraq and Libya. It was thus a zero-sum game, which states in the Persian Gulf have begun to realize is not helping them. China has deftly manoeuvred its relations with both Iran and Saudi Arabia, something which the Americans have not been able to do until recently with talks with Iranians and the Saudis on nuclear energy issues. With China being a huge and assured buyer of energy, it can use this hunger for oil and gas as an attractive market for Iran and lately Saudi Arabia. The Saudis can push back on US pressure because US arms companies need the attractive Saudi market for its products. Saudi Arabia under Salman bin Abdulaziz Al Saud is more forward-looking and seems to look at a world beyond fossil fuels. Recent events in the Middle East, including Saudi peace talks with Iran and Saudi Arabia's liberalization moves, would have changed Chinese priorities for the present.

There is clearly a movement away from the Atlantic set-up towards a Eurasian arrangement comprising Russia and China. Xi's three-day visit in December 2022 culminated with the first-ever China–Arab summit, described by the Chinese foreign office as an epochal milestone in China–Arab relations. The two nations signed deals worth $30 billion, coming on the back of several other vital agreements.

Prior to Xi's visit to Saudi Arabia in 2016, in their policy report issued in January that year, the Chinese declared that it was their intention to cooperate with all Arab states across the board on all development issues for mutual benefit and potential. This was wide-ranging, covering international production capacity cooperation and enhancing cooperation in infrastructure, trade, nuclear power, space, new energy, agriculture and finance. While Xi was ushering the BRI, the Saudi government led by the young Salman bin Abdulaziz Al Saud introduced his Vision 2030, which was a new foreign policy agenda, looked beyond a post-oil age and spoke of peaceful development, like the Chinese. Apparently, both had read the writing on the wall and had begun to prepare for a post-US phase. The Chinese began to build a 2.6 GW solar power station in Saudi Arabia of the kind they had built in the UAE. In 2016, China and Saudi Arabia signed a memorandum of understanding (MoU) to build fourth-generation gas-cooled reactors. Saudi–China trade surpassed Saudi–US trade in 2021.[102]

Some Saudi–Chinese trade payments are now likely to be in yuan, as like the Russia–China and Russia–India payments in roubles, which will undermine the dollar to some extent. The Chinese sit with a base in Djibouti at the mouth of the Red Sea and another in Gwadar overlooking the entrance to the Persian Gulf. It now seems that there is some forward movement in the Saudi–Pakistan deal to construct a $12 billion ARAMCO oil refinery in Gwadar. This deal could adversely affect Iran–China oil supplies, but as an emerging up-power China will have to juggle its relations with Iran and Saudi Arabia. The Americans will, as expected, respond to all these moves of reducing production and raising prices by OPEC by threatening to cease arms supply for a year and other harsh consequences, and vowing never to leave the fields of Arabia for the Chinese, Russians or Iranians.[103]

The Saudis may not be impressed by this, considering that their supply of crude oil to Asia accounts for 77 per cent of their exports as against 7 per cent to the US and 10 per cent to Europe, as per the US Energy Information Administration. Even so, it is unlikely that the US, with its massive military deployment in the Arabian peninsula under the Central Command, will make room for new competitors easily. Instability can be expected. Away from the Middle East, China has begun to secure itself further. The Russia–China gas pipeline reaches the Yangtze Delta from the Horgos Port in northwest Xinjiang and is the gateway for the China–Europe Highway. The Chinese have established ground space stations in many Latin American countries, from Venezuela to Patagonia in Argentina.

Between the time China was admitted to the WTO in 2001 to the end of 2022 its economy grew phenomenally. According to former Singapore Foreign Minister George Yeo, 'China's economy grew seven times in PPP terms, nine times in RMB and 11 times in USD. China was getting too big to hide even if it wanted to. In fact, China's GDP in PPP overtook the US a few years ago, around 2016.'[104] It was this golden period when China was winning without fighting and the US was fighting without winning. This was not just about theatres of war or territory; it was about economic growth, political influence and quality of life.[105]

Xi Jinping's government announced in 2015 that the Chinese goal was to become, by 2025, self-sufficient in all high-tech industries and that China had no intention of playing by America-led free trade rules. China was aiming to become not only the world's biggest, most advanced and most powerful country, but would revert to being the new imperial centre which in true Chinese tradition would have neighbouring vassal states paying tribute to the ruler – the Son of Heaven – who had authority over the rest of the world. 'In a word, China was "Ba" or great hegemon.'[106] It is this China that the present hegemon, the US, will have to face and try to counter in the years ahead.

While it is certain that the foreseeable future will be defined by US–China relations, it would be highly desirable that US and China are in a mutually beneficial global race that leads to stability and greater well-being – but it is likelier that the US–China collision course will lead to endless chaos. With the present situation in Europe extremely unstable, there are question marks about whether Europe can rebuild itself without external assistance.

Will the world see only more histrionics or will our leaders and their advisers lead us to the very real danger of pyrotechnics ending in mushroom clouds and then, shunya? Or will there be three statesmen and long-term thinkers at the same time who will look at Russia, China and India as one contiguous land mass and the consequent advantages for the world if they were to align? Even if a new world order takes shape, there cannot be one without the US playing a substantial role in it.

8

Clash of Civilizations

Islam is a revolutionary doctrine and program that overturns governments. It seeks to overturn the whole universal social order . . . it is not satisfied by a piece of land but demands the whole planet . . . Islamic Jihad is at the same time offensive and defensive . . . The Islamic party does not hesitate to utilise the means of war to implement its goal.'

– SAYYID ABUL A'LA MAUDUDI, *Jihad in Islam*, 1939

All empires that ruled over the present-day Middle East, from the time of the Babylonian Empire to the Ottoman Empire, had Jerusalem as their prized city, even though it had no strategic value. It is associated with the rise of three Abrahamic religions – Judaism, Christianity and Islam. The 3,000 years of history of the region have witnessed extreme faith, slaughter, fanaticism and, occasionally, peaceful coexistence. It has been a battlefield between three clashing civilizations. Western civilization became synonymous with Christian civilization with a geographical boundary that was mostly Europe, including Russia, by about the fourth century CE, while the Arab civilization became synonymous with Muslim civilization. Christianity spread to other continents along with imperial conquests of the globe after the unsuccessful Crusades.

Both Islam and Christianity originated in the same region about 700 years apart. Both have subsects and sometimes the differences between them are acute and violent. While the Christian faith has had reformations, the Muslim faith allows for no revision because it considers the Quran to be immutable. Judaism, Christianity and Islam, like all other religions, speak of peace and brotherhood. Although initially Jews, Christians and Muslims continued to live together in Jerusalem under Islamic rule in relative harmony, they fell out when the Jews refused to accept Mohammad as their prophet.

Fast forward to the British Mandate of Palestine, which Britain acquired in 1920 after the fall of the Ottoman Empire and promised that Palestine would eventually become a Jewish homeland. It took another world war for Palestine to be divided into an Arab Palestine and a Jewish Palestine in 1948. The Arabs opposed this, went to war and Jerusalem was divided between Israel and Jordan. From that point, there have been wars at regular intervals, intifada, a revolt against Israel by the Palestinians between 2000 and 2005 with occasional efforts at peace-making, but the Arab nations and other Islamic nations have largely refused to deal with Israel.

Christianity and Islam, extensively spread out over many countries and all continents, are the world's biggest religions. Islam is the fastest-growing religion in the world and will come close to Christianity by 2050, numbering 2.76 billion against the Christian population of 2.91 billion. The interesting aspect is that the Christian rate of growth is from 2.17 billion in 2010 while the Muslim growth for the same period is from 1.6 billion.[1] Christian and Muslim populations will constitute around 30 per cent each of the global population, while the Hindu population will barely change from 15 per cent of the global percentage in 2010 to 14.9 per cent in 2050. In Europe, the Muslim share of the population is expected to increase from 5.9 per cent in 2010 to 10.2 per cent in 2050, including migration and higher fertility rates as two of the factors. Jews have one country, Israel, surrounded by a hostile Muslim population. A little over a billion Hindus live in India and constitute about 80 per cent of its population. Additionally, about 95 per cent of the world's Hindus live in India. About half a billion Buddhists constitute less than 7 per cent of the world population and live mostly in Southeast Asia, Mongolia, Bhutan, Sri Lanka and India. India is a Hindu majority nation but not a Hindu republic.

The main civilizational debate has been between Islam and Christianity. Even though Judaism and Islam have many common practices, and Islam borrowed Judaism's prophets as its own, their long and tortuous history since the seventh century CE has left an embittered relationship.

From time immemorial, religion has been used a political weapon by the monarch, the ruler or the government in power, when considered expedient. Religion was used by Christian rulers for conversion and to divide other faiths to better exercise control over their followers. This was particularly so after the birth of Islam, which decreed that God was supreme over the entire world as it belonged to Him and all those who lived on that flat earth must adhere to His religion or be prepared to die a horrible death. The other Abrahamic religion, Judaism, like Hinduism, did not believe in conversion to the faith, but welcomed new adherents should they desire to join. Christianity and Islam, on the other hand, decreed it their duty to save the 'heathens' or 'infidels' and lead them to the salvation of their souls.

The Muslim in the seventh century CE was no different from the Christian when he preached peace and tolerance, but many of the new adherents of both were violent, ruthless and intolerant. The Roman Empire was the first to accept Christianity after the Crucifixion and new Christians were particularly severe on Greek civilization. Christian hordes entered the temple of the goddess Athena in Palmyra, Syria, in 385 CE, and smashed the exquisite statue of the gentle goddess. The temple fell silent as the decapitated head of Athena lay on the floor and gathered Syrian dust. 'The "triumph" of Christianity had begun,' writes British journalist Catherine Nixey in her 2017 book, *The Darkening Age*.[2] 'Parts of the destruction of Athenian works of art by freshly minted Christians on the ancient Greek civilization can be seen in Room no. 18 of the British Museum. These were described by some as an exhibition of paganism that was bound to end in submission to a higher creed.'[3]

Crusades for Christendom

Christianity did not spread on the wings of an angel. It spread on the tip of the sword and later, through good Christians out to salvage souls. The Crusades were launched by Pope Urban II of the Holy Roman Empire against the Saracens who had occupied the Holy Lands in the eleventh century, about a couple of centuries before Islamic marauders began travelling eastward to India. In 1095, Pope Urban II proclaimed the First Crusade in support of the Byzantine emperor against the Seljuk Turks and called for an armed pilgrimage to Jerusalem. They gave rise to legends like Richard the Lionheart battling the mighty Saladin in brutal wars, the emperors of Byzantium to the Knights Templar engaged in intrigue, in the ultimate Holy War between the Christian and Islamic worlds.

In Europe, the Crusades of the eleventh and twelfth CE made hatred of Judaism an incurable disease, and turned Islam into an irreconcilable enemy of Western civilization. Jerusalem's 40,000 Jews were butchered by the Crusaders. Saladin reconquered Jerusalem for Islam in 1187, but relations between the three religions of Abraham in Jerusalem were never the same again. Members of each faith eyed one another warily, constantly fearing assault or the expropriation of their shrines and homes.

The Crusades brought in a tragic sea change in Jerusalem, where coexistence that once prevailed became an impossible dream. 'These Western prejudices have certainly played their part in today's conflict and affect the way Western people view the Middle East today in highly complex ways,' says Karen Armstrong in her 2001 book, *Holy War*.[4] The Crusades also showed religion at its very worst. 'It is now over a Millennium since Pope Urban II called the First Crusade in 1095 but the hatred and suspicion that this expedition unleashed still reverberates, never more so than on September 11, 2001, and during the terrible days that followed. It is tragic that our holy wars continue.'[5]

The Iberian Crusades from the eleventh to thirteenth centuries to retake Spain from its Islamic conquerors failed.[6] Spain eventually threw out its Arab rulers more than 200 years later in 1492.[7] Islamic conquests had brought new followers to the faith. The good word was spread by swords, by bludgeoning with maces, or by letting arrows fly. That was the way it was for a long time, both in Islam and Christianity. Temple destruction was not just a pastime for the early Roman Christian, it was also an act of faith for Muslims.

Perhaps the next epochal year in the history of the three Abrahamic religions was 1492. In January that year, the armies of King Ferdinand of Aragon and Queen Isabella of Castile reconquered the city state of Granada. This was the last Muslim bastion to fall to Christendom. The Crusades in the Muslim east had failed but in Europe, they succeeded. A few years later, in 1499, Muslim inhabitants of Spain were given a choice of conversion to Christianity or deportation, which meant that for a few centuries Europe would become Muslim-free. In March 1492, Ferdinand and Isabella had also signed an edict to expel Jews, who were given a choice of baptism or deportation. Some of the Jews in Spain converted, others escaped to Portugal and those who remained fled to the new Muslim Ottoman empire where they were welcomed warmly.[8] The Inquisition against the Jews continued but later some converts were allowed to leave Spain in the sixteenth century, who then reverted to their Jewish faith in the Netherlands, Germany and Britain.

In August 1492, with the blessings and patronage of King Ferdinand and Queen Isabella, Christopher Columbus sailed out to discover India, but found North America instead. In 1498, the Portuguese Vasco da Gama landed in Goa. A few years later, in 1519, the Spanish explorer Hernan Cortes brought down the Aztec civilization in Mexico, and some years after that, in 1532, another Spaniard, Francisco Pizarro, led a campaign that defeated the Incas of Peru. Both used immense force to demolish the Aztecs and the Incas. These conquests laid the foundations for colonial regimes that would transform the Americas. The Mayans of Central America inhabited what are now parts of Mexico, Guatemala, Honduras and El Salvador, and were conquered by the Spaniards by the end of the sixteenth century. British explorers Francis Drake and Walter Raleigh made the conquest of North America their goal in order to counter Catholic Spain. By the end of the seventeenth century, the British had thirteen colonies in North America, from modern-day Maine to Georgia.

English Quakers, Catholics and Scottish-Irish Presbyterians – they were all seeking to establish a new civilization in pagan lands. They took their Biblical warrant from Genesis 1:28: 'Be fruitful and multiply, and fill the earth and subdue it.' It was not always peaceful or fair; in fact some accuse the new settlers and their successors of genocide hidden behind a narrative where the cowboys were law-abiding Christians, the Native Americans were evil, and the settlers invariably needed to be rescued by the US Cavalry. Until the mid-twentieth century, America had virtually no contact with the Islamic world.

A Very Christian Nation

Migration from Europe to America began as a trickle in the fifteenth century, but in the centuries that followed, it became a flood. The Native Americans were submerged into other identities, displaced, relocated or simply destroyed. All this was the result of the unrestricted expansion of European settlements, which included Roman Catholics from Spain and France and Protestants from England. Newcomers from England in the seventeenth century also brought many expressions of Protestant Christianity to the New World. Among the profit-seeking explorers were pastors with allegiances to the Church of England, and Puritan reformers rebelling against the Church and in search of religious freedom.

As Andrew Bacevich says in *The New American Militarism,* 'The United States of America remains today, as it has always been, a deeply, incorrigibly Christian nation.'[9] Americans have generally presumed that they have a special covenant with God and that they are His chosen people. Not much has changed from the time of the seventeenth-century Puritan leader John Winthrop, who dreamt of a 'city upon a hill' as the world's leading light – a term he used in a sermon delivered on the ship just before he and his fellow settlers reached America. It is a belief still held by innumerable Americans and their leaders.

It was assumed that God had assigned the newly settled Americans the task of carving out a New Jerusalem in the wilderness of America. This support for American exceptionalism was largely based on Christianity and still holds firm. Over time, the various denominations morphed and today, about one-third of the American population describes itself as Protestant Evangelical. White evangelicals tend to be conservative, have considerable political influence and vote Republican. The American right wing likes to believe that its government has been 'highly religious, specifically highly Christian, and even more specifically highly biblical'.[10] This is not quite so for the governments till about 2000 until the arrival of George W. Bush. During his presidential campaign, Bush would declare that his favourite philosopher was Jesus Christ because he had saved his life. He also felt that it was God who had asked him to contest the election in 2000.

Bush promised faith-based social services, education, medicine, science and even law enforcement. Faith-based justice was to be ensured with the help of a Pentecostal Christian, Attorney General John Ashcroft, a hero among evangelicals. Faith-based social services or 'compassionate conservatism' translated into federal aid to churches under faith-based initiatives. Faith-based science meant that the Bush government denied there was global warming. He even had his faith-based war, in Iraq. He packed his government agencies with born-again Christians like himself, replacing the previous lot. General William Gerard (Jerry) Boykin, Bush's deputy undersecretary of defence intelligence and a key planner of the War on Terror, made headlines for his comments in churches all over the country. After the 2000 election, he would tell audiences to ask themselves why Bush was in the White House even though most Americans did not vote for him. It was because God put him there to lead not only the nation but also the world, Boykin would say.[11]

A key twentieth-century belief was that modernization, science and capitalism, along with free democracies and markets, would create a more secular world. Instead, the historical dominance of faith-based institutions and the power of religion combined with that of modern media led to a religious rebirth. In the early years of capitalism it appeared as if capitalism would replace religion and science and technology would make people seek more scientific explanations about the unknown. For a time this was really happening. It appeared as if religion was receding and the American religious elite was losing its following. *Time* magazine carried a cover story in its 8 April 1966 issue asking, 'Is God Dead?', which was a reflection of this concern among the devout.[12]

Evangelicals in America

Evangelical Christians started to gain importance during the Second World War but even more so during the Cold War. The star performer those days was Billy Graham, who had rapidly acquired a national stature. By the 1950s, he was spiritual counsellor to American presidents and leading congressmen, and could make a difference between winning or losing an election. He was a Cold Warrior in Korea and Vietnam. However, Nixon, his favourite conservative, lost the election in 1960 and John F. Kennedy, a Roman Catholic, became president, much to the consternation of the evangelicals. After he became president, Nixon introduced a weekly religious service in the White House, which pleased the evangelicals immensely.

The US Congress organizes a National Prayer Breakfast on the first Thursday of February every year, but the event is put together by the Fellowship Foundation, a devoutly Christian organization.[13] In 2025, the Breakfast was on 6 February, and as always, since the time of Dwight

Eisenhower, the US president addressed the invitees. President Trump emphasized the importance of faith, unity, the role of prayer in guiding the nation, that God had a special plan for a glorious nation (the US) and it was going to happen sooner than later. In 2024, Joe Biden had spoken about the commandments of the scriptures and said, 'We have to remember who in God's name we are. We're the United States of America.' He did speak of other religions but essentially, the idea was to claim an American exclusivity with God.

The Vietnam War, which ended in 1975, presented a crisis of faith for Americans. The Protestant evangelicals were most perturbed by the direction in foreign policy their leaders had taken and the cultural upheaval that the war had caused. The old interpretation of the morality of force was abandoned, and replaced with a more permissive interpretation of 'just wars', which is a very Christian belief harking back to the Greco-Roman philosophical framework.

Christian conservatives, supporting a 'just' war in Vietnam, were dismayed at the rise of an anti-war movement in the US. Evangelicals asserted that military service was not only compatible with Christian belief and practice but was an obligation of American citizenship. Reverend Jerry Falwell, a committed evangelical, would assert that an American GI fighting in Vietnam was 'a champion for Christ'.[14] He ran a high-decibel campaign for just wars and in 1980 said that the grim truth was that America was indeed sick because the 'tide of permissiveness and moral decay' was crushing American society, including the military, from every side.[15] Falwell's harangue, couched in Christian terminology, sounded ominous and alarmist when he said that America was at the threshold of destruction or surrender. 'A political leader, as a minister of God, is a revenger to execute wrath upon those who do evil,' he said. 'Our government has the right to use its armaments to bring wrath upon those who would do evil by hurting other people.'[16]

The essence of much of the literature of the 1970s and 1980s argued that by turning away from God, the US was in the danger of the same fate as had befallen Babylon, Greece, Rome and other civilizations of the past. They feared that this would mean loss of global supremacy. Some would worry that the day of reckoning was upon the Americans and the Soviet Union was threatening not only American interests but also imperilling Christianity, communism being godless.

The relationship between Christianity and war has been intricate and 'Christians historically have slaughtered their fellow men, to include their fellow Christians, in breathtakingly large numbers'.[17] The two world wars, the Balkan Wars and the Ukraine War will account for the largest number of Christians – Roman Catholic, Protestants or Orthodox, Nazis or socialists – killed in battles with each other in the last hundred or more years.

Timothy Snyder's *Bloodlands* gives details of the 14 million killed by Stalin and Hitler between 1933 and 1945, and Stalin surely continued for some more years after that. Mao Zedong was responsible for the famine following his disastrous policy of the Great Leap Forward, which accounted for 45 million deaths between 1958 and 1962, and another 3 million killings during the Cultural Revolution in 1966–1967. Murderous and paranoid tyrants have been known to kill their own people to buy safety for themselves. Hitler thought of himself as God's gift to mankind, while Stalin and Mao thought they had descended on earth to create a socialist heaven. State-led or state-inspired killings and permanent disabilities in the last century have far outnumbered killings by terrorists.

The elevation of the Baptist Sunday-school teacher, Jimmy Carter, a born-again Christian, to the White House led many to believe that the time of the evangelists had come, even as Americans tuned to sermons of the new sensation, Jerry Falwell. Carter disappointed the believers and in 1980, most of his supporters voted for Ronald Reagan. Many white evangelicals moved away from the Democratic party. Ronald Reagan made the evangelicals happy when he targeted the 'Evil Empire' in Moscow, increased defence spending and pushed the missile-based Strategic Defence Initiative. *Star Wars* became the ultimate evangelical thrill. It was not long before the American military realized the advantages of joining hands with Christian conservatives to help them with their projects, gaining sympathy and admiration; eventually some in the armed forces would get convinced of the godliness of their actions. In 1972, the US Military Academy bestowed the Sylvanus Thayer medal on Billy Graham for exemplifying the academy's ideals of duty, honour and country.[18]

Vietnam and other events led to a revival of interest in Christianity and the economic globalization of the twentieth century, urbanization, education and democracy brought in more faithful. This simultaneous resurgence in the world of both Christianity and Islam, the two biggest denominations, brought in new conflicts of modernization and control. The Islamic revival in the Western world, often referred to as Islamism, in the late 1970s and 1980s was linked with the Arab oil embargo in the mid-1970s and the Iranian Revolution in 1979. These events, along with broader political and social changes, contributed to a shift in the political landscape of the Muslim world and a renewed interest in Islamic identity and politics. Both events were of great religious and economic significance, which soon acquired political and strategic overtones.

Church and State

In Britain, the Church of England has a special place. The very typical English word 'Establishment' is probably linked to it as the 'established church or state religion' with the monarch as its defender. The Archbishop of Canterbury is appointed by the prime minister on behalf of the crown.[19] Like the Iranian clergy, Britain also has unelected clerics sitting in the legislature and bishops in the House of Lords. The Church of England exercises significant power, even though just one in ten citizens attends church every week and nearly a quarter of the English population has no religion. This leads to two observations – one, that there are many vacant slots in the British religious world, leaving it open for aggressive Islamists to make a pitch. Two, if India were to try a similar system there would be prompt allegations of majoritarianism and Hindu domination.

The British always had a soft corner for extremism. During a debate in the British Parliament in 1843, Thomas Macaulay suggested a way to deal with the Hindu majority in India. He said Britain should not take part in any dispute between the 'Mohametans (sic) and the idolaters. But if our government does take a part there cannot be a doubt that Mohametanism is entitled to the preference'.[20] After the First War of Indian Independence in 1857, this became particularly serious because the British realized that Hindus and Muslims had united against the British and would sooner than later overwhelm them. The British had the guns but not the numbers, so they set about dividing Indians into regional, religious and caste identities. They simultaneously widened the rift between Hindus and Muslims, reflected in the history written by the English and later by their Indian acolytes to please the rulers. And so, that is how it was that they backed the idea of Pakistan in a subtle campaign led first by protagonists like Winston Churchill and later by Lord Mountbatten.

The British played the game of empire beyond India before and after surrendering India to Indians. Their support for Islamist forces was also meant to keep recalcitrant Arab rulers in check during the years of the Second World War and to continue to have access to their oil, while simultaneously pleasing the powerful and exacerbating the divide between Muslims and Hindu nationalists in another theatre.[21] British royalty favoured the idea of Pakistan, as Jinnah discovered when he went to the Buckingham Palace in 1946 and met King George. Queen Mary was even more enthusiastic about the creation of Pakistan. In December 1946 Churchill wrote to Jinnah, suggesting that they keep in touch secretly without arousing the suspicion of the Indians. He advised Jinnah to write to Gilliat (Elizabeth Gilliat), Churchill's secretary.[22]

After the Soviet Revolution in 1917, the Vatican had concluded that Bolshevism was going to be a threat to its ideology and to Christian civilization, even though Stalin was focused on 'socialism in one country'. Stalin even sought rapprochement with the West. Nevertheless, Pope Pius XII (1939–1958), sought Catholic forces to combat communism, with a global campaign against communism and the Soviet Union.

Communism in Poland eventually gave way to Pope John Paul's Catholicism into the 1990s. A meeting that Pope John Paul II had with Ronald Reagan in the Vatican Library on 7 June 1982 decided the course of action. This was later described by Reagan's National Security Adviser Richard Allen as the 'greatest secret alliance of all time'.[23] The two discussed Poland and Soviet dominance of Eastern Europe. Both were convinced that that if the Vatican and the US committed their resources, religious and material, Poland could be destabilized by keeping the outlawed Solidarity Movement alive.

That is how it eventually happened. American intelligence agencies got into the act. It helped that all the key administration players involved were Roman Catholics – CIA Chief William Casey, Richard Allen, William P. Clark, from the State Department and later Reagan's national security Adviser, and General Alexander Haig, secretary of state. Reagan, Casey and Clark would consult the Pope on issues relating to funding the movement. In December 1990, Lech Wałęsa, the leader of the Solidarity Movement, became the President of Poland. The Cold War was not yet over, but religion and statecraft had successfully effected regime change.

As an aside, mutual name-calling was a time-honoured Cold War practice. Iran's Ayatollah referred to America as the Great Satan in 1979. In 1983 Ronald Reagan described the Soviet Union as an Evil Empire, and in 1985 described the Afghan Mujahedeen as the moral equivalent of the Freedom Fathers. George W. Bush spoke of North Korea, Iraq and Iran as belonging to an 'Axis of Evil' in his State of the Union speech in January 2002.

The character of the Christian world is changing demographically. In 1900, 80 per cent of the world's Christian population lived in the West, but by 2000, this figure was down to 37 per cent and a majority lived in the rest of the world. That is where most of the growth has been in the last century, especially in sub-Saharan Africa, where the Christian population grew from 9 per cent to 45 per cent by 2000. Today, the largest churches are outside the Western world. The largest church congregation in the world is at the Yoido Full Gospel Church in Seoul with 480,000 members. The three largest Protestant churches in Paris are Afro-Caribbean evangelical mega-churches. With continuing immigration, the demographic pattern of these churches has changed, and they are more brown and black now than white.

In Africa, Latin America and Asia, while the traditional churches of Roman Catholics and Anglicans have increased, it is among the Pentecostals that the growth has been explosive. The migration of Christians from other countries to the US has also increased. American Christianity is a multiethnic community led by immigrants.[24]

The New Faith

Despite schisms in Islam after the death of Mohammad in 632 CE, a wave of Arab conquests swept across northern and eastern Arabia, attacking the outposts of the eastern Roman Empire in Transjordan and southern Iraq, then a part of the Persian Empire. All of Syria and Iraq were tributaries to Medina by 638 CE, and four years later, so was Egypt. In about a hundred years after this, conquests in parts of France, Spain, Morocco and up to the gates of Constantinople (Istanbul), brought Islam further into Central Asia and then on to the banks of the Indus. This reflected the force and power of the new religion.

The Wailing Wall of Jerusalem, the birthplace of Jesus Christ, and Al Aqsa Mosque are all in or near Jerusalem. Jerusalem eventually became a centre of the conflict among these three religions – Christianity versus Islam, and Judaism versus Islam. It was Christian infidel versus Muslim infidel, with both sides invoking divine providence for their victory over the other. Newly converted Catholics were regulated more strictly than before with the royal decrees of 1492 and 1502, which ordered Jews and Muslims to convert to Catholicism or leave Castile, Spain. There were massive expulsions too for those who refused to convert. And Jerusalem was conquered about twenty times by the three Abrahamic faiths.

In Islam, religion was law and Muhammad was the lawgiver.[25] Islamists' hatred for the Jews predates American policy in the Middle East or the birth of Israel. Verse 5:51 of the Quran sermonizes not to befriend or be befriended by Jews and Christians, 'O believers! Take neither Jews nor Christians as guardians – they are guardians of each other. Whoever does so will be counted as one of them. Surely Allah does not guide the wrongdoing people.'[26]

The Quran (5:65) says, 'And if only the People of the Scripture had believed and feared Allah, We would have removed from them their misdeeds and admitted them to Gardens of Pleasure.'[27] In 4:52, it is written, 'It is they who have been condemned by Allah. And whoever is condemned by Allah will have no helper.'[28] A genocidal war cry against Jews, *'Khaybar Khaybar ya yahud, Jaish Mohammad soufa ya'oud'*, has often been used in antisemitic contexts. It refers to 628 CE when the army of the Prophet Mohammad accused the Jews living in Khaybar of conspiring with other Jewish tribes and massacred them. It warns the Jews that the army of Mohammad will return.

Some of the lines in the Quran would appear opposing Jews and Christians. The versions interpreted or translated by various scholars give the same message. Like the Quran's Verse 9:5: 'When the sacred months are over, slay the pagans wherever you find them. Capture, besiege and ambush them. If they repent, perform prayers and pay the religious tax, set them free. God is All-forgiving and All-merciful.'[29] These verses were great enablers of the Muslim conquests in India. According to investigative journalist Daniel Greenfield, these led to 'the mass murder of as many as 80 million Hindus. The Hindu Kush Mountain range commemorates a small part of the genocide that took place. Likewise, the Buddhists were massacred in large numbers'. Islam achieves victory mostly through the Quranic command (9:29), 'Fight those who do not believe in Allah and the Last Day, nor comply with what Allah and His Messenger have forbidden, nor embrace the religion of truth from among those who were given the Scripture, until they pay the tax, willingly submitting, fully humbled,'[30] and not through any religious debate. This is not only ancient history; it is current practice.

Peace in Islam means peace within the Islamic world and among Muslims, and not necessarily peace with other religions and those who profess religions other than Islam. With the latter there has to be eternal war until everyone converts to Islam and the Islamic world wins. In the interregnum, there may be what is called 'hudna', a kind of temporary peace or truce.

Jihadis also practises what is known as taqiyya, which is essentially about self-preservation and used primarily in Shia Islam, although the concept exists in Sunni Islam too. Taqiyya is the practice of concealing one's true beliefs and religious practices, particularly when faced with danger or persecution. It permits not following the usual practices and rituals under these circumstances. The ultimate goal of jihad is to establish shariah all over the world. This is not the point of view of all Muslims but is the view of the aggressive Muslim religious factions like the Muslim Brotherhood, the ISIS, Al Qaeda, the Taliban that control considerable political and cultural activity in the Middle East, Afghanistan and Pakistan, and now we see it emerging in Bangladesh. The other aspect is that while other religions have moved with the times and have been upgraded, Islam's protagonists have kept it in seventh century since the Quran is immutable. When Hitler was on the rampage in Germany it was not because all Germans were Nazis. The good just kept quiet. Islam too is about conquest and control.[31] 'Hudna' (lying low when the enemy is on the ascendant, a truce) and 'taqiyya' (about concealing true intentions) are Adviseries to be found in the Quran. The Quran is as much a religious book as a political treatise. The Pledge of Aqaba was essentially a declaration of war against all mankind that would last until all people of the world adopted his religion and believed in him as God's messenger.[32]

Although ultimately, the main debate or conflict will be between

Islam and Christianity, for the moment, there seems to be some sort of an understanding between Western nations dependent on their riches and global control on a mostly unchallenged access to Middle Eastern energy resources, and the Middle East autocrats dependent on the sale of their product through Western agencies. There will be a time in future when this equation will change. At that stage, the convenient bonhomie will collapse, when Islam seeks to take total control of the West, to rule the West in their way, with their followers living in the style of the Westerner but without having to work for it. Aggressive Islamic attitudes are already visible in Europe at a time when the total Muslim population is less than 10 per cent. For the present, even though Judaism and Islam, two Abrahamic religions, have many common practices and Islam has borrowed Judaism's prophets as its own, the long and tortuous history since the seventh century has remained embittered.

The Conflict

Mohammad was forty years old in 610 CE when he began his communion with God, after he heard Angel Gabriel tell him in his dreams that he was the prophet of God as he sat in his cave near the summit of Mount Hira. Unconvinced at first, Mohammad's wife Khadija consulted her aging uncle Waraqa about Mohammad's dream, who confirmed this possibility because the same angel had visited Moses. Encouraged by his wife, Mohammad accepted he had indeed been commissioned by the God of Abraham to be His prophet. It was that one night on Mount Hira that showed Mohammad his destiny; it was later described as Laylat Al-Qadr, the Night of Power. Gone was the identity of a poor orphan, the goat herd and the husband of a wealthy Meccan woman.[33]

Surrounded by doubting Meccans and other Jews, Mohammad began writing his Quran. The greater the resistance, the more aggressive were Mohammad's Quranic verses. He warned Meccans, 'Indeed, Hell is lying in ambush as a home for the transgressors, where they will remain for endless ages. There they will not taste any coolness or drink, except boiling water and oozing pus – a fitting reward.'[34] Unable to win over numbers, Mohammad offered another Quranic verse that described his version of Paradise, 'But, for the God-fearing is a blissful abode, enclosed gardens and vineyards, and damsels ...'[35]

Resistance to Mohammad from the Meccans continued to grow while Mohammad dreamt of horrific torture for non-believers, when he would frighten them with stories of 'people burning in lakes of fire, boiling water or molten metal poured down their throats, women suspended over fire with a hook through their tongues'.[36] Eventually, the polytheist Meccans tired of Mohammad's monotheism and several of his followers fled to Abyssinia; Mohammad himself, fearing death, fled to Taif, where he was pelted with stones when he tried to convert people; eventually he performed hijra to (Yathrib) Medina in 622 CE. And then Mohammad went to wars against the Meccans and the Jews.

It was at Badr, an oasis east of Medina, that Mohammad's Muslims defeated the Meccans. The battles were brutal, and Mohammad's force had been motivated by visions of paradise and war booty. Eventually Mohammad's army won, followed by large-scale slaughter and looting. This is mentioned more than once in Surah Al-Anfal, which loosely translated into English mean 'The Spoils of War'. The Muslim victory in the Battle of Badr was because of divine intervention and not just because of the soldiers. This became the accepted rule of war. Reprisals against those Meccans whom Mohammad accused of insulting him were immediate and brutal. [37]

It was also after the Battle of Badr that Mohammad turned on the Jews and the initial bonhomie between the Jews and Mohammad ended forever.[38] The commonality between the two had dissipated fast when the Jews demurred from accepting Mohammad as the final prophet. He thereafter began a concerted campaign to demonize them. He had convinced his followers that his behaviour reflected the will of God. 'In their prayers, therefore, the faithful repeated his curses against the Jews; they memorised the Quran verses that condemned them. Mohammad's hatred became their hatred; his enemies became their enemies.'[39] He launched the ethnic cleansing of the Jews of Yathrib, the Qaymaqams Jews, immediately after this rebuff. Having done that, he expelled them from their lands where they had lived for a millennium. The Qurayza Jews were similarly exterminated/exiled, and Qurayza women and children made to witness beheadings. Between 400 to 900 Qurayza Jews were beheaded in a day and Mohammad's cousins, Ali and Zubayr, were the executioners.[40]

Violence or threats of violence were an important means of spreading the new religion. From early days, Christianity and Islam crossed each other, violently, along the lands surrounding the Mediterranean – Spain, the Levant and the Balkans. The world saw the Balkans go up in flames in the 1990s, but what happened in the fifteenth- and sixteenth-century Spanish Inquisition against the Moors has never been fully disclosed. The antagonism between Christianity and Islam began in the Mediterranean region from the first contact. They were religious, political, geographical and economic rivals – a rivalry which spread elsewhere and has been sustained ever since.[41]

Core Beliefs

The core Islamic belief is the Shahada, which says, 'I bear witness that there is no God but Allah and Mohammad is his messenger.' Regardless of which sect a Muslim may be from, the Shahada does not change, and it is not just a religious declaration but a political one as well. There is no conflict between religious and political violence, as we have seen from the early days of Islam, and the latter in support of the former is perfectly acceptable. Hardliners believe in this totally, including an Islamic duty to impose shariah by force. Those who belong to terror organizations like the Al Qaeda, Islamic State, Boko Haram, Lashkar-e-Tayyiba, Jaish-e-Mohammed, Tehrik-e Taliban Pakistan, the Afghan Taliban and a few hundred other such organizations, believe in the enforcement of the shariah by force.

Most Muslims who believe in the Shahada and are devout probably do not believe in violence. That is left to extremist groups or terror organizations, but these acts of violence or an Islamic apartheid are not condemned forcibly or loudly – at best, only obliquely and usually apologetically by most Muslims. The problem has been that this majority group is also unable to adjust its beliefs to the modernity of Europe and the West, and of late even to other religions. The West and other democracies have modernized to varying degrees and the economic, social, cultural and political norms have altered. Muslim immigrants can use the facilities of modern technologies but are unable and unwilling to accept modern Western value systems and secularism. They remain constricted to an essentially Islamic lifestyle by which they lock themselves out of local influences.

The unification of the Ummah in twentieth century was an American effort in its desire to destroy the Soviet presence in Afghanistan, where the Mujahedeen were brought together from all over the Muslim world to fight the Great Satan. There were copycat outfits that followed, with Al Qaeda, ISIS and Hay'at Tahrir al-Sham being accepted entities in the West because they served the local strategic interest of keeping Russia out, Syria under control and Iran that much more vulnerable to Israeli attacks across Syrian airspace. Meanwhile, it would prudent to remember that the ultimate identity of most Muslims is to be part of the global Islamic Ummah. This has no connection to a nation state nor to any culture that is not Islamic.[42]

The contrast between the Christian Bible, the Jewish Torah and the Islamic Quran is in the restrictions and punishments prescribed in the latter. Christianity and Judaism restrict themselves to the Ten Commandments for religious beliefs and leave the rest to secular rulers in the spirit of rendering to Caesar what is Caesar's. There have also been reformations in these two religions. Not so in Islam. In Islam, any law not in tune with its law is illegitimate. Its own law, the shariah, is derived from the Quran, the examples of Mohammad and the Hadith, and is therefore considered immutable.

Islam thus asserts that Jewish scripture had been changed by Jews over time and must be abandoned. The Quran is more forgiving towards Christians who might have forgotten some parts of their original scripture but had wrongly considered Jesus as the son of God (Quran 5:72; 112:2; 19:34–35; 4:171) or that Christians wrongly attributed Jesus as one of the three gods of the Trinity (Quran 5:73; 4:171). Muslims believe that Allah sent down an entirely different religion with the Prophet who got various verses from Angel Gabreel.

In her book, *Heretic: Why Islam Needs a Reform Now*, Ayaan Hirsi Ali, who escaped from Somalia to begin a new life in the Netherlands, urges a religious reformation of Islam to end the cycle of terrorism, sectarian violence and repression of women. It did not make her very popular with the Islamic fundamentalists and extremists. Hirsi Ali's chapter 'Shackled by Shariah' is very explicit about the rigidities of this religious code. She recounts the story of Meriam Ibrahim, a Sudanese and a Christian daughter of an Ethiopian Christian mother and a Sudanese Muslim father. She had married a Christian but was sentenced to 100 lashes after she delivered her child. She could be spared under shariah if she accepted the Islamic faith. It took the US State Department along with other European governments to help her eventually leave Sudan.[43]

Over time, the shariah was routinely applied across many Islamic countries like Saudi Arabia, Iran, Pakistan, Sudan and Somalia. Apostasy, or leaving the faith, is punishable with death, 'But if they turn away, then seize them and kill them wherever you find them, and do not take any of them as allies or helpers' (Quran, 4.89).[44] Blasphemy is punishable according to the Quran although the exact punishment is not defined except that Surah 9.74 says, 'If they repent, it will be better for them. But if they turn away, Allah will torment them with a painful punishment in this world and the Hereafter, and they will have no one on earth to protect or help them.'[45] The scope of this law has been recently made harsher in Pakistan, and in general, the punishment given for blasphemy is death.

Crucifixions are sanctioned in Surah 5:33: 'Indeed, the penalty for those who wage war against Allah and His Messenger and spread mischief in the land is death, crucifixion, cutting off their hands and feet on opposite sides, or exile from the land. This penalty is a disgrace for them in this world, and they will suffer a tremendous punishment in the Hereafter.'[46]

About a decade ago, the Pew Research Forum's report, 'The World's Muslims: Religion, Politics and Society' included a study in thirty-nine countries in Asia, Africa and Europe with 38,000 interviews in different languages. In response to the question, 'Do you favour or oppose making shariah law or Islamic law the official law of the land in our country?', five countries recorded an overwhelmingly favourable response from the Muslims – Indonesia (204 million; 72 per cent), Pakistan (178 million; 84 per cent), Bangladesh (149 million; 82 per cent), Egypt (80 million; 74 per cent), and Nigeria (76 million; 71 per cent). Pew also found that 99 per cent Afghans and 91 per cent Iraqis favoured shariah laws.[47] Several Shariah courts are already operational in Britain. The French have been under pressure to make polygamy acceptable for Muslims. As many as 86 per cent of Pakistanis favour death by stoning for adultery. In Hirsi Ali's words, 'There is probably no realistic chance that Muslims in countries such as Pakistan will agree to dispense with shariah.'[48]

European contact with the Muslim world increased as the European colonies spread in the Middle East and Africa. British, French and German empires vied for new territories to control and exploit. So long as the empire ruled, everything was under control of the emperor. As the empires faded away, they had to accommodate many from their former colonies. It was then that problems of assimilation of the former colony resident, now immigrant, with the erstwhile 'master' arose. Imported as cheap labour after World War II, with time they became competitors for space, lifestyles and upmarket jobs. Islam too entered the former imperial powers in ways they had not anticipated.

Geopolitics and total domination became the catchwords and local populations were accorded the same treatment as all empires in history had given alien populations – cannon fodder for their wars and cheap labour for their economies. The two world wars resulted in a change of global overlordship, as the US eased out Britain from global supremacy, especially in the oil-rich Middle East, and was confronted with a new menace challenging its supremacy, the Soviet Union. Islam and Communism were to become the Western alliance's nemeses.

Today no other Western nation draws so much Islamist rage as the US, especially since 11 September 2001. There were terror attacks in London, Madrid, Bali, Casablanca and elsewhere. Some 2,300 Muslims were arrested in Europe after 9/11 for suspected terrorist activity while in America there were only sixty such arrests. The 1990s did see aggressive US interventions in Iraq and the Balkans, and each time, the US earned a few more enemies. American Muslims may be more middle class than those in Europe but to presume that terrorism is the work of the dispossessed is not correct, because it can also be the weapon of the well-educated, middle-class professional.[49]

Christianity Versus Islam

Christianity versus Islam is an unhappy story that is 1,700 years old. The very Catholic historian Hilaire Belloc described Islam as a heresy and a permanent enemy of Christianity in 1938 in his book, *The Great Heresies*. He admired Islam's power to mobilize, its vitality and durability, but cautioned a world that was then involved with the rising storm in Europe, 'It has always seemed to me possible, and even probable, that there would be a resurrection of Islam and that our sons or our grandsons would see the renewal of that tremendous struggle between the Christian culture and what has been for more than a thousand years its greatest opponent.'[50]

Belloc added, 'The future always comes as a surprise, but political wisdom consists in attempting at least some partial judgment of what that surprise may be. And for my part I cannot but believe that a main unexpected thing of the future is the return of Islam. Since religion is at the root of all political movements and changes and since we have here a very great religion physically paralyzed but morally intensely alive, we are in the presence of an unstable equilibrium which cannot remain permanently unstable.'[51] No one paid any heed to this prophesy.

Even more, the so-called global War on Terror was led by people who neither knew nor cared to know their enemy. Yet they never ceased to tell others how to fight this war which essentially meant throwing in greater military power than that of the enemy, hoping for decimation by remote control. The terrorists simply melted away, leaving the innocent to face mortal danger. The global war was by declaration but not by intent, as it did not cover, for instance, the terrorist activity of Pakistan-based, Pakistan-assisted Islamic terror organizations like the India-specific Lashkar-e-Tayyiba and Jaish-e-Mohammed. They did not have global reach, was the convenient logic as Pakistan was once again a friend of the West as a major non-NATO ally. The tactics were wrong, the targets were wrong, and the place was wrong.

Belloc's prophesies were lost or ignored as America, relying on hubris, got involved in various conflicts in the Middle East, some of which, like the Yemen conflict, rage on. In pursuit of its imperial interests, the US had helped raise and equip the Afghan Mujahedeen to fight their guerrilla war or jihad against the Soviet Union in Afghanistan in the 1980s, and when the Soviets retreated, the Mujahedeen and Pakistan, indeed the Islamic world, celebrated it as a victory of Islam against the infidel.

Islam as a Weapon against Communism

In the modern era, interest in faith as a means to deliver political and strategic objectives was first tried successfully by Christian nations in 1979 by encouraging Muslims to adopt jihad as a means to get rid of 'godless communists' from Afghanistan. In time, the US, in pursuit of its global interests, won against its declared Evil Empire but not before it had encouraged another menace that would be far more difficult to tackle – radical Islamic terrorism. After vanquishing communism, it came after the Christian West, which as it turned out, had gifted Islamic jihad to itself and the world.

The Islamist narrative had been increasingly engaging the world since the last decades of the twentieth century. The Afghan Mujahedeen, an amorphous Islamic group fighting America's war against the Soviet Union, remained fundamentally Islamic. Then, the US supported Iraq against Iran in the 1980s, and its forces were involved in the First Gulf War (Operation Desert Storm) in 1991 with their troops stationed in Saudi Arabia permanently. The Afghan Jihad led to the creation of the Taliban and the conflicts in the Middle East led to Al Qaeda.

The next round of American intervention in the Middle East, from 2002 onwards, led to the creation of the ultra-radical Islamic State of Iraq and Syria commonly known ISIS or Daesh and designed to fight the infidel, including the Shias of Iraq, Syria and Iran, a country which had gained control of Iraq and substantially Syria. Each new Islamic organization was more virulent, more extremist and better equipped than the ones before. There were terror attacks against US interests in Nairobi, Dar es Salaam and the USS *Cole*, a US Navy vessel blown up by a suicide bomb attack in 2000. Osama bin Laden, a one-time CIA aide in Afghanistan, had announced jihad against the US in 1996. Eventually, the terror of 11 September 2001 happened. It has not stopped ever since.

Both Christianity and Islam have been imperial religions – they have been imposed on subjects with varying degree of success. Christianity went through its four centuries of upheaval, before accepting the principal of secularism and the separation of the church from the state. Not so in Islam, although there are periods of catharsis there, but the key word has been Islamophobia, a term first used in French literature early in the twentieth century but which gained widespread usage after 9/11. A kind of parallel to xenophobia, the flipside of Islamophobia is its use to describe any criticism or restriction as racism and victimization. Political correctness and vote bank issues take over to achieve what the Islamists want, their own way.

While there have been incidents of innocent Muslims being the target of hate crimes, Islamophobia has also been used as a shield to ward off criticism, legitimize its own aggressive actions with exaggerated rage and, more importantly, to silence criticism from within. This could include preventing women from discarding the burqa or hijab, or other shariah-based restrictions, and acting against those who disbelieve in the religion. Islamophobia is used as an excuse to continue to be aggressive against other religions, and spread the word of Allah. What is more, the word 'secular' does not exist in Islamic vocabulary or practice – something that Europe must understand, as should India. Muslims who want to adhere to a strict interpretation of Islam, have difficulty living in peace in a democracy; in any case there are few, if any, democracies that are also Muslim majority. They function best under strict dictatorships governed by Islamic laws. That is why military rule comes naturally to Pakistan.

The famous French author and philosopher, Voltaire, believed in the ideas of freedom of religion and speech, and a separation of church and state. He wrote a play in 1741, *Mohammad, the Prophet*, which was an attack on hypocrisy and fanaticism. Doubtless, Islamic censors disapproved, and the play can no longer be staged in France.[52] It is tragic, but not surprising, that several editors and staff members of the French magazine, *Charlie Hebdo*, were murdered by two Al Qaeda terrorists for publishing a cartoon on Mohammad. Five years later, in October 2020, when Samuel Paty, a teacher in France, showed his students the same cartoon from the *Charlie Hebdo* magazine during a moral and civic education class, an enraged Muslim refugee decapitated him. The authorities described it as an act of terror. The French President Emmanuel Macron was more explicit when he said, 'One of our compatriots was assassinated today because he taught. He taught his students about freedom of expression, freedom to believe or not believe. It was a cowardly attack. He was the victim of a terrorist Islamist attack.'[53]

Prior to this, the US government and the corporate world had little difficulty in engaging the powerful bin Ladens and the bin Mahfouz family of Saudi Arabia, as illustrated masterfully by Craig Unger in *The House of Bush, The House of Saud*. Quite early in the book, the reader is informed, 'The United States, sworn defender of Israel, was also the guarantor of security to the guardians of Wahhabi Islam, the fundamentalist religious sect that was one of Israel's and America's mortal enemies.' The massive contradiction that a global power countenanced and rationalized was astonishing, where the symbol of democracy was willing to not only be associated with a fundamentalist Islamic regime but also to 'arm and protect a brutal theocratic monarchy'.[54]

Black October

The Israel–Palestine and Arab conflict has its origins in early twentieth century when the Arabs and Palestinians objected to the formation of Israel under the UN Partition plan of 1947 and the first Arab–Israeli War was fought in 1948–1949. Since then, several wars, at first with Egypt and Syria, and then with Hamas in Gaza, two intifadas, endless terrorism first by Palestine Liberation Organization (PLO) then by Hamas and Hezbollah despite accords in Camp David and Oslo, have been the pattern despite Nobel prizes for Yasser Arafat and Israeli Prime Ministers Yitzhak Rabin and Shimon Peres, in 1994. The Nobel Peace Prize was also shared by Menachem Begin and Anwar Sadat in 1978; Sadat was assassinated by his own troops in 1981.

Jews were originally referred to as Palestinians in 1948; they who had escaped the traumatic events in Hitler's Europe lived on the Mediterranean coast. The Arabs have not been kind at all to the Palestinians of today. Soon after Israel's creation, five Arab nations – Egypt, Syria, Lebanon, Jordan and Iraq – invaded it and lost. From then on, nearly a million Jews were expelled from Arab countries including Iraq where they had lived since Babylonian times. Those who were expelled included Arabs from these countries that had gone to war with Israel in 1948–1949.

It was only after Yasser Arafat named his organization the Palestinian Liberation Organization in 1964 (which was described by the Americans as a terrorist organization till 1967) that the Arabs from the region came to be referred to as Palestinians. In September 1970, Jordan slaughtered thousands of Palestinians and this assault was led by Brig. Zia-ul-Haq who later became president of Pakistan and a great ally of the US during the Afghan Jihad. Similarly, Kuwait expelled hundreds of thousands of Arab Palestinians after they signed allegiance to Saddam Hussein. When Libya's Muammar Gaddafi expelled Palestinians in 1994, he advised other Arab nations not to accept them. Similarly, Syria never gave them citizenship. When Syrians fled their country during the civil war in 2013, Lebanon and Jordan accepted only Syrian refugees and not Palestinians. In normal parlance this would amount to apartheid, discrimination and even genocide, but no Arab talks about this.

In 2020–21, Israel succeeded in breaking through the Arab barrier by signing peace deals with the UAE, Bahrain, Sudan and Morocco, with attempts to have an understanding with Saudi Arabia, which have been shelved following the Hamas onslaught of October 2023. A Saudi Arabia–Israel agreement would have left Iran out on a limb. Chinese support for Hamas indicates its nervousness about the moves in the Middle East. It is relevant to refer to what the late Hossein Salami, head of the Islamic Revolutionary Guard Corps (IRGC), said in August 2022 – that the outcome of the battle would be determined when the brave and experienced people of Hezbollah and Palestine would move on the ground in a single military formation. Hezbollah, based in Lebanon, has been the other threat to Israel. The late Hassan Nasrallah, the Hezbollah leader, had told a meeting of Iran-backed groups in March 2023 to get ready for a ground invasion of Israel. According to the 10 October 2023 report in the *New York Times*, Iran was predicting that Israel would be destroyed.[55]

The massive and brutal 7 October 2023 attack on the Simchat Torah community in southern Israel by Hamas bears testimony to this recurrent theme in an area that is replete with contradictions, conflicting interests and political rivalries. Celebrations in New York, Toronto and Sydney by Islamic radicals, an attack on an Israeli diplomat in Beijing, a murder in Paris, two murdered in Brussels – all define the medieval attitude of the protestors celebrating the killing of innocents with vengeful individual attacks. This was followed by protests in Europe and America after Israeli retaliation. This has been possible only because Europeans and Americans surrendered their cities to so-called immigrants, imported as cheap labour, from the Muslim world; of the mosques that have sprung up in America, 85 per cent were built after 9/11. Unfortunately, powers that proclaim their right and ability to defend the world did not have the means to stop the nasty protests.

The inevitable and strong Israeli response was in extreme anger, and at another level, the goal seemed to be to destroy Hamas and terrorism. Policies of appeasement and concession had not worked; in fact, they never do with terrorists, and states never ever stop trying to appease, or worse, lionize. At the same time, revenge cannot be strategy. The Israeli reaction was also a perception battle that took the war to Hamas. The other worry in many Western capitals is escalation of the conflict. It has lasted longer than imagined, with no end in sight.

Subsequent Israeli tactics of moving further into southern Gaza indicated that their game was much wider than simply revenge. It is evident that the Israeli plan is to use the war for a total victory not just against the Hamas but also against Hezbollah operating from Lebanon and Syria with Iranian support. It was ironical that the US president disapproved of the Israeli invasion into Gaza, while continuing to supply weaponry to Israel and humanitarian assistance to Gaza. The advice for restraint without offering a solution to a country that has been the victim of terror since the first day of its existence makes the advice sound hollow.

The sad paradox is that after Israel withdrew from Gaza in 2005 as a goodwill gesture by Prime Minister Ariel Sharon, Gaza became a hotbed of conspiracy and terror against Israel. The other aspect is that the Israeli withdrawal from southern Lebanon more than two decades ago did not give Israel any peace. Despite this, or maybe because of this, Hamas has used Gaza as a base to attack Israel repeatedly. Meanwhile, Hamas leaders like Khaled Mashal, ensconced in luxury in Qatar, continue to threaten a fight for the end of Israel. Lebanon was a Christian majority, peace-loving democracy along with Israel in the 1950s, situated in the midst of Arab states ruled by dictators and monarchs. Today Lebanon is a Muslim majority country and a hotbed for anti-Jewish terror activities led by the Hezbollah and backed by Iran.

In October 2023, the surprise for Israel was not that Hamas attacked. Hamas has done this often enough in the past two decades even though Israel sealed the border in 2007. The real surprise was the scope and vehemence of the attack. Possibly no one estimated that Hamas could unleash so much death and destruction in a few hours. This, along with the surprise element, seemed to have stunned the Israeli state into a cold paralysis for some time. A terrorist organization or indeed any adversary's threat is determined by intent, capability and execution. Hamas always had the intent, they acquired capability with assistance from Iran and cashflows from Qatar, ironically first arranged by Netanyahu's government to divide the Palestinian movement.[56] It is useful to remember that in 2007, Hamas had killed hundreds of Palestinians (estimated about 400) inside Gaza because they were members of the Fatah Movement or the Palestinian Authority. If they could do this to their 'own', they would not hesitate to kill 1,300 Israelis.

The war in Gaza is a new game of power play where there are many players but no referee. In just one year, the US spent at least $22.76 billion on military aid to Israel and related US operations in the region up to September 2024.[57] This aid is not known to have stopped. The US, a stalwart ally of the Israelis, cannot sit this out and will remain involved one way or the other.

There could be realignment of interest groups with the liberal left combining with the Islamic groups, as was evident in some elite educational institutions of the US. The Hamas leadership has urged its followers to continue with the jihad. Israel will not stop the war till it has achieved its objective. If the jihad is profitable to the Hamas leadership, the war is also profitable to the powerful military–industrial complex, its infrastructure industry and the financial sectors that control the economy in the US. There are many who do not wish for the war to end. The war might slow down, but the various interests abide.

The Arab states' reaction varied from ambivalence to vociferous calls for revenge against Israel. Some of the strongest criticism against Israel came from Egypt, the home of the Muslim Brotherhood, exhibiting strong anti-Semitism, even more than Iran. The Saudis broke off their negotiations with Israel, but this may be temporary. Morocco, having normalized relations with Israel, also had protests against Israel even though it has been supplying military hardware to Morocco. Arab street reaction against the US and Israel is an offshoot of a mindset inculcated among young children that teaches them hatred against Israel and Jews (which in Pakistan is against India and Hindus).

The situation remains as complicated as it was decades ago. Israel's justification in bombing civilians in Gaza is based on credible intelligence that Hamas had been ruling in Gaza and planning its attacks on Israel, taking cover of civilians and stocking arsenals under hospitals. None of the Arab nations want to accept Palestinian refugees, having seen the havoc Palestinians created in Jordan and Lebanon with their aggression and eagerness to take to arms; also, when not fighting the Israelis, Palestinians created problems among themselves and the locals. If Arab nations want to live in peace with the rest of the world, be truly independent, if dreams like India–Middle East Economic Corridor (IMEC) are to come true, then Arab nations must themselves get rid of Hamas and its mindset. As Israel's former prime minister Golda Meir famously said, 'Peace will come when the Arabs love their children more than they hate us.'[58]

Yet at times like this, the question of Gazan rights becomes an Islamic issue and even Jordan, after having said that no Palestinian will be allowed to enter Jordan or Egypt, declined to let President Joe Biden visit Jordan. A territorial issue becomes an Islamic issue – and there is ambivalence in Cairo and Amman about Palestinians; there is support for Hamas there but not from the governments in Egypt or Jordan. The Hamas attack was designed to provoke and terrorize. The Hamas claims it is killing for Palestinian rights. Maybe millionaire Hamas leaders sitting in Qatar with bank accounts in Switzerland can explain these rights. This constant provocation along with threats often leads to policies of appeasement that lead to incremental concessions – and that is the terrorists' victory. Islamic sentiment is bound to be high all over the globe for quite some time now.

Instead, it is important for all Arabs to not sympathize with the Palestinians, to come forward and tell them that Arabs now want peace with Israel, and it is the Palestinians who are in the way. The world wants the Israelis to stop the attacks – not so much because the world is peace-loving but because the world fears the possible fallout on itself. Yet the world offers Israelis no guarantee that Hamas thugs will not attack Israel again. There are many facets and speculations about the October 2023 Hamas onslaught, but it is a confirmation that the clash of civilizations continues. More than that, the endgame is not clear, and it could easily get out of control. An Israel unable to control the situation could lead to escalation, forcing Arabs and Turks to join and the US to step in.

The US did step in ostensibly against Iran's nuclear facilities but more to help Israel get over its primary fear – Iran's nuclear capabilities. These attacks on 21 June 2025 were in support of Israeli attacks earlier on 13 June. By hitting Iran's nuclear facilities at Fordow, Natanz and Isfahan the idea was to cripple Iran's capabilities and make Israel feel safe after its massive retaliation against the Hamas in Gaza, the Hezbollah in Lebanon and Syria. This attack no doubt redeemed some of the prestige America had lost among its allies and friends that it was not doing enough to defend them. At the same time Russia, China and North Korea did precious little to show support to Iran. There is no happy ending visible yet.

A Very European Problem

Ever since the fall of the Berlin Wall, a strange sense of guilt seemed to have overtaken Europe. Possibly it is for all the atrocities and killings of the Second World War and even communism's excesses. Old Europe seemed to have gone into a shell and left the US to lead with its interventionist and meddlesome practices through NATO, primarily, aided by intelligence efforts, to keep the new Europeans on the straight and narrow anti-communist plank. The guilt is probably also related to Europe's silence during the Holocaust. It was perhaps subconscious atonement for this that led European nations to allow in roughly 20 million from the Middle East.

Inevitably, this form of appeasement has now become Europe's biggest problem. It arose partly from wanting to appear sensitive and understanding and not racist while dealing with migrants, and hope for their assimilation into European culture in time. Governments bent over backwards to accommodate Muslim demands for entry into Europe and special treatment. European governments also appeased Muslim heads of government who invariably lobbied to censor the press, universities, history books and even school curricula.

The early decades of the twenty-first century were a period of turmoil and violence in the Middle East, of conflicting interests between Sunni and Shia states, interests of Big Powers and rising Islamic extremism. The West, notably Europe, was caught between wanting to be liberal about allowing and even welcoming refugees from the troubled regions, and protecting their political constituencies. In contrast, six Middle Eastern countries – Kuwait, Bahrain, Qatar, the United Arab Emirates, Saudi Arabia and Oman – did not grant asylum to any Syrian refugee.[59]

Throughout the 1990s and early twenty-first century, the constant influx of refugees from the Middle East and North Africa was eagerly welcomed. Europe remained caught in its own political correctness as it sought to assume responsibility for the poverty and backwardness of Africa and Asia as a result of its colonial practices. The atheist Left and the Islamic radical had perfected the art of using the West's colonial past to seek a better way of life while simultaneously blaming it for its problems. Islamophobia and the victim card became part of an effective narrative.

As a result, in parts of urban Europe, there is a growing presence of aggressive Muslims who wish to stick to their own way of life without any assimilation in their country of residence. Europe might well have Islam become one among many religions, colliding with Christianity, or even the single main religion in some parts.[60]

European governments would invariably take care not to invite any Muslim dissident into their countries, fearing that doing so could spoil their relations with the Muslim world. Instead, they concentrated on calling representatives from the Council on American Islamic Relations (CAIR) known for its rabid Islamic leanings. Tearful handwringing and emotional speeches after a terror attack, saying that the religion of peace would never commit such a crime, became a pattern to avoid any clashes between Muslims and Christians. For the extremist this was a victory for Islam.

Weak reactions by the Spanish and British governments to the Madrid train bombing in 2004 and the London bus bombing in 2005 respectively helped terrorists draw their own conclusions. They had the opportunistic so-called liberal left on their side and governments of the day had no spine.[61] A spate of killings in France, Belgium, Netherlands and England took place in the first two decades of the twenty-first century, perpetrated by refugees or immigrants angered by perceived anti-Islamic activities, such as cartoons. These acts were explained away by politicians as criminal activity with reiterations that Islam was a religion of peace, faithfully reported in mainstream media. A poll in Britain in 2006 showed that 78 per cent of British Muslims believed the publishers of the Danish cartoons should be prosecuted. About 68 per cent felt that an insult to Islam should be prosecuted. According to the same poll, almost a fifth of British Muslims (19 per cent) respected Osama bin Laden, with 6 per cent saying they 'highly respected' him. Killing fellow human beings is a crime and a sin; but appeasement of those who sympathize with the perpetrators of such sins should count as a bigger sin.

It is a growing perception in the West today that Muslim immigrants tend to ghettoize in their adoptive countries. Many elements that form the essence of European life – free speech and thought, the arts, music, dancing, wine, performances – are taboo in Islam. Their socio-cultural leaders are not elected representatives but imams who enforce traditional practices. Ghettoization negates any chance of assimilation of the immigrant.

At a rally in Cologne in 2008, Turkish Prime Minister (later President) Recep Tayyip Erdoğan advised a crowd of 20,000 Turks living in Germany, Belgium, France and the Netherlands that assimilation was a crime against humanity, and that he did not expect Turks to assimilate. They should instead get involved in politics to gain influence. This was so the 5 million Turks then living in Europe would have constitutional strength and not just be 'guests'.[62] Major European cities today have Turkish, Moroccan, Tunisian and Algerian ghettoes, which insist on maintaining differences in social and religious norms, and some parts have become no-go areas for the police.

In 2004, historian Niall Ferguson wrote in his book, *Colossus*, 'With birth rates in Muslim societies more than double the European average, the Islamic countries of North Africa and the Middle East are bound to put some kind of pressure on Europe and the United States in the years ahead. If, for example, the population of Yemen could exceed that of Germany by 2050 (as the United Nations forecasts), there must either be dramatic improvements in the Middle East's economic performance or substantial immigration from the Arab world to aging Europe.'[63] The migration from the Middle East has continued but does not seem to reflect Fergusson's optimistic prediction. A twenty-first century crusade seemingly began in October 2001 with the American invasion of Afghanistan. It continues.

Simultaneously, another conversation was being constructed in Britain at the turn of this century – about building a multicultural society in a display of British tolerance. The Runneymede Trust, for instance, conceived of a community of communities in 2000 in its report, 'The Future of Multi-ethnic Britain'. The BBC appropriated the task of judging who was or was not racist. Dissent or stern action by the police, the courts, social workers and even by the medical profession began to be described as racist. Consequently, social workers and the police in Rotherham, Yorkshire, failed to investigate thoroughly cases of systematic rape of white women by men of Pakistani origin. Other issues were overlooked at the altar of tolerance and multi-ethnicity. For instance, a growing number of Muslim men were allowed to have more than one wife – one under British law and three under shariah. Despite the illegality of this, the mood of the nation was such that even feminists defended this Islamic right.[64]

In July 2017, the BBC broadcast a documentary called *The Betrayed Girls* about the Muslim grooming gangs in Rochdale in the Greater Manchester area of England. Just two months earlier, it had broadcast a three-hour drama about the trial of the same Muslim gang. This was rapid-fire, considering that when in 2004 grooming gangs in another town were exposed, the BBC asserted that only racists would believe that such a thing was happening. Four years later, when the BBC broadcast its first documentary on grooming gangs, it did not mention that the ethnicity of the rapists was different from that of the girls. The Muslim Council of Britain, which represents over 500 Muslim organizations, insisted that Muslim grooming gangs were a racist myth. Peter McLoughlin, author of the 2016 book, *Easy Meat: Inside the Grooming Gang Scandal*, cautions that although his book is written with care, it will shock and may not be easy to believe.

The response of political correctness aggravated the situation. 'Diversity, respect, dialogue: this, of course, was the mantra of political correctness, a habit of thought that in Europe is a veritable religion – its tenets instilled by teachers and professors, preached by politicians and journalists, and put into practice by armies of government paper-pushers. It was political correctness that had gotten Europe into its current mess, and only by repudiating political correctness did Europe stand a chance of averting what seemed, increasingly, to be its fate.'[65]

Until the British National Party and the English Defence League protested, it would seem that the British establishment was prepared to sacrifice a generation of schoolgirls at the altar of multiculturalism by concealing the ethnicity of the rapists to prevent Islam or Muslims from being seen negatively. This scandal was brewing since 1988; the authorities and the media saw a pattern but kept quiet. Muslim organizations, playing the victim card as usual, convinced the authorities that there should be a law in the UK to imprison those who tried to alert the public, as disclosure of identity might be interpreted as a racist act both by the person who raised it and for the authorities that pursued the complaint. For nearly ten years 1997 onwards, Labour governments in Britain tried to pass laws that would criminalize those who offended any Muslim. It was going to be a kind of Blasphemy Law that amounted to pre-censorship, which was fortunately never passed.[66]

Available figures suggested that UK could accept de facto decriminalization of rape as a result of the activities of the grooming gangs. The number of individuals prosecuted for and convicted of rape fell in 2019–2020 to the lowest level since records began. Police had recorded 55,130 rapes in England and Wales, but there were only 2,102 prosecutions and just 1,439 convictions – a mere 1.4 per cent, as mentioned by Ayaan Hirsi Ali in *Prey*.[67] This is beyond appeasement; this is abdication of state authority by encouraging inhuman behaviour and inviting chaos.

There was an optimistic belief in the West that the Muslim world was divided, and there was a huge gap between those seeking a peaceful coexistence with the West (embodied in the desire of the Turkish government to join the EU) and the extremist Islamists of the Osama bin Laden variety. Further, only a minority in Europe expressed sympathy with terrorist organizations and most young Muslims clearly preferred assimilation to jihad.

This is a false and convenient escapist argument. When logic fails, reality is ignored, optimism takes over. Most Germans did not support Nazis nor their anti-Jewish policies, but the Nazis still ruled. There is a world of difference between 2001 and 2025. The conclusion earlier was that the world was far away from a new caliphate that could pose a geopolitical threat to the Western world. Today, a caliphate might actually be nearer, after the Western invasions and violence in the Middle East since the beginning of this century.

There are concerns in the UK about demographic changes. For the first time, in a census of England and Wales, less than half of the population (46.2 per cent, 27.5 million people) described themselves as 'Christian', a 13.1 percentage point decrease from 59.3 per cent (33.3 million) in 2011. Nevertheless, 'Christian' remained the most common response to the religion question. 'No religion' was the second-most common response, increasing by 12 percentage points to 37.2 per cent (22.2 million) from 25.2 per cent (14.1 million) in 2011. There were increases in the number of people who described themselves as 'Muslim' (3.9 million or 6.5 per cent in 2021, up from 2.7 million or 4.9 per cent in 2011) and 'Hindu' (1 million or 1.7 per cent in 2021, up from 818,000 or 1.5 per cent in 2011).[68]

Wales had a greater decrease in people reporting their religion as 'Christian' (14.0 percentage point decrease, from 57.6 per cent in 2011 to 43.6 per cent in 2021) and increase in 'No religion' (14.5 percentage point increase, from 32.1 per cent in 2011 to 46.5 per cent in 2021) compared with England and Wales overall: in 2001, there were 1.55 million in England and Wales which rose to 2.71 million ten years later. According to data from the same year, Muslims made up 20 per cent or more of the electorate in twenty-six constituencies in England and Wales. In at least ten constituencies, they were more than 30 per cent of the electorate.[69] These are vital vote banks at election time.

These numbers explain the political appeasement of Muslims. For instance, in the aftermath of India's victory over Pakistan in an Asia Cup cricket match in 2022, violence broke out on the streets of Leicester, Birmingham and Wembley in London. The police watched helplessly as anti-India and anti-Hindu slogans were raised, and the politicians tried to cover the sinister ugliness. If this pattern continues, and if shariah becomes applicable in some parts of major English cities, this would mean a parallel judiciary system. It may not be long before Islamists insist even more forcefully on imposing their attire, language and faith as an essential part of their religious and cultural beliefs.

Despite political correctness, it is interesting to note that European prisons are overwhelmingly populated by Muslims. In France, the figure was 70 per cent. Across Europe, prisons have become centres of evangelism, where non-Muslims are converted to Islam and non-religious Muslims are indoctrinated into fanaticism.[70]

Post the Hamas attack on Israel, Islamic outrage against Israel spread to Europe. Maghreb prayers outside Downing Street in London, reciting Surah Fatiha, was a challenge to the West; it was also a statement: 'We have arrived.' According to Niall Ferguson, 'A youthful Muslim society to the south and east of the Mediterranean is poised to colonize a senescent Europe to the north and west.' Bassam Tibi, a liberal Muslim and teacher at a German university, warned that 'either Islam gets Europeanized, or Europe gets Islamized'. Tibi prefers the former outcome but it looks unlikely. More than two decades ago, in July 2004, Bernard Lewis, a distinguished Western expert on Islam, predicted that Europe would be Islamic by the end of the century. The historian Bat Ye'or (Gisèle Littman) coined a term in the early 2000s to designate the geographical entity that is taking shape as the result of Europe's Islamicization: 'Eurabia'.[71] She wrote about it in her 2005 book, *Eurabia: The Euro–Arab Axis*.[72]

Banking on political correctness, Europeans hoped that the problems of Islamic extremism would be solved if those who pointed out the problem stopped doing so. This did not happen even as the critics kept getting killed, chased into hiding in Europe or elsewhere. The problem did not go away. Not least, of course, because the immigrants stayed and had no intention of going anywhere. Many heeded the explicit as well as implicit advice in the countries they had come from to remain in Europe, but not become European. Europeans began to deal with an influx of immigrants from the Muslim world, first with a warm welcome and then with extreme trepidation, occasionally covered with the fig leaf of political correctness.

Religion and Power Politics

During Reagan's presidency, the Saudis received AWAC jets and Stinger missiles. In return, perhaps, the Saudis helped finance the Afghan Mujahedeen against the Soviet Union. There was Saudi money for Hamas opposing Israel, America's friend, and a good deal of money for new mosques in America where sermons were faxed directly from Saudi Arabia. Prior to the US, it was imperial Britain that helped create the Kingdom of Saudi Arabia in 1932 by bringing Saudi Wahhabism close to Sheikh Abdulaziz ibn Saud, who had earlier helped the British defeat the Ottoman Empire. Saudi Arabia's Wahhabi Islam became the founding ideology of radical Islam. Meanwhile, the Saudi kingdom spent billions of dollars through Islamic organizations and their own embassies to spread Wahhabism.

The 1990s saw the violent division of the Balkans into Christian and Muslim states, aided and abetted by NATO. In 2001, it took just nineteen fanatics from Saudi Arabia and Egypt to attack the mighty US and disturb the equilibrium of the presumed security of the Americans, in a spectacular, even catastrophic, terror attack. It was described as a dare and a revenge against US policies in the Middle East. The macho US image had been challenged, and the superpower had to be seen to be doing something. American retaliation was expectedly immediate and massive in Afghanistan.

When terrorists hit the World Trade Center in New York, there were more than a few chic members of the bin Laden family, other wealthy

Saudis and Saudi royals floating around the country. They had to be assembled at a safe place and taken out of the US as there were fears of a possible a backlash against Saudis. Even though there was a complete ban on flights from 11 September, some flights were allowed to bring in the Saudis from different parts of the country to Logan airport and fly them off to Saudi Arabia. Close, powerful connections between the Saudi royals and the Bush presidency, represented in America by the powerful Saudi ambassador, Prince Bandar, had helped.[73]

The attack on Iraq on manifestly spurious grounds merely gave the impression of a twenty-first century crusade against the Muslims of Iraq, after having already lost out on Iran several decades ago. Saddam may have become unlikeable in Washington, and politically expendable, but on the Arab street he was an Arab ruler. Hardliners in America, also known as neoconservatives, had been advocating an attack on Iraq to dethrone Saddam Hussein even before September 2001. They succeeded, and soon America was involved in two seemingly endless wars – in Afghanistan and Iraq.

This later spread into Syria. The Arab Spring did not flower; on the contrary, there was extreme violence. Well-equipped Islamist terror organizations like ISIS (Islamic State for Iraq and Syria) later named Daesh, even more powerful than the Al Qaeda, began proliferating in Syria and Iraq. By 2011, Daesh was controlling one-third of Syria, and it was not long before Iran and Russia stepped into the conflict, adding to the confusion. Refugees began to pour into Europe, and countries like Germany and Sweden, enamoured of their democratic and human rights ideals, let them in.

By June 2014, the political Islamic world and the jihad world had come together to seek a caliphate. In a statement entitled 'This is God's promise' (Quran 24: 55), Abou Mohamed al Adnani, a spokesperson of the jihadi Iraq-based group, proclaimed the establishment of an Islamic state, dropping the geographical reference to Iraq and Syria. Its Shura council elected Abu Bakr al-Baghdadi to the office of caliph. The ISIS took over from Al Qaeda in opposing the governments in Baghdad and Damascus as well as other Iran-sponsored Shia groups active in the region and also American forces. During their rise and existence, both Sunni organizations had the support of other powers; neither could have existed without it. In fact, the rise of ISIS as a mobile, well-armed and trained paramilitary force left no doubt about the massive support it must have received, mostly from Saudi Arabia and the Gulf kingdoms, all wary of the rise of Shia power in Iraq and Syria.

Both had their narrative-builders and used modern means to spread their message. They tailored their message according to the audience. In the West they played the victim card to great effect while also making a fiery and violent response to perceived grievances. The messaging was sophisticated, and they used the correct idiom of human rights and discrimination to attract sympathies in the West, particularly targeting young people who felt estranged from their communities.[74] At home, within the Muslim world, the ultimate Islamist slogan was about conquest and annihilation of unbelievers. Martyrdom was described as desirable and revenge was considered necessary, both for the cause of Allah. Arrogance and hatred towards other religions were defining tactics. The believers began to find the ISIS promise of an actual territory for an Islamic caliphate more attractive than Al Qaeda's vague promise of a global Islamist haven. Both practised extreme violence and cruelty, with ISIS being even more ruthless and exhibitionist.

The ISIS rose mysteriously and suddenly in 2014 with their flag of future ISIS territories of interest, which included all of India, Pakistan and Afghanistan, along with Central Asia and parts of China, in what it described as its Khorasan province. The Indian fear was that Kashmir would be the most vulnerable to Khorasan moves. Even so, it was the southern state of Kerala that clocked in with the largest number of pro-ISIS cases. Clearly the influence of the Gulf was showing.[75]

West-Sponsored Jihad

Ironically, in modern times, it was the pursuit of superpower global interests in Afghanistan that brought together Muslim volunteers/jihadists from various Muslim states in their fight against the godless Soviets. Earlier small-scale attempts from Pakistan, prior to the Soviet invasion in 1979, were deliberate provocations for just this Soviet reaction. It was Brzeziński, one-time national security Adviser of the US, who thought of playing the Islamic card to bring down the Soviet Union. The sword of Islam was unsheathed, as it were, and thousands of Muslims from all over the Islamic world answered to the call that Islam was in danger. The ummah had got together.

In pursuit of political and economic goals, a pattern emerged where the West, and specifically the US, favoured Islamist regimes to quarrelsome democracies. Destabilization of democracies become real priorities because monarchs, autocrats and dictators were easier to handle. As early as during the Second World War, the British were quite at ease funding the Muslim Brotherhood that enjoyed the patronage of the pro-British monarchy. The same geostrategic interests meant that there was also an intelligence-sharing arrangement with the Egyptian government which would share information about the brotherhood's activities.

States play this double game all the time. Hamas was supported by Israel at one time. Now Syria has been occupied by a group led by Al Qaeda adherents/successors with US knowledge and even assistance. Ahmed al-Sharaa, an Islamist leader of Hay'at Tahrir al-Sham, became president of Syria in November 2024, having ousted Bashar al-Assad. He has US backing because the aim is to keep Russia out and clear a path for access to Iran for the Israelis.

Al Qaeda was an offspring of the US interventions in the Middle East, as it functioned sheltered in Afghanistan. The ISIS was a Middle East-specific force that appeared, it seemed, almost out of the blue in Syria in June 2014. The Taliban was raised by Pakistan as an Afghan-specific force in 1994, but which had volunteers from Europe participating in jihad. The war cry 'Islam in Danger' has been a steady one ever since, and immigrants to Europe use this frequently in their violence on the continent. The formula of faith backed by the sword was replicated by Pakistan against India in the form of religious-terrorist organizations like the Lashkar-e-Tayyiba, Jaish-e-Mohammed and a host of others.

Radical organizations like Hamas purport to kill for their faith, as per Article 8 of its covenant, 'Allah is its goal, the Prophet is the model, the Qur'an its constitution, jihad its path, and death for the sake of Allah its most sublime belief.' This illustrates how jihadist thoughts on politics, theology and religion converge.[76] Jihadist violence goes beyond the aim of regime change. It aims at total Islamization. Islam's fundamental outlook is that it is the only complete religion (kamil) – perfect and sufficient, and the most comprehensive (shamil) – that includes all aspects of life. This is the reason for its adherents considering an Islamist regime as a complete regime for the totality of human life, which all Muslims must implement and execute.

In India, Islam was in conflict with Hinduism from the moment of its arrival. This was witnessed in temple destruction, which marked the onset and continuance of Islamic rule. Author Sita Ram Goel has meticulously tabulated this in two volumes, *Temples of India: What Happened to Them*. The second volume has two chapters written by Arun Shourie. Chapter 12, 'Takeover from the Experts', describes the obfuscation, prevarication, procrastination and, ultimately, total denial about the reality of Ram Janmabhoomi by the All India Babri Mosque Action Committee in 1990–1991. The issue was a matter of faith regarding the birth of Lord Rama at Ayodhya. Yet the twentieth century Muslim in India was not willing to concede something that was a matter of faith for another.

In today's context, in India, political Islamists who seek to impose their views through the ballot box are biding their time until they are able to access institutions of power from within. In contrast, revolutionary Islamists seek to change the system in one blow. They may be a minority, but their violence allows them to dominate. This organized minority is spread all over India and numerous cities and organizations are connected through the internet, giving rise to some internal Islamist insurgencies. The moderate Muslim who seeks secular, democratic and humane values is outnumbered and outmanoeuvred. Reform-minded Muslims find it increasingly difficult to challenge hardline Islamists.[77]

Given all this, followers of Islam must rethink their position in the modern world. No other religion even thinks of, let alone practises, the kind of seventh-century norms that they insist upon. Witness what happened in Pakistan where a mob burnt a man alive, allegedly for blasphemy for desecrating the Quran in June 2024.[78] As if this were not enough, the Pakistan government made the blasphemy law even more stringent; reform is not on their minds.

Islamic terrorism, often sponsored by states, cannot be described as a protest movement. It is a new way of religious conquest by spreading fear and death so that Dar al-Harb – the House of War – is converted into Dar al-Islam – the House of Peace or Islam.

A clash between Islam and Christianity is inevitable as both grapple for domination, while the Islam–Judaism clash is ongoing and will remain fierce. Samuel P. Huntington's prophecy of a clash of civilizations from a continuing and deeply conflictual relation between Islam and

Christianity looks increasingly closer. This will affect India, which is home to the second-largest Muslim population in the world after Indonesia.

In India, the Muslim population is home-grown and converted from other faiths, integrated in the different regions of the country they live in and following the languages and customs of that region. It has taken nearly a thousand years. True, there have been disturbances and differences settled on the streets on several occasions. These disputes are not between aliens who are bringing in other cultures and insisting on observing them against those who have belonged there for centuries, as in Europe. In India these are disputes between settled communities seeking political and economic domination. Religion becomes a convenient factor for the politician who seeks advantage by portraying wrongdoing and discrimination by the government.

It is Europe and now increasingly the US who are facing a situation that is the result of first ignoring the problem and pretending it did not exist, followed by wrong assumptions that the immigrants would amalgamate once they saw the advantages of living in Europe and then appeasement in the hope that this would solve the problem they face from immigrants largely from Islamic countries. The immigrants had come to enjoy a better life but not amalgamate and their leaders talk of ultimate victory because of their beliefs.

9

Obstacles to India's Destiny

How sweet it is to hate one's native land and avidly await its ruin... And in its ruin to discern the dawn of universal renaissance.

— JOHN LE CARRÉ, The Russia House[1]

In international affairs India has the most irritating problem with Pakistan, the most vexing with China and the most complicated with the US. Then, there is the enemy within.

A Curtain Raiser

Kashmir's tourist season had just begun. People from all over the country had begun to come to witness the beauty of the mountains and the amazing colours of the blossoming tulips. Life looked normal, indeed happy, for the sixth year running after the abrogation of Article 370 in 2019. But then tragedy of the most gruesome kind struck on 22 April 2025, when a group of four, some say six, descended on innocent civilians in Pahalgam. The terrorists separated the male tourists and shot the Hindus point blank in front of their wives, parents or children. Twenty-six Indian men were killed in the most horrific way. Many dreams died that day.

What happened from the early morning of 7 May under the rubric of Operation Sindoor was one of the most clinically organized military operations against Pakistan. In a matter of three days Pakistan was suing for peace after having launched unsuccessful counterattacks against

India. The Indian counter to these counterattacks was fierce, with the Indian Air Force targeting eleven military targets like airfields, even as air defence units neutralized their drones and radar systems on the night of 10 May 2025.

Pakistan and China have been the two major and well-known nuisances for India. Both wish to see us collapse. This fact will not change in the foreseeable future. Yet, if one were to evaluate which nation has the potential to do India the maximum harm or good, it would be the United States, a democracy and a promoter of democracy according to its own narrative.

On a good day, Indians see a lot in common with America. It is an extremely powerful country economically, technologically and militarily. All its actions are in its own interests and never in the interest of a so-called friend or ally. This definition of friend or foe also changes frequently, with no qualms – yesterday's terrorist with a price on his head can be today's friendly president, should the situation so desire. Other nations need to tread carefully. The Americans would have viewed the Pahalgam fallout as another opportunity to step in and stay relevant before China or Russia made that move. It is another matter that President Trump was clumsy in declaring the ceasefire, but this was an opportunity for American strategists to see how the military equipment performed comparatively in battle – especially Chinese and Russian. It was the Indian expertise and equipment that would have surprised them the most.

American equivalence between India and Pakistan goes back decades, even when India was under Chinese attack in 1962. Then US Secretary of State Averell Harriman and the British Foreign Secretary Duncan Sandys rushed to India to assess the assistance that could be given. They had a price for this – that India should negotiate on Kashmir. So it was in the 1965 War that Pakistan launched and more definitely so in 1971, when the Nixon government was positively hostile to India.

India's declared unambiguous adversary is China, far more powerful than India in many ways, with a border dispute, and it considers India a potential rival to its dominance in Asia. Pakistan is the noisy, irksome neighbour who has decided that it is equal to India and must conquer India.

The Indian counterattack into Pakistan Occupied Kashmir (POK) in 2016 after the Pakistani attack on the Uri brigade was kept clandestine till it was completed successfully. The air attack at Balakot by Indian Air Force planes, in response to the massacre of forty-one paramilitary soldiers in 2019 in Pulwama, was similarly clandestine and caused a lull in terrorism, barring a few low-end attacks.

The Pahalgam atrocity was presumably based on a Pakistani assessment that the Indian reaction would be similar to before – a clandestine one-off. They had not reckoned that the mood in New Delhi had changed.

Prime Minister Modi had tried to break the ice with Pakistan's political apparatus soon after he assumed charge in 2014 but the response from the military was singularly unhelpful as their 'assets' Jaish-e-Mohammed and Lashkar-e-Tayyiba and its front, the Resistance Front, had continued with terrorists attacks in Jammu and Kashmir. The Pahalgam attack was the last straw.

Peace has never suited the Pakistan Army as it fears a loss of its control on Pakistan, its lands, and its corporations where the army's business activities range from baking bread to building nuclear bombs, and virtually everything in between. They fear they would have to surrender Pakistan to Pakistanis if Kashmir became a non-issue and their country's enmity with India ended.

Over time, the Pakistan Armed Forces have also Islamized and the present army chief Asim Munir is a General Zia-ul-Haq clone, endowed with his puritanical Islamic zeal but without his guile. The present motto of the Pakistan Army is *'Iman, Taqwa, Jihad fi Sabilillah'* – 'Faith, Piety, Jihad in the Name of God'. It is easier to cultivate a future terrorist when the controller of the system is also of the same mindset – war in the name of faith. There has been a natural affinity between the Pakistan army, ISI and the terrorist. All seek the same goal.

In a manner of speaking, Pakistan began its Ghazwa-e-Hind (Arabic for the conquest of India) in 1947 when it sent in tribesmen from Northwest Pakistan along with its own troops into Kashmir and grabbed what is now POK. It repeatedly failed in its attempts in 1965, 1971 and 1999. Conventional war mixed with terror and hijacking were the tactics. The 1990s, after the collapse of the Soviet Union, were a period when the US was asserting itself as the sole superpower, and President Clinton was busy breaking up Yugoslavia in the hope of being able to control Russia, so America had no time for Pakistan-based terrorists running amok in Kashmir. There was no condemnation from the West, at best some equivocal comments, even as India was accused of human rights violations regardless of what the Americans and NATO did in Yugoslavia including a non-stop, seventy-eight-day bombardment of Belgrade.

The Pakistan Army became more adventurous and belligerent in February 1999. At a time when Prime Minister Atal Bihari Vajpayee was making his bus journey to Lahore on a peace mission, General Pervez Musharraf's men were climbing the hills of Kargil into Indian territory, once again under the guise of mujahedeen. Musharraf lost face, had to pull out and his misadventure under a newly acquired nuclear umbrella failed, but the mind was not chastized. The Indian Airlines flight IC 814, hijacked in December 1999, eventually landed in Kandahar and India had to surrender three terrorists for the passengers to be released. One of them was Masood Azhar, who founded the Jaish-e-Mohammed, and the other Ahmed Omar Saeed Sheikh, a British Muslim, who was in the group that assassinated the *Wall Street Journal* reporter, Daniel Pearl, in 2002. The third one, Mushtaq Ahmed Zargar aka Mushtaq Latram, the killer of several Kashmiris, disappeared into thin air, probably terminated with extreme prejudice, in other words disposed of after he had served his purpose or suspected of having turned.

On 13 December 2001, India's Parliament was attacked. Fortunately, a few brave policemen saved the day for the country. India mobilized the army to the western border and eventually pulled back without any major engagement. So, it went on, with serial train bombings in Mumbai 2006, when India did not react beyond the usual strong statements. This was followed by the massive orchestrated terror attack on Mumbai in November 2008 by terrorists from Pakistan, with a siege that lasted three days. It took a brave constable armed with just a stick to overpower one of the terrorists, Ajmal Kasab, who was caught alive. There was no counter from the Indian government. The imagery was not that of a powerful country willing to go to war or at least take some dynamic action. Clearly, it was a case of misplaced nobleness on India's part in trying to seek peace when the adversary was not interested.

So, after the Pahalgam atrocity in 2025, the rulers in Rawalpindi probably sat back, quite smug that the Indian reaction would be the usual one-off attack on some expendable terror target. Their assessment probably was that a limited Indian reaction, as in the past, would take the attention away from the massive economic issues plaguing Pakistan, not to mention the insurgency in Balochistan. Pakistan would also play the victim card if things went wrong for them.

This time, the Pakistani brass miscalculated. India had changed. The first Indian reaction was studied – besides the expected diplomatic moves, it suspended the Indus Water Treaty, which allows 80 per cent of the water from the six rivers of the Indus river system to Pakistan. In the early hours of 7 May, India initiated Operation Sindoor, aimed at targeting specific terrorist locations in Pakistan, from Muzaffarabad to Bahawalpur. Surely India must have war-gamed such a strike years in advance, and not merely in the fifteen days after 22 April. This would have included acquisition of weaponry, use of technology in war, streamlining intelligence and a calibrated selection of targets – both in the first response, and in response to an expected Pakistani reaction attack. Terrorism can only be overcome when its support systems – funding, arms and recruitment – are dismantled. Somewhere in our introspection, we have accepted that engaging Pakistan means engaging Pakistan with force, not across the table.[2]

As expected, Pakistan reacted but since they had no terrorist target, they chose military targets and civil targets including the Golden Temple[3], the much-revered place of pilgrimage for Sikhs and Hindus, with no success. The Indian response came in the early hours of 10 May. The Indian missile and aircraft attack hit eleven military targets across Pakistan, crippling their air attack and air defence capabilities in a display of Indian military capabilities. The unexpected had happened and the Pakistan Army chief Asim Munir informed his prime minster at 2.30 a.m. of 10 May about the Indian onslaught on the Nur Khan airbase and across the country.[4] Shehbaz Sharif said he was swimming when he got the second call from Asim Munir, saying that 'Pakistan had retaliated against India'. Possibly Sharif and his government are swimming in deeper and more turbulent waters than they care to admit.

Rudely awakened by the ferocity and precision of the Indian attacks, Pakistan sought a ceasefire. India offered a pause; Operation Sindoor would continue. This calibrated action had achieved Indian objectives, indicating that terror would be treated as war and responded to accordingly, hitting not only the terrorists but their source as well. 'Operation Sindoor should be remembered not as a dogfight between airframes, nor as a stumble towards strategic instability. It was a calibrated use of force, intended to signal resolve, degrade terrorist infrastructure and demonstrate capability – without crossing the line into broader war,' concluded Dr Walter Ladwig, a senior lecturer in the Department of War Studies at King's College London.[5]

On 12 May, Prime Minister Modi in his televised speech elaborated on a new doctrine[6] – that any future terrorist attack would be given a 'fitting reply',[7] India would not tolerate nuclear blackmail, and India will no longer differentiate between terrorists and their sponsors. He clarified a few things to the adversary, the adversary's international supporters and the doubters at home.

He was creating a new normal in India–Pakistan relations. To India's interlocutors, such as the US, it was clarified that terror and talks, or terror and trade, cannot go together. This was presumably in response to President Trump's offer of grand rewards to both the attacker and the victim. Blood and water cannot flow together, was also the Indian response. Talks with Pakistan, if ever, will be only about terrorism and they will be only about returning Pakistan Occupied Kashmir to India. Operation Sindoor was an exhibition of the new Modi Doctrine and a new narrative that said that any terror attack will receive a fitting response.

India had clearly won in the military space, but seemed to have lost the narrative to an audience that habitually tilts towards Pakistan. Our commentaries – political opposition and media – on such bilateral issues, tend to climb the escalatory ladder. The dispatch of special delegations to different parts of the world seem to have been successful but surely the Pakistanis will send their teams as well. This allows the West to play the role of a referee. President Trump assumed that role from the outset. What India needs is an all-time strong narrative that makes it difficult for the West to perpetually hyphenate India and Pakistan.

After the Pahalgam attack, it was not surprising that the West was not going to get involved on the Indian side. There was the usual diplomatic silence, obfuscation or equivocation that enabled Pakistan to continue its terror activities and then claim shelter under a nuclear umbrella. Then, in a diplomatically clumsy move, Trump unilaterally announced that India had agreed to a ceasefire on his say so before India did so on its own accord. Agreeing to Trump's claim means agreeing to an intervention, at a time when we had our own reasons to continue and would decide on our own terms about the ceasefire. This was then done on the request of the Pakistani DGMO. Additionally, Pakistan has found a good friend in China who has become Pakistan's main weapons supplier and supporter at international forums.

Pakistan was an American favourite from the days of the Cold War, which has changed very little as the US always had some use for Pakistan and Pakistan was willing to oblige. No wonder a senior American official reported to President Lyndon B. Johnson in a cable in April 1966, 'We have built up Pakistan's own independent position and sinews – to the tune of almost $5 billion in support. We've protected Pakistan against China.'[8] This was after the Pakistan invasion of India in 1965.

The reason for anger towards India in the US in the last couple of years, as reflected by comments from their secretary of state and the American national security Adviser in recent years lay in the fact that India has not toed its line on Russia. There was some sane advice coming America's way, as suggested by former Pentagon official Michael Rubin, that the US should not follow then Canadian Prime Minister Justin Trudeau in his anti-India postures, arguing that the India–US relationship was far too important to be sacrificed for Trudeau's venality.[9]

The usual snide references to Indian systems and politics in the US mainstream media were expected, but they did not temper Indian responses. Foreign Minister S. Jaishankar's comments at the Council on Foreign Relations, also known as Wall Street's think tank, were particularly telling. India was not backing down and was unprepared to accept the Western dictum, 'Do as I say and not do as I do.' Jaishankar's comment that India–Russia relations had been stable for decades was a message to the West. India was not going to walk out on Russia even as it sought to improve relations in many quarters, the US included.

At the seventy-eighth United Nations General Assembly (UNGA) session on 26 September 2023, Jaishankar said that political convenience cannot be the basis for response to terrorism; extremism and violence would have equally sharp and direct consequences. His statement, 'The days when a few nations set the agenda and expected others to fall in line are over,' did not go unnoticed.[10]

President Trump's intervention during Operation Sindoor exhibited the age-old American slant towards Pakistan and an inability to be fair. The US condemnation of Pakistan after Pahalgam was equivocal. Trump's declaration of ceasefire without consulting with India, the offer of trade as a reward to both sides if they stopped fighting, and his advice of various kinds (even suggesting that India and Pakistan have a 'nice dinner' to sort things out), were patronizing and frivolous.[11] This is going to put the India–US relationship under some introspection because if an American leader can offer the bait of trade at a juncture like this, he can easily withdraw military assistance or cooperation at a similar time later. His advice to Tim Cook of Apple not to make iPhones in India is a clear indication of the shape of things to come. It is quite clear that 'America First no matter what' will be the route Trump's America will follow, even more forcefully and erratically than in the years gone by. Meanwhile India–US relations remain in a trough as US leaders like Treasury Secretary Scott Bessent hold out threats

Despite the support, Pakistan's agenda remains unchanged. A response from Pakistan is likely soon before issues with water and Balochistan escalate. As claimed by others before Asim Munir, Kashmir is Pakistan's 'jugular vein'. He cannot now make a U-turn. Pakistan's politicians and generals play to the tune that without Kashmir, their country will remain eternally incomplete. Besides, the army fears that should peace between India and Pakistan ever happen, they will lose Pakistan to Pakistanis. In the past, Pakistan sought international relevance through constant delinquency and seemingly irrational behaviour. But the world is changing. India has changed while Pakistan may continue with its jihad. It will do that to its own peril. Although publicly China may have responded to the Indian attack with only a lukewarm statement, by declaring new names for places in Arunachal Pradesh, offering little comfort to Pakistan, but that would not change the basic equation between the two – 'keep India down'. China may also be assessing what went wrong with its equipment that could not deter Indian aircraft or missiles.

The speed with which organizations like the IMF and World Bank moved, with a promise of $2.3 billion by the first and a loan of $40 billion by the second, accompanied by an ADB loan of $800 million soon after Pakistan launched its terror attack, seems nothing more than a reward for services rendered. Add to this the alacrity with which President Trump claimed he had brought about a ceasefire was probably because he had been informed that the Indian reaction was one of calculated anger and was militarily professional. The media and some think tank commentary since then has been on familiar lines, trying to run down

Indian achievements and disregarding or, at best, underplaying Pakistan's original sin.

As India's profile rises, it will unsettle established powers. Obstacles will be home-grown or in tandem with external interests. Everybody is familiar with the nature of the external security threat that we face from two nuclear armed neighbours, China and Pakistan, who have displayed sustained hostility towards us from our early years. Neither can subjugate or conquer India. They can, however, try and slow down its progress at no mean cost to themselves. Obduracy being the DNA of these countries' rulers, armed incursions, by uniformed troops or through trained terrorists, are not expected to cease anytime soon.

Nevertheless, as a growing power India must look beyond its immediate neighbours. The Indian Ocean gains much greater importance in a time tectonic shifts in a changing world. India cannot continue to live in geographical insularity.[12]

Western Advances

There was a kind of a political revolution in India in 2014 when the dynasts and those 'entitled by birth' lost out to Narendra Modi's BJP, who was sneeringly referred to as the 'chaiwallah', harking to the official story of his beginnings. PM Modi's first task was to change the economics of the nation and the social segregation and deprivation, especially for women.

Commentaries emerging from the West underline an intense desire to see a new India minus Narendra Modi, whose principles of 'India first' and 'self-reliance' are anathema to their interests.[13] Daniel Markey, senior adviser in the South Asia Program at the United States Institute of Peace, and former member of the US State Department Policy Planning Staff, in 2023 summarized the goal thus, 'The country is instead led by an ethnonationalist who tolerates little dissent. It is in thrall to an illiberal and increasingly undemocratic party, and that party's grip on politics is only becoming firmer.'[14] Obviously, this and similar essays indicate that a new narrative must be churned out that would justify the need for a change of government in the interest of the country, of course, and succeed in installing a 'friendly' regime that looks after American, and maybe Western, interests more than Indian interests.

Given the overtly comfortable state of India–US relations at many levels, it may not be official policy to denigrate India but there are surely immensely powerful interests also at work. The spectre of two powerful economies and military powers in Asia haunts the West, even when relations between India and China are adversarial. The idea now is also to shift the narrative away from China and target India. The reason being that China is far too powerful now, and there are too many deep Western financial and trade entanglements with China so any harsh action against it could rebound on Western corporate interests. China knows this and the West knows this. So, pick on a country which has not attained a status equivalent to China, where blame can be fixed to change the narrative. The US needs India to safeguard American security interests in the Western Pacific; however, Indian interests are not what the US takes into consideration and there will be no quid pro quo for India either when the White House talks about continuing to work for improving and strengthening its strategic partnership with India.

The usual tactic is to create a narrative, and then let events unfold. Narratives do not have to be based on truth but need to have acceptability. Besides, the Western world has had the means to build and sustain its narratives of superiority, justify its actions or the righteousness of its causes, through its global dominance of the multiple means of communication. One classic example was the way the narrative for the Iraq War in March 2003 was built up. The world was told that Saddam Hussein was harbouring Al Qaeda and that he possessed weapons of mass destruction. None of this was true.[15]

In India's case, this kind of personalized targeting has other motives too. It seeks to demonize Narendra Modi, who is seen as a major impediment to Western corporate interests in a growing India. The Western corporate world, long used to laying down its own rules, probably views slogans like 'Make in India' and 'Aatmanirbharta' (Self-Reliance) as being competitive to their corporate interests, and thus undesirable. According to this standard Western script, India is a market and resource base, not a competitor or, much worse, a rival. It is great if it is a pliable democracy, even a pliable dictatorship will do, but a strong, independent, self-reliant democracy is an awkward entity and best prevented.

The Western media has long been at its game of Modi-baiting, overlooking that he was elected by a comfortable majority thrice. When anti-CAA protests broke out in India, the *New York Times* described the Act as Modi's push for a Hindu agenda,[16] the BBC asked why fear had gripped Muslims as a result,[17] *The Guardian*'s opinion was that the BJP wanted to silence Indian voices[18] and that Indian Muslims were speaking of police brutalities, while the *Washington Post* suggested that India's anti-CAA protests could be the tipping point against authoritarianism.[19]

The Citizenship Amendment Act (CAA) of 2019 amended the Citizenship Act of 1955 to grant citizenship to undocumented migrants from Afghanistan, Bangladesh and Pakistan who belonged to Hindu, Sikh, Buddhist, Jain, Parsi or Christian communities and had entered India before 31 December 2014. It was designed to facilitate the process of naturalization for these minorities who had sought refuge in India due to persecution or religious discrimination in their home countries. This offer was for Hindus, Sikhs and Buddhists who had been left behind and had fled to India because of persecution and discrimination in their country; the reason for not including Muslims was that since they had been a new country in the name of religion and many had migrated to a new homeland, there was no room for them to feel persecuted.

Violent protests broke out in Assam first and Bengal, where a large number of Bangladeshi Muslims had illegally migrated to India. The reasoning offered was that the Modi government was discriminating against Muslims who were excluded from the same neighbouring countries from being eligible for expedited citizenship. The violent protests were mainly limited to Aligarh Muslim University and Jamia Millia Islamia University in New Delhi. There was stone-pelting, some news of petrol bombs being hurled by the 'students' and sloganeering that would put the stone-pelters of Kashmir to shame. On Sunday, 15 December, the All India Students Association (AISA), a left-leaning student association, and the National Student Union of India (NSUI), organized an event marking five years of the anti-CAA protests at the Jamila Milia Islamia, a minority institution in Delhi. The students participating in the event raised Islamic slogans like, 'Tera Mera Rishta Kya, La Ilaha Illallah' and 'Hum Kya Chahte? Azadi'. They also criticized the PM Modi-led government and indicated that the country will never forget what happened in the year 2019.[20] The protests were politicized by religious groups, by political parties opposed to the ruling party, the BJP, and magnified on the social media. Some prominent journalists known for their views and political activists were participants.[21] The narrative that was spun by political parties like the Congress-affiliated National Students Union of India and some Islamists was that this act was against Indian Muslims. Violent mobs in Bengal were the first to ransack and destroy property and later police stations were also attacked. Some argued that the Act violated the principle of secularism by incorporating religious qualifications for citizenship. The government did not give in to the protests and the Ministry of Home Affairs notified the CAA Rules, 2024, to implement the Act. These rules outlined the procedures for applying for citizenship under the CAA, including the necessary documentation and timelines and was notified as the CAA Rules by the Indian government in December 2024.

A presumed one-election wonder in 2014, PM Modi has made a habit of winning elections in India. He has always had too much of India on his mind and too little of the West. Stopping him has become a serious venture, with no holds barred, short of a military invasion. Essentially, the US seeks obedience. In his visit to meet US President Biden in September 2023, Prime Minister Modi gave no ground to the US line on Russia. India also did not allow the G20 meeting as a venue to chastise Russia on Indian soil. Therefore, India had to be taught a lesson, indirectly through allies and vassals. Threats as commonly understood in India have been those arising from China, Pakistan and terrorism. But there has been another threat that has been brewing nearly ten years and is now easily visible.

Indians regularly show fashionable curiosity about the quadrennial jamboree that our friends hold in America for their presidential elections. Many of our intellectuals spend hours analysing implications for their drawing room followers; Americans pay little or no attention to what wise Indians have to say about them.

The West showed considerable interest in the Indian elections held in the summer of 2024. Only, that interest was not curiosity; it was visibly biased, well-coordinated across think tanks, media, anti-Indian elements living in their countries and mostly their citizens, raising religious issues as well as alleging discrimination by a Hindu majority. All false and inaccurate. Eventually the Modi-led BJP won but by a reduced majority and had to form a coalition, though unlike other coalitions in India in the past, this one seems to be considerably stable.

The West sees three major economic powers in Asia – Japan, China and India – rising, and the global balance of power shifting eastwards. It is really about protecting and promoting the West's vast commercial and global strategic interests which are under some peril with the present uncertainties. This would be in gross violation of their own 'rules-based order'. Therefore, today India is caught in a situation where its democracy and its desire to protect its national interests, led by a leader who has shown determination to further them, are seen as a threat by the West, by China and by Islamists. This is the real reason; others are part of the narrative being churned out now. It is almost Goebbelsian in nature.

BBC's two-part documentary against Modi, 'India: The Modi Question', was aired in February 2023.[22] It spoke about the Gujarat riots, the so-called anti-minority trends and the pro-Hindu 'nationalism', and was a hit job in the year before the general elections. The documentary was an example of disinformation and an attempt to strengthen a negative narrative. India's external affairs minister, S. Jaishankar, in an interview said that the timing of the BBC documentary was not accidental and called it 'politics by other means'. He further stated that 'sometimes, politics of India didn't even originate on its borders but came from outside', adding, 'I don't know if the election season has started in India, Delhi or not, but, for sure it has started in London, New York.'[23]

The way the Canadian government reacted, or did not react, to vile campaigns against India by some Sikh renegades had nothing to do with freedom of speech.[24] The BBC's attempt at creating an adverse narrative about Modi did not work. The West, especially Europe, is facing problems with its own minorities. There is also a fear in Europe that its diaspora from Islamic countries would create their own problems. Any anger or resentment needed to be diverted – to India by portraying it as a discriminatory Hindu regime.

India, China and even Turkey in Europe, are considered the main diaspora-creating countries, as they seek to increase their influence in international affairs. Diaspora are economic assets with their remittances and help in trade and foreign investment; they are soft power assets as they move up the social ladder and as diplomatic assets once they are strategically mobilized. There is concern in the West on implications of this for the global order in the long term.[25]

There was already a mysterious guiding hand. 'Anywhere you look, a White West narrative supremacy is running amok,' said Gautam Chikermane in an article in 2022 on the system of 'global rankings'.[26] Some of the supremacy – higher per capita income, technological prowess, a strong military–industrial complex and the ability to spend without regard to earnings – may be acceptable. 'But a large and increasingly vocal expression of that supremacy is accentuated by manipulated narratives.'

This is not the first time that narratives are being created without any basis and that is why these will not stand scrutiny.

A beginning to counter this mendacity was made through a paper by Sanjeev Sanyal and Akanksha Arora, 'Why India Does Poorly on Global Perception Indices', in 2022. They evaluated the indices Freedom in the World, Economic Intelligence Unit (EIU), Democracy Index and V-DEM.[27] The Freedom in the World index is supported, among others, by the National Endowment for Democracy, known to be funded by the CIA as explained earlier in this book. It is well known that the CIA has been in the business of moulding public opinion and the use of journalists at home.[28]

The Sanyal–Arora paper discusses the various methodologies used by surveys where the impression given is that they are based on objective parameters, and highlights the flaws in the reasoning and results. The parameters are subjective, indices are derived from perceptions and based on opinions of a few experts and many questions on democracy are not even meaningful indicators of democracy.[29]

Obviously, India needs not only remedial action but also pre-emptive action. Sanyal and Arora warn that once these indices enter World Bank records, they become acceptable and credible and can be weaponized to discourage or destroy investment in targeted countries. They suggest that 'independent Indian think tanks should be encouraged to do similar perception-based indices for the world in order to break the monopoly of a handful of western institutions'.

New, foreign and supposedly independent media outlets, backed by foundations and NGOs, can create fast-moving sensationalist high-impact content. This is part of the entire exercise to keep India off balance. To counter this there would be a need to keep a closer watch. Much more than the written word, the visual impact of what is seen on a screen, in a reasonable debate, a well-conducted podcast and, most of all, in a film, is immediate and long-lasting. The CIA and the Pentagon have used this method by liaising with Hollywood almost from the beginning of the Cold War, using fiction and fact to project the American view, giving suggestions and even monitoring projects. As John le Carré famously remarked, 'Secret agencies are a measure of a nation's political health and the only real expression of its subconscious.'

America never gave India any bonus points for remaining a democracy against all odds, and frequently favoured Pakistan over it or at best equated Pakistan with India. It will continue to support Pakistan to keep India in check and will also selectively support India as a bulwark against China. When a superpower talks of another nation as a friend or an ally, that smaller nation is on call and liable to be trampled under, if that becomes necessary, in the interests of the superpower. Support for democracy, liberty and human rights are part of the narrative, not the end goal. Democracy is described as rule by the majority of citizens, just as much as it is in any Western country where the majority is Christian. One does not hear of Christian majoritarianism but a great deal about Hindu majoritarianism. It is just that there are strong vested and entrenched interests at home and adverse interests abroad who do not want the new Indian enterprise to succeed.

Activist Agendas

At points in the past, activist groups have been used to obstruct development activity, new projects, critical infrastructure development like dams, mines, ports, border roads and highways in the country. The delay in the completion of the Sardar Sarovar Dam on the Narmada river and the Kudankulam nuclear power plant are two major examples of obstruction due to activists' agitations. Environmentalists did not want the dam to be built on humanitarian grounds while climate activists did not want the Russian-assisted Kudankulam power plant to be built out of concern of a possible nuclear mishap. If the activists had succeeded, large tracts of India would have been deprived of hydroelectricity and irrigation in the former case and power in the latter. In the case of the nuclear power plant, the hidden reason was that it was a Russian project, and it did not fit the post-Cold War narrative. India went through a seventeen-year ordeal of sanctions before it could build its own cryogenics and successfully launch the Chandrayan.

India's political opposition today does not have its own agenda beyond preventing the Modi government from succeeding. There is thus opposition to every move of the government. It was unfortunate and unexpected that the Indian government let mob protests determine its decision on the Farmers Bills which were withdrawn.

Disinformation or the selective use of facts must be countered with specific facts through Indian think tanks and universities where these subjects are studied, along with white papers and articles that can be cited in overwhelming numbers to counter any legal opposition as well. This must be a continuing process and needs an element of anticipation of every possible opposition and its source of support.

For instance, the sudden spurt of pro-Khalistan activities in the UK, Canada, US, Australia and New Zealand, with Germany following, is not a coincidence. It points to strategic planning, finances and manpower with somebody running their psychological warfare campaign, sometimes with the assistance or indulgence of the government of the country. An effective counter to this would be the revocation of OCI facility, freezing bank accounts and seizing properties of all signatories to the 2021 Khalistan referendum, and any Sikh gurudwara and media groups that have been known to lend support to a violent secessionist rhetoric must be put on notice. Following the Canadian fracas, it could be extended to other parts of the world where countries harbour Indian terrorists and criminal dodgers. Outside the country, it is a battle of narratives. In India it must be a security– security–intelligence and political response considering Khalistani activity in India. [30]

There is need for India to react – in the short term to wild stories and in the long term pre-emptively. There must be tactical responses to derogatory narratives and strategic responses to sell our own story in advance, for the future. The roadblock in this context is that all global communication – traditional and high technology – is controlled by the West. Reactions in anger or emotion, especially by the government, make little difference; in fact, they are taken as a confirmation of the original statement or report. As a people, we have invariably looked for approval from the West for our actions. We have now begun to discard this submissiveness and diffidence. Therefore, we should choose our time and our issue to react. All reactions need not be by the government either, but all reactions must be embellished by facts.

Government reactions must be strategic, credible and sustainable. Most American think tanks are well-endowed financially with big-name expertise. They interface with other similar think tanks, interact with the White House, the State Department and the Pentagon, the US government, the corporate sector, including the politically powerful military–industrial complex of the corporate world, which now includes technology and intelligence. Many of these think tanks have their outreach in other countries, essentially following their own schools of thought while proclaiming independence of thought. They provide long-term narratives on the target country about its domestic politics, its economic system and even geopolitics. Often, statistics are managed and manipulated to provide desired results. The recent Happiness Index may be laughable in India but there are enough people in the West who buy this line. The finding that India has less freedom, a component of the Happiness Index, and that only Cambodia and Bangladesh rank below India for 2025, is an absurdity and clearly indicates a massive manipulation of data.[31]

China and Pakistan's animosity towards India is normally considered the main external obstacle to its rise. This mindset fails to take into account other Big Power interests and Western alliances who come as friends but only pursue their own interests; they will change course abruptly, consort with India's enemy or adversary, or arrange for accusations, criticism and sanctimonious advice when they wish to change their narrative. Recent history is full of these examples, besides India. The Middle East is a classic case of policy changes and reinventing friends or alliances.

The Dragon in the Mountain

The formula that anything can be solved in international affairs through discussions and diplomacy has been tried with China over the years and again lately, but has not yielded any results and there are few indications that this will lead to satisfactory outcomes in future too. Chinese leadership made its intentions clear at the twentieth CCP Conference in October 2022. A Chinese film on the Galwan clashes between Indian and Chinese troops was shown to nearly 5,000 delegates at the conference, along with special invitees in the Great Hall of the People in Beijing. Many PLA officers familiar with the Chinese Western

Theatre Command were inducted to the newly constituted Party Central Committee and the Central Military Commission to enable them to shape their security posture, manage crises and conflicts and win local wars. Clearly this means pressure on India's borders will increase and there could be further clashes in future. The larger message to India is, push to develop and scale up indigenous capabilities across the board.

Chinese presence in Gwadar and Djibouti would enable controlling/watching access to the Persian Gulf and Europe through the Red Sea. Its increasing presence in Africa may bring it into conflict with the US, which already has an Africa Command to police the region. This may not be sufficient to keep the African nations on America's side. Chinese presence along Africa's east coast and internet connectivity provided by it with the help of Huawei, right from Pakistan to Africa and then branching off to Europe, is clearly indicative of growing Chinese presence and power. India's western naval flank and sea-bound trade to the west, from the Gulf onwards, could come under pressure, should the need arise for China because of its presence in Djibouti, Gwadar and Hambantota in Sri Lanka. China has developed an extensive presence on the east coast of Africa also. Even though many of them may be described as commercial ports, the Chinese presence does increase its influence.

The two countries are in military alertness along the land frontiers to India's north with no solution in sight, as the Chinese would want to drag this for as long as possible. It suits them to keep Indian Armed Forces deployed on the borders, which means additional strain on budgetary resources for India and constant pressure on the armed forces. The Chinese have developed a far better infrastructure on their side of the LAC and India has some distance to travel on this. The Chinese have considerable presence in Nepal, Myanmar, Bangladesh and Sri Lanka, and further into Southeast Asia. No country can or will ignore the People's Republic of China. Even Western airlines had to amend how they showed Taiwan on their itineraries – it could not be, 'Taipei, Taiwan', but only 'Taipei'; Daimler Benz had to withdraw its advertisement that showed the Dalai Lama. That is the power of money in the twenty-first century.[32]

Xi Jinping's rapid ascendancy into his all-powerful and aggressive stance comes at a time when the country faces no real external threat. His dream project, the BRI, had an eager signatory – Pakistan, under the China–Pakistan Economic Corridor (CPEC) in 2013. The One Belt One Road (OBOR) as BRI was initially called, was a hurried rejoinder to then US President Barack Obama's pivot to Asia. Pakistan would receive US $46 billion (raised to $65 billion in 2022) initially in projects that included a road from Gwadar through Gilgit-Baltistan into Xinjiang. This would mean increased Chinese presence in manpower and projects on India's western flank. This could become a two-front war for India by other means. Gwadar, as a naval base and connected to the proposed Gwadar–Kashgar highway, would immensely reduce the distance between the Persian Gulf and the eastern seaboard of China, compared to the sea route via the Malacca Straits.

Despite limited success, BRI remains Xi's pet dream because of the hope that this would lead to the realization of a bigger dream – of being the world's most powerful country by linking the Pacific coast to the Atlantic and the Arctic to the Indian Ocean. It would mean being in control of this vast landmass through dependencies created by trade and commerce, and the ocean through the might of the PLA Navy. It also entails Chinese forces being located in areas of BRI activity for protection of workers, infrastructure and materials.

There are some valid reasons why India cannot accept the BRI as it operates in Pakistan as CPEC. The Gwadar–Kashgar Road passes through the Gilgit–Baltistan region of Jammu and Kashmir, which belongs to India but is under illegal Pakistani occupation. The project was China-specific, and not designed to offer any advantage or opportunities to India or any other country; in fact, it was designed to push through a political and security agenda and exclude all economic rivals from similar benefits.

The PLA Navy had shown interest in building logistic points at key ports to protect its energy supply lines. The ports listed were Kyaukpyu (Myanmar port), Chittagong, Colombo, Aden and ports in the Maldives. These would be industrial hubs to support military operations, and bear a strong resemblance to China's 'string of pearls' strategy designed to encircle India and reduce its room to manoeuvre in the Indian Ocean region.

China seeks to consign India to a subordinate status in a China-led Asian order. There has been no change in its attitude since 1954, when India unequivocally accepted China's sovereignty over Tibet without an adequate quid pro quo, except for some polite meaningless statements. This Chinese intransigence has been a set pattern.[33]

It is important to remember that China is not interested in an early solution of the border issue. Between the tortuous and unending bilaterals, lofty nomenclatures and pressure tactics on the border have been the norm. One such agreement was in April 2005 when Prime Ministers Manmohan Singh and Wen Jiabao signed an agreement loftily described as the Agreement on Political Parameters Guiding Principles for Settling the Boundary Question. It also had a portion on 'Strategic and Cooperative Partnership'. One of its clauses said that both sides agreed that there was enough room in Asia and the world to accommodate the simultaneous and rapid rise of both the countries.[34] This must have sounded so comforting to the Indian government of the day, yet it was meaningless to the Chinese.

The reality at that time was that China was soaring high economically and militarily with the latest technology. They concluded that India was no threat of any kind to China and there was no need to observe any of the guiding principles agreed upon. Border intrusions and transgressions occurred at regular intervals and became more aggressive after Xi Jinping became the supremo.

A month ahead of Narendra Modi's visit to China in 2015, Xi was in Pakistan 'reaffirming the $46 billion investment in the 2,000-mile infrastructure and a connectivity push across the country'. Modi did raise the issue of the CPEC with Xi but it made no difference. India's external affairs minister put the BRI in an Indian perspective when he said, 'Where we are concerned, this is a national Chinese initiative. The Chinese devised it, created a blueprint. It wasn't an international initiative they discussed with the world, with countries that are interested or affected by it . . . A national initiative is devised with national interests, it's not incumbent on others to buy it.'[35]

In dealing with India, China adhered to its favourite tactic of creating border incidents to coincide, precede or follow an exchange of visits between the two countries. In September 2014, Xi Jinping paid his first visit to India. Amidst some forced bonhomie where the two leaders, Narendra Modi and Xi Jinping, were shown sitting on a swing in Gujarat, reports started to emerge that the Chinese had violated the LAC and were sitting in Chumar in Ladakh. The 2014 face-off started days before the Chinese leader Xi Jinping visited India and continued while he was in India. About 1,000 Chinese soldiers had entered Indian territory. Xi's visit continued and the Chinese vacated the intrusion only after Xi returned home. It must have taken Narendra Modi's government tremendous patience and equanimity not to downgrade the visit. Yet the deliberate and arrogant display of petulant imperialism by the Chinese was only telling India what the Chinese thought of it and what they wanted. Despite this, Modi visited China in 2015, knowing that Chumar would not have happened without Xi's approval. There was no independent-minded, trigger-happy commander who would launch into India at that juncture.

In May 2017, after India declined to attend the BRI Forum meet in Beijing where about twenty-eight leaders had been invited, Chinese troops intruded into Doklam on the Bhutanese plateau in June. The Indian military response was immediate and effective, with the Indian Army holding the advantage. This was followed in 2020 by a massive unprovoked Chinese escalation, with heavy casualties on both sides in Galwan in Ladakh. Chinese arrogance and militant behaviour met with a massive Indian response, diluting the Chinese message to India's neighbours, Asia and the world in general. China had difficulty claiming that it was the undisputed leader of Asia. It had to contend with a new India.

The most recent Chinese attempted intrusion in Yangtse, Tawang, in 2022, coming as it did without provocation and not too long after Galwan, should be taken as a declaration of intent by the Xi Jinping set-up. They will make more attempts to change the LAC before they think of discussing the dispute. It is best to expect the worst and hope for the best. Quite clearly, it indicates an intention to not solve the LAC issue and to let the boundary remain undemarcated, thus enabling China to take advantage of the ambiguity.[36]

Some might explain these incidents as a result of improved infrastructure on both sides of the LAC, which allows more frequent contact in areas where LAC perceptions overlap. Also, perhaps the Chinese assess that improved infrastructure on the Indian side may reduce their advantage on their side of the LAC. As expected, there was the usual criticism of the Indian Army being unprepared for this intrusion whereas the truth is that Indian soldiers were appropriately swift and aggressive.[37] A

China–India Cold War has been in the making and may intensify into an Asian Thucydides trap where a rising India challenges China's existing dominance.

India's reaction to Chinese activity on the LAC as well as along the McMahon Line in the Northeast was slow and inadequate for decades, but the pattern changed after 2014, with renewed multiple measures to improve infrastructure along the LAC. India has doubled the pace of construction of strategic infrastructure along the Himalayan border to match China's aggressive push in the region.[38] This may not be enough against Chinese build-ups, and India has a great deal of catching up to do. In addition, there have been reports from some Western countries of how the Chinese had established clandestine police stations in foreign countries, using their own countrymen to keep a watch on their own nationals, to coerce them into supplying intelligence, and even to suborn the native population for intelligence purposes. In April 2023 there were two of these clandestine police stations in New York City, two in California, one in Minnesota, one in Nebraska, and one in Texas. It would be negligence and complacency if India were to assume that this was not happening in India.

The Arunachal Frontier Highway, officially notified as the National Highway-913, and also called Bomdila–Vijaynagar Highway, would connect Bomdila in the northwest to Vijayanagar in the southeast of the state. All aspects of the project were approved in the financial year (FY) 2024– 2025 and construction is expected to be completed by 2027. This can be seen as another sign of Indian assertiveness, even though the terrain on the Indian side is much more difficult than in Tibet. Following the latest India–Pakistan clash in May 2025, China has stepped in with an attempt to provoke India by renaming twenty-seven locations in Arunachal Pradesh, which Beijing calls 'Zangnan'. As expected, India described this as a baseless political stunt. This is China's fourth such renaming exercise since 2017.[39] China's refusal to attend the G20 meet in Arunachal in March 2023 is just one indication. Xi's absence from the New Delhi G20 summit in September 2023, was not unexpected and was indicative of three main reasons – Xi was presumably sulking that the Indians were not succumbing to pressures on the border; he did not want Modi to steal the limelight – this was personal; and Xi did not want to be face-to-face with Joe Biden, who the Chinese had presumably assessed would not be president in 2025.

As it turned out, Xi's absence was an own goal for China since it afforded Modi the space to hold centre stage, even with Biden around.

The repeated incursions across the LAC since September 2014, a few months after Modi became prime minister, ensured China's continued stand-off with India despite Indian attempts to break the ice. China's leaders probably assess that this is the best way to keep a check on a rising India. At the same time, the Chinese are wary of the impact the continuing crisis with India would have on their regional and global strategic objectives. There is considerable debate in China about India's position and strength, and New Delhi should leverage this.[40] The debate has also focused on the growing India–US strategic partnership and the fear in Beijing is that the US is promoting India as the Pacific's western anchor specifically to contain China.[41]

In August 2008, the Indian National Congress (INC) signed a MoU with the Chinese Communist Party and agreed to discuss important bilateral, regional and international developments, in the hope it would improve high-level communication.[42] Possibly the INC did not realize that in China, the government perpetually belongs to the CCP. It is not so India, where governments belong to the country and not to political parties. It was not a party-to-party agreement in the conventional sense, and one wonders if the INC briefed the present government about what transpired between it and the CCP, which is unabashedly adversarial to Indian interests.

India will continue to face similar behaviour in the future due to its rise as an alternative power centre in Asia and a challenge to Chinese pre-eminence. The Chinese attitude is one of a government constantly trying to bully another. It also means that India must enhance its powers to defend and retaliate in every way. India cannot be an idle stakeholder in the region; it must become an active resident owner.

China's military strategy extends beyond conventional warfare and incorporates lessons from the West's recent operations in the Middle East and Ukraine. Ahead of any conflict breaking out, China would conceivably deploy the PLA's political commissars and other personnel to forward areas to soften the population in the adversary's border areas. This onslaught could be followed by a massive cyber offensive designed to disrupt communications in India among the military formations, the leadership of the forces and the political leadership, as well as vital logistic communication and infrastructure abilities. China's technological advances, both commercial and military, have been immense and that would be its preferred weapon in any future conflict with India – to disable or destroy systems. Pakistan's Armed Forces used Chinese weaponry during Operation Sindoor in May 2025 after the Indian Armed Forces responded to the Pahalgam terror attack by the Pakistan-based terror organization. Pakistan relied heavily on Chinese military hardware. Pakistan deployed the J-10C 'Vigorous Dragon' fighter jets armed with PL-15E air-to-air missiles and HQ-9 long-range surface-to-air missile systems with a 200-kilometre engagement envelope. These platforms were tested in actual combat for the first time. Chinese satellite reconnaissance reportedly supported Pakistani targeting, with Beijing even re-tasking satellites to enhance coverage over Indian military zones.[43] The PLA Air Force would then be introduced into the conflict together with China's missile force and, finally, an offensive by ground forces. This is what a coordinated Chinese onslaught might look like. Hardening of cyber defences and sharpening offensive capabilities would have to be one of India's priorities.[44]

It is crucial for India to remember that in 2017 during the Doklam crisis, the Chinese withheld data on both the Sutlej and Brahmaputra rivers. In March 2021, China announced plans to construct a massive hydroelectricity project on the Brahmaputra/Siang/Yarlung Tsangbo rivers, which would have eleven hydropower stations with a generating capacity of 60 GW (gigawatts) of power – thrice as much as its Three Gorges project.

Tibet is like a natural water tower for China's southern neighbours, and the main rivers like the Huang He and Yangtze in mainland China, and the Mekong, Brahmaputra, Indus, Sutlej and Salween that flow into India, Vietnam and Myanmar, all originate in Tibet. China has thus succeeded in extending its power and control over the rivers of Tibet as it goes about building more dams on them.[45] These rivers that flow out from the Greater Himalayas and the adjacent ranges like Kunlun, Karakoram, Tian Shan and others, feed all the rivers for half the global population living along the basins of these rivers and dams on the great river – Yarlung Tsangbo in Tibet, Siang in Arunachal Pradesh and Brahmaputra in Assam and beyond – will affect supplies to India.[46] The Chinese have constructed about 22,000 dams more than 15 m high as part of their plan to harness power and become carbon-neutral by 2060.[47] Given the state of India–China relations, and the absence of any formal water-sharing agreement, it would be naïve to expect China to behave like a responsible neighbour and consider India's needs.

Competition will become fierce. One is not sure if China will ever wage a conventional war with India; its preference would be to win without fighting, through cyber and telecommunications. The last war the Chinese Army fought, and where they did not do too well, was in 1979 when they took on their former ally, Vietnam. The Indian Armed Forces have fought more wars successfully and one could infer that Indian troops are better equipped to handle a hot conflict.

Xi Jinping is increasingly behaving like an emperor with a Middle Kingdom delusion, expecting smaller nations to pay obeisance. The present global churn – economic, political, military and technological – adds to uncertainties. His utility to Russia has increased after the Ukraine war. China's rise and America's relative inability to have its way as in the past, reflect a changing equation. China's smaller neighbours might begin to look to India to try and balance the power equilibrium.

Today, China suddenly has many more grave problems that its leaders have hidden from the world, and this includes a slowing down of the economy. The Covid mishandling has revealed scars in the country which Xi Jinping's hard control may not be able to heal. Despite fears in many Western circles, there is still no certainty that China will replace the US to become the world's sole hegemon by 2050. The world is changing – that is the main consideration, and we need to plan accordingly, during these global uncertainties, but living next door to a hegemonic China will not be pleasant for India. National interests, rather than shared values or wanting to merely look good internationally, should be India's guiding principle.

India and China need to find a way to break the impasse on the boundary issue. The earlier dictum let historical questions or differences be decided over time, but the economic engagement between the two countries has been unsatisfactory for India, giving it neither economic benefits through trade nor political gains. China has not missed any opportunity to be difficult with India on the boundary issue.

Dealing with Pakistan

The idea of Partition was not an accidental, spur-of-the-moment vague idea.[48] Pakistan was popularly imagined in UP (then known as United Provinces) as a sovereign Islamic state, a New Medina, as it was called by some of its proponents. Prominent ulema of the time, led by Maulana Shabbir Ahmad Usmani (founder of Jamiat Ulema-e-Islam and later acclaimed as Pakistan's Sheikhul Islam), sold the dream that Pakistan would create an Islamic utopia of the kind first promised by the Prophet in Medina. It would inaugurate an equal brotherhood of Islam, break down barriers of race, class, sect, language and region among Muslims, and establish an example worthy of emulation by the global ummah. All very pure and Islamic. Pakistan was dreamt of as the successor to the caliphate, that seemed attainable at one stage. But the dream soured soon enough. In recent years, Imran Khan, Pakistan's dethroned prime minister, also referred to the days of the Medina and said he would replicate them in his country.

India must face Pakistan's reality without any notion that India and Pakistan are alike. It suits Pakistan to remain permanently hostile to India so long as the army dominates the country. The attitude of the Pakistani Army's cabal of corps commanders will not change with any political change. The army has scant regard for politicians and civilians and make its disdain quite apparent. Its political leaders have remained either juvenile or in awe of the army or both. Pakistan's politicians are aware that their longevity on the seat of delusionary power is at the pleasure of the generals. The army and the Islamic fundamentalists have an understanding on how to run the country; the latter has immense street value in facilitating regime change.

India's biggest mistake has been gullibility and mistaken optimism that made it accept overtures that invariably come when Pakistan is in trouble, enticing Indians to make grand gestures to show magnanimity. The occasional sly gesture from Pakistan to talk of normalcy might increase the heartbeats of some Indians but is only designed to buy time for one reason or the other. It seems that the Indian state has finally stopped being delusional about Pakistan.

Pakistan's Army is now led by a man who was taught in General Zia-ul-Haq's jihadized military academy. General (now Field Marshal) Asim

Munir, who headed the ISI too in the past, is from a conservative family, has memorized the Quran (and therefore, is known as Hafiz-e-Quran). Munir and his predecessors treated all Islamic terrorists nurtured by them with great favour. Today there is hardly any difference between what a so-called moderate like Bilawal Bhutto or Imran Khan, formerly known as Taliban Khan, have to say about India and its leaders, or the Islamic fundamentalists. Islam in its pure form, something that the radicals adhere to, has taken firm root in Pakistan. Blasphemy, shariah, kafir and jihad are common terminologies in the country.

Pakistan has never been a 'normal' state; it was always a confused state unable to identify as a moderate democratic state and chose instead a distinctly Islamic identity. This is because Pakistan was really an Islamic idea formed on the basis of the argument that Muslims cannot co-exist with Hindus, and the two must live separately.[49] India has been irrationally ambivalent at best about Pakistan-sponsored terror, even forgiving, despite Pakistan's state-sponsored terror attacks. The Mumbai attack in 2008 was, in reality, an armed attack on India. India grandly and inexplicably accepted the Pakistani claim that both Pakistan and India were victims of terror. After the Indian counter-attacks in Uri and Balakot, there was a realization India and Pakistan could be in a two-sided sub-conventional conflict which might suddenly erupt – for instance, after another major terrorist attack on India. Indian retaliation was a part of the new policy, as demonstrated in May 2025.

Terrorism as a policy option for the Pakistan Army will not change. It will morph and adjust according to circumstance, regional, international and perceived need. The use of drones has already begun, and we can expect this to get more lethal. It is a matter of time before Pakistan renews its attention on Kashmir. There is an inevitability about this because the thought of Kashmir keeps Pakistan together. There is no freedom struggle in Kashmir but an externally inspired movement which, over the past seven and a half or so decades, kept itself alive by taking advantage of India's internal squabbling and policies of appeasement.

Pakistan's major interest is not the Muslim population of the Kashmir Valley, but the water that flows from Kashmir and irrigates the fields of Pakistan's Punjab. One can see the signs of an international campaign accompanied by heightened terrorism in Kashmir. Turkey's President Erdoğan has ambitions of establishing an Islamic caliphate, and he could tie this in with Pakistan and bring in China, whose larger game would include some control of the Middle East.

Meanwhile, Pakistan will continue its extensive, well-organized psychological war against India. It is a continuous sophisticated programme controlled by the Inter-Services Public Relations department of Pakistan's all powerful Inter-Services Intelligence Directorate. This agency quickly negated the gains India expected from its famous Balakot airstrike in retaliation to the Pulwama terrorist attack in February 2019. Our own Opposition politicians and sections of the mainstream media did not help the Indian cause by their adverse reactions to the airstrike by raising doubts about it.

Geography cannot be altered and Pakistan cannot be relocated. Strategically it will remain important especially as an adjunct to China. The Indian Ocean is now dotted with bases that permit Chinese warships to berth, which indicates a growing Chinese naval presence in the Indian Ocean. China endeavours to be the master of the Indian Ocean and a challenger to America in the Pacific Ocean.

Enmity is inevitable and permanent unless Pakistan suddenly discovers a statesman. Until then Pakistan's policy of unremitting enmity towards India and terror under a nuclear umbrella would remain a low-cost option for the Pakistan Army. There is little possibility of permanent peace or even normal neighbourly relations with India. The earlier doves in India are looking increasingly forlorn as the reality of Pakistan becomes apparent. As a country, Pakistan is in economic distress and political disarray. There is nothing India can do to alleviate Pakistan's misery, not even trade with them as some hopefuls would suggest. India needs to concentrate on increasing its own economic and military strength, move towards internal political cohesion and develop a narrative of its own, which should be heard loud and clear across the world. By a narrative, I don't mean a jingoistic one, but that of a strong, no-nonsense, responsible state.

Alongside having to handle two hostile nuclear-armed neighbours, some of India's other neighbours also want to play the China card while dealing with India. Myanmar is not averse to this as it struggles with its own insurgencies and economic crises. The Chinese presence in Nepal, Sri Lanka and the Maldives is substantial and will invariably work against Indian interests. Diplomacy, financial assistance and project-tied aid will not wean them away from China. Only our economic and military strength in the future and the way we deal with China will determine a change in the neighbourhood. India will remain vulnerable in the Indian Ocean unless it augments its capabilities rapidly.

Having said that, these are security threats and considerations. These may slow down India temporarily, but India will prevail in the end. What Indians need to curb is the tendency to thump their chests amidst proclamations of conquest. Deng Xiaoping's famous dictum to his party – 'Hide your strength, bide your time' – was essentially advice not to chest-thump too early till China was strong enough. This does not work in a democracy where politicians must loudly proclaim their achievements for a re-election.

The Enemy Within

'A nation can survive its fools, and even the ambitious. But it cannot survive treason from within. An enemy at the gates is less formidable, for he is known and carries his banner openly. But the traitor moves amongst those within the gate freely, his sly whispers rustling through all the alleys, heard in the very halls of government itself,' Marcus Tullius Cicero warned the Roman Senate.[50]

This is the sum of all fears.

While nations prepare to deal with external threats, the deadliest enemy is the enemy within – liberal, illiberal, communist, fascist, democrat or autocrat. Irrespective of ideology, they are the ones who pander to the outsider against their own country. This harks back to India's colonial past when it was more profitable and convenient and therefore more important, to side with the foreigner than with the neighbour. As a people, we allowed the foreigner to enter, loot, destroy and leave. This changed to conquering parts of a region and staying on to rule. With the arrival of the British there grew the culture of a coterie and courtiers who became enablers of the Raj and acted as middlemen to facilitate activities in favour of the Crown. They became the 'brown sahibs' created by the 'infamous' Macaulay system. The foreign ruler illegally acquired lands and gifted them to the natives if they behaved. There was rarely any issue of morality or ideals, more a question of survival. The foreigner eventually left, weakened or defeated; the coterie stayed on and quickly changed loyalties towards the new masters.

No conspiracies of regime change, subversion and terrorism can occur without some involvement of locals, willing to serve external masters in the name of their conscience and, of course, money. Anyone with a higher sense of devotion to his or her country would not turn it over to outsiders. In these cases, the outsider cannot succeed without cooperation, and often encouragement, from the insider. The Mumbai bomb blasts of 1993, the serial train bombings in 2006, and the November 2008 carnage in the same city could not have happened without there being a well-laid-out local support system. It would have taken months, if not years, to plan and execute these attacks without it.

The Citizenship Amendment Act 2019 sought to fast track citizenship for those who had arrived in India before 31 December 2014, were either Hindus, Sikhs, Christians, Jains and Buddhists and had faced religious persecution in the countries of residence, Afghanistan, Bangladesh or Afghanistan. Muslims were not included as they did not face religious discrimination or persecution in the country of choice. There was an immediate reaction first in Assam and then in Bengal where a large percentage of the population comprise illegal immigrants from Bangladesh and mostly Muslim. Protests in Delhi and other cities followed. Long-term riots are not spontaneous; they are planned, organized, financed and the logistics had been worked out including the supply of stones, kerosene for arson and even a catapult to hurl at targets. These riots were no different and had political support.

In February 2020, UN Chief António Guterres, on a three-day visit to Pakistan, was asked whether he was concerned about the new citizenship law in India. He said he was. 'It is absolutely essential when a nationality law is changed, the statelessness is prevented. Because when basic right of anyone anywhere is to have a country that a person calls his, then everything should be done in order to avoid statelessness.'[51] During the same time, the UN and the US government expressed concern regarding the 'discriminatory law'. 'We are concerned that India's Citizenship (Amendment) Act 2019 (CAA) is fundamentally discriminatory in nature and in breach of India's international human rights obligations,' a spokesperson of the Office of the United Nations High Commissioner for Human Rights told Reuters. A US State Department spokesperson was quoted as saying, 'We are concerned about the notification of the

Citizenship Amendment Act ... We are closely monitoring how this act will be implemented.'⁵²

These are all about creating narratives for influence-building or pre-empting a move to suit an agenda. Millions of rupees poured in and the scale of demonstrations, the massive logistic support for food, shelter and transport, the creation of temporary townships that came up, meant only one thing – these had been planned much earlier and had received tremendous local, political and financial support.

Every powerful country operates by suborning locals in countries it wishes to increase its influence in. They are known as 'useful idiots' through whom the powerful country operates citing noble principles of democracy, liberty, equality, progress and peace. In India, for instance, there are supporters of US and Pakistan who will periodically burst into sanctimonious sermons about the benefits of making peace with Pakistan, recommend that India should forgive and forget past terror attacks against Indians, many of them unarmed civilians, that a peace dividend will flow to the present government, India will be lauded in international circles and that resumption of trade will also benefit India. Indians must resist the perennial temptation of accepting policy changes just to look good in Western centres of power. Those pursuing the goal of domination and control are quite cynical of these starry-eyed Indian manoeuvres.

This was discussed in Chapter 2 how the US and European use NGOs as fronts for pushing their foreign policy and security agendas with considerable involvement of its intelligence agencies. Notable have been the USAID and National Endowment for Democracy.

Behind the façade of charity, American and European foundations weaponized philanthropy for statecraft. Selected NGOs and activist networks, were carefully funded to obstruct India's developmental trajectory. 'This strategy, subtle yet devastating, functions like the work of economic hitmen stalling nuclear reactors, halting coal projects, blocking industrial corridors, and sabotaging agricultural biotechnology, all under the garb of human rights and environmental justice.'⁵³

Powerful US-based foundations include the Ford Foundation, Rockefeller Foundation, Climate Works Foundation, Tides Foundation and George Soros' Open Society. These institutions fund global NGO platforms such as Greenpeace, Amnesty International, Action Aid, Survival International and others. From there, money is funnelled into local outfits that mobilize protests, litigations and global campaigns targeting India's most critical projects. What appears to be 'civil society activism' is, in fact, a coordinated mechanism of economic containment.[54]

This practice was largely curtailed in 2014–2015 following reports of the adverse effect that was being created on India's development.[55] It was found that many Indian NGOs funded by donors based in US, UK, Germany and the Netherlands were trying to create an environment that would stall development projects. A favourite method was prolonged agitations against nuclear power plants, uranium mines, GMOs, mega-industrial projects like POSCO and Vedanta, hydel projects (Narmada Sagar) and extractive industries like oil and limestone. Anti-coal activities targeted powerplants and the Russian-aided nuclear power plant at Kudankulam, which was stalled in 2011. This had an estimated negative impact on India GDP to about 2-3 per cent annually. Greenpeace had a substantial role in some of these activities.

Since January 2016, the Modi government embarked on a crackdown on foreign-funded NGOs found to have violated provisions of the FCRA, the Foreign Contribution (Regulation) Act 2010. As a result, licences of 6,677 NGOs were revoked between 2017 and 2021. Despite this, powerful NGOs like George Soros's Open Societies Foundation, Pierre Omidyar's Omidyar Network and the Henry Ford Foundation (founded by his son) were able to send funds into India by circumventing the law.[56]

Journalist Sandhya Ravishankar's 2024 report on the crackdown on foreign-funded NGOs is an eye-opener about their support to anti-government activities and the funding to certain media publications to write against the Indian government. All three foundations attract members and researchers through scholarships and fellowships, to create networks of other lavishly funded NGOs and advocacy groups. All three speak loftily about democracy and equality. The report also mentions that among the Indian NGOs funded by them are the Commonwealth Human Rights Initiative (CHRI), National Foundation of India (NFI) and the Centre for Policy Research (CPR), all of whom received funds from the Soros, Omidyar and Ford Foundations until restrictions were imposed by the Indian government by putting them in the prior approval category. Nevertheless, they received generous funding from the Big Three Donors, running into crores of rupees.[57]

Ravishankar's 2024 report also detailed how asymmetrical warfare had been organized in Tamil Nadu since 2017 through an intricate network of organizations arranging protests, like the pro-Jallikattu protests in 2017. A Delhi-based NGO, the Other Media, with FCRA clearance, received 30 per cent of its funds from various church organizations, including the Caritas Internationalis, reputedly one of the world's largest church-funded organizations. The list of players involved is virtually endless, and is as varied as their activities. [58]

It is true that a people get the government they deserve; it is also true that sometimes a people get the Opposition that they do not deserve. India today has an Opposition which, when in power earlier for nearly sixty years, promised the moon but delivered only moon dust. Ever since the general elections of 2014, this ragtag group of entitled underachievers has led protests to oppose every action of the elected government with violence, street fights, blockades and damage to property – all signifying traditional methods of left-wing destructive opportunism.

It is possible for people to love their country while hating its system. For such people there is nothing wrong or disloyal in betrayal of secrets and other views to the other. International movements, like communism and Islamic extremism, and many intellectuals work on this principle. Islamists have their version of their own supremacy and a sense of victimhood; communists have their ideology and infallibility, which clashes with the sense of infallibility and superiority of Western democracies.

India is at the cusp of history. We can attain greatness, if we get our act right. This opportunity will probably not come our way for several decades because the country's youth dividend will disappear. If we fail now, the danger is that we will be confined to a lowly life and possibly be colonized again. If we stumble, we might return to the position we were in for the first sixty years of independence, or worse. The fear that this will happen is not because of what the government is trying to do; it is what the opposition and its friends have been trying to undo, sometimes by themselves and their inanities, and sometimes with help from outside the country.

The definition of an Indian liberal today is that he or she must hate PM Modi, his cabinet and the BJP with uncontrollable passion, he or she must exult in every criticism of the Modi government by the Western media, never mind if this hurts national interests. Any national setback is a matter of celebration for them. If that is the hallmark of a liberal, then the country is full of illiberal individuals which does not necessarily make all of them 'bhakts' or even BJP supporters.

When the Covid virus emerged in 2020, there was hardly any scientific or medical knowledge about the pandemic and how to handle it. The initial handling might have been hesitant and flawed but in the end, we mastered the fear of the unknown and came out looking much better than many other developed countries. Yet there were politicians who would want to take advantage of the situation by spreading rumours and creating an exodus from Delhi. There were others who imported dubious experts who prophesied that the scale of the virus was so universal and devastating and given the Indian capacity to handle this for its huge population, there could be several hundred million dead as a result. Some of our TV channels telecast these interviews, hoping to create panic which would hurt the government, lead to its collapse and so on. This was the time when faced with a national crisis of undefinable magnitude, political parties should have united, instead of seeing it as an opportunity to regain power. Fortunately, nothing of the sort happened, despite the gloomy prognoses churned out by Western agencies. Indian resilience and fortitude triumphed in the end.

Further, it is an embarrassment, indeed a crying shame, when the pretenders to the throne are unable to give a single coherent statement about their vision for the country. Instead, what the country has seen is a constant attempt at a personalized debasement of the very office to which they so ardently aspire. Unable to find a powerful argument in defence of their actions, all the Opposition can do is to harp on the fact that the country is confronted with Hindu nationalism, also described as Hindu majoritarianism, something straight out of their Bibles – *The Economist* and *The Times* of London or the *New York Times*.

It has failed to see that sectoral appeasement, hypocritical promises, dynastic urges of leadership without vision and ignoring the vast majority while following a warped notion of 'secular' politics, can only lead to disaster. This is a conglomerate of failed politicians who see an opportunity to regain power not by solving problems but by obstructing policies. The ugly events during the anti-CAA protests in Delhi's Shaheen Bagh, Chand Bagh, Jamia and at the Jawaharlal Nehru University, and the despicable scenes at Red Fort during the anti-Farm Bill protests in 2021 and the kind of slogans that were raised will remain etched in many minds. The Opposition fears that unless this government is stopped anyhow, somehow, they will continue to be marginalized. Instead, India's opposition politicians, not blessed with any political ideology for the country beyond the dream of gaining power, would rather see the country in distress so long as they can occupy the throne.

Subversion of the Mind

The other fear is that we will be threatened through subversion of the mind, and not just cyber wars. Battles of the mind are designed to attain goals without having to fight gruelling bloody wars. Street protests, non-cooperation and fasting were valid means of protesting an illegal external government. We were using non-violence against a ruthless foreign occupier. India today has a democratically elected government, constitutionally elected through the same electoral process as its predecessors, by the people, through secret ballot under the norms laid down in the Constitution.

Our protests, expressions of dissent, must also be similarly constitutional within the law; anything else is unacceptable. The government in power must make it clear what is acceptable and what is not, and make this distinction obvious. One group's demands, however justified, do not permit disrupting the lives of others, prevent their access to their workplace, family, doctor, hospital or even recreation. Those who do this lose whatever sympathy they had to begin with. In many protest cases in the last few years in India, even this justification does not exist. Protests become events propped up by vested interests and supported by political opportunists who criticize and oppose the very norms they earlier wanted to adopt. An agitator must also accept that his or her freedoms are limited by another's rights and his or her own duties as a citizen.

Social media, made possible by modern technology, has meant the easy availability of 'free' platforms like X (formerly Twitter), Instagram or Facebook. These might be free for the user, yet the owner of the platform makes his billions. The gold mine is the data of the user – which is analysed and sold to corporate consumers and to interested government agencies, who can use the data or the platform to mould or restrict opinion and for advertisements from the corporate world.

Far away, out in the distance, one can see a gathering storm. Keen watchers of the scene had predicted that this storm would reach India's shores in the second half of 2023, ahead of the elections. There was no tsunami, but gusty winds to imbalance the government did hit India's shores. This storm was more on social media carried by new technologies and the activities of different political groups.

The entitled still feel that they have been wronged by the rest of the country because it elected someone from not just from outside their circle but one far removed from being an undeserving dynast, not once, not twice, but thrice. Ahead of the 2014 elections, the acidity of the liberal discourse had begun to grow as it 'feared' the result. It became a crescendo afterwards and has remained on a high decibel level ever since. No one from the entitled community wanted to know that the age of entitlement was over, and the age of the aspirational, street-smart, B-town boys and girls was here. The entitled lamented, returned their awards, though not the money nor the houses they stayed in. A small-scale industry wrote about the perils of Hindutva and benefits of secularism in the *Washington Post*, the *New York Times* and the BBC. There was horror about electoral fraud with the electronic voting machines every time the ruling party won, but such concerns disappeared when any other party won a state election. A new narrative, forecasting the sinister rise of Hindu nationalism, was created at home and embellished abroad.

External Combustion

A superpower has no friends, yet every country wants to be its friend. A superpower has only its interests in sight; no one else's interests' matter. No wonder Henry Kissinger had remarked, 'It may be dangerous to be America's enemy, but to be America's friend is fatal.'[59] India will be no exception to this rule.

The US Commission for International for Religious Freedom (USCIRF), one of those busybodies created by the US government under its own laws without any international approval arrogating to itself the right to meddle around in the world, was among the first to feel aggrieved when the Modi government introduced the Citizenship Amendment Bill in December 2019. It described it as neither accurate nor warranted. The USCIRF has been passing judgements on India in the past from 2001 to 2004 and then again in 2009 and 2010. One of its members, Tony Perkins, a commissioner in 2018, was known for his far-right Christian beliefs, and close connections with the Ku Klux Klan and other white supremacist groups. The Hindu American Foundation had pointed out Perkins's hateful stances against non-Christians. Despite lack of credibility, the Commission remains voluble.

The *New York Times* criticized the Supreme Court judgement on Ayodhya in November 2019, saying that by backing Hindus, the Court had handed Modi a victory to remake India, and might cause a rise in sectarian tensions. The article added that many Muslims feared they would be reduced to being second-class citizens and referred to frequent lynchings by Hindu mobs.[60] This kind of uncomfortable silence and selective reporting is intended to give a warped view of political realities in India and generate a negative world opinion about the country. Such narratives are strengthened further when Indians write against India in Western newspapers. *The Guardian* saw the decision to abolish Article 370 in Kashmir as another step against the Muslim community.[61] The *New York Times* published a report in August 2019 that cited critics who feared Modi was making India into a Hindu nation.[62]

It was not long before the issue of cow slaughter, smuggling of cattle and lynchings made the headlines. Modi's Hindu India had imposed a ban on cow slaughter, screamed the media, overlooking the inconvenient truth that it was the previous Congress government which had imposed these bans because this did not suit the narrative. There has been a concerted and coordinated attempt to depict the Narendra Modi government as presiding over an increasingly pro-Hindu government. Expressions like 'majoritarian Hindu rule', also described as Hindutva, or even the term 'fascist' have gained usage.

To protest the CAA, there was a series of street protests that quickly became violent and sectarian, as was intended by the agents provocateur, from the Jawaharlal Nehru University to Jamia Millia towards the end of 2019, leading to the Shaheen Bagh women's demonstrations in New Delhi, and then the riots of northeast Delhi in February 2020 in which fifty-five persons were killed. These were part of a grand sinister design, not just to destabilize and discredit the government by unconstitutional means but to create a sectarian divide and blame Hindus for it. R. Jagannathan, editorial director of the RSS magazine *Swarajya*, described the Shaheen Bagh women's demonstrations as a thinly disguised passive-aggressive jihad against the majority in India using the Citizenship Amendment Act as the trigger.[63]

Some Muslims left at the time Pakistan was created, while many more stayed behind. By condemning the exclusion of Muslim refugees from neighbouring countries as being eligible for Indian citizenship under the CAA, those who stayed behind wanted the Government of India to allow those who voted against staying in India to be allowed to return under the provisions of this Act. This is absurd and no government will allow it for any number of reasons, security and demography being primary ones. At moments like this, the sane voice invariably gets muted and a wrong impression – the one that the fundamentalists, obscurantists and their supporters want – gains unopposed visibility and acceptance. Voices of sanity and rationality need to be heard loud and clear, by this I do not mean the bigoted ones that are shown on TV channels. Controversy may be good for TRP ratings but can be costly for the nation if it encourages bigotry by normalizing the extreme or retrograde point of view.

The Indian liberal is perhaps no different from those who are considered global liberals. They display paternalistic attitudes towards the rest arising from a sense of entitlement. The assumption is that the liberal, sitting in his or her exclusive gilded echo chamber, knows what is best for the common man on the street. If this common man does at all have an opinion contrary to the salon advice, then it is promptly dubbed nonsensical or at best dismissed as a conspiracy theory.

Since 2014, a concerted attempt at undermining the present Indian system – political, economic and cultural – has been organized in the West. It is almost as if it is a Christian West versus a Hindu India match. Why is this being done – one democracy to another, one might wonder? In international relations the accent is on national, economic, strategic and security interests. There is no such thing as democracy of nations. If we did believe in such concepts, we would not have the P-5 at the UN, nor one hegemon imposing its domestic laws on the rest of the world (sanctions for instance) or go to war on false pretexts.

China would like supremacy over India without having to fight long bloody wars. Therefore, the only alternative is to try and organize a regime change. This method is more acceptable if a regime change is tried against an autocratic, dictatorial regime or a declared enemy. India is neither; on the other hand, it is the world's largest democracy where all elections have been held regularly and have always led to a peaceful transfer of power. The press is free and allowed to say what it likes; it gets away with a great deal more here than in other countries. India has never had the situation where for instance, Al Gore won the vote, but George Bush became President owing to a sleight of hand. So, Klaus Schwab and George Soros, the latter a sworn enemy of Narendra Modi, have been toying with their Great Reset where in a new world of capitalism, the world will be managed for the poor by the rich and powerful.

Prime Minister Modi pushed the G20 to replace ideological fluff and bias-laden chaos with an intellectual and facts-based order. More than that, India should also develop means and capacities to develop narratives of its own about other countries, particularly when in this age of social media and instant narratives, it is important to speak of other countries and our own interests in a manner that suits India. Our stories must come from us, and not from outside.

India was good so long as it did not believe in weird notions like nationalism and self-reliance or try to become a hub of manufactured products. India was supposed to be a market and a resource ruled by flabby innocents and acolytes of the West, not a rival to the West's dwindling share in the global cake. It is impossible to conquer or defeat India militarily; Pakistan has limited capabilities and is a nuisance, most of the time. It would be unwise of the West to rely on China to militarily take on India; recall that Kissinger tried to persuade China to attack India during the Bangladesh War, but the Chinese did not oblige.

India will have to improve the quantity and digital reach as well as the quality of research literature produced by its own think tanks. Taking a leaf from how foreign think tanks work, Indian think tanks should begin to concentrate on the domestic political landscapes in the US, selected European countries and a host of other nations. The picture that normally emerges is not as rosy as is made out; there is acute poverty, deprivation, discrimination, race conflicts and many social problems that are normally swept under the carpet. Private think tanks could then produce detailed rankings and reports on the political, economic, security, social and religious conditions of each country. The Government of India could produce a comprehensive international religious freedom report like the US state department does. This would provide enough material for discussions over months in seminars and workshops, involving experts from the countries concerned.

India's other problem is that we have nothing similar or even close to media companies like the CNN, BBC, Reuters, AFP and others. We must deal with the internet and social media platforms that have their yardsticks of censorship, often quite biased; unlike China, India has not developed its own social media platforms. The Ukraine War has been covered in India mostly from reports from Western agencies; there is no Russian point of view. Without a voice of our own and means of communication that are our own, we will remain handicapped in selling our story. Our media simply has to get more professional and not merely serve the agenda of the owner of the medium. As India's economic and general strength increase, our external interests will also increase. A $3- or $5-trillion economy would need an extensive, all-source professional media portraying India favourably. The narrative must be ours and not that of others.

The road ahead is bumpy with roadblocks and it is steep. It is a road India must navigate towards its glorious destiny.

10

Awakening, and India Has Risen

Arise, awake, and stop not till the goal is reached.

— SWAMI VIVEKANANDA[1]

False Dawn

In the first fifteen centuries of current era, India had the largest economy in the world. It was 28 per cent of the global GDP in 1000 CE, which came down to 24 per cent in 1500.[2] The country remained prosperous during the rule of the Mughals.[3] Then the British got into the act of colonizing, and our GDP had plummeted to about 4 per cent of global GDP by the time they left in 1947. Economist Utsa Patnaik's research has put the figure drained from India over roughly 200 years at US $45 trillion.[4] After inflicting this manufactured poverty on India, the narrative in the West blamed India for it and offered aid – which no doubt was rooted in the stolen money.

In 2025, the same impoverished India stands as the fourth-largest economy in the world by its GDP figures and third by PPP figures, having doubled in the last ten years. It is self-reliant in food; its armed forces are amongst the most formidable in the world; the country provides some of the most efficient information technology; and the world has access to India's young professionals. Its youth cohort is amongst the youngest in the world, and the future looks bright. Yet it stands in the middle of a global chaos of endless wars and conflicts as one empire declines and others rise. India still hopes to continue doing well for itself in its economic growth and all that comes with it. Hurdles will continue; we simply must overcome them.

The British left India after ensuring the implementation of a convoluted plan to secure their own imperial interests in the northwest region of undivided India. Months or even some years ahead of Partition, the British had concluded that the northwestern part of India, what would become Pakistan, was strategically more important to them than the rest of India. Most British security requirements would be met by Pakistan. The Kashmir crisis had begun to brew quite early and subsequent developments need to be seen in the context of British and US strategic interests in India and Pakistan.[5] The British departed not just because of a non-violent struggle. They also found that India was becoming unmanageable, and they did not have the means to control a possible violent uprising. The armed forces were restless. There had been a revolt by the Indian Navy in Bombay in 1946, with similar uprisings in Calcutta against the British Raj. This convinced the Raj that it could not manage India without the help of the Indian soldier or bureaucrat; it would be far better to hand over power before it was snatched, and also try to keep some control. Prime Minister Clement Attlee, on a visit to Calcutta in 1956, when asked about the influence of the Indian freedom movement on the British decision to quit India, said it was 'minimal'.[6] Attlee's belief was that Netaji Subhash Bose had a bigger role than the Indian National Congress in India attaining freedom.

So began the thought process of creating a united Pakistan and a weak, divided and confused India. In the process Pakistan got two parts, East and West. Add to this the possibility that Kashmir might have remained independent or even joined Pakistan, while the British had already ensured that there was a revolt in Gilgit–Baltistan, led by a British Army major, to declare it independent of Jammu and Kashmir.

The Sun Also Rises

India has changed rather dramatically since its early years as an independent nation. A few years ago, apart from being a media event and the usual handwringing, little would have been possibly done to rescue 41 men trapped in a collapsed tunnel in Silkyara in Uttarakhand in November 2023. For over a fortnight, men and women from different agencies and different parts of the country, led by the National Disaster Management Authority (NDMA) and the Indian Army worked nonstop to rescue all of the with the help of the miner's experts in rathole mining who ultimately helped in the rescue.[7] It was no ordinary feat, and it took extraordinary grit and determination. The country trusted these men and they lived up to this trust. This is another example of India coming of age when all lives matter and the task is professionally accomplished.

In contrast, the abiding image at the end of the first decade of this century was of an India that was a chaotic soft state without a strategic culture that could not even respond forcefully to the devastating terrorist attack on Mumbai in November 2008. Having been ruled for centuries, Indians seemed to have forgotten the science and art of statecraft and were seen to prefer taking the line of least resistance.[8]

One of the consequences of globalization is the continued struggle and competition for resources, vital minerals and so on that would shape military policies of nations that have vulnerable supply-line choke points. With time, globalization was not just an economic model ensuring Western economic dominance. It went beyond that with unlimited greed and became a form of absentee colonialism. This was ultimately an undesirable way of managing the globe, when with most manufacturing transferred to China, it led to lost jobs and began to affect domestic politics in the Global North.

Other problems came before India along the way – some global, like climate change, terrorism and energy; some regional, like water shortages and migrations; and some purely our own: our abysmal law and order – delayed justice leading to social discomfort and insurgencies in many cases, and issues of poor health, education and infrastructure, which were not attended to by successive governments with any great tenacity and sincerity. Rapid economic growth will create socio-economic pressures arising from exploding expectations and demographic pressures on urban areas.

There is however potentially an even greater crisis brewing; the fear of a US–China hot war at a time when US interests are engaged in Ukraine and West Asia. Should the Chinese leadership, involved as it is with its own internal political squabbles, and equipped with a navy that is bigger than the American navy, decide to invade Taiwan as a diversion at this time, the US will have to retaliate.[9] This would mean America could be involved in three simultaneous conflicts against formidable adversaries – Russia, Iran and China. It is also doubtful if the US has the financial capacity today, given the state of its national debt, to sustain these conflicts or even the ability to re-arm and re-equip its allies. Should that happen, the world will be staring at an Armageddon while the Islamic world prepares for its own final battle – Al-Malhama Al-Kubra.

So far, the India–Pakistan conflict has been restrained after India agreed to pause its reprisals against Pakistan for the terror attack on innocent tourists in Pahalgam in April 2025. The sharp and professional Indian reaction in a carefully calibrated response indicated that future attempts would invite a similar response. India is not going to roll over and accept any violations. The extremely professional response by our armed forces on 7 and 10 May 2025 unnerved many doubters. There was a close alliance of interest between China and the US about how they handled India's reaction which signalled a definite rise. The US wants India's rise on its own terms against China, and that India should be on its side but obedient without acting on its own. China wants to be the undisputed hegemon in Asia and eventually the only one to replace the US as the next global hegemon. This adds to instability in South Asia apart from that in Pakistan, in the Middle East and in the Ukraine theatre. There is extreme political disequilibrium where the existing hegemon, US, is losing its grip, while the heir apparent, China, is not widely acceptable, and the state of global finance is unsteady. These developments will test the strained US–India bonhomie.

Undoubtedly, India needs a partner in the US and to simultaneously manage its relations with China.[10] Apart from this, India needs to sustain ties with Russia, engage Europe for trade and technology, orchestrate strategic and trade tie-ups with the kingdoms of Saudi Arabia and the United Arab Emirates, without souring relations with Iran, and at the same time strengthen ties with Israel. This entire exercise is going to be a complicated and stressful diplomatic and strategic manoeuvre, but that is the state of the world today.

Ties with the US always have an air of uncertainty about them. US interests in India, apart from limited (for them) economic interests, are in helping US deal with China, which is America's prime strategic interest; it is not about protecting or helping India. Throughout the two-and-a-half-year Himalayan stand-off between India and China, President Biden remained silent about supporting India. Instead, he went out of his way to be nice to Xi during their summit meeting in San Francisco.

Yet there is hope for India. Today Indian industry is beginning to stand up to international giants, household savings are seeing a positive shift towards risk-taking and will move to riskier ventures like equities, and internationally, India will emerge as a new face in the next ten years. As India journeys to becoming a $10 trillion economy, foreign policy priorities will work into the system for protection of economic interests like markets and resources. Acquisition of latest technology with its security aspect will be a constant endeavour. India will have transited from a low-income to middle-income economy as the technology-driven Fourth Industrial Revolution matures. Disenchantment with globalization and the reality checks of pandemics have already revealed the 'frail ethics and malicious influence' that have defined global governance all these years.[11]

India is today poised for bigger things, as it looks at becoming the third-largest economy and the fourth-largest military machine globally. Even the latter could change, and India could replace Russia for the third spot. One would expect that other democracies would look forward to India's rising star, but not without reservations or doubts. India will be seen as a rival, both by the declining West and a rising China.

The US Dollar and Chinese Ambitions

The global financial system has been changing for some decades now. The US economy was a consumption-driven model supported by the US dollar, backed by American force and global presence, and supported by cheap Chinese labour that kept costs for Americans low. This model is now facing questions from other nations that are looking for their place in the sun. This comes at a time when the global balance of power is shifting from the West to the East at the fastest rate since the Industrial Revolution. The kind of equilibrium achieved by major and emerging powers after this period of transition will depend on how they de-risk supply chains, re-globalize trade and mitigate conflicts.[12]

Having the dollar as the global currency helped the US become a militarized hegemon that carried out its forever wars. There has been frequent chatter about the end of the dollar as a global reserve, which would reduce the American ability to control a global empire. Apart from this, 2008 marked the beginning of its financial decline amid increased uncertainties.[13]

Chinese global ambitions have become more pronounced as the US seems increasingly incompetent to protect democracy or its own interests. There was a time about two decades ago when the US was willing to share supremacy with China in a G2 kind of arrangement, but America quickly backtracked and today it seeks to edge out China even from East Asia. There is a new stress on supply chain security and changed labour arbitrage, keeping India in mind. Tensions continue and both have their own fears of the other. Trump's foreign policy moves have left most nations perplexed but there seems to be more swagger and bluff than action, as wars in Ukraine, Gaza and Yemen continue. Uncertainties enhance the dangers of a Thucydides trap as partnerships move to intense rivalry.[14]

China will remain the West's prime fixation as well as India's. China wants a unipolar Asia and a multipolar world, India wants a multipolar Asia and a multipolar world, and the US wants a unipolar world and a multipolar Asia. The prospect of two economic powers with considerable military might – China and India – is worrying for the US. It is too late to overpower China, but India can be hobbled.

Both the US and China and their interplay will determine strategies of other major nations – Russia, India, Australia, Japan and France, which will take into account economic growth, power shifts and changing priorities.[15] India will have to keep in mind that China's rise may not be peaceful as its influence rises in Asia. America and the West continue to work on a strategy to retain supremacy while China aims to snatch it from them. India is caught in the crossfire. The Americans will have to deal with the growing global perception that sees the US as a declining power with its supremacy challenged.

The West is not ready to accept the assessment of India's Minister for External Affairs S. Jaishankar that the world is seeing the end of a 'world order which is still very, very deeply Western' and his prediction that looking ahead, countries like India pursuing their particular policies and preferences and interests was acceptable.[16] As India's rise continues, making its economy the third largest, it would be anachronistic to exclude it from G7.

To stay ahead of the competition, India would need a first-rate external intelligence mechanism, manned by men and women of appropriate skills for the mid-twenty-first century. An intelligence system must remain relevant in and for the future.[17] Preparations for this need to begin now, bearing in mind what may lie ahead and that such systems cannot be created or refurbished during crises but in times of peace with time in hand.[18] It is not going to be easy. Secret intelligence will never be able to match up unless it starts reinventing itself now.

Step In and Step Up

The elections of 2014 marked the beginning of great change. Many intellectuals and self-styled political analysts, mostly on TV, predicted a coalition government and were surprised at the results. Congress leader Mani Shankar Aiyar's ill-advised chaiwallah jibe at Narendra Modi did swing a few seats in favour of the BJP.[19] But it did more than that; it aroused the can-do spirit in many Indians, young and not-so-young. The sky had become reachable for those deprived for centuries, and their dreams too could come true.

Despite the global problems, pandemics and politically inspired internal protests, India became a $4-trillion economy in 2025, almost double of what it was in 2015. India's economic boom will mean that India will overtake Germany to become the third-largest by 2027 and the number of households with an annual income of over $1,000 are expected to rise from 26 per cent in 2021 to 53 per cent in 2031.[20] India's economic prospects look seriously bright according to international assessments, something that gives Indians great comfort. In April 2025, *Forbes* listed Inda as the world's fourth-largest economy in its listing of the world's ten largest economies[21] and the country's GDP is expected to grow at 6–7.1 per cent during 2024–2026 according to Standard & Poor.[22] Standard & Poor, in their review of Credit Conditions Asia Pacific Q1 2024, stated that there was a shift in the growth pattern from China to South and Southeast Asia.[23] The report projects China's GDP growth to slow down to 4.6 per cent in 2024 and marginally increase in 2025 and slide back to 4.6 per cent in 2026 while India would be touching 7 per cent by 2026.

The IMF, despite some reservations in India, predicted that India will become the world's third-largest economy by 2027, surpassing Japan and Germany with a GDP exceeding $5 trillion. India aspires to be a developed economy by 2047, an achievement that is restricted to only a few countries.²⁴ The expectation is that India's economic growth will outpace all other G20 countries for at least the next two years and will be driven by domestic demand.²⁵ According to JP Morgan, India could be a $7 trillion economy by 2030, the third-biggest in the world.²⁶

It has not been all negativity in the West. There has been positive commentary about India's economic prospects, where India's economy and population are expected to grow, and could be considered as a counter to China, as a global economic heavyweight,²⁷ and that by 2030 the G3 of global economies, US, China and India, will have a greater share of global economic activity than the next twenty countries, including European ones.²⁸ Commenting on the G20 meet in India in 2023, Walter Russell Mead, a distinguished fellow at the Hudson Institute, spoke about a rising India and a shifting world order, where China and Russia seethe, Europe shrinks, US dithers and India rises.²⁹

The American investor Ray Dalio, after meeting the Indian prime minister in New York in 2023, commented on India's economic prospects. 'Prime Minister Narendra Modi is a man whose time has come when India's time has come. The potential of India is enormous, and you have now a reformer who has the ability to transform and the popularity to transform. India and Prime Minister Modi are at a juncture in which a lot of opportunities will be created.'³⁰

Ahead of the results of the 2019 elections in India there was general scepticism about the BJP's and particularly Modi's ability to win the second term on their own. Commentators were either out of touch with reality or optimistic without reason. Ian Bremmer wrote in *Time* about the possibility of a coalition arrangement but redeemed himself by pointing out, at some length, the positive improvement brought by the Modi government – tax collection, stern action against fraud, massive infrastructure development, use of technology for biometric identification, zero-balance bank accounts to help direct payment of subsidies, the Swachh Bharat programme that provided toilets to hundreds of millions, the Ujjwala Yojana that provided cooking gas to women in the countryside and healthcare reform for the half a billion poor for treatment of cancer and cardiac diseases.³¹ Bremmer gave up his optimism about India in a subsequent column.³² There have been many others who have held a negative viewpoint about India and continue to do so. It is time India stopped looking for Western approval and buckled down to the task ahead.

In the past decade, it would be prudent to summarize India's progress as a change in the slope of the curve of change, from a flattish Congress rate of growth to an accelerated Bharat rate of growth. This status has been achieved by Indians in one decade or less. By 2030, India would still be a work in progress but the real take off to 2040 will come after that.[33] Investors are increasingly seeking real and stable economic growth. This is something few countries can provide in the current macroeconomic and geopolitical environment. According to the World Bank, India and China will dominate global investments and savings by 2030. It also believes India's share of global growth will rise to 18 per cent by 2028. Absolute wealth held by households will grow exponentially in India.[34]

This buoyancy in the economy allows India to borrow from local and international debt markets to expand its infrastructure. This means the domestic markets for goods and services get better integrated, leading to a multiplier effect on GDP. This in turn reduces inflation, increases purchasing power and productivity. Stability and strength in the Indian rupee incentivizes greater use of the currency in international transactions, a move that would further consolidate the rupee as a major global currency. This attracts more foreign investment in a country that offers significant opportunities for labour arbitrage, lending tailwinds to growth. The country is in a happy upward spiral.

India will play a significant role on the global stage, which will involve addressing broader security concerns and preserving larger interests. Pushbacks from adversaries and competition from rivals are to be expected, but in the real world of heightened national interest, pushbacks can also come from 'frenemies'. These are mostly from Europe and North America, who find India useful on their terms but there is no real camaraderie or commitment. International conviviality can also be just an opportunistic attitude. Attempts have already begun to pull India down in the competition for resources, markets, influence and domination. This is already happening as our Western democratic friends look at India's insistence on self-reliance and national interest with grave concern, as also suspicion and envy. This could even mean confrontation and conflict. The US policy is to try to co-opt India into treaties and arrangements that suit the US, and simultaneously try to undermine Indian legitimacy and image. Unsubstantiated allegations of human rights violations, ill-treatment of minorities and curtailment of freedoms and negative reporting in the media (described as neutral) continue alongside attempts to co-opt. The short-term fear lies in the continuance of the present leadership in New Delhi; the long-term fear is that once India attains its GDP target of $10 trillion, it may have little empathy for US interests.[35]

Despite attempts to disrupt, delay or reverse India's progress, it is assessed that India will remain the fastest growing economy in the world for the moment, the World Bank said in its June 2025 Global Economic Prospects Report.[36] China and India account for more than a third of the world's population, have the highest rates of economic growth. They will remain the biggest guzzlers of energy, will compete for resources and markets and there will be occasions of competition and even confrontation, although conflict will be avoided. An undemarcated border between the two largest armies and nuclear nations does not make for comfortable relations and prevents the development of a full association. Astute diplomacy, especially when the energy market went into a spin at the start of the Ukraine War, showed that India has matured enough to prevent a domestic economic crisis.

India's economic fortunes were subdued for more than six decades, the 1991 reforms being the only hesitant break from the past. India failed to rise to the occasion till 2014. Economic well-being, including infrastructure, multilayered social cohesion and upliftment, accompanied by a strong security apparatus without losing contact with your roots, only multiplies a nation's strength. A new world began to unfold for India and Indians from 2014 onwards – much to the chagrin of long-established self-interests and their inherited rights of entitlement. In rural India, the huge spend on roads and infrastructure, has ensured access to facilities comparable to cities.[37] The New Indians too had dreams and they have begun to see an opportunity like never before. People would make their own space and opportunities for dreams, which they were beginning to feel were attainable. India is clearly coming of age at a time when all around, we see turbulence; yet India has become a beacon of hope.

The shifting of gears in the Indian corporate world and the government has been possible because, at last, after seventy years of rudderless governance, we have a government that thinks ahead coherently and acts on what it promises. Not everything turns out the way it was intended, there are miscalculations or, simply, wrong decisions. One of the criticisms of the Modi cabinet used to be that it was a collection of inexperienced politicians and would not be able to run a complex country like India. Only the Congress could, and how.

Indians' quality of life has changed with the coming of Narendra Modi. His entry to Parliament that morning of 2014 was impressive and his speech inside the hall was memorable. Equally extraordinary was his speech on Independence Day, where the listener got a clear idea of how his mind was working. It was not the usual uninspired reading from a script speech. He was electrifying and even left many squirming with his brutal frankness when he described the social conditions of women in India. He was therefore going to provide comfort and dignity to India's women. He spoke of providing toilets for women in the villages. Only a man who had lived a life of deprivation and struggle, and seen how this degraded human beings, could empathize with this. Later he would have zero-balance bank accounts for direct transfer of subsidies to those who were entitled; gas cylinders at discounts to provide relief to the women who had to spend entire days collecting firewood. It had taken Indian governments more than seventy years to provide these basic amenities.

Modi took all reform – political, social, economic, fiscal and financial, seriously. Make in India and Aatmanirbharta were articles of faith, and to put India on the global map as a country that mattered was the goal. Along the way he would make mistakes – the jury is still out on the currency demonetization, but it was designed to jolt the few; the start to GST regulations was clumsy but the bureaucracy got it right ultimately. Today the GST revenues are up and soaring. If we have reached a situation where the tax data shows income tax returns doubled between 2011–2012 and 2020–2021, it could mean only two things – that the Income Tax Department was doing it right for the people to file returns and that the average taxpayer felt that his or her tax was being appropriately spent, as was evidenced in the amazing improvement in infrastructure, health and education. 'It was the growth roar of India's middle class.'[38] The tax-paying numbers also increased; obviously, the country was doing well

India will have to understand the trinity of disruptions – technology, geopolitics and narratives – interacting with producers, consumers and regulators as catalysts of growth. It is when all this works together that

India will discard the colonial era infrastructure to become one of the major fulcrums of global economy, an influential rule-maker and one of those redrafting the new world order.[39]

Narratives will have to be an essential part of our armoury as we deal with rising challenges and opposition. Narratives are necessary for creating favourable perceptions and preventing the proliferation of wrong perceptions about India. Narratives are also a part of the business of control, dominance and influence. Sending delegations after an accomplishment or a success are inadequate as they are event or episode related. They have little long-term impact on those negatively disposed towards India or who are at best neutral.

We should take a page from the Chinese book of practices to deal with the West, especially in the US. We need to think long-term, be patient and consistent, because changes in perception or review of interests do not happen overnight. We need to invest heavily to create dependencies, so that withdrawal would hurt. The Harvard University story is an example. The Trump Government in 2025 has accused Harvard University that its campus is following Beijing-backed influence operations. These suspicions are not new, and many Republican Congressmen have been worried that China was using this channel to access advanced technology. According to a White House official, Harvard had allowed the Chinese Communist Party to exploit it and the school had turned a blind eye to these activities.[40] Angered by this, the Trump government has reduced funding to Harvard heavily. This does not mean others should not try influence-building, which is part of statecraft.

Dealing with the US administration in the short term is going to be problematic because we are dealing with a temperamental person (Trump) who possesses an outsized ego. If India–US are in this for the long game, India needs to remember that any deal with America has to be mostly in America's favour; what the co-signatory gets is his good luck. MAGA, or 'America First', as John F. Kennedy said in his election campaign, are the same thing.

Handling the Economic Future

Addressing the nation on 12 May 2020, Narendra Modi outlined the nation's priorities for economic growth. The first was – Aatmanirbhar

Bharat, self-reliant India. 'Economy, which brings in quantum jump and not incremental change; infrastructure, which should become the identity of India; systems based on twenty-first century technology driven arrangements; vibrant demography, which is our source of energy for a self-reliant India; and demand, whereby the strength of our demand and supply chain should be utilized to full capacity.'[41]

It is not the primary job of the state to create opportunities of employment, but it must provide facilities – for training, skills-development and higher education – so that the talent remains at home in a high-technology world. The state must provide security, welfare, health and education, and its delivery systems should break out of bureaucratic mindsets. The state and the corporate sector have an equal role in the emancipation of women. The fact that that income tax revenue has increased, along with the number of returns filed, and that GST is working, is a positive indication. There is increased mobility of population because of improved infrastructure. The government must be doing something right. Among other things, it has remembered that if a government wants to rule effectively, it must build roads and such infrastructure. The farmer is a phone call away from the market to judge the day's price for his product; all he needs is last mile-connectivity.

Bottlenecks exist in substantial numbers and often have an old history. Acquiring land in India is still a challenge. The experience of the Tata group in Singur in 2008 revealed that both political and legal risks still exist. Similarly, convoluted labour laws make hiring and firing onerous, rendering companies inflexible and unable to respond quickly to market demand. Liberalization in 1991 improved matters, but the state continues to choke the supply side of the Indian economy. Reservations for employment are an obstacle to qualified technology, medical or engineering disciplines. There are separate laws governing the handling of religious places; there are separate regulations for minorities. It is time to have a uniform law for every aspect of our lives. The bane of freebies being offered at the time of elections should be prohibited by law.

The first thing that India needs is an overhaul of its colonial-era bureaucracy that retains the commanding heights of the economy. It still foists endless red tape on business, strangles entrepreneurship and takes too long to make most decisions. Ease of doing business has improved, but is still not fast or deep enough. Performance-linked promotions and dismissal for underperformance are long overdue. India needs sound economic policymaking, directed by domain experts in each administrative department.

If the bureaucracy holds India back, so does the judiciary. As of end-2023, over 50 million cases are pending in courts.[42] It takes around six years for a case to be resolved in a subordinate court, over three years in the high courts and another three years in the Supreme Court. A case that goes all the way to the Supreme Court takes an average of ten years to resolve. Many cases get stuck for twenty to thirty years or more.[43]

Indian agricultural practices are extremely inefficient, which has reduced groundwater, emptied government coffers through endless subsidies and lowered farm productivity. The government's agricultural reforms were designed to allow farmers to grow what they wanted and sell wherever they wanted, bypassing extractive middlemen. The new legislation aimed to boost agricultural production, lower inflation and increase exports, while potentially reducing rural hunger and improving India's human capital long-term. But this was not to be.

Global conditions are still favourable despite the turbulence. Western economies seeking to decouple from China without triggering inflation see India as the only country with the size and the scale to be an alternative. India's large youth population and rising middle class are powerful tailwinds for high economic growth, and it be a force for global stability – provided the West can somehow, from its perspective, control India.

One great success has been the government dealing with the Kashmir issue by revoking Article 370. This article was inserted into the Indian Constitution by Jawaharlal Nehru in a unilateral action to appease the Muslim majority in Kashmir. Ending the special status of Jammu and Kashmir, bifurcating the state into two union territories, Jammu–Kashmir and Ladakh, on 5 August 2019, also had the advantage of leaving Pakistan shell-shocked.[44]

At first there was disbelief that the government had done away with the temporary article that had survived for seventy years and there was fear of violence. Nothing of the sort happened and today, nothing seems more logical and rational.[45] There was no upsurge; no street violence except the tears of those who had benefited from the continuation of

Article 370. Its abrogation destroyed the intifada factory and dismantled the echo chamber that created conditions conducive to a terror ecosystem in the state.[46] The unfair special privileges that were misused by Kashmiri politicians for seventy years while pretending that this article was the only instrument that linked Kashmir to India, has become a story of the past. Jammu and Kashmir is now as much integrated with India as any other state of the union.

The State of Our World

An optimist besotted with the new technology of artificial sntelligence, and in control of communications and information, believes the world is at the cusp of greater things. However, a realist assesses that the world may be facing a great upheaval and it will ultimately settle down to a new equilibrium. It would be safe to say that the world is transiting through a difficult and treacherous phase of intense rivalries and declining fortunes.

Almost every crisis or change is taking place simultaneously, and not just in geopolitics. Other factors are becoming increasingly important – economic order, military engagements, massive terror and retaliation, issues relating to education, health and pandemics, access to food and energy sources and climate change – and at the same time, the existing global pecking order of power and domination is being challenged.

Carl Sagan says that the most crucial elements for human existence and well-being are transportation, communications and basic industries. Food and agriculture, medicine, education, entertainment, environment – nowadays, even the democratic institution of voting – all depend on science and technology. 'We have also arranged things so that almost no one understands science and technology. This is a prescription for disaster. We might get away with it for a while but sooner or later this combustible mixture of ignorance and power is going to blow up in our faces.'[47]

The United States, as a significant global power, has encountered various strategic challenges in Iraq, Syria and Afghanistan. Additionally, proxy wars in Ukraine and in the conflict involving Israel, Hamas, Hezbollah and Iran, are anticipated to persist for decades. The financial crisis of 2008 was unexpected but is expected to repeat itself in various forms. American inability to have its own way as before, meant that it was in relative decline. This was a major change in perceptions around and about it.

Past global disagreements have resurfaced. The world order that has dominated since the Second World War is now crumbling. It appears as if the American adventure in forcing Ukraine to take on Russia is now going to end sadly for Ukraine and Europe, and reflect badly on America. No hegemon gives up power easily as they see their rule under threat, but post Ukraine, China is likely to be more assertive. In which case it may assert itself about Taiwan, a favourite dream of Xi Jinping.

China seeks equality with the US for the moment, which the Americans do not want to accept, and regional supremacy in Asia with the long-term goal of global supremacy. Quite tellingly, at the Xi–Biden summit in San Francisco in 2023, Xi was looking for a bilateral arrangement between them while the US was looking for arrangements that did not lead to conflict in the Western Pacific.[48]

Technology – A Frenemy

We are living in an era of individual ambitions, exploding aspirations, heightened societal expectations and limited abilities to fulfil all these, despite a technology blitzkrieg that is gathering speed exponentially. Early inventions, from the wheel to the steam engine, revolutionized movement from place to place, in war and in peace. Technology has given mankind unimaginable medical cures, benefits in agriculture, space exploration. People do not write letters, they use email. People do not speak but send messages with symbols. Alongside traditional threats, there will be new threats from the misuse of AI. As the recent sharp Indian reaction to Pakistan's misadventure in Pahalgam has shown, use of technology has taken military warfare to a new level.

The twenty-first century technology blitz will be known as the period which adapted the computer age in all its aspects. Artificial Intelligence (AI), ChatGPT, the ability to morph and create lifelike deep-fake images and videos – all these are still to reach their limits; meanwhile, truth has become a huge victim. The distinction between what is true or fake has become blurred. AI will have to be regulated before its exploding capabilities play havoc. Accountability and regulation through a specialist regulator need to be thought out.[49]

The US and China have already created their own systems. Unless India develops its own system, it will become a consumer of this technology, rather than a leader. As consumers, our data will reside in either of these countries, who will have data ownership. There would be no one to build in Indian languages – 70 per cent of Indians do not know English, and if Indians do not build it, the Indian versions will be available at huge costs. Building our own large language models (LLMs) – a type of AI algorithm that uses deep learning techniques and massively large data sets to understand, summarize, generate and predict new content – is essential. Only then will India begin to compete with China where technology is concerned.[50] Self-reliance is not easy but it is essential if we want to follow an independent policy and be a power of some stature. Or else, we remain dependent on those who are creating these. Artificial intelligence embedded in nanotechnologies will make the task of intelligence agencies that much more complicated. They will also have to deal with a combination of radical Islam and Islamic terror, as well as gun runners, narcotics traders, human traffickers and anything illegal and lethal, all using every available modern technique, including artificial intelligence.[51]

India's rise is happening at a time when the global situation remains tense, and the chances are that it might get worse. Yet despite these uncertainties, India today is poised for greatness that is rightfully hers. There have been several foreign policy successes. India is now seen as an active member of various groups like BRICS, SCO, QUAD, and bilateral discussions between the Pentagon and State department and India's external and defence ministers, is a measure of the lines of communication being free and easy most of the time. India fully utilized its presidency of G20 in 2023 to extend its reach and influence. India's outreach into West Asia has been phenomenal and goes beyond the mundane. The skill and agility with which we managed to stay out of the campaign to stop energy purchase from Russia following the American diktat, while maintaining a smooth relationship with Washington, is an indication of the growing strength of India's diplomacy. Neither the US nor China would want a militarily and economically powerful India that challenges them and Pakistan would happily oblige in keeping both these powers happy by creating situations for India.

India is in the process of finding its well-deserved position in the world and not the kind some wealthy individuals in the West are trying to evolve by 2030, designed to preserve the dominance of the West.

Once India's economy emerges as one of the largest in the world in the years ahead, there will a fundamental redefinition of twenty-first century relationships. India will not get there just by dreaming of it; no one will help India become a major power. We will have to work for it all the time. It will take climbing a mountain, or perhaps breaking a mountain, to get there.

Ideology or territorial conquests are not the slogans of the emerging new world order. Ideologies have become obscure and territorial conquests are expensive and difficult to maintain. Wars will not be eliminated as the hunt for energy, critical materials and rare earth that help economic growth, technological superiority and enable continuance of hegemony, will continue. Resource wars in different categories, fought with technological superiority and AI-aided weaponry, to ensure control over resource flows will be the pattern. The US would like to ensure that no other nation challenges its grip on energy or rare earths.

Today China with its extended reach globally through its BRI initiative, having acquired rare earth contracts and energy corridors across Africa, Latin America and Central Asia. Its semiconductor capacity challenges the US. Russia with its massive oil, gas and Arctic reserves is another threat to continued US hegemony.[52] However, there is considerable informed commentary in the US that the ground is slipping away from America.

Trump's inability to secure peace in Ukraine after eight months in power, far away from the one day he had boasted, has led the US establishment to look for scapegoats. India is one of them pushing the India–US relations to a new low. Allegations against India for extending the Ukraine War by buying Russian oil,[53] not adhering to US sanctions and refusing to give Trump the credit for bringing about a cease fire between India and Pakistan, are factors that have played into the system. This is partly pique and mostly frustration that is pushing the argument and driving India away from the US. What if Russia, India and China get together as members of BRICS for some honest talk. This situation of a breakdown in India–US trust may have unintended benefits for India in the long run. The notion that a flailing superpower, facing a relative decline in the world order can be a reliable partner has been finally put to rest.[54]

Robert D. Kaplan's latest book, *Wasteland: A World in Permanent Crisis*, speaks of a world which is facing a deadly mix of war, climate change, great power rivalry, rapid technological changes, the end of monarchies and empires. It all will lead to chaos. It is a grim story but true. These forever wars must cease even though they may be profitable to certain sections of the industry.

It is possible that the Americans tried to pull Russia from China when Putin and Trump met in Alaska on August 15 just as Nixon had done in 1972 when he visited Bejing and met Mao and pulled China away from the Soviet Union. Apparently, the Trump magic did not work on Putin. Three days later, on 18 August the Chinese Foreign minister was in India talking to his Indian counterpart. Putin gave no indication he was going to abandon Xi Jinping, but made sure Prime Minister Modi visited China for SCO meeting. Before visiting Beijing Narendra Modi visited Japan. Modi's visit to China eased considerable tension in the China-India stand off and the highly visible camaraderie between the three leaders was most encouraging. [55]

Maybe the three leaders – Russian, Indian and Chinese – assisted by their able foreign ministers and national security advisers need to sit down together and look at the changing world to find some new roads to permanent peace. If Palmerston said Britain had no permanent friends or enemies at least we can say we have no permanent enemies. Friends do not really exist in the real world of geopolitics.

A country run by banks will always be in debt. Healthcare run by Big Pharma will never cure disease. A state run by war will never know peace. A nation run by media will never know the truth.[1]

— ROB MOORE

Acknowledgements

This book took a long time coming and just seemed to continue to grow as I tried to fill in a large canvas. Ultimately I had to remove three chapters. The rapid changes globally made the writing more complicated.

I was able to complete the book with the unceasing support, patience and encouragement from Urvashi, my wife and friend for 55 years.

There were others who helped me with the project. I took advantage of the Switzerland-based Surya Kanegaonkar and his knowledge about virtually everything related to global affairs. Of great value was the research and commentary by young Bengaluru-based Vedesh Gangur.

I must also thank Chiki Sarkar who invited me to write for Juggernaut Books. Swati Chopra, editorial director, helped me with her invaluable advice and patience. It was her enthusiasm that was infectious and kept me going. Swati was very closely associated with both my earlier books *The Unending Game* and *The Ultimate Goal*. This greatly helped me for the third one.

Padmini Smetacek was impressive with her attention to detail and was of immense help in the final stages of the book. My thanks also to Krishna Sawant for her contribution to the copy editing process. The cover designer Antra K. gave some excellent choices for the book's jacket.

See detailed endnotes by scanning the QR code above